Sardonic Smile

Sardonic Smile

Nonverbal Behavior
in Homeric Epic

Donald Lateiner

Ann Arbor
THE UNIVERSITY OF MICHIGAN PRESS

First paperback edition 1998
Copyright © by the University of Michigan 1995
All rights reserved
Published in the United States of America by
The University of Michigan Press
Manufactured in the United States of America
∞ Printed on acid-free paper

2001 2000 1999 1998   4 3 2 1

*A CIP catalogue record for this book is available
from the British Library.*

Library of Congress Cataloging-in-Publication Data

Lateiner, Donald.
   Sardonic smile : nonverbal behavior in Homeric epic / Donald Lateiner.
     p. cm.
   Includes bibliographical references (p.) and index.
   ISBN 0-472-10598-1 (alk. paper)
   1. Homer—Knowledge—Psychology. 2. Nonverbal communication (Psychology) in literature. 3. Epic poetry, Greek—History and criticism. 4. Social interaction in literature. 5. Human behavior in literature. I. Title.
PA4037.L44   1995
883'.01—dc20
                                                95-1704
                                                    CIP

ISBN 0-472-08490-9 (pbk : alk. paper)

No part of this publication may be reproduced, stored in a retrieval system, or transmitted in any form or by any means, electronic, mechanical, or otherwise, without the written permission of the publisher.

To three generations of my fractious family.

First, to that sine qua non, my wily mother, Mary Schaffer, and to my enduring stepfather, Stanley Schaffer, who together have supported unblinkingly my love of antiquity materially—for instance, by presenting me with an unabridged Greek-English lexicon thirty years ago—and spiritually—by meeting my quirky enthusiasms with encouragement.

ὣς ἐφάμην, ἡ δ' αὐτίκ' ἀμείβετο πότνια μήτηρ·

Then, to my wife, E. Marianne Gabel, Esq., who suffered and learned to produce (sometimes gladly) microanalyses of our family's every angry gesture, loving posture, and dopey face.

. . . ὁμοφρονέοντε νοήμασιν οἶκον ἔχητον
ἀνὴρ ἠδὲ γυνή· πόλλ' ἄλγεα δυσμενέεσσι,
χάρματα δ' εὐμενέτῃσι· . . .

Finally, to my energetic and excessively expressive sons, Ulysses and Abraham, who sketched impressive book covers, sometimes kept quiet, and often raucously ejected me from academic obsession with smiles, grunts, and persistent taps on the arm. Our face-to-face interactions might momentarily have impeded the product now at last in your hands, but without the *nepioi*, there may well not have been anything at all.

καί ποτέ τις εἴποι 'πατρός γ' ὅδε πολλὸν ἀμείνων' . . .

Preface

This book boldly barges into an interdisciplinary and frighteningly technical domain of research—into two actually, Homeric studies and nonverbal communication. I was formally trained in neither, but in ancient history, Greek literature, and social thought. Moreover, and to my regret, students of eyelid-flutter rarely read Homer, and students of Homer too infrequently devour *American Ethnography* or the *Journal of Clinical Psychology* to explore nonverbal behavior.[1] Delightful exceptions come to mind for selected formulae, rituals, and, especially, stylized epic environments, such as supplication, gift-exchange, and "looking darkly."

Homeric monographs often dissect either speakers of words or doers of deeds—a comfortable Hellenic antithesis and Homeric complementary dyad. My target consists of a third, *in-between,* but very wide, nonverbal channel that communicates character and motivation as presented in literature. I mean reported nonverbal acts, purposely performed or uncontrollably leaked, that enhance, devalue, or disguise verbal messages. Nonverbal behavior can replace, duplicate, or complement language: a nod can replace a "hello," a smile can duplicate it, and a handshake may complement or confirm it. Since the philological world welcomes so many studies of formulaic epithets, repetitions, and patterns, it may tolerate one book on Homer that addresses the human race's principal mode of human interaction and one that the bard frequently "records."

Face-to-face interaction, a multichannel bodily activity including taunting as well as chatting, incorporates many acts that remain below *both* parties' level of awareness. These acts (for example, micromomentary grimaces of

---

1. Ye olde analyst Sir Denys Page once disarmingly introduced lectures on the *Odyssey* disclaiming originality (1955, preface). He wittily arraigned in Bryn Mawr many mechanical faults and alleged illogicalities of narrative and character in the *Odyssey,* as he had done before in Berkeley for the *Iliad.* Here, he modestly asserted that he was "contributing little of my own except (occasionally) a glitter of rhetoric round the fringes of the self-evident." Sir Denys earned Homeric credentials as the last of the old-style "analysts" in three valuable, if sometimes inaccurate, books (cf. F. Combellack's review in *Gnomon* 28 [1956]: 411–19) and preserves them now, the most convenient whipping boy of English-speaking "unitarians" who discover and uncover bizarrely seamless constructs.

distaste or raised eyebrows of disbelief) regulate interactive flow and comment on others' speech. Conversation often demands a high level of awareness, leaving little attention available for nonverbal behavior. But a friendly handshake, an offered refreshment, and relaxed postures, or a locked-on gaze, gaze aversion, or hostile glare are equally, or more, affecting alternants for speech. Body language, intended or not, whenever perceived by another, communicates affect and influences others' behavior.

Part 1 of this study validates these propositions by an extensive investigation of the texts of an influential, if idiosyncratic,[2] ancient author. Let's call him, for short, "Homer." Part 1 subsequently maps out contours of the communicative Homeric body—the nonverbal channel of the speech-laden text (nearly one-third *oratio recta*). After an introduction to basic terminology (relatively inconsistent among researchers in this rich, but as yet unbounded, area), concepts, and categories of nonverbal behavior,[3] the reader finds a detailed study of an adequately varied and representative sample, *Iliad* 24. Other probes of other books can dislodge different, but similarly frequent, data, but the reader here finds one chosen for intrinsic interest and sharply varied activity, Akhaians and Trojans, humans and gods expressing

---

2. The latter modifier should conjure up the two uniquely monumental texts of paradoxically traditional, oral, formulaic poetry extruded by the catastrophes of Mycenaean to archaic Greece. I assume that the accounts in the *Iliad* and the *Odyssey* of specifically nonverbal behavior reflect moments of social reality, particularly the interactions of generations close to the transcriptions. I candidly assert this as assumption, but it seems sound because the Homeric epics grew and took shape over many generations and before live audiences. Donlan 1993, 156–59, lays out more reasons to reject the view of this literary world as totally artificial and eclectic, and to accept a "socio-cultural reading" that reflects a coherent social milieu and provides a consistent sociology of Homeric society. Cf. recently Van Wees 1992, 5–23, "History in Poetry"; and Nagy 1979, 15, on the genesis of these poems, "the culmination of perhaps over a thousand years of performer-audience interaction." Those who reject the Parry-Lord complex of oral and formulaic hypotheses may relax, however, since the thesis of this essay does not require any particular view of the genesis of the poems. The oral-formulaic hypothesis, it seems to me, only strengthens my arguments for gestural realism. The more the poems result from bard-audience interaction, the more likely the bard or rhapsode would include only nonverbal behavior that was instantly cognizable. The following discussion sidesteps significant and knotty problems of how the present *Iliad* and *Odyssey* texts reached their current incarnation. I have nothing to add to the extensive literature, recently reviewed by Nagy 1992. I might note that the self-conscious creations of Sophokles, Thukydides, and Plato, never tested in performance before frequent audiences, are less likely to record nonverbal behavior accurately. *One possible* reason for Herodotos' unusually high frequency of nonverbal behavior in historical prose is allegedly frequent performance before large and varied audiences.

3. Lexica of descriptive terms for Greek and Roman nonverbal behaviors remain desiderata. Thorough inventories and review of vocabulary may alert us to patterns and absence of patterns in verbal descriptions of nonverbal behavior. Sittl's 1890 index provides a beginning; cf. Holoka 1992, 243–44.

grief and (some) joy. This principled procedure of grounding every generalization in specific loci automatically aborts, I hope, unsubstantiated, airy, or theoretical claims that might suit modern literary or political ideologies or "essentialist" paradigms but do not suit philology. Without dense documentation and description, students of ancient society and literature cannot advance appreciation and understanding of actual ancient behavior or its quasi-reflex, literature. So we survey all types of Homeric nonverbal behavior before tightening the focus.

Part 2 examines the *Odyssey* for expressions of honor and dishonor organized by several categories of nonverbal analysis. Every *persona* in the *Odyssey* profits and suffers from his or her own and others' gestures and postures of respect and disrespect. This middle part of the book concentrates on these selected and significant nonverbal rituals of accommodation, investigating voluntary and involuntary kinesics (including gestures, facial expressions, and postures), proxemics, and other nonverbal behaviors as the *Odyssey* presents them. The exploration cannot exhaust the seemingly infinite Odyssean variety and frequency of such behavior. Nor does it pause to completely explicate single scenes. I hope to excavate a hidden dimension of Homer's social finesse.[4]

Part 2, then, intensively examines this one, limited topic in the field of nonverbal behavior to illuminate a shadowy, but important, corner of face-to-face, social interaction and status manipulation in the *Odyssey*. The separate wordless, or word-supplementing, communicative channel of bodily expressions of respect and disrespect demonstrates a distinct major dimension of Homeric characterization, psychology, and sociology. These textual clues to heroic outer and inner life confirm the sincerity, or subvert the hypocrisy, of minor and major figures.

The reader will notice that chapters in part 2, which concerns the *Odyssey*, roughly correspond in topics and order to part 1, chapter 3, which concerns the *Iliad*: chapter 4 corresponds to section 1 of chapter 3, chapter 5 to section 2, and chapters 6 and 7 to section 4. Odyssean materials that correspond to sections 3 and 5 in chapter 3 are found in part 3, especially in chapters 9 and 11. Exploration of the same topics—organizing parallel evidence amassed from both epics—may, by cumulative arguments, persuade dubious literati about small and large communicative acts in an oral-traditional text. The

---

4. The Oxford texts of Monro and Allen, the lexica of Cunliff and Ebeling, the concordances of Prendergast and Dunbar, and the translations of Lattimore (to know them is to love them) have been gratefully employed, if rarely quoted, throughout. I have tried, often with no success, to improve on Lattimore's versions.

x Preface

Odyssey more often remarks behaviors that the *Iliad* takes for granted, but both poems inscribe speech and instrumental act in the regulation of nonverbal dynamics in ordinary business. Some incidents necessarily emerge for analysis more than once as we examine co-occurrent nonverbal behavior from different characters' and classes' points of view. I have generally eschewed recapitulating the narrative. As Odysseus at the end of his included stories phrases the idea: ἐχθρὸν δέ μοί ἐστιν / αὖτις ἀριζήλως εἰρημένα μυθολογεύειν, "I just hate describing again stories already clearly told" (*Od.* 12.453).

Part 3 modifies apertures. It replaces the filter of categories of nonverbal behavior with one selecting leading "personalities" of the *Odyssey*. The change will be congenial to literary critics because it dwells among individuals (poetic constructs) rather than social groups and expectations (anthropological constructs). It engages Homer's presentation of "character," the sets of textual actions, reactions, words, and gestures that he denominates Telemakhos, Aithon, the suitors, and Penelope. Characters are considered here for intrinsic importance and frequency in the plot and also, specifically, as representatives of an age-group, an excluded socioeconomic class, a privileged one, and sexual otherness, or gender. The four chapters in part 3, devoted to four important players who struggle for social dominance and respect, examine the specific body-talk of the insider turned out, Telemakhos;[5] of humble beggar Odysseus, stigmatized by near zero-grade status; of the pushy, neglected suitors, most awkwardly jockeying for supremacy; and of the unempowered grand prize, Penelope, the hard-pressed, polyvalent woman—mother/prestator/queen/bride-to-be/wife. "Longinus" (9.15) observes the *Odyssey*'s sketches of routinized life around the house in a "comedy of manners": τὰ περὶ τὴν τοῦ Ὀδυσσέως ἠθικῶς αὐτῷ βιολογούμενα οἰκίαν. The *Odyssey* is a very funny poem.

It assisted my discussion to refer throughout, in the text and in the notes, to the commentaries on the *Odyssey* and the *Iliad* by Russo (in Russo et al. 1992), Macleod (1982), Hoekstra (in Hoekstra and Heubeck 1989), Stanford (1965), and Heubeck (in Heubeck et al. 1988–92). References to these commentaries are abbreviated as Russo ad loc., Macleod ad loc., and so forth.

No apology is extended for my Hellenic, rather than Latinate or Anglican, transliteration of names: the heroic world of the Akhaians is not Latin or

---

5. Teenagers represent a seriously disadvantaged group, as my fifteen-year-old son Ulysses often reminds me. Intermittently adult Telemakhos and equally liminal girl/woman Nausikaa, important secondary characters, offer well-observed age-based nonverbal behavior, as do elderly Nestor, Eurykleia, and Laertes.

American. Let the weird warriors and wives of an alien world keep their exotic patina. I did yield to the seduction of the familiar for the name of Crete. And such adjectives as Mycenaean seem too awkward or not even English as Mykenean or Mykenaian. Quibblers for consistency may feast on these hors d'oeuvres, if nothing substantial appears more outrageous.

Acknowledgments

Friends and colleagues have assisted me over the last decade in finding rare articles and philological dissertations as well as unfamiliar social science materials. Bill Beck and Sarah Iles Johnston have performed this locative service in Hamburg, Germany, and on several well-stocked campuses, respectively. So has Greg Crane. Judy Hallett, Jennifer Roberts, and Carolyn Dewald, who help so many colleagues and students, helped me all the way through this delightful project just by being there. They are like the heroes of yore. Rachel Kitzinger, my friend of a quarter century, studiously ignored this entire project in a peculiar way helpful to me.

I thank the unflappable Homerists Mark Edwards, Jim Holoka, and Dan Levine for scrutinizing a nearly prehistorical version of part 1. Jenny Clay and Nancy Felson-Rubin commented on drafts of chapters 6 and 11, respectively. Our fruitful and exciting conversations on paper and by electronic mail have left me a little uncertain where their work leaves off and mine begins, but I claim all the errors. Joseph O'Connor responded publicly to a lecture that borrowed examples from what later became part 2. It was delivered in a series organized by Lillian Doherty in honor of the retirement of Professor Rolf Hubbe at the University of Maryland, College Park. Princeton University and, in particular, Jim Luce invited me to present some material from what is now part 3. Duke University, through the kind offices of my friend Dr. Georgia Machemer, generously listened to a presentation concerning Telemakhos and the suitors. At Indiana University, curious students, my collegial hosts, and especially Matt Christ audited a risky venture into vulnerability and insult in the "Telemakheia." Elements of chapters 4 and 7 were presented at the 1991 Chicago meeting of the American Philological Association. Several cozily anonymous readers for the University of Michigan Press have significantly improved this essay on literary anthropology (a better term than most for this investigation).

Dr. Ellen Bauerle, native of Delaware, Ohio, and editor at the University of Michigan Press, carefully read the entire manuscript, posed many queries, and improved the exposition. I thank her for a hundred provocative stick-on notes. The press's copy editor, Jill Butler Wilson, regularized many eccentric sentences. Ruth Bauerle retaught me to index by computer.

A few other Homerists—Gil Rose of Swarthmore College, Joe Russo of Haverford College, and Bill Beck (again) of the renowned Hamburg Lexikon der frügriechischen Epos—have provided collegial encouragement and spiritual support to an explorer of archaic pragmatics and oral poetics. Reviewers are not to blame any of them for my precocious generalizations, incautious remarks, and hardy stylistic infelicities. Nearly all of them have wondered about the wisdom of pursuing across the darkling plain this rivulet meandering away from the mainstream, even the main streams, of Homeric scholarship. The inexplicable lack of attention paid to Homeric nonverbal behavior, even by those pushing studies beyond "word and deed," is my joy and justification.

Ohio Wesleyan University (through Provost William Louthan and the faculty personnel committee) awarded me an eccentric additional sabbatical leave to complete this manuscript, for which time and confidence I express my profoundest gratitude. My tiny university has supported my scholarly interests in every possible way that it could. No learned society has yet felt obliged to rush to my succor.

An expanded section of chapter 3, section 2, comparing Homer's treatment of stupefaction to Vergil's and Ovid's, appeared under Fernando Poyatos' editorship in *Advances in Nonverbal Communication* (1992). An earlier version of chapter 7 appears in *TAPA* 122 (1992), edited by Sander Goldberg. I thank Professors Poyatos and Goldberg for editorial help. A version of chapter 10 appeared in the elegant—but, for classicists, obscure—1993 issue of *The Colby Quarterly* edited by Professors Hanna and Joseph Roisman and dedicated to Homeric epic. Their critical acumen made it better.

My onetime student and eternal gadfly Eliot Wirshbo of the University of California, San Diego, was there to look dubious, shrug his shoulders, and abrasively say, "So what?" both at meetings of the American Philological Association and thereafter in the margins of my imagination and revisions. The critical reader owes some small thanks to this California scholar who braked some wilder hypotheses. Rosaria Munson of Swarthmore College, another former student, helped me by always asking about, but never questioning, the enterprise. I acknowledge and embrace these friends for the listed services and others that I would blush to publish.

Contents

Glossary   xvii

Part 1. Nonverbal Behaviors

1. Introduction: Nonverbal Behavior in Life and Literature   3
2. Apprehending Homeric Character(s): Gesture and Criticism   19
3. Probe and Survey: Nonverbal Behaviors in *Iliad* 24   31

Part 2. Nonverbal Respect and Disrespect in the *Odyssey*

4. Heroic Etiquette: Salutation, Encounter, and Valediction   65
5. Leaking Heroic Sentiment: "Face" and "Tone"   83
6. "Standing Tall": Posture, Elevation, and Deference   93
7. Heroic Proxemics: Social Space and Distance   105

Part 3. Nonverbal Characterization in the *Odyssey*

8. Youth: The Boy-Man's Body-Talk   139
9. Status: Odysseus' Body and the Beggar's Stigma   167
10. The Suitors' Take: Manners and Power in Ithaka   203
11. Gendered Weapons: Penelope's Nonverbal Behaviors   243

Conclusion: "More Than Words Can Say . . ."   281

Appendix: Chronemics   291

Bibliography 297

Index of Passages Cited 311

Index of Important Subjects and Persons 321

Glossary

Adaptors. Habitual nonverbal behaviors that communicate, though often unintentionally, the emitter's emotional condition or attitude. Ekman and Friesen 1969b provides the most useful divisions of categories (see, e.g., *alter-adaptors, object-adaptors,* and *self-adaptors*) although others (for example, Poyatos 1986) have modified their decisions.

Affect Display. Visible, audible, or tactile emotional expression, intended or not. For example, foot-stomping appreciation, a confused stutter, or an embarrassed blush.

Alter-adaptors. Symbolic acts and positions that communicate affiliative desire or its opposites. For example, handshaking, embracing, or back-slapping, as well as leaning in, locking a gaze, and bowing.

Alternants. Movement, expression, or nonlexical sound that can substitute for or reinforce words.

Awareness, in- or **out-of-.** Behavior can be perceived or not perceived by the emitter or subject (the ego). In-awareness behavior is conscious but not necessarily voluntary. Out-of-awareness behavior is not perceived by the subject and is therefore necessarily involuntary, although sometimes subject to subsequent control (consider tears, squints, or guffaws).

Body-talk. Synonym for nonverbal behavior, but less appropriate for paralinguistic phenomena.

Body tonus. Muscular tension, relaxed or alert, conveying mood (anxiety levels) and/or social status in an interaction—that is, one's attitude toward a situation, whether one is stiff or at ease. Compare Telemakhos in the company of the suitors with Polyphemos after some good Maroneian wine.

Chronemics. The human use, perception, and manipulation of time. For example, how many minutes late you may calibrate a meeting with your boss or *basileus,* or a meaningful pause before answering a personal question.

Coverbal gesture. Body-talk that accompanies—usually to emphasize, sometimes to undercut—speech.

Dyssemia. Deficient abilities in sending and/or receiving nonverbal messages.

Emblem. Actions that replace words. For example, an American hitchhiker jerks his thumb back and over his shoulder. See Ekman and Friesen 1969b, 63–68, 94–95.

Ethnogest. Nonverbal symbolic act peculiar to one or a few ethnic groups. For example, the Hellenic chin-raise to indicate "No" or the Italian and Hellenic hidden-palm wave (see D. Morris 1979, 241–59).

Face. The persona or character an individual presents to his or her public(s) and the standing or respect this wins the individual in the community. See Goffman's studies.

Gesture. A movement of some part of the body that conveys a message: body-talk or body language narrowly construed. Gesture provides symbolic meaning rather than instrumental acts. For example, a raised, open palm, when it conveys the evil eye or "Stop!" or the number five, rather than when it holds down a napkin or softens an incoming blow. Gestures can be modulated and measured by intensity, vibratility or degree of expansiveness, repetition, limited or extensive body involvement, and so forth.

Greet up or **down.** The practices of conveying status differences when meeting a person of a different social standing; mostly similar to but still significantly different from those used when greeting an equal. A bow to a superior and a nod to an inferior offer ancient and modern examples. See Goody 1972.

Idiogest. A nonverbal behavior unique to an individual, common in modern literature (such as the quirks of Captain Ahab or Dr. Strangelove) but rare—or hard to prove—in ancient oral and formulaic epic.

Illustrator. Gestures tied to speech, usually in-awareness and informative. For example, gestures that demonstrate the nature of a circular staircase or how to light a match and cigarette.

Instrumental. A "goal-directed" action or word (also "performative utterance") that aims at a desired result. For example, chopping firewood with an ax or reciting "I thee wed" in a marriage ceremony. Cf. *symbolic*.

Intention; intended and unintended behaviors. Communicative behavior may be enacted purposefully or unpurposefully. When the subject wills a smile or a wave of the hand, it is intended; when a blush or tear is "leaked" despite all volition, it is termed "unintended."

Interactants. The persons involved in an interchange, who nearly always employ both verbal and nonverbal signal systems.

Kinesics. Movements, in-awareness and out-of-awareness, that accompany or replace language. Kinesics etymologically includes gesture but inclines to focus on less conscious and less explicit body and facial micromotions, as originally defined by Birdwhistell.

Leakage. Accidental and unintentional revelation of information—frequently by facial expression, limb displacement, or tone—that is neither intentionally nor consciously communicated to other parties in an interchange. In literature, authors often indicate such signals to the audience, as when Homer reports a bitten lip, Plato a blush induced by Socratic interrogation, and Aristophanes a fart.

Lexeme. The spoken word; verbal communication.

Nonverbal behavior. Useful umbrella, or covering, term for all human acts and responses capable of communication—conscious, intentional, voluntary, or otherwise—and including gesture, posture, body-talk, paralinguistics, chronemics, and proxemics. Events include somatic, vocal (nonverbal), dermal, thermal, and olfactory messages and experiences.

Object-adaptors. Separate objects employed by an individual or group to indicate condition (age, health, gender), status, intention, or mood. For example, a smoking pipe, sunglasses or a cane, a scepter and throne, rouge and lipstick, or ragged clothes. Also called body-adaptors.

Paralinguistics. Any communicable emotion or communicative event produced by the vocal apparatus except for the very words themselves. For example, tone, volume, pitch, and pace; nasalization, hoarseness, whistling, and accents; pauses and breathing accompaniments, such as panting and wheezing.

Performative force. The matrix and context of a "speech act," as well as the nonverbal behavior that accompanies it, shape the form of communication and the effect that it has. Ridicule, blame, and praise statements, and also supplications from mendicants or defeated warriors, take power from the "who," "when," and "where" that situate them (cf. Martin 1989). Not to be confused with "performative utterance," a linguistic term for words that make happen what they name (e.g., "I thee wed"); compare *instrumental*.

Prestation. The protocols and process of gift-exchange, giving and receiving valued objects, services, emoluments, and expressions of debt, esteem, and favor. See Mauss 1967.

Protocols. Taught customs, or social practices, that govern interaction between and among members recognizing a common affiliation. "Distant approach" protocols refer to the folkways about which Telemakhos claims perfect ignorance when he hangs back from approaching and greeting Nestor, or what people usually do when they sight a friend one hundred meters away.

Proxemics. The human use, perception, and manipulation of space. Topic includes distancing zones (public, social, personal, and intimate), elevation (abased, seated, standing, etc.), orientation (face-to-face, turned back, etc.), and posture in the personal sphere; house and community layout in the social sphere. See Lateiner 1992b.

Psychophysical. Combinations of mental and bodily reactions that produce involuntary and voluntary responses. For example, a wince may indicate physical pain and/or emotional discomfort—say, embarrassment at dietary weakness or distaste and discomfort at an overloud party from which one cannot escape.

Regulators. Nonverbal behaviors, in-awareness peripherally, that establish and control conversational precedence and turn taking. For example, lip licking, gaze directing, winking, paralinguistic "um"-ing, and even hand raising to obtain recognition in parliamentary or academic settings.

Relations management. Verbal and nonverbal establishment and re-establishment of hierarchy or parity between individuals at every encounter; often affirmations of good will or reminders of former services and shared experiences.

Self-adaptors. Typically unawares movements to prepare or modulate an interaction, such as children's lip licking, male belt hitching, and female hair adjusting.

Significant objects. Tokens, gifts, prizes, clothing, memorials, talismans, and divine portents, such as prodigies, inter alia, that communicate authority, status, belief, gender, age, and so forth. In life, for example, a necktie might be a significant object that determines whether you will be admitted to a fancy restaurant. In literature, significant objects (e.g., a beggar's costume of rags) often help an author to key a scene or conflict for an audience.

Speech act. The total Gestalt of a person communicating in words to another or a group. Thus, the verbal element is embedded in a context of social interaction (status, gender, age, time, and place) as well as in nonverbal behaviors (dress, posture, distance, tone and volume, etc.).

Symbolic. An act, word, or gesture that evokes a referent and conveys a meaning, attitude, or disposition beyond the apparent, at some level of abstraction. Such events communicate thought and emotion but usually do not achieve or satisfy an immediately functional end. They constitute a signal or sign rather than an accomplishment. For example, a wave or parting handshake that conveys affection rather than use of the hand to eat a meal, although that activity, like almost all other functional acts, has symbolic as well as instrumental dimensions. Compare *instrumental*.

Turn-taking protocols. Conversation is regulated in terms of length, volume, intensity, and speaker-listener roles by interactants' gaze and gaze breaking, orientation, distance, hand movements, confirming nods, nonverbal sounds ("unh-huh," "hmmm," "ummh"), eyebrow motion, and so forth. Age, gender, and status often determine who speaks first, longest, last, loudest, and so forth.

Verboids. Vocal but nonverbal sounds or their absence, usually graphed in English with imitations ("huh?" "ugh!"), descriptions (he fell with a grunt), and/or typefaces and punctuation marks indicating tone, emphasis, pause, and so forth (e.g., italics, a question mark or exclamation point, and ellipses). Compare *paralinguistics* and *vocalics*.

Vocalics. Larynx effects that modify lexemes. For example, whispers or shouts; slurred, clipped, or nasalized enunciation of words; sarcastic or preachy intonation; and so forth.

Voluntary behaviors. A nonverbal behavior both conscious and intended by the emitter. Affect displays on the slippery continuum from intentional and voluntary to out-of-awareness behaviors often defy simple taxonomies.

Part 1
Nonverbal Behaviors

Chapter 1
Introduction: Nonverbal Behavior in Life and Literature

1. Significance of the Subject

Every body, by its distinguishing characteristics, gender, age, motions, and positions, sends and oozes thousands of messages at every moment in "ordinary" life. These appearances, placements, and displacements accompany, reinforce, contradict, and even replace words and ordinary deeds. Nonverbal behavior supplies the interpersonal climate for communicative words and instrumental acts. Gesture, posture, and vocalic variation subconsciously structure human interchange and modulate its dynamics. It includes in-awareness and out-of-awareness behaviors, intended and unintended "symbolic" movements, posture, position relative to others, and nonverbal sounds and voice modifications. Such gestures as looking down and such sounds as whistling and laughter (e.g., a "forced" laugh) may be in-awareness or out-of-awareness, that is, such nonverbal behaviors may belong to category B1, B2, or E discussed in section 2 in this chapter. The context will clarify and stabilize the category. The topic by definition excludes speech, direct and indirect, and instrumental, goal-directed actions like cooking boar-steaks or spearing an enemy.

Nonverbal behavior refers, above all, to gestures, visible bodily acts both conventional and informal, more or less conscious and deliberate, that express some attitude or response. "As the tongue speaketh to the ear, so the gesture [and similar nonverbal behaviors] speaketh to the eye . . . ," said Francis Bacon in 1605. Nonverbal behavior also comprehends seemingly inadvertent movements that inform interactants about covert intentions; involuntary reactions express emotions and responses. Vocal nonverbal variations during verbal expression, such as throat clearing or erratic pitch, frequently betray covert sentiments and override explicit statements (even to the contrary). "Telltale" objects, clothing and appurtenances, such as jewelry and leather jackets, can identify a person and his or her assigned or chosen social roles. Modifications to appearance, clothing, "accessories," or smell

4   *Sardonic Smile*

(body- and self-adaptors) communicate self-image. Beyond visible movements of the stationary body and vocal nonverbal sounds, nonverbal behavior encompasses carriage or deportment, alterations of the entire body, and mannerisms both idiosyncratic and age-, gender-, or class-determined. This category of proxemics includes posture, elevation, orientation, and distance from others. Later on, this introductory chapter spells out the contents of each major subdivision of nonverbal behavior in greater detail. This taxonomy alerts us to various otherwise somewhat obscured channels of human communication.

Despite the popular press's fascination with body language (especially involuntary or unconscious nonverbal behavior), relatively few and isolated recent studies have been devoted to analysis of gesture proper, because it seems "rhetorical" (in the derogatory sense) and contrived. Gesture finds itself in the "wastebasket of performance," because the psychological century has devalued theatricality. Recent studies of pragmatics and of speech acts, however, have begun to revalorize, for us devotees of supposedly unrehearsed expression at least, "the poetics of manhood."[1]

The creators of ancient narrative encoded a vast range of social information and psychological perception in speeches, acts, and descriptions of behavior. Students have profitably analyzed political organization, verbal speech-ways, religious beliefs, and many other significant aspects of Homeric society and literary achievement. Incidents of nonverbal communication, however, have generally been glossed only on an ad hoc basis by commentators and critics and have not been systematically collected and analyzed in terms of social conventions and aesthetic contribution. Part 1 of this book responds to this lacuna: it proposes comprehensive working categories and a survey of *Iliad* 24, an interesting and representative sample of Homeric technique.[2]

---

1. Kendon 1982, 53, 55, and n. 2, citing Ekman and Friesen 1969b. See Herzfeld 1985, 141–49, and Martin 1989, for masculine performance aesthetics in modern and ancient Greek contexts.

2. Chapter 3 does not address "analytic," neoanalytic, or Parryite issues concerning the date(s) at which, or the methods by which, *Iliad* 24 was composed. I would like to endorse (and lack competence to disprove) Macleod's position (1982, 16–17, 35): in spirit and echoes, and as a frame and ending for the whole, book 24 supplies tragic and fitting conclusion to "the grand design of the *Iliad*." The relevance and congruence of book 24 to both book 1 and the architecture of the entire *Iliad* are also discussed by Peppmüller 1876, with parallels, and diagrammed by Myres 1932, esp. 284–94, and Whitman [1958] 1965. Furthermore, the fact that some—or many—nonverbal behaviors are expressed through formulae is irrelevant to narrative function and nondeterminative of aesthetic, literary effect. Austin 1975, chap. 1, demonstrates this pleasant truth with verve and wit. Therefore, this study does not address controversies about the utility or consequences of formulae, as such, for which Nagler 1974 and Austin are helpful. We

No single interdisciplinary definition for this multidimensional phenomenon of communication has yet won wide acceptance. No one doubts the existence of the silent language of (voluntary) gesture. Unintended movements and postures communicate no less; a licked lip, sudden wince, or catch in the voice carries as much meaning and affect as words, indeed more. Therefore, this study prefers inclusiveness so that future research in literary anthropology does not overlook any possible source of edification about one of the complex ways that cultures nonverbally store, communicate, and impose attitudes and ideas on their members.[3]

Modern fictions and parafictions take for granted the utility of everyday gestures, postures, and voicings in developing fictional realities.[4] Small contemporary theaters for intimate, drawing-room drama and the large screen but close-in camera of the cinema exploit meaningful gestures to the hilt. Basic narrative techniques of exposition, dialogue, and characterization by description have always been enriched by expressive body movements or bearings that translate hidden, internal emotion and verbal messages into visible, external manifestations and passive, often unintended bodily expressions, or *affect displays*. Symbolic behaviors enact social relations, sometimes through ceremony or ritual, or nuance individual activities or sounds that informally (intentionally or not) communicate information. Nonverbal behavior provides the artist with an additional instrument to dramatize, characterize, and structure decisive conflict, contact, and cohesion. The described nonspeech acts serve as organic parts of the story—natural, inevitable concomitants of speech and instrumental action.

The face most capably and prominently reveals emotions, but the hands, voice, limbs, and body posture are also eloquent. Such displays often appear suddenly and briefly. As they communicate information about human responses in real-life situations, so in oral and written literature, they supplement the verbal messages of characters. They enrich the narrative by showing the reader what people look like ordinarily and at moments of crisis. They expose how they react, how they feel (cold or sweaty, sensitive or calloused, etc.), how different sexes, ages, classes, cities, and races conform to, or play against, type. Reported nonverbal behavior can confirm, modify, or subvert explicit words of characters and internal narrators. The normally austere,

---

quote Homeric episodes from other books when they best illustrate the described phenomena.

3. See the following for different attempts at comprehensive definition of meaning-bearing movement, symbolic demeanor, and sound "effects.: e.g., Grajew 1934, 3–5, Hall 1959; Burgoon and Saine 1978; Poyatos 1983, and others; and Nöth [1985] 1990. As with definitions of smut or obscenity, difficulties of demarcation do not abort useful and illuminating discussion.

4. A glance at the works of Meredith, Dickens, Tolstoy, Isaac B. Singer, or Margaret Atwood shows this. See recently the brief comparison of ancient and modern fictions in Newbold 1992.

objective style of Homer supplies this unobtrusive vehicle for recording emotion and sometimes relies on it to express meaning for otherwise restricted characters, such as Telemakhos or Penelope.

Nonverbal behavior in literature raises broader and comparative questions: Why does one poet represent one kind of nonverbal behavior more than another? Which poet reports the greatest, and which the least, variety of nonverbal behavior? How does nonverbal behavior affect readers' responses? Before we can answer such questions, we must query specific texts and authors thoroughly. First, we inventory varieties of nonverbal behavior. Then, we explore Homer's exploitation of this symbol world of human behavior. In the course of the inquiry, we note some differences between Homeric and North Atlantic gestural communities. For instance, Homer pays less attention to facial expression than we do, and Homeric characters often act as if more forms of control exist in the situation than in the person. This dictatorship of the ruling sociability is the case today in other contemporary cultures more traditional than ours. We must discipline ourselves to respect the pastness of the past and the otherness of the other, while learning what we can about ourselves and our own manipulations of body and voice.

Ancient epic bards do not include details of nonverbal behavior to enhance authenticity or realism, to flaunt knowledge of arcane or subliminal activities that were not systematically studied until almost yesterday. Rather, the description of bodily reactions and relevant artifacts makes vivid the lively web and texture of human interrelations and interactions. Nonverbal behavior in the text often supplies internal feedback that tells coparticipants and the audience how they might react in such a situation, like a chorus in Attic tragedy. Helen's beauty or Priam's grief produces noticeable nonverbal effects on others. Homer's notation of nonverbal action and reaction behaviors conveys direct and accessible information about etiquette, folklore, social life, and heroic human nature. His characterization through gesture proves to be as subtle as static descriptions or psychological analyses of characters' spiritual and emotional states.

The present study profits from nearly three millennia of Homeric textual and contextual critics. Somatic semiosis has been observed in the earliest Western creative texts (*Gilgamesh,* the Hebrew Bible, and Homeric poetry) and has been studied occasionally by ancient and later analysts, including Plato, Aristotle, Cicero, Dionysios of Halikarnassos, Quintilian, and Eustathios.[5] Internal and external, but humanly modifiable, aspects of our

---

5. For examples, see Plato *Ion* 535b-c (character and rhapsode); Aristotle *Rhet.* 3.1 = 1403b20; Cicero *de Orat.* 3.59.213–21; Quint. *Inst.* 1.11.17, 11.3.65–184. Eustathios, ad *Od.*

world constitute the "triple structure of human communication": language, paralanguage, and kinesics (cf. Poyatos 1983, 346). Formal and informal patterns of handling space, time, and external body-adaptors more recently entered the field of nonverbal behavior studies. We wield ourselves and the environment in symbolic ways that enlarge communicative resources, perceptions, and participation for message senders and receivers. Faced with the fact that the modern interdisciplinary science of nonverbal behavior suffers from difficulties of definition, methodology, taxonomy, and even excessive nomenclature, I endorse the "pansemiotic" view of Goffman: the body, and therefore the person, can *never* not communicate. Everything short of *praxis* (self-realization through instrumental acts, e.g., a punch in the nose) provides *semiosis,* a potential message, whether or not intended, received, or understood (unilaterally, bilaterally, multilaterally); and it may be understood consciously or (as so often) subconsciously (Nöth 1990, 388–91; Poyatos 1983, chapter 4).

The following pages owe little directly to textual semiotics, a branch of cultural and literary criticism descended from structuralism, Russian formalism, Saussure's linguistics ("the life of signs"), and Roland Barthes' perceptive, but unsystematic, insights, or to discourse analysis (a division of sociolinguistics).[6] Classical philology and literary criticism have rarely engaged in any systematic study of body-talk. A brief review of the modern authorities that intellectually midwived this essay may help readers understand its unfamiliar interdisciplinary debts. We may hope to have understood their complex approaches and not just to have borrowed their specialized terminology. My greatest obligations are owed to the microsociologies of Erving Goffman and to Edward Hall's anthropological essays on aspects of nonverbal behavior (e.g., chronemics and proxemics). Sociologists and anthropologists have shown much greater interest in body messages than literary scholars, or word-people, classical and modern. Erving Goffman in particular (and somewhat eccentrically for his discipline) developed the study of the "presentation of self in everyday life." Anthropological field studies of nonverbal behavior published by Edward Hall, Weston LaBarre, Michael Herzfeld, and Esther Goody also helped me articulate the ancient "silent

---

6.363, equates Helen's anodyne (significant, defining object) and her speech. Dionysios (*Dem.* 53) underlines the relevance of delivery for Demosthenes' speeches: τί δὴ ταῦτα [sc. τὰ πάθη τὰ τῆς φωνῆς καὶ τὰ σχήματα τοῦ σώματος] πρὸς τὴν λέξιν αὐτοῦ συντείνει; φαίη τις ἄν. ἡ λέξις μὲν οὖν, εἴποιμι ἄν, οἰκείως κατασκευάσεται πρὸς ταῦτα, μεστὴ πολλῶν οὖσα ἠθῶν καὶ παθῶν καὶ διδάσκουσα, οἴας ὑποκρίσεως αὐτῇ δεῖ.

6. Culler 1981 and Nöth [1985] 1990 survey these academic movements. Burns 1992 evaluates Goffman's many contributions.

language." The psychologies of face and limbs produced by Ray Birdwhistell and Paul Ekman enhance "deception studies," a bailiwick of interest to governmental clandestine agencies and students of informal persuasion.

A post-postmodern humanist no longer needs to justify a license to poach on the social sciences, especially anthropology and sociology. Prehistoric, preliterate epic society and social conventions are unsurprisingly opaque to the unaware, or, more dangerously, deceptively familiar—a problem which led, for instance, to the extended misunderstanding of why Akhilleus refuses Agamemnon's cornucopia of reparations or why Agamemnon remains seated when he eventually does offer his version of an apology. It enables, or at least invigorates, the reading of Homer to recognize his extensive vocabulary for bodily and vocal signals and his subtle descriptions, by visual cues and acts, of social difference. We begin to grasp the different, archaic Greek rules of symbolic interaction at funerals and feasts, between equals and across hierarchies, conventional more often than idiosyncratic ways to manipulate status.

For this task of making sense of social interaction in the *Iliad* and the *Odyssey*, Hall's social anthropology and Goffman's face-to-face sociology are particularly helpful. These two students of social interaction are theory-poor, one of their less obvious virtues. They are preternaturally conscious of bodily enactment of social and personal meaning. Body habits differ by rank, age, society, gender, and (least often) individual. Symbolic systems of the word, the body, and the group clarify each other. Attention to status manipulation and body language enables us to abandon comfortable, but questionable, psychologizing for more demonstrable sociological analysis. Such studies stick to the attested surface rather than diving below with the aid of artificial psychological analyses of what a subject "must have thought." Anatomies of Penelope's thought and emotional processes are especially liable to essentialist reductionism.

Political discrimination (homeless outcasts and local potentates), gender expectations, damage limitation, and status rejiggering in Homer frequently present reciprocal and immediate verbal interchange and instrumental actions. The striking speech and act, however, are frequently modulated by body language and significant trivia of self-presentation. The consonance of the three communicative systems (verbal, gestural, and paralinguistic) satisfies expectations of convergence in life and in creative literature, in religion and sport as well as in epic and drama. Social bodies require education and socialization in techniques of attention, movement, and even repose. We inflict queer postures on youth; sitting up in a chair is unnatural, as any parent knows. Initiation into adulthood's social enforcement systems changes forever our use and care of our bodies, in response to food, sexual allure, and other external sources of agitation.[7]

Goffman studied social relations as "expression games" and theatrical performances with casts, cues, audience(s), props, stages, and so forth. Between the primary, presumed veracious (1.1–10) narrator's narration of the *Odyssey* and those inner tales mocked as lies by the inner or narrative audience,[8] there are self-conscious and unself-conscious roles played, in which certain character enactments are preciously and definitively described as fraudulent—for instance, Odysseus as Outis, Aithon, and a tramp; Athene as Mentes, Mentor, a waif on Skheria, and Penelope's sister Iphthime (4.796–810). The omniscience of bard or goddess allows the audience confident access to the "dark secrets" of behaviors, distinctions between assumed and real social roles. The characters, through dress, conduct, mien, words, and associates, express their chosen images of themselves; the audience is more, or less, impressed. A character is known by "the expression that he *gives* [true and false], and the expression that he *gives off*." By verbal deceit and nonverbal feigning, Telemakhos, Penelope, and Odysseus shape and attempt to shape the reality of their social situations (Goffman 1959, 254, 2, 66 and 66 n.15, 169).

The stagelike qualities of the public Homeric *megaron* are underscored by many exits and entrances. The suitors hold center stage, but their comportment, verbal and nonverbal, profoundly reveals how precarious their position is. Penelope descends to their level, always attended by serving women and remaining only briefly subjected to male gaze; Telemakhos comes in and out but is never allowed to feel "at home." The vagrant's entry is most extended, most impeded (by Melanthios, Argos, and the suitors), and most obstructed by social expectations. He has nowhere to retreat to, nowhere to prepare his show. To increase his security and to spy on his household's miscreants, Odysseus creates a new, anomalous, and not unquestioned position, by arrogating to himself new duties.

Social friction provides the most telling situations for nonverbal decoding. Odysseus' disguise, Penelope's struggle to remain uncommitted, and Telemakhos' scrambling to maintain his precarious rank and property uncover the brutal gestural codes of the heroic world's jostling "status warriors" (as Van Wees 1992 calls them). Homer's varied cast of guests and hosts constitute a study of manners in the vital borderland between "in's" and "out's," strangers and friends. We can compile the "dos" and "don'ts" of archaic

---

7. Cf. Mauss 1935, 275, 284, 291–92; Douglas 1970, 66–70, Burns 1992, 36–41.
8. E.g., by Euryalos at 8.158–64; Athene at 13.287–301; Eumaios at 14.122–31, 165–70, 363–66, 387–92, 508–10; Antinoos at 17.446–49(?); and Penelope at 19.309–16.

Greece's extended visits. Odysseus, accoutred as a beggar, claims former noble identity and shows the courtly manners and deportment that should prove it (14.109–20, 193–200; 19.107–22, 183–98). In conversation with Penelope, he must perform simultaneously as prince and beggar; he lets her know he is equally adept at both. This too wins her approbation.

Odysseus' disguises, by their explicit adoption, clarify what Homer regarded as socially determined, culturally assumed, and inescapably characteristic of the human condition. His certified frauds, "discrepant characters," and contrived performances establish crucial and lucid evidence for Homeric "impression management." Thus trained in the school of traditional epic, we can distinguish definitive falsehood from debatable examples in everyday life, where one encounters spontaneous whim, inherently labile human nature, or duplicitous instrumental acts of the sort that characterizes con-men.[9]

2. Categories of Nonverbal Behaviors

Five categories for the study of nonverbal behavior in ancient epic have been constructed from the findings of psychologists, anthropologists, semiologists, and kinesiologists.[10] The exigencies imposed by a vanished society obviously allow us to examine only those nonverbal behaviors that Greek and Roman writers and artists thought worth reporting. Subject to this grievous loss of undocumented, everyday nonverbal behaviors, the data inventoried here require but these five categories (see also glossary). Chapter 3 addresses these categories again in order and at length for *Iliad* 24. Certain types of highly stylized, ancient nonverbal behaviors are set aside in this study because they do not appear in Homer or constitute independent art forms performed in "stop-time" for large audiences, so they usually lack meaning for personal, spontaneous interaction. These include the sign languages (emblems) that Ovid used to communicate privately with his girlfriends and publicly with the Getae, who spoke little or no Greek or Latin; the standard dance-steps and lascivious gestures of mime and burlesque actors; the formal etiquette of institutional diplomacy; and the imitative movements of an actor parodying a known person.[11] This sample ex-

---

9. Goffman 1959, 66–67, with note on literary applications. My next book addresses epistemological and historical issues of sincerity and duplicity among "entrepreneurs of the supernatural," such as historical Peregrinos, Alexander, and Apollonios and fictional characters in Petronius and Apuleius, primarily in the eastern half of the Roman Empire.

10. Ekman and Friesen 1969b, esp. 63–92; Hall 1959; and Birdwhistell 1970. Lateiner 1987, 108–12, offers an earlier Homeric inventory on the principles enunciated here.

11. For examples, see *Am.* 1.4.15–38; *Tr.* 5.10.36 and *Met.* 6.5.79; *Od.* 8.263–65, 370–84; *Am.* 2.4.29; *Ars* 3.755; *Met.* 11.673. They deserve separate study.

cludes a reductive popular expression of nonverbal behavior, ancient and medieval allegorical personages, such as Lust or Avarice. The categories addressed are the following:

A. Ritualized and conventional gestures, postures, and vocalics
B1. Affect display: psychophysical, out-of-awareness emotional signs
 2. Subconscious, out-of-awareness gesticulation and vocalics
C. Objects, tokens, clothes (external adaptors)
D. Social manipulation of space and time (proxemics and chronemics)
E. Informal, in-awareness gestures, postures, and verboids

A. Ritualized or conventional behaviors permeate Homeric epic. They are common in type-scenes (e.g., setting sail, dreams, and sacrifice) and are often articulated by formulae and patterns that assist the reciting bard. The leisurely, if highly traditional, report of common acts confers solemnity on both sacred and secular occasions, such as toasting, bedding down, bathing, and divine visitation. Ritualized political and juridical acts, such as grasping the scepter, exchanging gifts, and swearing an oath on an object, confirm that even men at war still have civilizing rules and conventions. Ceremonial gestures, such as prayers and libations, mark a crisis, signal the character's focused involvement, and invite readers' heightened attention. Finally, especially in the *Odyssey,* some rituals invite nuanced parody and social critique—for example, when unwelcome Olympian messenger Hermes or humble Eumaios, Iros, and the beggar Odysseus arrive at a host's and are greeted and treated as honored guests. Many of these behaviors, in type-scenes or unique situations, will be examined in this book.[12]

Suppliancy, one such type-scene, offers a thematic key to both epics, as the following confrontations reveal: Agamemnon's proxies proffering reparations in the embassy scene of *Iliad* 9; Lykaon and Priam beseeching all-powerful Akhilleus; and Odysseus requesting succor of Polyphemos, then of Alkinoos and Arete, and finally of the outrageously tightfisted suitors. Indeed, the complete failure of all Trojan battlefield suppliants and the perfect success of divine suppliants in the *Iliad* heightens Priam's unique Trojan success before the most relentless Akhaian killer (Gould 1973, 74; Pedrick 1982, 132, 135, 139–40). Sharing food provides another privileged mode of social reintegration, rejected by Akhilleus, Priam, and the suitors at various moments, but later grudgingly accepted on limited terms as a sign of some

---

12. M. Edwards 1991, 11–23, concisely surveys "composition by theme"; Williams 1986, illuminates Homeric parody.

12   *Sardonic Smile*

hard-won understanding, a ritualized—that is, clearly bounded—de-alienation from human companionship.

B1. Imaginative writers record some nonverbal behaviors that are entirely unconscious, beyond control, or involuntary (psychophysical expressions, in the jargon of psychology and ethology). Examples include blushing, trembling, and convulsive twitching. Other examples that are somewhat or variably conscious, intended, and controllable (affect displays) include sighing, collapsing to the ground, weeping, and lip licking or lip biting. Such events display emotional and situational responses that, intentionally emitted or not, provide others with "body clues," messages about our psychological state or perception of relative status.[13]

B2. Akhilleus aggressively directs dark looks first at Agamemnon and later at other status and space invaders. These penetrating glances telegraph angry mood and threatening intentions to both the interactants and the audience. Beetled brows rebuke and menace those who violate his personal space or inexplicit concepts of ceremony, decorum, or dignity. For instance, the idea that material considerations might determine his actions offends him when Odysseus and Priam tot up their "unrefusable" offers (9.378–92; 24.559–60, 568–71). Homer employs a rich, calibrated vocabulary of words *and* gestures to depict anger and pain. In the *Odyssey,* the suitors and the handmaids laugh in glee or hysteria, but Odysseus only smiles, and sometimes only inwardly, a very self-controlled response.[14] Penelope collapses and weeps, as do Briseis and Thetis, to express women's pain and their often otherwise inexpressible suffering. Male heroes weep also, more actively; Akhilleus' frequent tears and his openness to pain contribute to his special heroism and attraction. His body expresses his heroism; his vulnerability and the expression of his suffering is verbal and nonverbal, physical and psychological. This discussion combines in category B both active and passive, unintended and half-intended self-revelation, topics that current studies of

---

13. The works cited by Ekman and Friesen 1969b, Hall 1959 and 1966, and Poyatos 1983 et al. survey phenomena for psychologists, sociologists, and anthropologists. For the effect of gender, see Henley [1977] 1986; for demeanor, see Goffman [1955] 1967c; for hierarchy, see Firth 1969, 1972. See Poyatos 1983 for European literature, Portch 1985 for American literature, and Lateiner 1987 for selected works of ancient literature. Evans 1930 discusses physique, gestures, and facial expression, as well as the ancient psychological treatises that attempt to "read" character from appearance; see also Evans in *HSCP* 58/59 (1948); 189–217; Evans 1969.

14. Fenik 1974, 180–87; Levine 1982a, 1983a, 1984, 1987; Russo ad 20.301–2. The sardonic smile within (?), μείδησε δὲ θυμῷ σάρδανιον (Homeric hapax), puzzles not only philologically but physically and psychologically. Note the inverted, nonverbal metaphor: the verbal description of a facial expression "in his heart" describes—as it substitutes for—an emotion. I discuss this involuted, eponymous smile in chapter 9.

real-life behavior reasonably keep distinct. This "leakage" includes pallor, teeth chattering, crying, and sweating; certain groans, whines, cringes, and laughter; and so forth.[15]

Silence and stillness themselves can powerfully convey inner strength, severe annoyance, or fearful dumbfoundedness. When the Akhaians' silent advance is contrasted with the swarming Trojans' piercing cacophony (σιγῇ and κλαγγῇ, 3.2–9; cf. 10.523), both the order of the battle line and the paralinguistic contrast transmit differences between two fighting forces. The semanticity of silence marks fear and crisis: Helen in fearful silence leaves to pray, the proxies of Agamemnon are stricken at Akhilleus' outburst, and Odysseus orders the kingliest king to shut his mouth (*Il.* 3.418–20, 9.430, 14.90). The choreography of ancient conversations has become terra incognita: who begins and ends it, who changes and polices topics (forbidden subjects), who nods the head or mumbles "uh-huh," who interrupts whom and how often, and so forth. The "flow" rules of conversation regulation are almost involuntary and peripheral to awareness.[16] Silence indicates prudent disengagement or, more often, involuntary emotional overload and incapacity in the face of threatening situations. Eurylokhos' stunned aphony when he wants to report Kirke's dirty work (*Od.* 10.245–48) presents a fine compact example: οὐδέ τι ἐκφάσθαι δύνατο ἔπος, ἱέμενός περ, "Nor could he speak out a word, though he very much wanted to." Antilokhos' aphony (*Il.* 17.694–700) after he hears of Patroklos' death portrays emotional and muscular paralysis. His difficulty in expressing the news to Akhilleus seems second only to Akhilleus' profound silences (18.22–34).

C. The employment of significant objects weightily displays authority in religious and temporal ceremonies. Consider the scepters of kings, the protective crosiers and fillets of the priest Khryses in *Iliad* 1, and special goblets, such as Nestor's, Akhilleus', Hera's, and Priam's (11.631–36; 16.225–30; 24.101–2, 233–37). The stemware is flourished for prizes, toasts, and libations (23.656; 9.176, 203, 224; 16.225). Agamemnon brandishes his ancient, genealogized scepter, emblem of government and divine sanction, to shore up visibly shaken authority; Odysseus wields it as a humiliating weapon; and Akhilleus italicizes his departure from the Danaans by hurling

---

15. Holoka 1983, 6, 15; Monsacré 1984, 59, 61, 65. Levine 1984 and Colakis 1986 anatomize Homeric smiles and laughter. In Latin literature, Vergil reports Lavinia's *one* blush, an uncontrollable reaction. Lyne 1983 shows how this affect display reflects both Lavinia's feelings and Turnus' noteworthy behavior. Ovid, on the contrary, frequently notes (women's) blushes.

16. Cramer 1976, 203, investigates the only such imperative in Homer. Ekman and Friesen 1969b, 82, describe conversational "regulators;" see also Henley [1977] 1986 and Henley et al. 1985. Lateiner 1992a discusses stupefaction in Greek and Roman epic.

it down. Chairs are deployed symbolically to characterize Zeus' superior power and Priam's insatiable grief (see chapter 6). Hektor's corpse itself and the gifts that ransom it constitute the climactic objects of the *Iliad*'s object-filled narrative.

In the *Odyssey*, the honorific guest-gifts and banquets that Odysseus craves structure every encounter on his wanderings. His scar, bow, and bed uniquely identify him and his prized prerogatives, just as body badges of decrepit age and the walking staff and ragged clothes of vagrant status previously disguised his "true" personal and social identities. In fact, references to women weaving cloth and the wearing of clothing everywhere punctuate the *Odyssey*. One textile's fabrication preserves Penelope's chastity and another Odysseus' life (2.94–110 [thrice reviewed]; 5.346–50, 372–73, 459–60). Other (dirty) garments justify Nausikaa's jaunt to the seashore. These, when clean and on Odysseus' back, expose Nausikaa's covert assistance for the vagrant to another perceptive woman, clever Queen Arete. Weavers (who are always women) are also associated with obstacles to Odysseus' *nostos:* Kalypso sings as she shuttles before the loom with Odysseus in thrall, Arete recognizes her work at another dangerous moment, deceptive Kirke and her maidservants are encountered while working at the loom, and even Ino's lifesaving buoyant *kredemnon* is feared as a woven trick. Kalypso's parting gift of clothes nearly drowns Odysseus (5.346, 356–64, 372). A golden brooch to fasten a mantle allows the beggar to prove to Penelope (by ecphrastic description) that he has known and entertained her husband. Finally the misleading rags are removed by the "beggar" to confirm a version of heroic nudity and to slaughter the suitors. The hero casts off one persona (established by body-adapters, textile degradations) and resumes another, socially elevated identity, by the significant absence of any such identifying social sign.[17]

D. Proxemics, both in-awareness and out-of-awareness, studies formal and informal orientation, elevation, and distance-manipulating activities in daily transactions (e.g., presidential declarations of war from the Capitol dais in Congress or buttonholing to offer emergency directions). Chronemics does the same for time-management activities in interchanges (e.g., the stately pace of Catholic mass or hurried office gossip). The arrangements can be permanent or impermanent (e.g., classroom layout and taxicab queues versus cocktail-party clumping and time-out football huddles). One may examine private, nearby, and distant communicative spaces or slow and rapid uses of time-taking and time-sharing in particular cultures. Ter-

---

17. Griffin 1980 (17–19), Combellack 1948, and Benardete 1963 (15–16) enriched this paragraph. On textiles and clothes, see Schadewaldt 1959, Hölscher 1960, and Jenkins 1985.

ritoriality and its transgressions (exclusion, 16.361–62; violation, occupation, and pollution, 22.480–94) offer ethological aspects of proxemics. Ordinary examples of chronemics include calculated tardiness for assignations and academic classes and interruptions and accelerated "tailgating" responses during heated disputes. Literary examples include the compressed reports of many adventures in books 9–12 and the retarded pace of the narrative in the bow contest. Hurriedness or slowness can be reported of characters as well as of dilated or compressed narration: Telemakhos strides quickly back to the palace, whereas tardy suitors need to be summoned (17.26–30, 170–77).

E. Gesture is the best known and a most highly aware category of nonverbal behavior, both when emitted and when received. Limb and face movements are easiest to control, and we are taught early on to do so, when we smile, wave, or wrinkle the nose in disgust. Words alone are not enough, or rarely are. But gestures may themselves suffice. We "read" bodies and voices to understand "living" words from babyhood on. When we read "dead" words on a page (as Homer's audiences did *not*), we reimagine interlocutors with all their bodily cues and signals. Likewise, with voices, we mentally recreate appropriate timbres, pitches, and vocalic hints; modern creative writers notice these more often than Homer or other ancients. Crucial to the communicative repertory, gestures furnish unambiguous, explicit, and visual messages. Gestures often belong to and complement the verbal message (e.g., a "redundant" handgrasp of greeting). They sometimes provide the entire communicative significance of interaction on their own (e.g., Odysseus' deferred nod to Telemakhos). They can also mark advancing stages in the plot. For example, Odysseus twangs the bowstring to mark success in stage one and to announce the start of stage two.

Body language is a popular term for gesture, gesticulation (which often means no more than large gestures), and posture. *Kinesics* offers a modern synonym usually restricted to out-of-awareness micromotions of the face and limbs. This term usefully avoids the confusing analogies to verbal messages implicit in the popular term. The widest descriptor, *nonverbal behaviors,* has the virtue of including both intended nonverbal *communication* and the many unintentional acts or sounds, often out-of-awareness, that reveal so much of us. The term further comprehends tactemics, proxemics, and chronemics (the symbolic use of touch, distance, and time), strepistics (nonvocal body sounds like clapping and knee slapping), and paralanguage (vocal but nonverbal factors beyond lexemes).

Gesture, facial expression, and vocal (eventually verbal) utterance develop together in the infant and have equal significance. Communication involves mental processes of idea formation and emotional response and also social processes of interaction. Nonverbal behavior facilitates speech production. It certainly provides symbolic representation as well as qualifiers for verbal expression. Emphatic head and hand movements can replace talk entirely; posture and pacing give words a weight or added "spin" otherwise not present. Alternatively, a sour facial expression and sarcastic tone can entirely subvert friendly statements or laudatory speech.

Paralanguage—the sonic and temporal "how" rather than the denotational "what" of a verbal message—contributes to literature as well as to life. *Phonostylistics,* a subdivision of the category, includes intended personal and socially determined vocal tone, pace and volume, clipping and nasalization, emotional expressiveness, and so forth. Paralanguage, of course, always accompanies verbal messages, but nonverbal "segregates"—such as preverbal grunts—and nonlexical acoustic messages—such as "mmmh" (tell me more), "*uh*-uh" (no), and "unh-*huh*" (yes)—supply perfectly adequate messages and "ordinary English." Any modification of phonemes that differentiates meanings (suprasegmentals), such as stress, juncture, pitch, tempo, and intonation, constitute additional paralinguistic data. Consider "I don't know" and "I don't, no." Here, juncture and accent determine meaning for the hearer.[18]

Paralanguage often codes affective states, reactions to situations (e.g., boredom or anxiety), by volume, pitch, and resonance; "informative" semipermanent or permanent features, such as regional origin (by nasalization and clipping), age, gender, or race; and variables (as we see it) of class origin (by precise articulation versus slurring), momentary social ex/inclusivity (by whispers, shouts, and voice projection efforts), or physiological excitation (by hoarseness, moan, breathlessness, pain, etc.).

3. Previous Research

The line between symbolic communication and instrumental action is sometimes hard to draw—unlike the difference between a fist shaken in your face and the punch that bloodies it. Such difficulty does not invalidate attempts to analyze archaic social behavior patterns. The fluidity among the many symbolic categories of nonverbal behavior (variously defined by communicative function, organ of expression, nature of emotion expressed, or degree of awareness) has produced a frustrating variety of classificatory systems.[19]

---

18. Adapted from Nöth's description ([1985] 1990, 247–50). Wescott 1966, following Trager's 1958 lead on paralinguistic sounds, contributed the term *strepistics,* communicative body noise, e.g., clapping, spitting, slapping, burping, and stomping.

19. Ekman 1969b and Poyatos 1983 offer relevant discussions of problems of categoriza-

Introduction   17

The first and only attempt to produce a comprehensive catalog of gesture in Greek and Roman life through literature and art is Sittl's impressively extensive, but long antiquated (1890) survey.[20] His field is so wide that he cannot long discuss any one phenomenon, and his synoptic collection treats all periods of antiquity as one. Among studies of ritualized behavior in literature, the following deserve special notice: Redfield, the son of an anthropologist, on purification and funeral games; Gould, Pedrick, Thornton, and Sullivan on supplications; Williams on formal receptions; and Combellack on assembly etiquette. Other helpful studies of informal gestures include Holoka on dark looks, one of the most frequent forms of visual aggression; Muecke on turning away and looking down; Adkins on insulting tones and expressive physical agitation; Cramer on the uses of silence; Levine, Colakis, and Arnould on laughter; and Monsacré and Arnould on weeping. The following *significant objects,* communicative social artifacts, have received several insightful studies: scepters and other indicia of power; ransom and other, less compelled types of "gifts"; food and drink; heirlooms; textiles of quality; ornamental goblets; bows; and brandished weapons.[21]

---

tion. The same scholars have best typologized gestures: Ekman and Friesen 1969b, 1972; Poyatos 1983, 1986. The former team's categories of "emblems, illustrators, regulators," etc. need further refinement for ethological universality versus (a North Atlantic) cultural specificity. This last issue attracts semioticians who continue to debate—following Charles Darwin's pioneer essay, *The Expression of the Emotions in Man and Animals* (1872)—the arbitrariness and spread of a given sign, e.g., horizontal and vertical head-nods for "yes" and "no." Some gestures seem phylogenetic or "hard-wired," e.g., smiles and pupil dilating or eye widening; some are clearly ritualized, culturally learned, e.g., the curtsy (see its etymology) of respect, the geographically limited thumb-jerk of the (vanishing) American hitchhiker, or the use and duration of direct gaze eye contact between sexes and races. This last nonverbal behavior is often socially disrespectful, even challenging or lethal in certain cultures or subgroups [see chap. 5 n. 8], except in carefully bounded situations.

20. Ohio Wesleyan's Beeghly Library has the German author's annotated copy of *Die Gebärden*. Grajew 1934 focuses on Homer (1–32) and Apollonios (33–55) in a Freiburg dissertation acquired for me by Jim Holoka. Grajew agrees that Homer's gestures are mostly "rituell-konventionelle" (our category A) rather than "Abbilden einer Innerlichkeit" (B and E). Holoka 1992 lays out various useful investigations that classical philologists might undertake in the study of nonverbal behavior.

21. See Combellack 1948; Redfield 1975, 161–65, 203–10; and Griffin 1980, chap. 1, "Symbolic Scenes and Significant Objects," esp. 9–12, 14–20. Griffin's thoughtful survey underutilizes *Iliad* 24 for this topic and scants the *Odyssey,* a mine of nonverbal subtleties. Adam Parry (1956), Motto and Clark (1969), the ever insightful Walter Donlan (1982a, 1989, 1993), Steve Nimis (1986), J.A. Arieti (1986), and Richard P. Martin (1989) discuss Akhilleus' celebrated and calibrated responses to Agamemnon's dangerous gifts and the role of shared meals in negotiations. Consult my bibliography and Holoka 1992 for additional items. Morris et al. 1979, 275–92, offers extensive bibliographical assistance for modern gestural studies.

Chapter 2
Apprehending Homeric Character(s): Gesture and Criticism

In all situations, live or literary, every body poses statements, questions, imperatives, and wishes for others to observe, understand, ignore, or respond to. Observable traits are typological (sex, build, age), somatic (head cold, cleft palate), individual (throat-clearing tic), and expressive (anger, ecstasy). Every day, everyone renegotiates his or her status, presenting a "text," the self on exhibit, more or less in control, the upper lip stiff or not. The voice also, aside from words, which might amount to 1 percent of the total information provided by the vocal tract, is an eminently flexible instrument of communication. We delicately employ these communicative registers without knowing how, or often even when. We can never, as noted before, *not* communicate nonverbally. Only the blind cannot *see* what we say. Literature of every epoch mirrors this reality but (un)naturally selects and highlights certain deeds, words, communicative body movements, and vocal effects.

All the more, literature that began, developed, and matured as dramatic, visible, bardic oral performance includes nonverbal behavior, however such processes of development, transmission, and delivery came to be definitively transcribed. In written form, the inclusion of gestures is highly marked, for now only the unilinear, one-channel text can convey it. Our highly verbal culture should not overlook or undervalue the significant report of body-talk, of elaborate native dances of host and guest, for example—of Odysseus as the suppliant, vagrant, and revealed king, and of the suitors, when they swagger or cower. The body communicates power and oppression.

Heuristics and hermeneutics both tend to flail about uncertainly when facing "Homer"—now a graphed text in a "dead" tongue, but once, and for centuries, an unbounded set of traditional and unfixed performances that empowered groups and cemented values. Has a multichanneled event now been reduced to a lifeless skeleton in a "textual cenotaph"? Has a densely intersemiotic experience, a charged and vital social event, been frozen into a flat, two-dimensional tomb, as some ethnopoeticists claim? Is the written text only a "manuscript-prison" of a once powerful, three-dimensional traditional performance? Certainly the bards and even the rhapsodes once were enabled by a living social context, a breathing coparticipating audience in an arena of interaction, such as one encounters in still functioning oral and semioral cultures. Epic performance is, and was, a social event and institution, not an amusement for the isolated. Our monumental, but ink-only, lettered texts have undergone several "intersemiotic translations," from major communal celebrations to a private, ivory-tower exercise. But to treat these texts as virtually "literary" may blind us to specific virtues of "this special tale-telling idiom." Questions of original format and re-creation engage the folklorist, the comparatist, and now even the philologist. As John Foley (1992, 277, 283, 289–90), Gregory Nagy (1992), and some others have realized, the consequences of oral-formulaic theory and ethnopoetics may gain informed respect for the *Iliad* and the *Odyssey*.

Homeric meaning will not be impoverished, that is, by oral poetics. Repetition in Homer, fully one-third of the two poems (cf. Scott 1921, 264: 9,253 of 27,853 verses), is a dynamic story-way, an element of densely coded energy that activates worlds of association—not a primitive fault inviting the literary critic's benighted judgment of sleepy inattention (Horace) or ineptitude (Pope). Performance perspectives (and experiences, I am told by those who have been there) allow swift access to meanings "charged with associative values," "back-channels" sometimes denied to readers three millennia later but entirely real for the original bard's audience. These cocreators, by their reactions, suggestions, and material appreciation, shape each telling and showing—a fact of life observed repeatedly through the internal audiences in the *Odyssey*. Repetition, economical placement of formulae (Parry), composition by theme (Arend and Edwards), formula clusters, parataxis, *Kunstsprache* (Meister), and the multiform motif-Gestalt (Nagler) fertilize the oral-traditional bard's repertory. Henceforth, the contribution of nonverbal behavior should be factored in as well, a highly affective and focused form of human expression allotted to persons in the text and presumably—but for us irretrievably—employed by the performers of the text. We can observe not only marked movements of face and hand but also expressive body tonus and orientation, whispers, pace, and posture.[1]

---

1. J. Foley 1992, 283; at 288, he briefly alludes to bardic nonverbal performance behaviors. Bérard 1918 (6, 25, 35) and Boegehold 1986 and *Gestures and the Interpretation of Ancient Greek Literature,* forthcoming, suggest other pointers in the text (deictic pronouns, e.g.) of bardic nonverbal behavior. Herzfeld 1985 offers performance photographs; cf. nos. 5, 23; also V. Edwards and Sienkewicz 1990, nos. 8, 10. On Homeric language, see M. Parry's collected papers (1971), with xxi n. 2, and Meister 1921.

The oral-aural-visual and proxemic experience of epic-telling and epic-hearing enjoy and employ expressive and perceptual channels—necessarily. An uninflected, voice-only performance *in person* would come across as desiccated and dead. The print reader can experience these communicative amplifications in imagination only. To decode all the remaining (written) signals, the "value-added signification" of, for example, gestures and postures, we must alert ourselves to alien and subtle forms of expression. Oral epic is "untextual" originally, while we philologists are "hypertextual" (J. Foley 1992, 293–94). To appreciate a multichanneled, communicative dynamic that can appear more minimal than Groucho Marx's eyebrows, Charlie Chaplin's twisted mouth or cane, or Katharine Hepburn's strut, we grasp every expressive hint and milk it. The nonverbal behavior of Homer encodes taken-for-granted behaviors—a shared table etiquette (food-ways at feasts), perhaps, or a gendered social response (Penelope's entries into and retreats from the hubbub or Nausikaa's companions' flight from a naked male stranger). Odysseus' "hand on another's wrist" to signify social control is not "natural" but conventional and enculturated. Any one example of a nonverbal behavior should evoke not only all similar scenes in Homer (formulaic and literary parallels) but, ideally, real moments of the lived social experience of Homer's audiences. Those Hellenes would construe the performed narrative from resources of memory and from immersion in the live tradition, whose texture our time-numbed fingers can barely distinguish. More universal emotional displays like Iros' trembling and more individual gestures like Odysseus' heroic tears are still immediately accessible to us, but the culturally specific gestures are equally important for full appreciation of the epic's great sensitivity and impact on antiquity.

Men and women in verbal (not visual) texts are both like and unlike people on the streets. Gesture, tone, posture, confident swaggers, and body adaptors (pipes, tuxedos, see-through blouses, porkpie hats, and baseball caps) reflect and project not only the inner life of individuals but social pretensions and oppressions of genders, age cohorts, social strata, races, and economic and political classes. Self-image incorporates and emits values and worldviews, class and status. This totality of personal communication, accessible to analysis by modern sociologists, anthropologists, and social historians, finds expression in Homer too. Not only the major players but minor characters, such as Arete and Eumaios, advertise nonverbally their constructed sense of identity and, by their responses, their perception of others' roles.

Frequent and significant for the main plot's development are reported gestures and ephemeral postures that enrich the narrative with incidental detail. These micromotions almost get lost in the epics' main action, as they tend to do in everyday life. They are easy to miss and are sometimes no more than the body's static or chatter, underlining explicit messages or providing confusing counterproposals (communicative dissonance—e.g., Kalypso politely greets Hermes verbally but questions him *before* feeding him, a definite no-no of heroic etiquette). Their total effect, however, on our sense of the reality of Homeric social textures, his constructed literary cosmos, ought not to be underestimated. The humdrum habits of routinized living complement the spontaneous and revealing gesture, antithetical to abstraction and cerebration. The thoughtless impulse, condensed and externalized as a startle or gasp, and the artificial comportment and pompous, preordained motions of the orator or priest all communicate personal and social meaning, significance and affect, to the audience.

Body-talk supplies Homer with an indirect dramatic technique for depicting personalities and concentrating reader attention. "Longinus" (9.2) calls Aias' silence μέγα καὶ παντὸς ὑψηλότερον λόγου, "grand and more sublime than any speech." Odysseus' eloquent body, by movement or position, often tells us all we need to know of his mood and intent. Reticent Homer thus eschews narratorial intervention and the need for intrusive psychologizing. The social person has precedence over psychological man, in any case.

Gestures and reports of nongestures ("he did not flinch," 17.463–64) also illustrate the following unenunciated, but often demonstrated, principle of heroic success in the *Odyssey*. The more uncontrolled or uncontrollable a person's nonverbal behavior reported by Homer is, the less admirable the person displaying it is, a principle to which we shall return frequently. Odysseus and his family in Homer provide models of self-control and self-conscious manipulation of body-language information. Laertids emit few messages that damage their image. Odyssean heroism assumes delayed gratification, long-range investment, and the potency of voice and body management—as well as Iliadic skill with conventional weapons, stamina, and guts. The following pages substantiate these assertions.

Other studies will dissect other expressive Homeric characters, such as Akhilleus, but no Homeric figure is as thoroughly and variously characterized as Odysseus(es). His donning and doffing of guises also offers the narrator and audience a "reality check"; we know when he is feigning social and familial roles. Even careful Odysseus and publicly reserved Penelope, however, at inconvenient times betray inner states and sentiments, ironize their fair or disinterested words by dissonant body language, and subvert their projected "cool" selves by a tic, a twitch, tears, or a shudder. Iros and the suitors—and, to an important degree, all interactants (and indeed animals like Argos and the gods)—do the same.[2]

Expansive elaboration of speech, simile, or instrumental act signals crises of values and lives. "Circumferential details," occupying half a line or several lines, shift time into slow motion and obliquely draw our focus to them. "Social amenities are played out at length, and their elaborate execution is Homer's stylized form of emphasis." The detailed nonverbal behavior specifics of ritualized welcome for foreigners or even apparently spontaneous greetings of long lost family members provide a microscopy, an extraordinary close-up of the matrix of significant moments. Such symbolic sequences set a horizon of expectation. Violations then shock the original audience, immersed in these values, or the modern audience, attuned to protocols of arrival and departure. The disguised beggar's manipulation of interiority, elevation, and bodily orientation as he crosses the palace threshold and penetrates social envelopes (proxemics), or the slow description of his stringing the already genealogized bow (object-adaptor), concentrates tension and attention, conveys a moment's urgency, or locks the reader's mind onto another dimension of *kairos* (Austin 1966, 307–9 [= 1978, 80–81]). In oral and written literature, the report of such "secondary" signs always has salience for the external reader, and often for the internal interactants themselves. A poem that meditates on dubious social rank and personal identity, ambiguous moral worth and social standing, deserves close attention from both fluid and fixed societies.

Odysseus brandishes his sword in the Otherworld to ward off the shades; Eumaios kisses Telemakhos' head as a sign of greeting a superior. In addition to such relatively straightforward nonverbal behavior, however, the power of nonverbal behavior to conceal, distort, lie, and control is highly prized in the *Odyssey*. Bodies and positions mislead as well as words—or better. Objects and postures "speak." Old dog Argos' very ears are eloquent.

After a generation of oralists has inadvertently impoverished the legitimate pursuit of Homer's social pageants and parodies, critics—some unnecessarily devoted to the "one great genius-creator" hypothesis—once again regard every detail as potentially consequential and worthy of atten-

---

2. These emotional expressions are best termed *affect displays*. We call them that here and elsewhere, cheerfully employing the innovative work and noun-crowded lingo of ethologists, anthropologists, and sociolinguists. The glossary assists readers. The initially cumbrous terminology allows for finer distinctions and clearer concepts than the classical philologist's usual working vocabulary. Ekman and Friesen 1969b, Hall 1984, and Nöth [1985] 1990 provide more and fuller definitions.

tion. The attention is merited, although the unitarian hypothesis is unprovable and unnecessary. Consider an example from the level of the word. In a concisely elegant analysis of chairs in Homer, Houston (1975, 212–14) points out that of six words for this body-adaptor, the *Odyssey* reserves *thronos* for privileged males (and goddesses). This stately, large, and covered seat is not used by women—even Penelope—, by servants, or by Odysseus when he feigns being a vagrant. As such, he obtains only the meaner *diphros*. When he attends as a ranking visitor, the *thronos* is his seat and reflects exalted social status. When he discards his mean costume with its imputed proletarian identity (21.420 and 434; cf. *Il.* 11.623 and 645), the same chair changes from the no-count's *diphros* to the master's *thronos*. The delicacy and unobtrusive character of such micromeasures of honor justify attention to the literary expression of the "dust of ordinary life."

Thus, meaning adheres even to characters' inattention, because this ordinary, essential procedure often saves face. Odysseus and Arete both know that Odysseus is borrowing clothes from Nausikaa but leave it long unsaid. Eurykleia is brutally forced to disattend to the scar on Odysseus' thigh. Discredited Odysseus, as stigmatized vagrant, must disregard the missiles thrown at his head and the many insults. Telemakhos cannot respond to every taunt, snicker, and invasion of his "personal space," although as a young man of disputed rank, he resents each one keenly. Sometimes both sides know an embarrassing fact and know the other knows it, but neither openly admits it. This may be the case in the upstairs interview of mistress and mendicant in *Odyssey* 19 or in the pigsty poker-faced parley and counterbidding of Eumaios and Odyseus.[3] It certainly applies to Telemakhos and Helen's awareness of each other's identity, Helen and Menelaos' wary marital truce, and the pins-and-needles conversational confrontations of Kirke and Odysseus.

How do we read Homer's traditional poems—drenched in hoary and not-so-hoary formulae as Milman Parry proved—in the post-Parry period? Parry, Combellack, and others have powerfully expressed the pressure of the general that prevails over the particular in orally derived poetry. Parryists all, know it or not, we recognize traditional, oral formulae. But now, with the insights of Adam Parry and Norman Austin as well as a generation of Parryist formulae-modification studies, we also respect the more flexible genera-

---

3. Harsh 1950; see Amory 1963 and Russo 1983 for Penelope's mental processes in book 19; Roisman 1990a for Eumaios. In the close-up camera shots of modern cinema, shared glances, licked lips, twitching mouth muscles, and raised eyebrows (as well as strictly intrusive, energized bass viols that should offend the modern audience's hyperactive canon of realism) powerfully signal these unholy, unspoken communions.

tive Gestalt, prototypes of formulae, modified formulae, formulae in untraditional contexts, and even significant variants.

The Homeric "nods" that bothered poetic craftspersons of earlier centuries are now justified, or even admired, as results of inherited expectations, oral performance, traditional composition, type-scenes, and so forth. Comparative study of oral epic, then, has not, and cannot, determine satisfactorily when, where, and most importantly how Homer, Homers, pseudo-Homer, Homer's daughter, Homer II, and/or Team Homer composed the *Odyssey*, that is, the *Odyssey* that I am reading this sunny February Ohio morning in a battered library copy of Monro and Allen's 1919 maroon, onionskin OCT or Stanford's 1965 Macmillan "red." Traditional oral epics do not recognize *a* date of composition in any case, only of transcription. Naive, mechanistic analysis of oral composition has evolved into more sophisticated oralist investigations[4] that allow unlimited artistic control to the "final" poet(s). We no longer try to follow Parry's perfect "economies" or explain away perceptible and affecting subtleties as nonexistent, imaginary, and coincidental. Oral poetics does not browbeat readers to forgo observing complex and subtle characterization and plot construction. This situation has led to neo-analysis and neo-unitarianism, both of which elegantly bypass the perhaps no longer worthwhile issue of Homeric "nods" and clear discrepancies versus "unified artistry." The former argue that older themes and other, discrete stories present in our texts have been refined and expanded; the latter switch the spotlight from joints and fissures to seamless development, cross-references, and remarkable consistency. The interesting questions have changed. Are current texts a (literate?) poet's spectacular, monumental version of an already ancient oral tradition's diverse lays? Given the nature of oral poetry, traditional diction, wide illiteracy with co-occurrent conserving gifts of memory, and given a listening (not reading) audience, both the occasional incompatible elements and the delicate subtleties that the modern scholar finds can have coexisted for the poet or even the rhapsode, and for the listeners who advanced the plot along with their "singer."[5]

---

4. Such as Nagler 1974, Shive 1987, Webber 1989; cf. Wender 1977 on the literacy of Homer and the special exigencies of oral composition; see also Adam Parry's remarks in M. Parry 1971, x–xxii, and the rest of his substantial introduction (ix–lxii) to his father's brief, but revolutionary, lifework. Lloyd-Jones 1992, 52–57, composed an informative review of the current state of the question. For the best recent survey from the point of view of oral poetics and comparative folklore, see J. Foley 1992.

5. See Combellack 1965, esp. 46, 49, 53–54, for an amusing presentation of "oralism." Holoka 1991 elegantly summarizes the Parryist contribution and limitations. Wender 1977 wittily evaluates ancient and modern oral epic. Kullmann 1984 generously acknowledges oral poetics while presenting and addressing the different problems that neoanalysis tries to solve.

While social historians, linguists, and students of comparative creative forms try to establish place and time for bard and audience, literary critics may pursue a different agenda and comprehend what exists in the only *Odyssey* they have, the industrially printed *Odyssey*. We meet Homer only on type-set, uniform pages—the frozen art-object that enables private re-creation. Unlike hearers, we can flip back and forth, and we do. Unlike the original audiences' oral performance, the current text of Homer permits the same sort of analysis as texts of Vergil, Ovid, Kazantzakis, and Derek Walcott. Contemporary response to an autonomous text may discover effects unintended by Homer and Company, but who can define what one (or more) genius was capable of? Such a misguided attempt would appear to be one version of the "intentionalist fallacy." No one asserts that Shakespeare could not have written *Julius Caesar* because the tragedy shows more knowledge of Roman society and human psychology than he or another Elizabethan Briton could master. The same is even more true for the fleshed-out social world of Homer and Homers. To restrict critical discussion of the *Odyssey* on a priori assumptions of oral tradition and performance—about which non-Serbs and most Serbs know little for the present and essentially nothing for 700 B.C.E.—is to miss the mark on Homer, to forestall interpretive progress.[6] This book happily bypasses these real and major issues to attend to other essential phenomena that politely request a modicum of scholarly attention.

The study of nonverbal behavior secures and identifies a refreshingly new dimension of the Homeric epics. It may not create a new hero, since it is not a character study as such or a new oral poetics. This book does not, as someone might object, amount to a new interpretation. The book's sufficient justification would be to demonstrate that attention to body-talk confirms and italicizes existing, already subtle expositions of the world's favorite story—of Penelope's bounded independence or of Telemakhos' social and legal conflicts. But more than character analysis and sociology can be unearthed. Body-talk identifies unobserved ironies and psychological italics, as body and voice undermine or confirm verbal messages. Sometimes, nonverbal behavior contradicts explicit messages, and, as in real life, the noted

---

Austin 1991, 235, emphasizes the self-referential world of a very conservative tradition. Nagy 1992 compares ancient Hellenic with living epic traditions.

6. Lowenstam 1992 suggests that ancient vases can assist Homerists on select issues concerning the chronology and development of epic tradition. Holoka 1991, 477–81, and J. Foley 1992 identify the leading interpretive issues. Kullmann 1984, 315, 319, emphasizes the unique scale of the *Iliad*'s one episode and its debt to the *Aithiopis*. Parallels with medieval European epic show the likely (Near Eastern) influence of writing on the composition of the Homeric poems; see Mondi (1990).

gesture overrides the spoken word for the audiences, internal and external. Homer teaches us to trust everybody but to cut the cards.

Whether or not the modern literary text is an autonomous and closed system, the Homeric text—oral and preliterate in origin, traditional and educational in performance—reflects and purveys a paradigm, or a congeries of paradigms, of meaningful behavior for the ancient audiences (late Bronze Age, Dark Age, archaic, classical, and even later) that listened to each and every version, preversion, or perversion.

Therefore, we can, and will, assume the text "reports" reputable and disreputable, certainly recognizable, nonverbal behaviors, be they handshakes and chin-grasps (category A), tears and laughter (B1), cries and twitching limbs (B2), ratty wallets and rags (C), impatient looks and crowding (D), or whispers and nods (E). Homeric texts not only provide a coherent, integrated and meaningful world of their own (literature); they also "report"[7] ways of verbally and nonverbally behaving and communicating that were decodable by at least seventh-century B.C.E. to fourth-century C.E. audiences, and perhaps by fourteenth-century B.C.E. to sixth-century C.E. audiences.

Nonverbal behavior contributes to the pleasure of the *Odyssey* in several ways. First, the audience is flattered by Homer's implicit trust in its ability to "read" passing gestures and postures without extensive exegesis or comparison. The hearer/reader constructs a satisfactory mental picture or paratext that enriches the words (heard or read). The narrator is reticent, stingy in expressing values, judgments, and opinions (cf. M. Edwards 1991, 1–6); but his reports of nonverbal behavior imply judgments. An eccentric experiment might strip a book of all such bodily clues and find the text seriously impoverished.

Second, although Homeric epic is expansive and digressive (the scar, the scepter, the shield, the bow, the "inserted" wanderings), nonverbal behavior speeds the narrative. Gestures efficiently signal emotions and intentions without extended description or psychological analysis. As in daily life, they are an effective and affective shorthand.

Third, actions can speak louder than words—or can "say" the unspeakable. Odysseus' twanging test of the strung bow sends shivers down *my*

---

7. Albeit they do not offer an easily demonstrable chronological unity, Homer's poems portray a remarkably consistent social, economic, and political world. Finley 1978, Qviller 1981, Geddes 1984, and, with outstanding bibliography, I. Morris 1986 and Van Wees 1992 survey the vast literature on the coherence prerequisite to claims of historicity for Homer's society(ies?). The issue of whether any past social reality obtains reflection *in* the poems involves dating the epoch(s) of both performances and eventual transcription.

spine—and I am not facing imminent puncture. This gratuitous but telling gesture[8] renders otiose the narrator's or critic's strategic or psychological analysis of the various contestants.

The body sends and receives messages, mediates all human communication, and helps to control the rhythm of social interaction. Gestures form part of public rituals and are necessary to the orderly reproduction of the social order. Normally the physical channel supports and agrees with the spoken one, but it constitutes an entirely separate medium with its own syntax. A laugh or a tearful sob can be small and can appear on the face alone, or it can involve the whole body, depending always on the person, the social occasion, and the relationship of the individual to the group. Consider the implicit meanings that structure Telemakhos' or Penelope's social interchanges with each other and the freewheeling suitors.

For example, laughter in the *Odyssey* reflects pressures on the individual and the group from the social situation. When "the general social control settings are slack," laughter erupts more freely.[9] The suitors' gang-laughter emblematizes their false sense of security. It caps a series of aggressively possessive postures, proxemic stances, and invasive acts. They have lowered the threshold to cross before exhibiting their arrogated freedom. They exercise unimpeded mobility on another's turf, express attitudes of scorn, and seem to exude a sense of homey comfort—unmodulated relaxation inappropriate in another *basileus'* house.

Peter Rose has categorized critics' responses to character and situation in Homer under three heads: "unmediated empiricist," "ideological," and literary—the last again subdivided into "belles-lettrist" and "thematic."[10] A brief doxography of attitudes toward the foul body and tongue of the social critic Thersites in *Iliad* 2 illustrates these approaches' attribution of various "univocal intention[s to] the bard." Arguably unaware of the "poet's" self-insertion and the critics' own assumptions about Homer's social and ethical views, such attitudes preclude a range of responses to antiheroic Thersites'

---

8. I mean that the act is instrumentally gratuitous, not advancing the agenda of any of his recuperative goals. In literary terms, it both reaffirms his untrusting character—everything, even the bow, as well as everyone, even Penelope, must be tested—and marks the completion of stage number one in the life-or-death bride contest. It communicates this and more to the audience(s) and is therefore not gratuitous as a literary strategy.

9. Douglas [1971] 1975, 83, 85, 87; Levine 1982a. The gods' unquenchable laughter shows precisely their unquenchable humanness. "Longinus" *de Subl.* 9.8: "Homer, as far as he can, has made men gods and gods men." On the bounds and distance that separate these two species, cf. Clay 1972; 1983, 13–25.

10. P. Rose 1988, 6–11; cf. Thalmann 1988. Both discuss Thersites and ideology, and both find a subversive Homer in the *Iliad* as well as the *Odyssey*.

abnormal disruption of heroic political protocols. Thersites' eloquent performance indicts Agamemnon "Most Kingly," a view parallel to Akhilleus' previous and subsequent vociferations. He expresses the grudges and discontents shared by the mass of soldiers. His explicitly ugly appearance has been reductively understood to undercut his perfectly rational and logical challenge, as though many-minded Homer is unaware that appearance and reality do not always jibe.[11]

One may reasonably propose that the oral poets of the *Odyssey* tradition drew their repertoire of speech, movement, and nonverbal communication from life experience. It cannot be proven, absent other contemporary literary and comparable ceramic evidence, but the burden should lie on those who dispute the proposition and assert that Homer's world is naught but fantasy. But who would hypothesize the *artificiality* of everyday heroic conduct toward thanes and strangers, with mother, at table, or with guests? Deconstructionists and others who enlighten us on the peculiar status of literature and all art performances do not deny that the power of art, in part, derives from some interesting, however asymmetrical, relation to lived reality. While gestures can be idiosyncratic to the person or culture-specific (ethnogests), some are universal; other forms of nonverbal behavior cross cultures and remain relatively constant through time.[12] The oral epic *Odyssey* frequently utilizes audience experience of manners for heightened vividness, energy, irony, and (presumably) evocation of audience response, then and now. Let us now observe which nonverbal behaviors emerge in *Iliad* 24, as well as where, when, and how.

---

11. This slippage is hardly a later Arkhilokhean discovery of the mind. Akhilleus' response to the glozing, desperate Odysseus in *Il.* 9.312–13 or the very ancient, even primitive theme of the return of the disguised husband in the *Odyssey* retorts otherwise.

12. The historian of ancient visual images candidly realizes that archaic and classical Greek visual art derives primarily from myth: significant act, attribute, and gesture do not thereby lose semantic content or social comprehensibility. The observable conventions of early Greek representation and iconography, however, prevent and preclude the unargued assumption that painted and marble gestures always, or even frequently, conform to and reproduce real-life, contemporary practices. (Genre scenes on Attic vases constitute an exception.) The presentation of flying Medusa by a "kneeling run" or Hektor and Akhilleus dueling stark naked and the anachronism of chariot battles in fifth-century vase painting serve as sufficient warnings. We grant that the *Odyssey* contains a plethora of fantasy in the "wanderings" of books 9–13, and both poems reveal some anachronistic archaisms (like *Il.* 11.19–42: Agamemnon's gold and silver breastplate, etc.). This is true whatever date we assign to the existing text. Critics nevertheless generally agree that the *Odyssey*'s images of social and economic life cleave closely to everyday life and institutions of bard and audience, more so than those of the *Iliad* or most early representational art. See Sittl 1890, the disappointing dissertation of Kapsalis 1946, the telegraphic prose of Neumann 1965, and Lowenstam 1992 on art; I. Morris 1986, 94–115, and Donlan 1993, 155–59, on social life and *Realien* reproduced in the current text; D. Morris et al. 1979 on modern gestural transmission and migrations.

Chapter 3
Probe and Survey: Nonverbal Behaviors in *Iliad* 24

Homer undergirds his swift, vivid narrative through body language. The Homeric epics deploy nonverbal behavior to characterize leading figures, to make their reactions instantly intelligible, and to provide a third "language" that supplements their own words and the narrator's description of their martial and political deeds. This is true in the *Iliad* as in the *Odyssey*. Akhilleus and Priam in *Iliad* 24, through their bodies and unplanned motions, become clearer and more intelligible to each other and to the reader. Gestures, postures, and nonverbal sounds in the *Iliad* both supplement and contradict words and acts. In the *Odyssey* also, they provide something that words cannot say, or they undercut and render problematic both instrumental acts and words. Nonverbal behaviors provide Homeric epic, and literature in general, with enriching detail and decisive information. They furnish unobtrusive signals that confirm or deny characters' automatic responses, self-management, and received ideas of human nature. The survey of Iliadic examples that follows will conform to the categories described in chapter 2. It is meant to suggest the importance and ubiquity of nonverbal communication in another, comparable text. It will demonstrate the saturation of epic by nonverbal behavior, while later chapters focus on specific matters limited by category of etiquette, characters, or type of behavior.

1. Ritualized and Conventional Gestures

Ritual commands a central and pervasive place in ancient, even as in modern, life. Hundreds of communal, religious, and secular events fill nearly every day of the ancient calendar. Patterns of learned behavior, secular rituals, structure daily activities, such as eating, dealing with strangers and acquaintances in friendly or hostile ways (honor and degradation), setting out from home for the day's farmwork, entertaining dependents with one's marginal surplus to cement bonds, upholding one's code of honor, and recreation. Communal, even religious, rites, daily, monthly, and yearly, fill up life. The chief personal rites of passage (birth, puberty, marriage, and death) submerge and swathe the individual in social, ritualized activities. These essential, affective, and honor-calibrating events, and their individual deformations, frequently determine and redirect the plots of the Homeric poems.

Iliad 1, the commencement of the narrative and the wrath, treats many initiatory rituals, including approach ceremonies, propitiations of the god Apollo and the earthly Akhaian king, calling political assembly, displaying and challenging warrior honor, commencing diplomatic negotiations, purification, supplication, gifts, sacrifices, libations, feasts, and so forth. The corresponding end-frame book,[1] *Iliad* 24, offers as many ceremonial acts and exchanges, but here Homer concludes the story of wrath, so defilement, death, and rituals of sorrow,[2] burial, and closure are thematic.[3] *Iliad* 24, a narrative of closures, foregrounds personal and communal rituals of closure with attendant nonverbal behavior.

Human rituals depend for their power, in part, on the participation of the celebrants' whole bodies. Will and words gain expression by symbolic nonverbal behaviors: gestures and postures, nonspeech sounds and tones, clothes and artifacts (body-adaptors), and a disruption of ordinary space and time that powerfully affects interactants. Proper attention to etiquette and altered behaviors in altered situations partly defines the adequate hero in Homer. Inattention to, or abuse of, ritual procedures produces dishonor, even death. *Iliad* 24 richly illustrates these assertions.[4] We cannot survey every ritualized Homeric behavior,[5] but we can suggest the pervasiveness of noteworthy gestures, postures, and paralinguistic indicators of a ritual or conventional nature in *Iliad* 24. The last book reintroduces and reaffirms conventions of

---

1. Homer's balance and ring-composition are described by Myres 1932, a study of "palindromic structure" (271) in book 24, and Whitman [1958] 1965, 257–60. More recently, see Macleod 1982, 32; Lohmann 1970, 12–30 discusses its use in speeches.

2. In book 24, the Phthian hero's paralyzing grief balances King Priam's hyperkinetic sorrow. Display rules for betraying pain and sorrow vary widely cross-culturally. Odysseus is the most frequent weeper, as Waern 1985, 223, notes: *am meisten weinerlich*.

3. All other human business momentarily becomes peripheral to unarguable death. Nonverbal ceremonies of the happier past are briefly mentioned: Trojan dancers and singers (a negative reference), Akhilleus' sex life, Apollo's lyre playing, and the dancing nymphs of Akheloios. Their joy counterpoints the doom-drenched present (261, 130–31, 63, 616; on dance, see Quint. *Inst. Or.* 11.3.66).

4. Edwards 1987, 152–54, introduces patterns of heroic conduct; J. Foley 1990, 243, explains "plastic compositional units." Book references in this chapter apply to the *Iliad*; references without book numbers apply to *Iliad* 24.

5. For instance, formulae for ritual handwashing occur five times in the *Iliad*, fourteen times in the *Odyssey*, six times with an identical five-line cluster (e.g., *Od.* 1.136–40) or type-scene. The ritual celebrates (guest) inclusion before the first shared meal. This nonverbal initiation deserves separate analysis, more attention than philological identification of traditional verbal elements. Compare passionate hand-clasping formulae, ἔν τ' ἄρα οἱ φῦ χειρί (6.253 and ten other passages).

community and peace through a range of secular rituals, verbal and nonverbal. The narrative, speeches, and nonverbal behavior remind bloodied and angry participants of the "prizes" for which men fight and die. The contrast to the preceding days of hacking and hewing in battle somewhat elevates the dehumanizing gore, rage, outrageous revenge, and depressing destruction (Macleod 1982, 45–46).

The nonverbal behaviors of religious devotion are prominent. Apollo and Zeus mention Hektor's regular sacrifices and gifts to the gods. Priam lifts his hands and eyes to Zeus, after purifying his body and pouring wine as a libation to the latter (lines 34, 68–70, 301–7, 284–87). Trojan bodies are instruments of communication.

Sharing food establishes a material symbol of acceptance, a ritual bond of solidarity, especially in Homeric redistributive economies. Com*pan*ionship (in the original sense) employs the body's communicative symbolic resources. Procedures of human alimentation have always been highly ritualized in terms of content, occasion, constraints or "style," and invited participants. Book 24 tells of Peleus' celebrated wedding feast, Thetis' drink and toast of welcome, Priam's fast (a negative feast, another nonverbal behavior), Akhilleus and Priam's ratification of agreement and closure of personal isolation(s) by sharing supper, Niobe's paradigmatic return to human conditions (symbolized by breakfast eating), and finally the funeral feast that honored Hektor.[6] Sharing food is richly symbolic and multivalent. The meanings of mourning are more limited but as highly affective.

Iliad 24 provides a handbook for archaic mourning procedures. Homer articulates the stages and action that perform grief—that honor the dead and give closure to the living. Akhilleus expresses his grief and graces his dead friend Patroklos by obsessively mutilating Hektor's corpse (15–17, 51–52, 416–21). Hektor's extended family weeps profusely. Priam veils himself and spreads dung on his body by rolling in it and smearing it about himself. Priam's kinsmen follow him in prescribed lament when he departs Troy for the Akhaian camp as if to his own certain death (ὡς εἰ θάνατόνδε κιόντα).[7]

---

6. 62, 102, 641–42, 627–28, 613, 803; cf. Finley 1978, 123–26, on feasting; also Saïd 1979; Motto and Clark 1969; Griffin 1980, 16. Akhilleus earlier (19.200–210) unyieldingly rejected food and ransom. His meal sharing and conversations in book 9 confirm social solidarity and accepted reciprocity with select Akhaian leaders. Lykaon appeals to the bond of former clemency (Akhilleus already owns a debt) and a meal once shared with his killer-to-be (21.76). His later failure in supplication marks Akhilleus' exceptional rejection of hallowed and civilized *xenos*-bonding, formerly and formally certified by nonverbal rituals. From the huge bibliography on shared meals and their rituals, note Visser 1991, esp. chap. 5.

7. Elsewhere the word "to his death" appears only twice, of (other) great warrior heroes: Patroklos and Hektor (328; Macleod ad loc).

Priam fasts continually and keeps vigil for his dear son (160–65, cf. 510–12; 328; 637–42). Self-defilement (body-adaptor behavior) and self-deprivation (of food and sleep) best perform—that is, externalize for others—his feelings, his verbally inexpressible paternal grief.

Once agreement has been struck by the sorrowful survivors, Hektor's corpse is properly washed, anointed with olive oil, shrouded in a cloak and tunic by Akhilleus' domestic staff, and then brought back to its native public, Troy-town, with further funeral lament (581–82, 587–88, 696–97, 709). The mourning period for the hero Hektor is fixed at an abnormal nine days (in part to compensate for pyre-fuel shortage), with burial and feast on the tenth (cf. the burial of Niobe's children mentioned by Akhilleus, 612). The monument to the dead man will rise on the eleventh.[8]

The kinswomen tear their hair and touch Hektor's head (gendered nonverbal behavior); the multitude, unrelated by blood, crowds around (proxemics), the expressive gesture of concern allotted them. The *oikos* lays out his body, professional male singers lead the dirge (θρῆνος), and females wail in unison (στενάχοντο). His wife Andromakhe ritually leads the kin-lament (γόος), while she holds her husband's head in her arms. His wife and mother perform the duty and exercise the right to *sing* (paralinguistics) their own unique laments. His sister-in-law Helen also, in her last appearance, croons and keens for her Trojan protector (710–12, 719–24, 747, 761).[9] These nonverbal and paralinguistic behaviors "speak" as loudly as the words themselves. Hands speak. The movements and sounds physically perform the experience of loss for the community, while they help the survivors emotionally and socially adjust to an emptier world.

For the funeral—both a cremation and an inhumation—a pyre is erected in public, fired, then extinguished finally with wine (cf. 38). The bones are collected and placed in a mortuary casket. The casket is itself enfolded in a purple cloth before being set in the ground and topped with a mound of stones. Lastly, the Trojans gather for a sumptuous feast in accord with tradi-

---

8. Thus, Priam responds to Akhilleus' inquiries about death rituals in ancient Troy (664–66). The actual burial rites in 783–803 are slightly different: no cremation had been mentioned, and the periods are one day wrong.

9. Female hair tearing often appears on roughly contemporary Attic Dipylon vases of the Geometric period, part of the luxurious grave goods for the dead. Kakridis 1949, 67–75, and Lowenstam 1981, 32–35, 60–61, consider the Homeric head-holding gesture. For notable millennial continuities of gesture in Hellenic funeral lament, see Alexiou 1974 and Danforth 1982 with photographs. The English language seems less endowed with nuance for grief language as well as for funeral procedures and nonlexemic, formal manifestations of grief. This poverty may mirror North Atlantic reserve in self-revelation and graveside practice, not to mention the antiseptic and lonely deaths we choose to endure in modern hospitals.

tional procedures—εὖ (802). Death and the pain of survival thematize the *Iliad*: Thetis mourns for her son alive in books 1 and 18, Akhilleus mourns Patroklos dead from 18 to 24 (at least), and the death of Hektor dissolves the spirit of the great Trojan personages as it spells the doom of Troy (22 passim).

Two forms of ritualized nonverbal behavior prominent in *Iliad* 24, salutation and supplication of an enemy, require greater detail. Nonverbal protocols of heroic greeting[10] and parting provide one barometer of touchy *basileis* civility. *Iliad* 1 and 9 also pivot on nuances of welcome, the observance and rupture of well-understood patterns of reception. Thus, the three books that are arguably most central to the plot and most developed thematically (latest?) locate issues of exchange and reciprocity at their focus. The visitor must be greeted and seated, then offered wine and food, which will be consumed before any inquiries are made as to his name and provenience (394, 397). The good hosts of the *Odyssey*—namely, Telemakhos, Nestor, Menelaos, and Eumaios—provide the pattern, while Polyphemos and Alkinoos show themselves inept, if not dangerous, by violations of these and other rules of hospitality, such as protecting guests and their honor from others' abuse (at dinner and the games). These rules that go without saying are honored and violated repeatedly by knowledgeable interactants in *Iliad* 1, 9, and 24.

Nonverbal, proxemic postures and gestures enable initiation and termination of verbal communication between equals and unequals on earth as in heaven (see chapter 6). First, Iris comes close to Thetis to parley; then, nymph Thetis sits next to Zeus, because Athena makes (proxemic) room for her. Hera personally offers her a goblet of ambrosia and comforting words (cf. 15.84–89). The two divinities implacably hostile to Trojans cooperate in the process of arranging the return of the chief Trojan's corpse. Immortal Thetis then approaches her mortal son, Akhilleus. She sits immediately next to him to stroke and soothe him in sorrow. Meanwhile, Iris approaches Priam and whispers in his ear (24.87, 100–102, 126–27, 169–70). The disguised Hermes subsequently emerges and takes badly frightened Priam's hand to reassure him of safe conduct. Divine-human traffic is very heavy in the battle's brief hiatus.[11] Finally, after the tragic rapprochement of the leading

---

10. G. Rose 1969, 387–406, lists Homeric protocols for greeting strangers; Williams 1986 considers Odyssean parodies of the pattern; Levine 1982a, 100–101 examines the greeting of close acquaintances.

11. Macleod ad 463–64, observes that gods "do not customarily even appear to men in their true shape." Exceptional book 24 perhaps questions this rule. Human-divine encounters are sometimes bracketed by the poet with comments on divinity's opacity to men (*Il.* 5.127–28,

survivors, the sorrow-stricken Trojan crowd huddles around their returned friend and fallen leader. They salute the corpse and express their loss (361, 478, 515, 707–12).

The crucial encounter between Priam and Akhilleus aborts, in several ways, the usual procedure. It is thus marked by absence of greeting protocols: Priam's sneak-arrival at the feet of Akhilleus. Priam closes in on unsuspecting Akhilleus to supplicate before awareness is mutual. Supplication permeates the lethal encounters of the *Iliad,* on and off the battlefield, but in combat "it is always rejected or cut short," and the suppliant is slain. Akhilleus embodies and realizes that ethic of relentless and merciless war (9.632, 16.33, 21.198). Thus, the "values of humanity and fellow feeling" exhibited in the uniquely successful supplication of 24 heighten its power (Macleod 1982, 15–16). The elaborate description of nonverbal behaviors produces the cinematic effect of slow motion and emphasizes the reversal of business as usual by reasserting humane and generous sentiments. Nonverbal behavior gives visual substance to the momentous *Umkehr;* it provides the counterweight to unremitting killing everywhere before (and after, by clear implication).[12]

Supplication structures the trajectory of Akhilleus' wrath and its eventual extinction. Khryses and Agamemnon originally set the pattern of suppliance and rejection, then Akhilleus develops it with his mother. Menelaos, almost human, yields once to a suppliant (6.51–53), but his brother brings him back to his (pitiless) battlefield senses. Phoinix narrates the story of Kleopatra's failed suppliancy before Meleagros; the semisupppliant Patroklos and the pseudosuppliant Agamemnon vary it. Priam finally succeeds in restoring its important terrestrial potency.[13] Priam's self-degradation, his postural abasement before Akhilleus, is the necessary price for recovery of his son's dead body, the supremely valuable "social artifact." Every formality of gesture, every nuance of acknowledged status-manipulation, is observed.

Priam's divinely contrived and uniquely unnoticed entrance into Akhilleus' presence enacts the varied functions of salutation but without otherwise standard greetings.[14] Supplication atypically *opens* the unequal communication. Priam defines and affirms—by his body's reduced

---

845; 10.573–75; 20.131; *Od.* 3.222–23, 4.653–56, 16.161, 17.483–87; cf. Clay 1983, 16–17).

12. Macleod 1982, 20–21, 30, with 16 n. 1 for references; also Pedrick 1982, 132, 139–40; Thornton 1984, 138–41.

13. Other, but not earthling, successful supplications include Thetis' requests of Zeus and of Hephaistos to honor her son. Hera also gets her way with minor gods.

14. Goody 1972 and Firth 1972 survey cross-cultural greeting rituals. Further, see Firth 1969; Gould 1973, 91–95, 100.

elevation—the imbalance of the interlocutors' status and his own lower rank. Thus, he identifies himself as a suppliant (in this situation). He manipulates the awful garb of humility that he has assumed by kissing the hand of his son's killer, even more than by his subsequently initiating the delayed verbal exchange and the verbal honorifics: θεοῖς ἐπιείκελε, διοτρεφές (486). The approach and abasement establish the situational hierarchy by proxemic, chronemic, and kinesic protocols.

The ritual of supplication here regularizes a constrained communication that would otherwise have been socially unacceptable and even physically dangerous. The absence of any words of greeting or even reassuring gazes and identification before the enemy penetrates the "intimate" distance of "personal space" produces a unique triple anaphora of wordless amazement (θάμβος, θάμβησεν, θάμβησαν, 482–84). Old Priam has shown a new heroism, as "hard-hearted" young Akhilleus will show a new humanity and gain a unique κῦδος.[15] The audience waits for a sign of reciprocal willingness and generosity from Akhilleus: will he accept this assertive demonstration of abased status from an enemy king; will he respond in kind and with reasonable words, however brusque, rather than with his usual hair-trigger, bloody fury? Priam's vulnerability when he violates Akhilleus' body-envelope rightly arouses our fears. He rejects, however, the competitive ethos of Homeric conduct between equal-status non-*philoi*. He adopts the posture of a submissive inferior. This forestalling of proxemic permit and preemption of low elevation enable him to impose himself aggressively on Akhilleus' heroic code. Zeus, sending orders through Thetis, can be no more compelling. The powerless have their own (social) power, a theme of the *Odyssey*.

Gestures and postures of deference and supplication emotionally enrich, as they ritually satisfy, the narrative of mutual grief and the supreme commercial exchange between heroic enemies. The material quid pro quo (corpse for heaped up items of value and esteem) symbolizes a momentary spiritual, even physical, bridge between two shattered and isolated human souls. Bodies reveal what words cannot say. Words here are truly secondary; they merely ratify the language of bodies and the manipulation of distance and temporal intervals. Rather than a verbal agreement ratified by the formality of a handshake, we experience a nonverbal bonding between powerful presences sealed with verbal confirmations.

Hermes advised Priam to close in immediately and seize the Akhaian by the knees—as if on a battlefield. The Trojan trumps that humble posture of

---

15. 24.110, with Macleod's note. Reciprocal wonder (629–31) and mutual esteem indicate their equal heroism.

surrender by the gesture of kissing the hands that have slaughtered his many sons. The lowered body, physical contact, and self-abasing words may logically be viewed as redundant, but communicating simultaneously through all channels conveys both unique urgency and sincerity. His humility is startling in any Greek context (465, 478, 506; cf. 357), but here it conforms precisely to Phoinix' persuasive "anticipatory echo." He had described the personified divinities, the lame, aged, indirectly glancing, but well-connected Supplications.[16]

The pathetic affect is so strong that Akhilleus loses speech (*aphonia*). The intimated image of his own father is too painful. Since Priam has not yet spoken a word, his appearance itself and nonverbal behavior must account for Akhilleus' incapacitating emotion, the pity of the man called "pitiless." Akhilleus shows ambivalence. He takes Priam's hand to reassure him that interchange will be peaceful, but at the same time he pushes him away (508–9; ἀπωθεῖν is formulaic for rejection of suppliants). Sharing a deep sense of human limitation and weakness, the two bereaved men weep together, entrained in paroxysmic pain. Then Akhilleus again touches Priam's arm, grants protection, and exercises dominance by making him stand. Finally finding words, he invites him to be seated. These are social signs of both the ritual of accepting suppliants and that of welcoming honored guests (507–22; cf. Akhilleus and Odysseus at *Il.* 11.765–79 and *Od.* 7.153). He has been touched by and has touched his enemy—vital heroic contact. He has restored him—physically—upright (elevation).

This nonverbal behavior expresses his patent sympathy. This ordinary ritual signaling that suppliancy is granted and a guest received amounts to recognition, honor, and welcome, even without ratifying words. Yet it affronts Priam's heightened sense of ritual obligation to his son's abused corpse. He will not sit in a chair (normality) while Hektor's corpse lies neglected.[17] Priam uniquely supplicates a victor not for consideration of his own body but for return of another's corpse. Two sets of nonverbal behaviors and rituals conflict; Priam's postures of grief do not suit postures of the successful suppliant and guest. But to underline Priam's totally dependent position (both in terms of suppliants' ritual and raw power), Akhilleus, through his beetled brows, threatens the recalcitrant visitor and acknowledged inferior with violence. Even he whom he pities may arouse wrath again, if he will not obey an order to be seated. The frightened King obeys

---

16. 9.501–14; Gould 1973, 76; Thornton 1984, 116–19; M. Edwards 1991, 19–23, on anticipation.

17. 553, the momentary reality; cf. Odysseus' refusal to eat Kirke's food until his men regain human form (*Od.* 10.383–87).

(559–60).[18] As in *Iliad* 9, but more so, supplication is complemented by guest-friendship. These two social institutions exhibit certain parallel ceremonial acts that "permit the acceptance of the outsider within the group." In both rites, exchange of gifts, a form of nonverbal behavior, facilitates accepting the otherwise unacceptable, even the alien person or the known enemy.[19] It is one of the many recombinative units that structure social life no less than oral epic.

The body is a prime instrument and point of reception for social intercourse. (Here, e.g., the "haptics" [contact behaviors] include Priam's dropping to the floor to seize the knees and kiss the hand of Akhilleus. No less communicative, Akhilleus lays hold of his enemy's arm.) In this climactic scene, the suppliant's reduced elevation, by its severe disturbance of normal position, reveals how low majestic Priam will sink in social honor to recover his son's body. The relation of young, less kingly Akhilleus, still sitting on his throne (ἵζεσκε, 472), to elderly, dignified, and otherwise kinglier Priam, curled up on the ground at his feet (ἐλυσθείς, 510), expresses concretely, and in a single image, the untraditional, nonreciprocal greeting in terms of distance, movement, gesture, elevation, and posture. A minor gesture will "italicize" a message; here, a major gesture, a complex of bodily messages that drastically alters Priam's position, compels attention, reduces uncertainty as to the stranger's identity and intention, and initiates the transaction: an exchange of objects and also an unexpected social reciprocity, the sharing of grief at human loss. The generic commonplaces and the horizon of expectations set up by the multiforms of battlefield savagery have created patterns that neatly augment the astonishing features of this unexpected scene.

For the ancient Hellenes, gestures of limb and bodily position conveyed nonverbal messages more frequently and effectively than the face.[20] Priam therefore performs his nearly unconditional respect by utterly abject posture and orientation to Akhilleus. He nevertheless asserts some residual dignity, his equality as a suffering human being, by aggressive reduction of the sepa-

---

18. The imbalance of power extends even to their seats: Akhilleus sits on a throne, Priam on a stool (θρόνος, 515, 553; δίφρος, 578). The point is lost in many translations; cf. Houston 1975 on Odyssean seating. "Seating in prominence," a prominent detail of even the most conventional feast, here is weighted by a unique context.

19. See Pitt-Rivers 1977, esp. 98, on how honor is gained by being paid to a superior. Gould 1973, 93; 80 n. 39 lists all Homeric examples of supplication. See also, chap. 3, section 4, and chap. 7.

20. Cf. chap. 3, section 2. Modern Westerners, especially those on the North Atlantic rim, deprecate "theatrical" bodily gestures of respect and bodily contact in public in favor of "face-work"; cf. Goffman 1967a, 5–45, an essential study; Driessen in Bremmer and Roodenburg 1991, 245.

rating distance—proxemic penetration of Akhilleus' body-envelope—and by seizing turn-taking precedence in speech (μνῆσαι πατρὸς σοῖο, 486). His complete array of submissive ritual acts paradoxically compels physically powerful, yet socially punctilious, Akhilleus to accept his request.

The situation enforces his extraordinary claims. By nonverbally abdicating status and power, he requires Akhilleus to grant him the honor that the elder seems to disclaim. This body-persuasion provides one major reason why he succeeds where Agamemnon had failed with "persuasive" gifts.[21] Agamemnon's deference is either false or shoddy or both; Priam's is unarguable. Body language prevails over words or wealth when the two conflict. Akhilleus' own complementary gestures demonstrate two things: first, that he well understands the moves of the game; and second, that he realizes his essential identity with his enemy—or any other man.

Formal and informal public addresses in Homer draw attention to nonverbal elements of both speaker's delivery and audience reception, two aspects of secular, "political" ritual. Nonverbal behavior, under the later rubric of "delivery" (ὑπόκρισις or *actio*), had a serious impact on the ancient study of persuasion.[22] Homer's attention to *kudos*-winning speech and oratory (*Il.* 1.490, 9.443) is patent in the high frequency and importance of his dialogues, group discussions, and assemblies; in his implicit, and sometimes explicit, attention to different persuasive styles of orators (3.216–24); and in the evaluations of Akhilleus' reckless and Odysseus' prudent speeches.[23]

Akhilleus admires both Priam's heroic appearance and his powers of persuasion, verbal and nonverbal (ὄψιν . . . καὶ μῦθον, 632). Homer has already characterized him by various speech acts: for example, he scolded his sons (237, 248–49, 251), and he flattered the stranger Hermes (375–77). Now he beseeches his most dangerous interactant, an enemy, effectively (ὑφ' ἵμερον

---

21. Gould 1973, 94–95, 100. Motto and Clark 1969 argue well for the Phthian's observance of Akhaian etiquette in every particular. Considering supplication in Attic drama clarifies this point about the power of "compelling gestures." The exigencies, however, of hearing and seeing in the large, open theater of Dionysos entirely invalidate attempts to draw any conclusions thence about ordinary body-talk. A. Spitzbarth 1946 (*non vidi*) and M. Kaimio 1988 discuss gesture in Attic drama.

22. Quintilian opines (*Inst. Or.* 11.3.65) that in public speaking, *Is* [sc. *gestus*] . . . *pleraque etiam citra verba significat,* "gesture means more than the words themselves." The Romans divided its materializing power into *vox* (paralinguistic phenomena), *vultus* (facial expression), *gestus* (= *motus corporis*), and *cultus* (= *habitus corporis,* or posture). *Vox, vultus, cultus,* and *gestus* must be calculated to suit a serious speaker's subject and intent. Cic. *Or.* 17.55; Quint. *Inst. Or.* 11.3.2, 9; chaps. 65–184 minutely consider gesture and dress. Volkmann 1885, 573–80, summarizes ancient references.

23. M. Edwards 1987, 88–97, notes that two-thirds of the hexameters consist of direct speech; Fingerle 1939 provides statistics book by book.

ὦρσε, 507; οἰκτίρων, 516). He mounts clever appeals and manipulates gaze and eye-lock, proximity, supplicatory postures, touch, and gestures:

ἄγχι δ' ἄρα στὰς
χερσίν Ἀχιλλῆος λάβε γούνατα καὶ κύσε χεῖρας. . . .
(477–78)

ἔτλην . . .
ἀνδρὸς παιδοφόνοιο ποτὶ στόμα χεῖρ' ὀρέγεσθαι.
(505–6)

κλαῖ' ἀδινὰ προπάροιθε ποδῶν Ἀχιλλῆος ἐλυσθείς. . . .
(510)

The effective orator escapes the ghetto of language and exploits the spectrum of nonverbal behavior:[24] emblems (knee-grasp); illustrators (bent-over body); affect displays (tears); conversation regulators (such as supplicant initiation, lock-on gaze termination, establishing speaker precedence, and turn taking: twice, 483–85, 633–35); adaptors (steady gaze); physical appearance (ὄψιν; stature and beauty);[25] touch (hand-kiss); paralinguistics (silence, volume, pitch); proxemics (coming into the "intimate distance," stillness), chronemics (late at night, delay in speaking, keeping speech short); alter-adaptors (gifts for ransom, food and chair [offers and] refusals).

Less dignified behavior better suits comedic than tragic genres. Comic and adventure literature enlist more expressive activity and drastic, not to say spastic, movement than tragic texts, because our jerky bodies often betray or "leak" spiritual pretenses and foolish or criminal plans. Conflict between word and gesture is sometimes read as irony in epic, as when Polyphemos interprets Odysseus' grandiose claims on *xenia* while the hero scuttles into dark corners or when Iros replaces threatening words with a cowering body when push comes to shove. Such internal conflicts or conflicts between

---

24. The technical categories, differently divided by semiotic, psychological, and linguistic specialists, are well defined and explained for my purposes in Ekman and Friesen 1969b and some later textbooks, e.g., Burgoon and Saine 1978. Other studies (e.g., Poyatos 1986) divide the phenomena differently, often into more precise, limited categories, such as "kinephonographs" and "ideographs."

25. The narrator characterizes the verbal content and style of Thersites' speech as "unmeasured, disorderly, unorganized, indecent, and amusing to the troops." Nonverbal features are also mentioned: Thersites' ugliness, demeanor, and offensive paralinguistics—"scolding, shouting, abusive, shrill." See 2.212–46; the last line includes Odysseus' sarcastic rebuke of his inferior's putative status claims to obtain the speaker's floor: Θερσῖτ' ἀκριτόμυθε, λιγύς περ ἐὼν ἀγορητής, "Thersites you thoughtless speaker, however clearly and easily you orate."

classes sometimes suggest slapstick—for instance, Odysseus' elegant speech while beating Thersites in the *Iliad* or the comic, if fatal, ballistic attacks by the suitors on the beggar.

Homer provides the narrative with such comic variety—with tension between word and performance, or between status and assumed roles. For further instance, we mention Hephaistos' desire to calm the Olympian feasters' threatening eruption into a brawl as he hobbles around the table in *Iliad* 1 and lowly, ugly, and irascible Thersites' jeremiad against the high command and then his punishment in *Iliad* 2. Hera's unholy seduction (employing stimulating olfactory, dermal, thermal, and body-adaptor nonverbal behaviors) overwhelms Zeus. The male spouts a vain verbal catalog of sexual conquest as he lusts for and grabs at his wife in *Iliad* 14. The poet often cues our response by internal laughter, as we note when Zeus laughs at Hera's boxing Artemis' ears in *Iliad* 21 or when the suitors laugh at Iros' nonverbal and verbal insolence and consequent put-downs in *Odyssey* 18. Heroic quarrels over prizes that make even Akhilleus and the Akhaians smile (23.556) repeatedly interrupt Patroklos' funeral games.[26]

The heroic dignity of a king like Agamemnon or Priam, in his own estimation if not the poet's, demands restrained comportment. *Comic* characters, including Antilokhos and the suitors, cannot "carry it off" and leak their affect. In the *Odyssey,* Odysseus' facial demeanor often prefaces or replaces verbal expressions.[27] He smiles the most. He even "manages" a smile when others are rebuking his wife Penelope. His smiles (especially the sardonic one) characterize menacing resources and mark each context as a significant, if ambivalent, moment. His famous sardonic smile and Penelope's puzzling, embarrassed laughter (20.301–2, 18.163) both underline concealment of plans from all others and the heroic control and inwardness of their selves, a Greek ideal (see chapter 11). The tranquillity of a self-assured queen like Arete or the self-controlled smiles of Odysseus, when confident of the assistance of Olympians or steadfast in the face of blows (e.g., *Od.* 17.234–35), contrast to the agitated speech and coltish movements of nervous Paris or angry Antilokhos, the hysteria of the cocky suitors, and the leaping to rise, crying, and sneezing of young Telemakhos.

---

26. Levine 1982b neatly demonstrates how the Odyssean suitors and the established beggar Iros comically mirror each other. They share insolence in word, gesture, and deed. Odysseus and Iros contest for a monogamous relationship to the suitors, as the suitors contest for sole possession of the imaginary bride. "Ares and Aphrodite Get Caught" (*Od.* 8.266–366) provides another comic misadventure, this time a divine interlude packed with nonverbal embellishment between Demodokos' two tear-evoking human (Trojan) tableaux.

27. For example, *Od.* 8.165, 17.304–5, 19.389, 23.111–12; see Levine 1984; contrast Eurykleia's incautious moves at 19.476–94, 22.407–12, 23.1–14.

However, intense kinesic activity can portray unbearable emotion and the rejection of a group's conventional standards of behavior. Traumatized and enraged Akhilleus gnashes his teeth, rolls on the ground, weeps, and otherwise disports his hated body.[28]

2. Affect Displays: Emotional Betrayal

Portraits in oral epic present fairly constant appearance and characters, often in formulaic, even fossilized, phrases. Sometimes the narratives describe dramatic, momentary, emotional disequilibria, characteristically conveyed by mien, posture, demeanor, gaze, and gesture. Idomeneus effectively describes cowards by changes in skin color, frequent postural alterations, fast heartbeat, and teeth chattering, a quasi-paralinguistic leakage (*Il.* 13.278–86). Visible arousal, like these or perspiration and blushing, "leak" affect. The physiognomy and bearing of the praiseworthy hero is, above all, calm and steady. The eyes index the spirit, as the following phrases, all from a short stretch in *Iliad* 1, prove: κακ' ὀσσόμενος, ὄσσε δέ οἱ πυρὶ λαμπετόωντι ἐίκτην, ὑπόδρα ἰδών, κυνὸς ὄμματ' ἔχων (105, 104, 148, 225). Baleful looks, blazing eyes, glaring glances, and, elsewhere, admiring or loving gazes concretely convey emotional states. Physiognomic consciousness is essential to Homeric characterization of emotional states.[29]

Iliad 24 narrates the disputed disposition and transfer of Hektor's corpse. The gods discuss the problem; mortal Priam is dispatched from Troy to claim the body, and Akhilleus and Priam experience and express parallel sorrow for their dead beloveds. The corpse is washed by the Akhaians, returned to Troy by Priam, and accorded "last rites" by the Trojans. As we have seen, the commercial exchange is devalued compared to the emotional bonding, but both are expressed nonverbally as well as verbally.

Expressions of uncontrollable grief amid the rituals of mourning dominate the book on both sides of the big ditch. Tears are noted for seven subject-

---

28. *Il.* 24.9–13; *Od.* 10.496–99. Benson 1980, esp. "Gesture and Genre," 41–58, applies contemporary rules of decorum, philosophical, religious, and literary, to hagiography, *The Clerk's Tale*, and medieval romance. Windeatt 1979 describes Chaucer's deployment of nonverbal behavior as suggestive of inner feelings. Nonverbal behaviors in Chaucer do not offer cognitive self-awareness or self-analysis (143) but supply emotional leakage that gauges sincerity of characters' words and deeds (151). In addition, gestures enliven the narrative with "incidental observation" (159). In ancient epic, however, fewer examples of such incidental data emerge, because interest focuses on decisive acts (such as Chaucer's kneeling and fainting), not on characteristic idiogest—idiosyncratic, symbolic body movement (humming, coughing, nail biting, etc.). Roman fictions (e.g., from Seneca Maior, Petronius, and Apuleius) offer more material for that aspect of ancient literature.

29. Evans 1969, 58–67, catalogs facial expression and orientation; see also Holoka 1983.

object dyads: Akhilleus for Patroklos and Peleus; and for Hektor, Priam's sons and his wife Hekabe, Andromakhe, the Trojan public, and Priam himself (4, 9, 511–12, 162, 794, 209, 745, 714, 786, 509–10). The tears of Niobe express unquenchable, but necessarily endurable, human grief (613, 49). Mortals constitute a community of ephemeral sufferers.[30] Our *pathe* establish our specialness. Priam himself is benumbed, except with (literally) sympathetic Akhilleus. He seems to be beyond the comfort of tears, both when he is self-isolated and when he is surrounded by his grieving palace, family, and subjects (cf. Waern 1985).

While wrenching verbal articulations of sorrow most fully explain to audiences Akhilleus' sentiments and those of Priam, Hekabe, and Andromakhe, the nonverbal affect-displays complement the words. Apostrophes, eulogies, and keening speeches of bereavement gain force from the emotion-laden physical and paralinguistic phenomena that accompany them here. *Iliad* 24 conveys Akhilleus' anguish and anger in a rich variety of nonverbal behaviors: his out-of-awareness scowl at Priam's importuning, his groaning at the thought of Patroklos' honor diminished, his writhing on the ground in grief, his frustrated search for a bearable posture and place to be still, his compulsive repetitions, and his startled and startling movements (559, 591, 5; cf. Priam: 165, 10–12, 572, 621). The grief of Priam is expressed both formally, through ritualized body-fouling, and informally through affect displays, such as sobbing while huddled at Akhilleus' feet (509–10).

Others too impart their inner states by visible behaviors. Priam, twice approached by gods, suffers uncontrollable shivering (170, 359). His hair stands on end—a unique involuntary reaction in Homer. He is dumbfounded by Hermes' approach and later struck with stilled wonder by Akhilleus' godlike appearance, as is Akhilleus by the astounding sight of the enemy chief (360, 629–32). Helen's presence, because of her beauty and the disasters that it had evoked, disturbed nearly all Trojans. She was ostracized almost by instinct. The shuddering withdrawal (περιφρίκασι, 775) that she mentions in describing the involuntary effect she produces in others appears but once elsewhere. There it describes Diomedes' surreal effect in his *aristeia* at the cost of Trojan opponents (11.382–83). Homer notes other nonverbal features of crowd psychology. Book 2 characterized the Akhaian host: shaking, shouting, running, laughing at Thersites, and scattering (2.144–53, 270,

---

30. Young Pisistratos opines that mourning is the sole *geras*, honorific prize, of humans at *Od.* 4.195–98; see Redfield [1967] 1973, 153, on mourning as a source of delight and a mastery of sorrow, a constructive source of song and story (19.518–22, 15.398–401). Thus, emotions expressed through the nonverbal, paraverbal, and winged verbal realms generate mythic figures.

398). The Trojans in book 24 informally and instinctually swarm, like calves or children, toward Priam as he wheels in Hektor's corpse, the body of their defender. Their clustering betrays self-aware helplessness, their need. They gather again, before having been summoned, to prepare formally for Hektor's entombment (709, 790; cf. *Od.* 10.410–15).[31]

A sharp contrast to agitation, various physical movements that replace or transcend words, is sudden cessation of word and motion. Such unmeditated, dramatic, and communicative stillness, denoted by Greek τέθηπα, signifies a nonverbal damming of the stream of reassuring motions, parallel to no longer verbal silence, otherwise known as "speaking degree zero."[32] Only Akhilleus experiences θάμβος, this extreme alteration of consciousness and responsiveness (1.199, 24.483). The epic utilizes this infrequent, but potent, affect-display, to signify the ceasing of human responses. Such a communications vacuum, a hiatus in the usual dependable human emissions, strikes interactants most forcibly.

For the articulate heroes of Homer's *Iliad*, such paralysis usually occurs in military struggles, when men are compared to frightened deer (4.243, 246; 21.29; Lykaon at 21.64 remains relatively rational). Stupefaction more "naturally" comes about from theophany and supernatural interference, the inexplicable and irremediable change that befalls Aias at Zeus' hands, Patroklos at Apollo's, and Priam at Hermes' (11.545, 16.806, 24.360).

The three other of ten Homeric examples, describing neither victims in war nor hapless sufferers of the gods' will, concern Akhilleus, the most

---

31. Levine 1987 (also note his other studies in the bibliography and as discussed in chap. 10) has explored the expressions of the opposite class of emotions, smiles and laughter, as well as tears in the *Odyssey*. The gleeful suitors' and Penelope's maids' laughter reveal their presumption of putative status and blindness to approaching destruction (cf. Herodotus in Lateiner 1987, 94–95). Melantho's affect displays in particular exacerbate her sexual promiscuity and amplify, in another mode, her disloyalty to master, mistress, and house. Homer contrasts her behavior to Penelope's: the mistress frequently weeps out of love for Telemakhos and Odysseus. Odysseus' controlled smiles anticipate the suitors' defeat; they express a justified sense of superiority. The offending suitors, the subversive maids, and even loyal Eurykleia enjoy and exult improperly (22.409–34; 23.58–84). All other females serve as foils to faithful, modest, and cunning Penelope. Wohl 1993 suggests that even Penelope, as a non-kin female, possessing productive and reproductive power, threatens insecure and distrustful Odysseus. *Homophrosyne*, however, Homer's "romantic" notion, neutralizes their apparent conflicts and suppresses our notice of his patriarchal and violent domination.

32. Perhaps the word τέθηπα is related to θάμβος and its verb, which would add eleven examples, but these latter words seem to mark the initial surprise rather than the consequent disorientation. Vergil and Ovid employ the Latin equivalent, *obstipesco*, "to be stunned by an emotion," "to become stupefied, paralyzed, silent and numb." Lateiner 1992a provides further details.

emotional, agonistic, and voluble hero.[33] The arrival of the Akhaian embassy at his tent, of an earlier one in Phthia (in Nestor's report), and of otherworldly Patroklos in a dream all bewilder him at first (9.193, 11.776, 23.101). But before each verse is finished, he has roused himself to heroic hospitality or response.

Homer the narrator distinguishes at least three types, degrees perhaps, of astonishment. There is bewildered surprise, θαμβέω, when Priam first arrives at Akhilleus' lodge (three times in 24.482–84); the awestruck wonder conveyed by θαυμάζω when Akhilleus and Priam mirror gazes with each other after first words (twice in 629–31; cf. Macleod ad loc.); and the thunderstruck paralysis of τέθηπα when Olympian Hermes appears to and stupifies Priam in the dead of night (360).

3. Tokens and Dress: Telltale Objects

Homer sows his poetic field with objects, tokens, and other external signifiers that identify and situate persons for their interactants. As the introduction made clear, associated objects—self-adaptors and other-adaptors—inform interactants who we are and how we feel. The bride's clothes say as much as her blush or smile; so do Priam's ritually filthy clothes in book 24. Communicative objects commence in Greek literature with Khryses' tassled staff and Agamemnon's elaborate and genealogized scepter. Akhilleus' hurling of this scepter to the ground (*Il.* 1.245) clearly communicates by gesture both immediate dissatisfaction and dissociation and also immanent withdrawal. His honor has been transgressed; his humiliation requires symbolic response and retaliation. As such, the failure to honor the king's power-symbol was more significant than its de-elevated landing place. By distancing himself—swiftly, intensely, and violently—from the communal power-object, he abuses it and them, and thus ruptures his bond with the assembly and its convener to preserve his independence, honor, and dignity.[34] Homer's intensely narrow focus in *Iliad* 24 on the grief of a father and a son similarly capitalizes on several significant objects.

Hektor's is the only corpse ever successfully ransomed in Homer. Objects express emotion. Hektor's princely ransom of objects, exchanged here for a

---

33. Martin 1989, 206–15, 220, quantifies and accounts for Homer's oral "expansion aesthetic," Akhilleus' distinctive verbal characteristic along with moral trumping and efficient killing. When Akhilleus appears in a book (1, 9, 18, 23, 24), he tends to talk more frequently and in larger blocks than anyone else. See Fingerle's 1939 statistics (9–10, 19, 29, 34, 36–37).

34. Other meaningful Homeric projectiles that serve as the social sign can be noted: the stone discus by which Odysseus surpassed the best Phaiakian throw (*Od.* 8.186–98) and the suitors' ballistics, for which see chap. 10.

"useless" corpse, suggests the incalculable value of the living leader.[35] Since Hektor now is and is not a person, is and is not an object, he therefore can and cannot be "equated" with spoil, gifts, goods, recompense, and ransom. The "objective" style of Homer does not speechify about the value of life—Akhilleus' observations on life and nonlife at 9.400–409 were enough anyway. The subliminal effect of δῶρα ἄποινα, words for lifeless, but symbolically resurrecting, objects—words repeated by gods, victor, vanquished, and narrator—transforms "neutral" into "value" terms. Dispassionate report has become expressive; the cool, objective style more effectively provokes strong emotional response.[36]

Lifeless things in Homer have a "discreet but intelligible language"; sometimes their vicissitudes equal or excel in *pathos* those of human beings.[37] They provide vivid description but also physically communicate emotion and exert force on characters. The blackest veil of mother Thetis states precisely her bereaved emotions. Priam's filthy body and tattered mourning garments proclaim a "darkly" emotional condition and distance him from family, not to mention his fellow citizens (93–94, 163). He still wields his staff of office, but now only in the private realm, shaking it menacingly at his sons (247).

The chair that host Akhilleus gently offers to indicate welcome and fellowship is refused by Priam (522, 553), as the food would have been, had not Akhilleus first nonverbally and verbally supplemented the offer. He restores the corpse of Hektor and relates—inversely paternal as he now is—the parable of Niobe. Only then does Priam end his fast (641–42), a self-destructive, and therefore all the more powerful, nonverbal behavior. Priam's isolated dissociation from the human condition encompasses rejection of conversation, ease (elevation and posture), food, clean and decent clothes and body, and even sleep (635–40). Once he has recovered the corpse, his intense anguish is lessened sufficiently so that he can associate himself with a different set of significant objects, now those relating to the reintegrative niceties of funerals and burial. The tomb and monument (666, 799, 801) are

---

35. Macleod 1982, 20 (deleting verse 232); Griffin 1980, 19. δῶρα appears thirteen times, ἄποινα eight (e.g., for both, see 118–19, 139, 555, 594). Ransom lexemes emerge once every thirty-eight lines. Not only cash value, so to speak (e.g., the ten gold talents of 232), but Priam's specially won and specially worked tankard (234–37) are packed up—anything to obtain his dead son's body.

36. Herodotos 1.45 and 7.225, Thukydides 7.86, and Semonides' epitaphs well display the power of reticence.

37. Fränkel [1962] 1975, 38; Griffin 1980, 136, on 16.793–805: Akhilleus' helmet, here worn by doomed Patroklos. The African Tuareg enjoy an entire additional language of male veil manipulation; see Hawad-Claudot in Poyatos 1992a, 197–211.

mentioned, not only Hektor's, but those of Patroklos and old Ilos also. Troy has become a cemetery and a burning pyre. Hektor has become bones in a golden *larnax* (795), dead and buried, but at least his corpse has received its due objects of ethnic honor and value, proper ritualized treatment.[38]

One unique form of nonverbal behavior, augury, possesses a separate, divine, but recognized, syntax. This "visible speech" of gods to humans includes all wordless, divine messages to earth below: portents, dreams, "unnatural" thunder, lightning, rain, timely earthquakes, rains of blood, and weird noises (13.59, 11.53–54, 18.217–18; also miracles, such as the petrification of Alkinoos' ship and men at *Od*. 13.163–64).[39] At *Il*. 24.305–21, Priam washes, prays for success and security in a selected, open spot in his courtyard, pours libation, and requests a telegraphic bird on the right, a nonverbal semasiological message (πέμψον δ'οἰωνόν, ταχὺν ἄγγελον ... δεξιόν). Zeus duly provides his eagle, and Homer measures his wingspread in a simile that describes the strongly barred door of a rich man's treasure chamber. Power as well as size and future safety as well as expense are conveyed by the mighty auspice and the simile, by the nonverbal bird and portal. Some readers may question the inclusion of object-adaptors among my categories of nonverbal behavior, but they provide literature, a medium of words, with a potent "concrete" dimension by which to communicate feeling, thought, and meaning. They are therefore especially indispensible to a nonmimetic (nontheatrical) medium.

Separate, "lifeless" objects are at times invested with social value (like the scepters of Agamemnon and Priam), emotional power (how clothing is worn

---

38. Odysseus' repeated "before-and-after" grooming and clean clothes sequence, his first grubby and then magnificent appearance, patterns his series of visits: Ogygia, Skheria, and the palace on Ithaka. Odysseus' tawny hair is set by Athene to appeal to Nausikaa; later, she again ruins it for disguise, and his baldness is mocked by Eurymakhos (6.230–31, 13.399, 431; 18.355). Baldness exemplifies "body badges," nonverbal expressions of identity beyond the subject's control. Penelope also deploys appearance to express emotional state: she refuses to beautify, or even wash, herself. She only presents herself to the suitors veiled and accompanied by loyal servants, two nonverbal expressions of shame, modesty, status(?), and personal reserve that distinguish her from all other women (18.178–84, 207–11). See Levine 1987, 25, and chaps. 7 and 11 in this book for Penelope's proxemics.

39. To exclude these phenomena from *human* nonverbal behavior seems harmfully pedantic. Epic's anthropomorphic gods have access to more means of sending messages than humans do, but the modes are no different (or we would not understand them). If the color of a stoplight, the shape of a highway "yield" sign, or the "forbidden behavior" symbol of a circle with a slanted diameter line are acceptable semiosis, nonverbal communicative symbols of our legislatures, so should be Zeus' clear-sky thunder or Athena's varied birds. I here disavow solutions to the meaning(s) of divine intervention in Homeric epic (e.g., Athene stays Akhilleus' hand at the early assembly and advises Telemakhos to get out of Sparta and to avoid the suitors' assassination squad when approaching Ithaka).

and how personal expression varies the face), or divine sanction. Such nonverbal signals (even portents) can support, supplant, or contradict a character's words or actions. Object-adaptors from on-high or down-below are informative, communicative, and interactive. Economy of affect makes ancient epic crisp, rapid, and revelatory. The control of personal appearance powerfully affects Odysseus', Penelope's, and Akhilleus' interactions. These nonverbal messages sometimes decide the narrative.[40]

4. Proxemics: The Human Use of Space

Distance structures human relations. Hall (1966, 113–30) divides social space into four "regions": the intimate, personal, social, and public distances. The lines between paired-off people vary from culture to culture but may vary less between Akhilleus and middle-class Americans than between contemporary Middle Easterners and the same. The stages of Akhilleus' wrath can be schematically represented as violations and restorations of his territory (and significant objects, like Briseis). He draws a series of very clear boundaries between himself and Agamemnon. Agamemnon's ambassadors (as we oddly call them, as if they were representing separate states) gingerly enter the posted grounds of their alienated colleague. Priam manages to penetrate his "turf" and, more emotively, his social and personal being. Akhilleus' body-envelope is very large and is sensitive to the slightest slight.

Intimate distance allows Homer's characters and others to feel and smell other bodies. Skin texture (touch), body heat or cold (with or without touch), and acrid and sweet odors inflect and deflect intercourse. At this distance (and at each of the others), we respond differently to stimuli because we have different sensations (olfactory space) and a different concept of physical self and other. We hear sighs and whispers and see objects in great detail. Humans possess four "situation personalities," depending on how we imagine our personal bubble of inviolable space in every social transaction—in bed or on the subway. At the closest distance, people make love, comfort children and the bereaved, and embrace close friends. We immerse ourselves in each

---

40. In addition to object-adaptors, such as crowns, brandished weapons, low-cut blouses, and chairs, there are self-adaptors, such as (in-awareness) perfuming and other grooming, including hair, and (out-of-awareness) nail biting, lip licking, etc. Furthermore, note alter-adaptors, such as flirting (coy smiles or close approach with or without touch) and visible signs of impatience (foot tapping or clock checking as at *Od.* 13.29–30). Ekman and Friesen 1969b, 85–90, describe further subcategories. One major difference between deployment of nonverbal behavior in ancient and in modern fictions is that current literary convention stresses the idiosyncratic gesture or mannerism, as Portch 1985 shows for Flannery O'Connor, while ancient poetry emphasizes communal acts, visible evidence of status, other social phenomena, and nonlexical, but socially approved, "leakage."

other's sensorium; the sensory input is stepped up. At this distance, Akhilles and Briseis take their rest (676), Hekabe and Andromakhe bewail their dear Hektor (712, 724), and Thetis soothes Akhilleus as Athene strokes her favorite earthling.

At the *personal distance,* we still touch or grasp one another. The "kinaesthetic sense of closeness" varies from culture to culture, even from nation to nation, and even between ethnic sub-divisions,[41] but this is the distance of one-to-one relations, the friend, the go-between, and the client, relative, or servant. One can still physically dominate the interlocutor. Only trusted acquaintances come this close and transact private business. Conversations at this range expect intermittent eye contact and facing bodies (unless the participants are in motion).

Social distance, four to seven feet, facilitates impersonal business and casual social relations. There is an insulation of the person, a welcome sense of separateness. Sometimes tables and chairs structure this space and affect behavior, as in Akhilleus' lodge. The voice remains at normal volume, and facial expressions can be read clearly. At this distance, the gaze of another can be intensely annoying or can convey the rapt attention of lovers in public venues.

Public distance affects people's choice of words and phrasing as well as their pace and volume. Others are observed without facial detail, and, to be lucid, nonverbal clues must be fairly emphatic: whole arm movements or major changes of posture, as in the Attic theater or the American presidential inauguration. The spatial envelope determining crowded or pushed or claustrophobic feelings varies West to East, North to South.

Every narrative perforce indicates spatial relationships, because proxemics names one of the few basic, unavoidable aspects of human intercourse. (Chronemics, another such aspect, is discussed in the appendix.) This section largely confines itself to examples that most clearly affect mood and events. Homer manipulates to unusual effect the social and psychological meanings of space. Proxemic behaviors cut across all the categories described in chapter 1, so some repetition is unavoidable. That they can be ceremonial, informal, intended, subconscious or unconscious, and voluntary or even enforced comes as no surprise. The quest for *Lebensraum* (elbowroom) and "personal space" currently expresses political and psychological craving for defined comfortable distances. In this section, we examine the four proxemic zones

---

41. Hall 1966, 131–64 gathers remarkable examples of groups misreading other groups' measures of proper distance. Lateiner 1992b more fully discusses heroic proxemics; cf. chap. 7 in this book.

in *Iliad* 24 and then briefly consider proxemic dimensions of perhaps the central ritual, supplication, in the *Iliad*.

Thetis deals with her son, Akhilleus, in the *intimate* zone (126). Hermes is described by Priam's henchman, Idaios, at the *public* distance, but the god comes closer for *social* interchange and even into bodily contact, the *intimate zone* (ἀγχιμόλοιο, 352, 360–61; ἄγχι, 477). Hekabe has also approached her spouse, Priam, just as closely (283). Priam defenselessly apposes himself to his son's killer, a startling violation of protocols between enemies on and off the battlefield. Priam supplicates Akhilleus, then they touch each other—first unidirectional knee-grasp, then bidirectional hand-work (478, 508, 515, 671). The usual regulation of *verbal* back-and-forth interaction between the unacquainted (an almost involuntary, out-of-awareness set of rules) shifts—because of Priam's location—to a different pattern, an intimately shared, largely *unverbal* understanding. Interchange of a fixed gaze (face-work) conveys instant sympathy and rejection at the intimate distance. Normal heroic conversational protocols also involve hard looks and smiles at the personal or even social distance. Posture, distance, and body orientation that on other occasions would be rude, ill-mannered, or likely to invite attack express urgency and extreme emotion in Akhilleus' tent (Ekman and Friesen 1969b, 82–84). So does Akhilleus' parentlike setting of Priam on his feet again (515), although this act primarily confirms, in a ritual mode, successful supplication performance.

The close but untouching personal distance measures the herald Iris' approach to Thetis, Thetis' approach to Zeus, Iris' message delivered to Priam, Hekabe's help for Priam, his housekeeper's assistance in ritual, Hermes as Priam's escort, and Akhilleus' unusual permission for his two closest comrades' presence at dinner (παρέοντε). Akhilleus acknowledges the enemy's suppliancy but gently distances Priam from himself by force: ἁψάμενος δ' ἄρα χειρὸς ἀπώσατο ἦκα γέροντα (508, cf. 515). Distance talks; he has expressed proxemic need for "personal space" and reduced for himself the "volume" or intensity of Priam's unanswerable plea. That "claustrophobic" reaction also impels him to insist that Priam be seated—that is, keep his distance. Priam's reluctance to do so reflects his desire to maintain the proxemic pressure. Such elevational alterations create a different distance, different postures and bodily orientations, and thus a different situation and ethos (522, 553).

Social distance positions the leisured Olympians' table-talk that opens *Iliad* 24 (μεταυδάω, 32—Apollo's dinner speech). Priam chases off male relatives from his home at even this unwelcome proximity (247–52). Akhilleus' warriors remain at this distance to mark respect for acknowledged hierarchy and their companion's will (ἀπάνευθε, 473).

Priam and Akhilleus, the heroic principals, move apart, from *intimate* to *personal* to, finally, *social* space, after Akhilleus returns from loading Hektor's corpse on the wagon (597). He sits on his couch, then he and the imposing father share a meal (ξενία). They become companions in warm food and in cold grief. Finally, they separate for their nightly rest, Akhilleus inside, and Priam and his herald outside the shelter (673–75). Proxemic procedures articulate phases of their difficult interaction and now signify the completion of intimate business. The midnight distancing, however rationalized, avoids "morning after" problems, the necessarily "sticky" ceremonial of enemies' restoring intercourse and face-to-face valediction.

This central and crucial encounter of *Iliad* 24, Priam's intimate visit with Akhilleus, is bracketed by the social events on Olympos and the public mourning in Troy, the unquenchable shoulder-to-shoulder feasting above (98–103) and the mournful public-distance gathering and obsequies below. Book 1 began with the public-distance confrontation of a local priest and an alien army but ends with the intimate distance of Zeus and Hera in bed. Book 24 begins with the end of the Akhaian games at public distances, with Hektor lying far away from his parents (ἀπάνευθε, 211), dishonored on the battlefield. Akhaian burial celebrations begin the book that ends with the end of another public-distance burial ceremony, the departure of Hektor's mortal remains. Homer characterizes variously stressed participants and situations by the use of space.

Supplication, a ritual partly dependent on elevational and proxemic protocols, pervades the *Iliad*. The poem opens with Khryses' failure with Agamemnon and success with Apollo. Agamemnon's "space becomes off-limits." He mercilessly taunts the old man with distance: he must not *come near* again, his daughter will be *far away, inside* Agamemnon's house, indeed *intimately sharing* his bed (1.26–31; Holoka 1992, 246). Thetis' suppliant request at the knees and chin of Zeus sets the plot in motion. The embassy to Akhilleus is the most extensive supplication in ancient epic. At the crisis of the Akhaian defense, "big fool" Patroklos, while standing, semisupplicates Akhilleus (16.46–47), and the poem closes with "a full traditional supplication . . . in the fullest ritual detail." Physical contact establishes a particularly awesome bond between suppliant and supplicated. Proximity is an essential factor in every case (except Khryses' prayer to Apollo, where the man-God situation allows certain telephonic fantasies). So space as well as posture structures this essential reintegrative ritual where social bonds have never existed or have been ruptured (Thornton 1984, 117, 120–29, 138, 141).

Akhilleus, "squatting" on Priam's Trojan territory, holds by force a delimited beachhead. Control of Trojan land constitutes the plot's immediate incentive. When Priam enters the Akhaian's lodge, he violates the territorial integrity of the violator. The spatial aggression and unexpected proximity communicate his urgency, just as gestures of "full suppliancy" communicate nearly unlimited deference to his son's killer. Akhilleus' claustrophobia and impotence are little diminished by gestures attempting to break Priam's ritual hold. The proxemic coup limits Akhilleus' options. Priam could not express his urgent plea beyond the intimate zone, where no plea can be barred, if performed correctly. Perhaps this is why he finally succeeds where the priest Khryses initially had failed. Trojan elder Priam exacts from Akhaian Akhilleus by touch (haptics) and proximity his child that distanced Khrysan or Theban elder Khryses (1.366–80) failed to extract from Akhaian Agamemnon.

The way characters "handle" time and space, often automatically and rarely after thinking, tells us what they feel. The text conveys the latent messages of "real" life, brought to awareness by authorial description. In Akhilleus' lodge, gestures and spatial manipulation introduce and embody messages about helplessness and compassion. In many cultures, social controls exist in the situation rather than in the person.[42] The personal element is subordinated to communal norms or is expressed through ritualized or public acts. What seems to us private, inward, secular, and psychological appears as shared, outwardly experienced, and "social" in the Homeric poems. The last generation of scholars, following E.R. Dodds, contrasted these "shame" cultures to "guilt" cultures. Others speak of situational as opposed to psychological analyses. A sympathetic response to the challenges of the *Iliad* recognizes that humans of every culture and era *always* respond (in informal quarrels and flirting as well as at formal weddings and funerals) through socially recognizable and acceptable forms, not directly expressed emotions—if such a thing is even imaginable (and I doubt it). Some acculturated reactions are ceremonial, while others are more actively or passively affect-revealing; often one observes both together. Human negotiations in any case are constructed from each culture's own toolbox. The Homeric example includes tools like scepter hurling and dirt smearing, as well as more "transparent" gambits like smiling, stroking, and (ethologically constant) horripilation.

Akhilleus' social space teems with ceremonies and restrictions whose limitations he perceives. He rigorously adheres to his code and calls to account those who try to elude it. Sometimes he manipulates these rules cleverly, if

---

42. Hall 1959, 92; Gould 1973, 94–95; Griffin 1980, 24–26, 53–56; Thornton 1984, chaps. 8–9. In Aristotelian terms, *praxis* has priority over *ethos*.

not courteously, to his own advantage. Some situations stymie him. The flawed stratagems of Agamemnon lead to the more gravely flawed responses of Akhilleus (a pattern repeated for Telemakhos and the suitors, but with our sympathies reversed). In their visit to Akhilleus' lodge in book 9, Odysseus, Phoinix, and Aias describe, with increasing fervor and effect, the institutions and code of heroic behavior. While boasts, taunts, and even logical arguments suggest that Akhilleus will persist in violating the heroic code, his actual behavior carefully conforms to it. He knows his proper "place" and the limits of his social freedom.

Agamemnon publicly threatens to come personally to Akhilleus' lodge to seize his subordinate's prize, Briseis (*Il.* 1.185). The act would doubly violate the lesser *basileus'* intimate space, by face-to-face challenge and by theft of a gift "freely" given.[43] He does not come in person to Akhilleus then, for prudential as well as ceremonial reasons. More importantly, he again chooses to avoid the personal visit later, when he realizes it is past time to make amends, that is, to offer apology and restitution (*Il.* 9). Nestor, in anticipation perhaps of both the delicate negotiations to come and the commander's clumsiness, proposes delegates. Agamemnon never opposes the convenient idea. Thus, he expects to keep his social "face" intact and his haughty (and safe) "distance." But the ceremonious element is not a frill but is essential to heal the rupture. Agamemnon's change of heart is limited (9.160–61), flawed. Akhilleus rightly calculates that the apology is spoiled. Only an abortive ceremony of restitution of property by proxies occurs. Akhilleus experiences no complete social and public ritual, no adequate face-to-face personal admission of fault here or even later (*Il.* 19.51, 76–77).

In that crucial scene of rapprochement, Agamemnon's late(st) arrival and his remaining seated omits the essential approach of the party in the wrong to the offended party. Making the first move, displacement of self, and direct, face-to-face apology are necessary elements in negating offense; these negotiations of self-presentation restore honor to the dishonored interactant. Agamemnon's repeated failure to apologize, distribute, and supplicate rightly and ritely (εὖ, "duly;" Latin *rite*) dishonors Akhilleus. The situation forces unromantic and uncomfortable Akhilleus to maintain his honor. Invective and boast, and threat and apartheid, offer effective tools from the heroic toolbox. Within the heroic code, his spatial, ergo social, isolation is the most politic response (and the Olympian preference voiced by Athene) to his humiliation in *Iliad* 1. Akhilleus' return does not hinge on and does not

---

43. The quotation marks remind the reader that no gift is free, a truism of sociological anthropology, if not Perikles' funeral oration.

result from Agamemnon's material and paternal generosity with a "catch" (18.111–15; 19.67, 137–50: ἄποινα). When he eventually accepts Agamemnon's contorted, defective formalistic apology, the reasons are quite different from those that his peers or many modern readers are able to imagine. In sum, Akhilleus rigorously adheres to the warriors' code; Agamemnon repeatedly violates it (by apportionment, titrated insolence or deference to subordinates, and vaunting). Zeus never faults Akhilleus' behavior in the quarrel with Agamemnon.[44]

Priam performs the sacred institution of supplication to perfection. "The power of this sacred institution [of *hiketeia*] is inescapable."[45] *Iliad* 24 moves finally from the enclosed intimacy of the Olympian clubhouse, Priam's palace courtyard, and Akhilleus' lodgings, outdoors to the cooler, open-sky, public distances of state funeral. The civic reception of the body is followed by family mourning in public (707–20). Other mourners, women from outside the family, are present, and the whole community echoes Helen's lament (δῆμος ἀπείρων, 776). Priam, as king, orders the assembled soldiers to pile wood for the obsequies, and the townsmen gather for the cremation and consequent funeral banquet (777, 786, 790, 802). As any funeral and burial separate the bereaved survivors from the deceased, physically as well as emotionally, so Homer separates the hearer/reader from Troy. In cinematic jargon, the final scenes of *Iliad* 24 hold tight focus on facial close-ups at the *intimate* and *personal* distance in Akhilleus' hut, then draw back to the *social* and *public* distances of the living Trojan community in mourning. Finally, it withdraws even farther, beyond a *public* distance, to the noncommunicative dispersal. The community's social dynamic automatically carries life forward after the leader's death, however, at a reintegrative banquet (24.802).

Both Homeric epics "comment" unobtrusively on protagonists' acts by

---

44. Motto and Clark 1969, 115, 119; Martin 1989 on the poetics and pragmatics of power. Chap. 6 in this book discusses deference and demeanor in Agamemnon's splendidly inadequate performance of restitution, verbal fobbing off of blame (19.86–90) on innocent gods, nonappearance in his first offer of restitution, and later, nonverbally offensive, seated posture (nonelevation) in public assembly. See Donlan 1971 and 1993; Clay 1995.

45. Motto and Clark 1969, 109–10, on rank and arrangement; Thornton 1984, 113–14, 141 for the quote. Modern Americans' apparently casual rules concerning supplication (favor requesting) are no less elaborately deferential and fixed in sequence, but the procedures of a pseudoegalitarian society are designed to seem more informal. The contortions of the failing student before a teacher, the scorned lover, the employee about to be dismissed, or the child who wants more television time may illustrate. Because Euro-Americans want and expect requests to come from the "heart," we reject even the appearance of ritual. This we wrongly regard as "insincere performance," cultural fabrication. The paradoxical result is that Euro-Americans are more inhibited in the expression of emotion—the formal rules of informality are too confusing to risk disclosure.

noting their mobility or lack of it, the extent of their body-envelopes, and the degrees of their penetration of others' "turf." They achieve physical proximity as prerequisite to spiritual recognition. The privileges of shared space signal sorrow or joy. While Trojan and Akhaian protagonists voice grief in eloquent words, their bodies—by position and distance—also eloquently articulate inner states and intentions. The *Odyssey*, especially the second half, revels in the intricacies of space manipulation (see chapter 7).

5. In-awareness, Informal Body Language

The nonverbal behavior that we most consciously notice consists of the illustrative and emblematic gestures, postures, and sounds that one subject intends to send to another. When Thetis strokes her sole child (24.127), the act is both intentional and in-awareness; it communicates sympathy and satisfies the affectionate parent's need for closeness and touch (haptics). Priam's beating another person (247) communicates his mood and attitude, his anger and hostility, while it (more instrumentally) inflicts pain. Touch by hand or mouth is a conscious and intense mode of communication, obviously within the intimate distance. Touch generally provokes more response than equally conscious modulations of the voice—meaningful, so-called paralinguistic phenomena.

Homer mentions affective larynx effects. The shrieking pitch and raised volume of Hekabe's voice express frustration and intentional violation of normal female vocal expectations. Iris' whisper transmits an intimate, private, and privileged thought. Kassandra the prophet also shrieks, a paralinguistic sign of demonic inspiration, doom, or both (κώκυσεν, 200; 170, 703). Three women lament Hektor in tearful voices (στενάχοντο, 746: ὣς ἔφατο κλαίουσα, 760, 776). Groans punctuate and articulate the grieving (591, 696).[46]

The eyes are as eloquent as the voice: the locked gazes of Priam and Akhilleus communicate their mutual awe; the "dark" glance threatens an inferior; exchanged glances and maintained silence among Akhilleus' henchmen preclude the need for authorial analysis of heroic psychology; the act betrays their tact. "Telling" laryngeal and ophthalmic behaviors, not lengthy descriptions of emotional states, audibly and visibly convey attitudes of

---

46. Priam's angry, scolding words, a type of speech accompanied by tonal nonverbal behavior that Helen says Hektor never used in twenty years, are regretfully excluded from this survey by the criterion of explicit textual evidence. Homer does not specify here the expectable paralinguistic attributes (248–49, 767). Similarly, Hera comforts Thetis by means of a goblet of refreshment, an object-adaptor accompanied, we here can only surmise, by appropriate tones (101–2).

protagonists and "extras" both to internal and external audiences (629–32, 559, 484; cf. Cic. *de Orat.* 3.221 or Nestor's knowing glance at *Il.* 9.179–81).

Informal and informative, in-awareness nonverbal behavior is rare in *Iliad* 24, relative to the other types discussed in this chapter. References to Akhilleus' semiritualistic warrior-trophy displays and then mutilations of Hektor's corpse (15–17, 51–52, 417–18) meant more for his mood earlier, in book 22. Here, their continuation symbolizes Akhilleus' pathetic inability to "snap out of it," to accept a displeasing reality and get on with life. He remains frozen in bereavement until Priam holds up a mirror of equal grief and breaks the spell. Similarly, Hekabe's verbally expressed wish to eat Akhilleus' uncooked liver more likely preserves a popular idiom of cannabalistic hostility than a description of real, nonverbal, but communicative, ritual.[47]

Responsibility of affines, legal control, and gendered power and dependence are signaled by arm-grasping hands. The husband ceremonially grasps his bride's wrist during the marriage rite as a sign of control. The female (gendered) correlate is to cling to the arm of a spouse or man-child. This example makes clear that one gesture can have different, even opposite, meanings depending on who does it to whom.[48] An eloquent, informal gesture in *Iliad* 24, persuasive to participants and compactly communicative to the audience, is this hand- or wrist-grasp. Thus, Hermes and Akhilleus both guide Priam, indeed assert their control over Priam's postures and distance, while reassuring him verbally and nonverbally of friendly attitude (361, 515, 671–72, specifying ἐπὶ καρπῷ). Hera grabs Artemis by the same wrists with one hand before boxing the child's ears. Thus, and with a provocative smile, Hera visibly reminds Artemis of her "minor" or inferior status and reproaches her as a naughty child (21.489–92; at 508, father Zeus laughs at her situation).

---

47. 24.212–13; Segal 1971, chaps. 5–7; Combellack 1981.
48. *Od.* 18.258; Sittl 1890, 131–32. For clinging to a husband, see Andromakhe at 6.406. For clinging to a man-child, see 6.253 (Hekabe) = 19.7 (Thetis). For other variants see 18.384 (two women greet each other), 14.232 (Hera greets Sleep). The formula at 18.423 is applied to Hephaistos' greeting Thetis. The gendered act characterizes this exchange as surprisingly urgent and conveys his hierarchical superiority in the divine pecking order. Modern advertisements transmit similar gender asymmetry in companionate couple's power by showing male arms over female shoulders while females cling to males; cf. Goffman 1976, "Function Ranking," "The Ritualization of Subordination," and illustrations 24, 58, 83, etc. In post-Homeric Attic vase painting (as Neumann 1965, 59–60, notes), men continue to lead, by the wrist and hand, the very young, the very old, drunkards, prisoners, and brides. All these creatures are subject to patriarchal authority, in need of guidance, or both. Lowenstam 1992 surveys the uses of ceramic evidence in Homeric studies. The ritualized and conscious gesture has analogues in primate behavior that may lie behind human formality.

Astyanax had earlier "screamed and shrunk back" from the extended hands and helmeted face of his fiercely armored father. The child's nonverbal behavior transmits an age-based, infantile feeling: uncomprehending fear (but nonetheless suitably clairvoyant, 6.466–70). Ascribing ostracizing, symbolic intent, Andromakhe earlier predicted that a *Trojan* would someday thrust her orphaned son from the communal table. Now she predicts his death, grabbed by an overpowering Akhaian (22.491–99). This Akhaian who someday seizes Astyanax to hurl him to death performs an instrumental act, but the death of the young prince, real enough, supplies a synecdoche for the death of the Iliadic community (24.735).

Andromakhe's anticipatory fears for herself and her child arouse pathos. No less passionate is her lament that Hektor had no chance to stretch out his arms to her at home, on his death bed, in his final moment before dying. The unrealized, momentary, nearly instinctual gesture of need serves as another synecdoche for Hektor's indefinitely needy condition and unfulfilled love. The preliminary gesture and the aborted embrace characterize the intimacy of Homeric families and companionate marriage, for Trojans as for Ithakans (ἐκ χεῖρας ὄρεξας, 743; *Od.* 8.527, 16.214, 17.38, 23.207–8, 23.240, 24.347).

The greatest grief of Akhilleus, Priam, and Penelope appears unrestrained, because their extremes of passion and consequent disregard of social convention in these moments present the central action. Their sounds, gestures, and collapsed postures are vivid and economical communications that reveal psychological states, confirm feelings by act, and advance the narrative toward the next development. Equanimity, emotional stability, and self-sufficiency (ἀταραξία and αὐτάρκεια) are themes and ideals of philosophers, not of epic poets who portray the power of passions. Nearly automatically and unself-consciously, these characters express grief, while artful and calculating Aithon/Odysseus explicitly represses and defers his.

6. Conclusions

Nonverbal behaviors provide humans and other sentient creatures with a necessary redundancy: "information received from one system [e.g., the verbal] is backed up by other systems in case of failure. . . . [T]alk suppl[ies] only part of the message. The rest is filled in by the listener" (Hall 1966, 102). In 1927, Edward Sapir ignored achievements of literature, when he elegantly described nonverbal phenomena as "an elaborate and secret code that is written nowhere, known by none, and understood by all" (Portch 1985, 7).

The ancient epic poets find nonverbal behavior a succinct and distinct dimension for their characters and action. They deploy it frequently; it contributes to the varied texture of their mimesis. It is not episodic or extraneous but essential to the drama and to the expression of individual and group personality. It fleshes out narrative and description; it provides counterpoint and emphasis. Such dramatic coloring speeds or slows the narrational pace. When Odysseus alleges that the bard Demodokos must have been present for or must have heard from an eyewitness his account of the sufferings of the Akhaians, the praised vividness and authenticity derives (in part) from his report of nonverbal behaviors (e.g., *Od.* 8.80, 291, 305, 310, 324, 344, 361, 366, 505–6). No mere chronicle or summary, devoid of persuasive speech or insistent gesture, would possess this power or convey such ethos.[49]

All nonverbal behavior reported in literature is, in some sense, conventional, narrowed in its channels to become comprehensible by strangers unfamiliar with an individual and his idiogests. Furthermore, the medium, like any other, must be selective, since verbal accounts, texting, requires "channel reduction." Every teller's narrative strategy selects certain significant facts: only some behaviors, some deeds, and some words "deserve" attention. Even the modern kinesiologists' fixed-focus video camera has a more limited scope and sensorium than a live interactant.[50] Who communicates what to whom and how are questions essential to any reading of the epics. Homeric "facts" are often nothing other than nonverbal behaviors.[51]

Homer operates with patterns of formula, theme, and type-scene for purposes of literary coherence, intelligibility, and drama, as well as for consider-

---

49. The historian Herodotos, the Attic orator Lysias, and Plato also realized this power and indeed borrowed it from Homer. For Herodotos, see Lateiner 1987. For the Bible, see Mackie 1899, cols. 162b–163b. He indicates ethnic differences between Near Eastern and Anglo-Saxon usages. Gruber 1980 offers a detailed survey.

50. Tabulated book-by-book statistics on the number and location, internal audience, and length of speeches, the speakers, the type of speech, etc. for both Homeric epics are collected in the valuable 1939 dissertation of Fingerle. It is hard to locate and deserves printing. My graduate school colleague and Homeric companion William Beck, now of the Hamburg *Lexikon der frühgriechischen Epos,* supplied extracts and tables from this valuable study. For book 24, consult Fingerle's pp. 36–37: 804 verses contain 47 speeches composed of 452 verses (Fingerle wrongly typed 252 on pp. 36–37). The average length of a speech is 9.62 verses; the average percentage of a book occupied by *oratio recta* is 56.22 percent. My total number of speech verses is slightly different. Fingerle compares numbers for the entire epics in various useful ways on pp. 68–78; pp. 79–80 summarize results.

51. This self-evident assertion, as Daniel Levine points out to me, contradicts the influential formulation of Auerbach 1953, chap. 1, "Odysseus' Scar." Auerbach claims that Homer puts everything in a perpetual foreground, uniformly illuminated, where "thoughts and feeling [are] completely expressed" (9).

ations based on the nature of oral epic performance. Gestures also structure his world and ours. He is "persuasive" because he produces a rounded, three-dimensional image that neglects few descriptive and narrative techniques. The lesser authors of the later epic cycle seem to have employed a thin and flat diction, uninspired repetitions, and fantastic elements of romance. They lack the delights of direct speech, tragic characters, and dramatic construction.[52] Few traces of nonverbal behavior can be discerned. Nonverbal behavior, seldom if ever before appreciated by Homeric critics as a ubiquitous element in the epics, contributes importantly to Homer's preeminence. His range of nonverbal behavior is unmatched, and its occurrence, never perfunctory, adds depth to the Homeric stage.

Iliad 24 includes all major categories of nonverbal behavior but is richest in ritual (category A), in part because the final book swaddles us in ceremonious reintegration and closure: the gods and men, the dead and the living, and even the Akhaian besieger and the Trojan besieged. The family unit reasserts itself in the intimacy of human habitats, removed from the blasted, barren fields of battle and brutal Olympian bullying.

Nonverbal behaviors identify emotions and their intensity. They articulate the soul through the body. Many nonverbal behaviors are easily controlled; all normally capable, that is nondyssemic humans employ them daily to supplement or replace words and to ease and effect interchanges with others. In critical situations, often depicted by Homer, posture and gesture have a propriety, truthfulness, and creative expressiveness of their own that transcend words. In particular, the coordination of bodily kinetics with strong feelings (as in family feuds, parting, and mourning procedures) can have either centrifugal or restorative effects. Repair of persons emerges in *Iliad* 24, where the nonverbal expression of emotion italicizes the inherent pathos, verbal information-sharing, and communal healing. Nonverbal behavior, whether underlining or undermining, transmits essential expression of individual and communal attitudes and feelings. Our bodies and voices suggest or assert that which the speaker fears to declare or cannot find words for.[53] Occurrence of nonverbal behavior in Homer, then, "silently" supplies another, independent and cooperative channel of communication for charac-

---

52. Griffin 1977, esp. 48–53. I first developed some of these generalizations in an unpublished comparison of *Iliad* 24, Vergil *Aen.* 2, and Ovid *Met.* 14.

53. The unthinking prejudice of our hyperverbal culture has misstated the topic's unappreciated importance, in part by employing negative and metaphoric terminology like *nonverbal, body language,* etc. Cf. Gombrich 1972, esp. 377–82. At this point in the development of the field, it has become difficult to disseminate effectively a less misleading taxonomy.

ters' status, general attitudes, immediate conscious responses, and unconscious feelings. Certain authors, following Homer, summarily reveal by nonverbal behavior significant signs of character and interaction, a "hidden dimension." Oral literature is thus the richer, and the student of ancient personality and social life uncovers enriching contextual information.

Part 2

Nonverbal Respect and Disrespect in the *Odyssey*

Chapter 4

Heroic Etiquette: Salutation, Encounter, and Valediction

1. Etiquette

Ceremonial observances regulate social intercourse among friends and strangers (ἅ τε ξείνοις θέμις ἐστίν). Civility, neighborly good will, and conventional pieties provide the infrastructure of involvement. "Footing" establishes speaker-audience alignment. Tone, posture, distance, orientation, and demeanor determine friends and enemies. When Odysseus is repeatedly asked his name, father, place of origin, and current purposes, we have Homeric "grooming talk," ritualized courtesies to situate interactants. When Odysseus' son, nurse, swains, father, and wife throw arms about him in greeting, we have rituals of ratification, reassurance displays, that declare, despite change, that essential gender, age, and status hierarchies have survived acknowledged separation. Parting rituals affirm the acceptability of interdependence and expectations for future reciprocal hosting and guesting. In the *Odyssey*, few partners in parting actually will have a future relationship, but the essential element of valediction remains the promise of hospitable reciprocity, should present host become future guest.[1]

Relations management depends on affirmations of good will and on acting out unignorable parity and disparity. Encounter etiquette recognizes or recalibrates status established or renewed at every meeting, however recent or distant the last instance was. Nonverbal behavior provides a "gloss," an echo or a sign, for supportive, offensive, and remedial exchanges. The Ho-

---

1. Greetings in antiquity, their verbal and nonverbal forms, comprise Sittl 1890, chap. 5, "Konventionelle Begrüssung." Arend's 1933 study of type-scenes includes arrivals (simple, by visitors and by messengers), departures, libations, etc., although not gift giving and unique greetings (28–34, 34–54, 54–61, 86–91, 76–78). M. Edwards 1975 (71–72, 58–59 on *Od.* 4.150–53; 64–67 on 5.28–95) discusses apparent inconsistencies in Homeric hospitality (Menelaos' belated toast to the young travelers and Hermes' arrival at Kirke's). He explains them as imperfect conflations of two common type-scenes. Miner 1956, 503–5, an anthopological classic, parodies American grooming rituals from an alien, scholarly perspective. Pitt-Rivers 1977 offers an "imaginary ethnography" of honor gained and lost in hospitality exchanges in the *Odyssey* and of honorary social incorporation.

meric stranger is reassured by being taken by the hand (*Od.* 1.121, 3.37, 7.168); warm welcome (invitation, guidance, seating with honor) is fully appreciated (*Od.* 14.45–52). Menelaos experienced a Phthian, pre-Troy version of proper hosting and reports it briefly (*Il.* 11.775–80). The exigencies of Homeric travel and precommercial tourism mean that hosts furnish guests with beds, baths, oils, towels, and clothes (*Od.* 4.48–50, 8.449–56, 17.85–97, 19.317–20). Hosts offer libations, then food, and drink to visitors' health; gifts follow.[2] Other, less welcoming and hostile encounters are fully reported, complete with congruent "negative" nonverbal behavior. Skherian abuse, Kyklopian detention, Aiolian rejection (on the rebound), Laistrygonian assault, and Kirkean deception—omitting for the nonce the panoply of suitors' miscues—exemplify perverted paradigms and nonhospitality.

Salutation, valediction, and the talk and action that they bracket—necessary, ubiquitous rituals of occasion—vary considerably across cultures. Americans stand while Tongans sit to perform respect for a newcomer. Homer's heroes rouse themselves to the vertical for a visitor of stature. When ambassadors or guests of stature arrive, Akhilleus and Telemakhos quickly rise from their chairs (*Il.* 9.192–94, *Od.* 1.113–20). To channel and program an interchange, Homer provides initiatory kinesic markers: Odysseus' or Telemakhos' eye-contact management and nods (*Od.* 20.385, 21.129, 17.330), body contact like Pisistratos' and Odysseus' firm handclasp, or Odysseus' knee-grasp that supplicates Arete (*Od.* 3.37, 17.263, 7.142). Entire encounters are micromanaged by semiautomatic turn-taking and turn-granting procedures.

All public orders benefit from encounter rituals that recognize interactant acceptability. Reciprocity and signs of mutual acceptability are essential to demonstrate acceptance, although often both parties will define and affirm inequality of rank during interaction. The party that approaches, prostrates himself or herself, and initiates conversation often is demonstrating social inferiority by postures, orientation, and gestures—metatalk. Relative posture, especially body elevation, reveals identity and rank: the more you disturb yourself to greet another, the lower you acknowledge your relative status. Thus, Odysseus as noble suppliant or minimally recognized beggar betakes himself around Skherian and Ithakan mansions and tables, while dyarchs and suitors keep their seats and composure. We will briefly consider Homeric openings, encounters, and closures—frequent and significant components of interpersonal performance in face-to-face Homeric society.

---

2. 3.40–43; 7.179–84; 13.66–69; 7.175–77, 335; 18.121; 15.123–27. Goffman's 1971 essay on "supportive interchanges" informed this paragraph. See also Pedrick 1988, 85; Williams 1986; Gutglueck 1988; briefly West 1993.

2. Arrivals

Greetings—arbitrary verbal and nonverbal initiation of communications—draw attention, establish identification, and reduce uncertainty.[3] Awakening as a stranger on one more unfamiliar shore, Odysseus accepts the role of inferior. He first "greets up" the presumed local, Athene (disguised as a shepherd's boy, but a wealthy one, to judge by his fancy mantle). The newcomer approaches the resident, because his situation demands supplication to gain aid for a helpless, abandoned foreigner. Thus, he displaces himself and opens the verbal encounter. Rank and address here are principally determined by territoriality, haberdashery, and perceived need, not by age or gender (13.19–90). The verbal greeting exchanges situational "facts"—why the stranger has come—but the nonverbal proxemics reassures, ingratiates, and acknowledges dependency on the young man. After Athene returns to maiden-goddess form, revealing her undeniable existential superiority, and admits her identity, she smiles parentally at her protégé and strokes his arm. These positive coverbal gestures, smiling and stroking, endorse and emphasize her comforting speech.[4]

In addition to preexisting personal relations between greeters and the messages they intend to convey, social context constrains the nature and form of greetings. Status (determined by age, gender, class, and occupation), external audience for the encounter (if any), and ends (explicit or implied) for which they meet shape the event and calibrate level of formality in gesture and elaboration of address, verbal and nonverbal.[5] Young Telemakhos has no heroic credentials when he goes abroad, but because he is the son of their honored comrade Odysseus, the older heroes Nestor and Menelaos provide him with red-carpet treatment. They acknowledge that they owe his father's son no less. Odysseus as outlander and beggar, per contra, is lucky to be noticed at all with anything other than abuse and abusive words.

Greetings not only bracket and validate increased access; they function as markers of politeness and respect, denial or affirmation of threats, petition preliminaries, and—most essentially—identity establishment. Greetings, however highly formulaic, communicate perceptions of a relationship or footing—self-image and estimation of the greeted other. They hint at both parties' intent for the business that follows the initialized interchange.

---

3. Roth 1889, Firth 1972, Goody 1972, Youssouf et al. 1976, Schiffrin 1977.

4. On formulae for affectionate caress in the *Iliad* and the *Odyssey*, see Levine 1982a, 100–101.

5. Firth 1969, 1972; Goffman 1971; Goody 1972; Youssouf et al. 1976, 815–16.

68 *Sardonic Smile*

Three types of interactants confront us: familiars, entirely unknown strangers, and those previously heard of but not yet met. Ceremonies vary accordingly. Odysseus' encounters with Agamemnon, Aiolos, and Hermes serve as examples of the three categories, as do Kyklops' exchanges with his fellow inhabitants, with Odysseus in disguise, and with Odysseus revealed. The dynamics of such meetings are determined in part by whether they occur on our turf, on the other's turf, or on neutral turf, such as the agora or the battlefield (which can be friendly to both or to neither).

The heartiness of salutations differs even when verbal and "polite fictions," formal ceremonious elements, remain constant. Informal nonverbal behavior establishes degrees of warmth. Involvement can be "polite or rude, frosty or warm, formal or casual, stilted or relaxed, obsequious or condescending, insulting or complimentary, perfunctory or painstaking, . . . genuine or spurious." Posture, tone of voice, and facial composition clarify the greeters' inner attitudes. Every society's communicative registers include these expressive modes or "keys" as well as formalized forms of address and gestures. We evaluate others' social skills and maturity by their ability to manage both semiotic behaviors and dialogic words (Youssouf, Grimshaw, and Bird 1976, 799–800, 812, 815). The concatenation of type-scenes of "arrival, reception, deception, and revelation" in the *Odyssey* offers many examples and tests of Homeric nonverbal procedures. Departures are nearly as numerous but have received less poetic and scholarly attention.[6]

Greetings reciprocally affirm differential allocation of status: subordinates take the initiative in greeting acknowledged superordinates. Eumaios and Philoitios kiss the revealed master Odysseus before he returns the greeting (21.223–25). The embracing and kissing signify love, respect, and hierarchy, and also increased access both sought and granted. So old Eumaios warmly greets the returned master's son Telemakhos (16.14–16; cf. 17.35, 39–40; the wrist kiss at 24.398). Reciprocity sits at the heart of the epic. Nearly thoughtless rituals affirm and deny it. "Negative" (i.e., expected but unfulfilled) reciprocity in the cases of Akhilleus with Agamemnon (in both directions) and Odysseus with the suitors focuses conflict in a way that not even mortal combat can match. Homer's method is to show as much as to tell. Bodies perform the heroes' feelings. Insult and outrage reach their peak with violation of god-sanctioned rituals of exchange.

Systematic description of Homeric greetings includes distant sighting,

---

6. Homer humorously exploits Telemakhos' difficult departure from Menelaos, as G. Rose 1971 shows. See also section 4 in this chapter.

salutations at a public distance, then salutations at an intimate distance, if clearance is granted for close approach (χερσίν τ' ἠσπάζοντο [wave, embrace, or handshake?], 3.35; 4.22–24, 24.391–411). The approacher usually has de facto lower status and cautiously penetrates the other party's airspace or territory. Salutation may take the form of no physical contact, especially with cross-gender greetings, as when Odysseus nears but does not touch Nausikaa, or when Penelope descends to the unruly companions. Salutation may lead the man on his own turf to take a stranger-guest by the hand or to proffer a manly handshake, as Autolykos once greeted his grandson Odysseus or as Philoitios later welcomes the beggar. More intimate greetings may produce an embrace or embraces with a kissing of the head, eyes, shoulders, and hand, as young Odysseus' grandmother greeted him. The wraith Agamemnon pathetically "throws himself" into Odysseus' arms. Gender, age, and status rules determine the appropriate nonverbal form of welcome (6.145–47, 18.206–12; 1.121, 3.37, 9.280; 11.392; 19.415, 20.197; 24.347; 19.417–18, cf. 16.15–16, 23.207–8).

Lachrymose leakage, weeping for joy, frequently accompanies rituals of return. Here no effort to dam the affect is wanted or exerted, so the exhibition of emotion does not belong with the unintended display, or "leakage," of deception clues described in chapter 5. Male and female slaves greet Telemakhos and Odysseus thus; Odysseus and Telemakhos cry uncontrollably in each other's arms. Agamemnon, when he finally returned to Argos, wept in this manner. Penelope cries when young Telemakhos returns, and Odysseus weeps when he descries companion Elpenor among the dead. Odysseus weeps at his reunion with the ghosts of Antikleia and Agamemnon, as does the Argive royal ghost; and like-minded Odysseus, Telemakhos, and Penelope like-nonverbally weep in each other's arms.[7]

Homeric royal greeting rituals reflect the exigencies of ancient life. The anxious transition of unknown and possibly dangerous stranger to guest is effected partly by preliminary ceremonies of reception. These include escorting over the threshold and the washing, anointing, and clean dressing of the

---

7. 17.33; 21.223–25; 22.498–500; 16.214–16; 4.523; 17.38; 11.55, 87, 392, 395; 23.207, 232. Waern 1985, Monsacré 1984, and Arnould 1990 survey Homeric weeping and grief beyond that. Indeed, one might postulate this weeping of the reunited as de rigueur, genuine and spontaneous outpouring of excess emotion, but verging on ceremonial rather than unique, unexpected, or unwillingly revelatory. However natural, the act is culturally validated for the Ithakans but not for North American males. Epic performance draws tears from Penelope and Odysseus, even he who has requested this very tale (1.336; 8.84–88, 521–32). Penelope's delight in tears is formulaic: τάρφθη πολυδακρύτοιο γόοιο (19.213 = 19.251 = 21.57; Redfield [1967] 1973, 153). Kendon 1973 articulates six stages of American greeting rituals.

guest.[8] After the ablutions, the noble host must again greet and seat the stranger, must regale him with wine and food, and must not make inquiries about identity and purpose before the meal's end (cf. 3.69). This summarizes the behavior of Telemakhos as Mentor/Athene's host; of Nestor and Menelaos as Telemakhos' host; of Nausikaa, Alkinoos, and Arete as Odysseus' hosts; and of knowledgeable Eumaios as Odysseus' host. Some hosts who behave otherwise, such as Kyklops, Kirke, and the suitors, are accounted hostile, while others, such as (originally) Alkinoos or the presumptive, self-appointed doorkeeper Iros, are considered inept and dangerous for the precarious status of a Homeric guest. Lowly Eumaios the (once regal) pig-herd is the perfect host for a complete stranger, providing food, proximity to the fire, and clothes (14.45–48). This suggests a social comedy of manners and points to the inversions of class-based civility and etiquette on Ithaka between pigsty and palace (Williams 1986, 395; cf. G. Rose 1980). Ithaka's acephalous society and leading household are barely held together by the suitors' party—a truce in an obviously competitive situation—and by Penelope's womanly manipulation of stressed hosting rituals. Nonverbal ceremonies in the anomalous situation maintain a degree of civility, while most words between suitors and Laertids are "fighting words."

The woman of authority in stable heroic households has three gestures of hospitality: she arranges the guest's bed; she supervises the elaborate prebanquet bath; and, at departure, she offers gifts of cloth made by her industrious hands. These wholesome complements to male hospitality appear in the behavior of Arete, Helen, and sometimes Penelope. Women who are not so clearly subject to male control, such as Kalypso, Nausikaa, Kirke, and sometimes Penelope, threaten patriarchy, even male mobility, precisely when they appear most hospitable. Kirke perverts hospitality by enslaving every man who appears on her doorstep. Kalypso intends to imprison and "disappear" Odysseus. Likewise, Nausikaa wishes to demobilize Odysseus, but she has little maneuvering room. Penelope arrests forever the suitors' hopes of wealth and children.[9]

---

8. Gutglueck 1988 discusses the secular rite (n. 13 lists thirteen examples) but oddly ascribes to castration anxiety Odysseus' insistence on bathing himself on Skheria (rather than letting the usual, if to us surprising, noble young women do it). Rather, the place (raw nature, at the culturally undefined seaside) and the company (unintroduced women without watchful, protecting males) cannot adequately structure or regulate bathing etiquette. The sociosexual parameters of the heroic, mixed-gender, and naked ritual would not be clear; thus, Odysseus is "embarrassed." In a modern parallel, adolescent male and female students who proudly sport bikinis at the swimming pool would blush to wear them (*ut speram*) to the classroom.

9. See Pedrick 1988, 85–86, on domestic amenities; 91–93, on baleful effects.

Greeting postures, distances, and forms of address manipulate encounters. Odysseus expresses uncertainty as to whether he should address Nausikaa as a queen or goddess, after pondering whether to approach her closely or keep his distance. Along with deferential approach and extended palms as a beggar in Ithaka, he coverbally cajoles the suitor Antinoos as a man of uncommon sense. Both sets of behaviors allege the wealth, rank, and aristocratic virtues of Odysseus' interlocutors (6.149–57, 17.415–17). His distance, elevation, and orientation to these two superiors focus their attention on him. They impose requests almost as demands.

Hands constitute the most versatile organ of in-awareness nonverbal behavior. Eurykleia moves her hands to cover her face and so blots out a hateful present situation. Odysseus grabs her throat to reinforce, both symbolically and instrumentally, his urgent command of silence. His hands fondle and manipulate the bow and shoot the first symbolic arrow (also a penetrating and instrumental sign for the bride contest). The handiwork appears eloquently equivalent or superior communication to *verbal* claims for Penelope's "hand" (synecdochic here for her person). The nonverbal communication's success is acknowledged nonverbally by the suitors' dramatic leak of affect—they immediately blanch, the blood and color departing from their faces (19.361, 480–81; 21.412–13).

Hand movements extend Homer's sensitive repertoire of human expression. One hand grasping another's hand may convey a warm welcome, earnest concern, strong support, or motherly affection when accompanied by sympathetic caress. Elsewhere in Homeric poetry, such manual maneuvers communicate confirmation of marriage, angry disapproval, or beseeching dependency. Akhilleus and others contrast meaningful hand-acts to empty words. The elevation of hands and arms initiate prayer, supplication, and readiness to fight.[10]

In the presence of more than one person, the choice of whom to greet, when, and how (with a gift?) poses delicate questions that can determine whether an encounter succeeds or fails. Thus, we tend to address any members of the police force as "officer" when requesting help to gain entry to a locked automobile or forgiveness for excessive freeway alacrity. Not all decisions require politesse, however. Odysseus' decision to greet Nausikaa at the

---

10. *Il.* 18.384; *Od.* 1.121, 3.37, 19.415; *Il.* 5.30, 14.136–38, 21.286; *Od.* 3.374, 24.398; *Il.* 1.361; *Od.* 4.610, 5.181, 13.288; *Il.* 15.126–127; 6.253, 406; 1.77, 298; *Od.* 17.239; *Il.* 1.501, 8.371, 10.454; *Od.* 18.89, 19.473. Martin 1989, 18, collects Iliadic exempla. *Od.* 18.258 reports a marriage ritual wrist-grasp; 8.106 reports instrumental aid to a blind singer. Bates 1975 examines gestures of blessing and cursing; Scheflen 1964 catalogs expressive use of head, hands, and legs/feet, signifiers of varying degrees of eloquence but ranked thus in usefulness in contemporary Euro-American civilization.

beach was not shrewd, since the other girls had already scattered out of fear and run into the bush. His choice of Arete to approach at the palace was her daughter's logical advice. In all cases where a choice must be made, however, Odysseus knows the right person, the right distance, and the right time to "greet up" and to ask for what he wants or needs.[11]

Exceptional circumstances engender exceptional greetings. Eurykleia grasps by the beard her just-recognized nursling and master, a form of deferential supplication. A groom grasps his bride by the wrist as a symbol of control in Greek marriage ritual, and thus Odysseus had once "captured" Penelope. Agamemnon and Odysseus osculate the dry soil of their homelands on debarkation, in effect treating it like family (19.473, 18.258, 4.522, 13.354, cf. 5.463). Odysseus tries to embrace the shade of his mother and his commander-in-chief in the Otherworld (11.205–11, 392–94). Animal greetings, both friendly fawning and unfriendly growling, appear in the poem (20.14–15, a bitch; 14.29–30; 17.291, 302, Argos; 9.214–19, Kirke's zoo). When divinity alights, mortal dogs cower and whimper in necessarily nonverbal recognition. Sluttish maids, "bitches" in Odysseus' terminology, indecorously greet each other with inappropriate and complicitous laughter (16.162–63, 18.338, 20.8).

3. Hospitality, Including Gifts

Odysseus the stranger meets either hostile, and sometimes lethal, reception or honor and kindness. The elevation of *xenia* to the care of Zeus almighty marks Hellenic awareness of the fragility of such goodness. Odysseus' gentle reminders to Kyklops, Alkinoos, and Antinoos (9.270–71, 367–68, 475–76, etc.) suggest the nonuniversality of hospitality. *Hostis* meant any "stranger" before it developed the limited sense of "enemy" to the insecure Latins (Cic. *de Off.* 1.37; cf. French *hôte,* "guest" and "host"), but the two concepts seem close in any society with weak or nonexistent police authority.

Gift-exchange, meals in common and a bed-linen for the night, body-contact rituals, and shared sacrifice are four types of nonverbal symmetry that bind two previously unacquainted parties. Glaukos and Diomedes have time on the battlefield to clasp hands and exchange gifts (*Il.* 6.224–33). Strangers have unknown powers that must be appeased or conquered at arrival and separation. Hostility and strangeness must be surmounted to establish a permanent bond. The institution of *xenia* supplied a successful

---

11. 6.135–36, 142–48. His disastrous engagement with Polyphemos, it must be allowed, exhibits a textbook of etiquette errors. See Goody 1972, 40–43. Youssouf et al. 1976, 799, regret the absence of studies of cross-societal uniformities.

means to overcome natural anxiety in Homer's report and in later Greek history. The exceptions are notorious because they were exceptional. Aigisthos, Polyphemos, and the suitors abuse *xenia* and suffer accordingly in the moral romance of Homer. The vicious parodies of guest-gifts offered by Polyphemos and Antinoos provide one of the many ominous nonverbal parallels between the monster and the monstrous suitors in mistreating the stranger.

Rituals of friendship between members of separate groups constitute necessary glue in centrifugal Homeric society. They are more bonding than mere acquaintance and similar to social contracts among married kin. The stylized etiquette of initiating a compact, creating an enduring bond, and arranging services and benefactions in adversity or in the other person's territory connect by pseudokinship otherwise insulated and isolated leaders, travelers, and even whole communities. "Gifts" establish a bilateral nonverbal contract and always imply eventual return. The compact extends far beyond items of exchange value and even across generations.[12]

Zeus oversees hospitality, central to the verbal formulae, nonverbal themes, and type-scenes. A structural pattern of arrival, reception, and departure articulates and concatenates the *Odyssey*, particularly books 9–12. The etiquette of hospitality that gives substance to this pattern can be violated by either host or guest, neither, or both. The ritualized acts of welcome handshakes, companionable feasting, guest-gifts, and farewell embraces are presented formulaically, but they nevertheless express essential meaning and sentiments. The words are the more otiose constituent. Ritualized acts develop semiotic glosses and nuances everywhere to key interactants to performers' sentiments and precise attitudes.

Homeric manners incorporate six usual stages of formal reception: a stranger approaches and stops, attendants respond, the host greets, the host offers a seat of honor and friendly companionship, the host feeds, and finally

---

12. van Gennep [1908] 1960, 29; Mauss 1967, 1, 3, 18, 40, on the contractual ethos; Schein 1970, 81–82; Herman 1987, 16, 49, and passim on *xenia* in the later polis. Donlan 1989, 8 cites "the rub": the giver "owns a debt." Telemakhos' visits to Akhaian heroes are kept short because he seeks news of his father. We cannot say how long Mycenaean or archaic princely visits typically extended. Even this visit's length is debated: Delebecque 1980 and Olson 1992a. Certainly Odysseus' rest-stops with Kirke and Kalypso last longer than usual chronemic protocols demanded, but he would legitimately refer to extenuating circumstances, divine demands. He stays with Aiolos for a month (10.14). The house call to which Americans devote a scant hour lasts at least three days among Arab bedouin; Hall 1984, Bogucka 1991, and Benjamin Constant in *Adolphe* describe the extent of visits among nineteenth-century Polish gentry. Nestor's and Menelaos' protestations against Telemakhos' departure are candid enough, but the formulaic discourse of valediction is laced with polite fictions in all societies: no one wants guests to stay indefinitely.

the host inquires the guest's identity.[13] Hospitality often recognizes the guest by offering the seat of honor: Akhilleus offers Priam his own throne, and Nestor and Athene make room for Patroklos and Thetis on earth as in heaven (*Il.* 24.515–22, 11.645–46, 24.100; *Od.* 7.169–71, 16.42, perhaps 1.130). Eumaios has only a kindling pile to offer a beggar for sedentary comfort, but he covers it with goatskin from his own bed and thereby demonstrates paradigmatic hospitality. He elicits an appreciative Odysseus' admiration. Odysseus' interest and skill in manipulating gift customs are humorously patent to the experienced noble swineherd (14.508–11).[14]

One proof of aristocratic nature has always been the host's ability to respond appropriately to unexpected visitors. Young Nausikaa and Telemakhos, although not yet empowered householders, show poise in entertaining surf-scarred Odysseus and Mentes/Athene and, later, disguised Odysseus back on Ithaka. Both acknowledge difficulties in fulfilling hostly duties because of age, gender, and/or position in the household, but they share without stint, in a rough-and-ready way, whatever they can (6.246–62; 16.69–72, 79–89). Odysseus, the experienced guest, appreciates their precociously couth behavior.

Telemakhos "grows up" from a babied, lethargic adolescent (1.113–20; χαλίφρων, 16. 310, 19.530; Penelope thus must protect him) to an abrasive teenager rebuking the noxious "guests" and his own mother (17.45–51; 21.344–55, 372–75; 19.159–61, 532–34). During his tour of the lower Peloponnese, he is half-ignorant of visitors' protocols when he arrives at Pylos. Here, fatherly Athene must encourage the helpless scion out of his timorous modesty, across the beach, and into the heroes' feast. She screws up his courage, while he hangs back, excusing himself by ignorance of introductions and other good manners (3.14–24). He does not know the words or the right nonverbal moves for getting up close and eliciting serious discourse from an elder. No father has taught him. He finally follows, literally, in Athene's footsteps: ὁ δ' ἔπειτα μετ' ἴχνια βαῖνε θεοῖο (3.30).

Later, returning home, Telemakhos crudely, though understandably, breaches protocol by choosing *not* to pay the expected and usual respects again to Nestor at Pylos. He upsets the old man's son, Pisistratos, who will have to remedy the gaffe as best he can (15.199–214). Gawky Telamakhos' adolescent outbursts, abrupt, choppy remarks (e.g., 2.80–81, 17.400), and aggressive postures toward the Ithakan suitors elicit several laughs and

---

13. Levy 1963; Newton 1983. E.g., see *Il.* 11.775–80, *Od.* 1.118–58. For feasts, see 4.66; 5.92, 196–99; 6.248, 20.257–62.

14. 14.48–54. M. Edwards 1975, 70, offers most of these examples. G. Rose 1980, Williams 1986, and Roisman 1990a discuss Eumaios' wonderful manners.

taunts from that oafish band. The challenges are verbal but also accompany nonverbal (proxemics, condescending smiles, and guffaws) and paralinguistic challenges to his competence: intonation and tailgating comebacks are crucial (2.301, 17.407–9, 20.373–84). Delicate but firm is the nonverbal and verbal characterization of the precocious youth with regard to the intrusive ruffians.[15]

After the initial reception of guests, there follow numerous libations to gods, entertainments (dancers, jugglers, etc.), polite requests made of the host, expensive presents, and nonverbal and verbal expressions of gratitude. *Xenia*—guest-gifts, nonverbal communications of wealth and prestige—constitute moral transactions—objects that convey emotion and mementos of the giver (15.54–55, 21.40). Nestor is appalled that Telemakhos in his haste nearly leaves Nestor's house before receiving gifts of carpets and blankets (3.343–55). Such guest-gifts also establish obligations on the gifted for future reciprocity. The customs of theatrical prestation are assumed and varied to effect in the *Odyssey*. Homer treats the symbolic performance of wealth, gift-exchange, hospitality, and charitable donations with some humor. Royal Menelaos looks ludicrous and mercenary when he praises aristocratic tourism as a way to get rich. Inexperienced as a beggar and/or intentionally "pushy," Odysseus, to get a rise, presses Antinoos more blatantly than beggars' etiquette might permit. Polyphemos taunts Odysseus, who is greedy for guest-gifts, for his sermons on hospitality by granting him the "gift" of momentary survival—he will be the last crunchy visitor to be eaten. Ktesippos ironically invokes heroic customs of honorable exchange as he launches the hostile ox-hoof at Odysseus.[16]

Gifts are objects pulsing with social energy; they nonverbally encode sentiment, obligation, and esteem. Homer's most significant gift-object (a rich and relatively noticed category of nonverbal behavior; cf. chapter 3, section 3)—leaving out the vile and precious merchandise of women—might be Odysseus' bow. This "thing" of stored murder and death was once a pawn in a reciprocity system, a guest-gift central to the only actually *equal* gift-exchange in the Homeric poems. Odysseus obtained it from Iphitos when

---

15. Millar and Carmichael 1954 read too much spiritual development into the word πεπ-νυμένος, "vigorous (mentally)," a participle first applied to Telemakhos at 1.361. It may, however, indicate growing verbal and nonverbal interpersonal assertiveness.

16. 15.78–79, 17.414–18, 9.369–70, 20.296. Hoekstra ad loc. finds Menelaos' remark unheroic; he degrades the line as very late. That explanation may be otiose, however, given the otherwise scathing characterization of inert, inept, and inane Menelaos. While it is clear that the heroic economy allows guests to expect lavish parting gifts, Odysseus is characterized, especially on Skheria, Kyklops' isle, and on awakening in Ithaka, as unusually obsessed with his "loot."

neither man hosted the other, as its own weight-giving digression explains.[17] Iphitos, its former owner, was murdered in one of thieving Herakles' gross and symptomatic violations of hospitality. Odysseus never took it abroad; the bow was left to protect the house, almost as a talisman, in his absence. Performing successfully with the bow will amount to winning the bow, the wife, and the estate. The bow can sing like a bird, but the song spells death, as the suitors' nonverbal, uncontrollable, psychosomatic loss of color demonstrates.

Status management and conflict, and resolutions through prestation, are thematic in the Akhaian camp at Troy, in the Skherian challenge of Euryalos, and in Odysseus' house. The *Basileis'* jostling for primacy is not a sign of political degeneracy but a symptom of prepolitical systems without clearly defined arenas of competition. The *basileus'* surplus of goods must be redistributed as "gifts" to maintain the "big man's" credibility and therefore his public esteem and tribal control. Noneconomic exchange of goods bonds a social network and power structure coherently pictured in the poems (e.g., 14.230–34; 19.194–98, 239–43; cf. chapter 10). Women's textiles and men's metals keep circulating throughout the Homeric poems to maintain the social organism, to pay remediation and repay respect.

Agamemnon violates customary prestation with Akhilleus. His faults of manners dramatically alter the war's progress. Although his offer of reparation is economically impressive, the nonverbal packaging torpedoes the effort. It is not the "what" but the "how" that fails. Agamemnon's absence from the offer invalidates its cash redemption value by social gaucherie or, worse, by mean intent. Gifts can also, therefore, dishonor, depending on the circumstances of the giving. The irrelevant economics of the aborted transaction is emphasized by Akhilleus' repeated lack of interest in reparations—even after he decides to return to battle. Furthermore, as status-sensitive Akhilleus realizes, gifts establish both honor and obligation. Becoming Agamemnon's son-in-law is not pure gain. Indebtedness follows the carrot, the horse, and the carriage.

Big King Agamemnon's inappropriate reappropriation of Briseis was worse than no gift at all (*Il.* 1.299). His later attempts in *Iliad* 9 at repairing relations would demote Akhilleus institutionally to his liege. Donlan (1993) exposes the trickery of the "gifts" included in the marriage of his daughter:

---

17. 21.11–41. Austin 1966 elegantly explains the nature of digressions; Mauss 1967 describes the enduring social reality but ignores the helpful Greek evidence, which Finley 1978, 61–66, 145, well exploits; see also Donlan 1989, 9–12. The history of the bow and its owners encapsulates a mini-epic of Tirynthian hospitality extended and betrayed. Merciless Herakles dishonors the host's table and murders Iphitos, his invited guest.

towns and extensive turf. These incentives to return to war are astutely and rightly rejected by Akhilleus as a political ploy and therefore as inappropriate compensation for status insult, however adequate in other respects. Skherian Euryalos, for his part, makes suitable amends to Odysseus for lesser offense by both generous word (proper proxemics and elevation) and a valuable gift (8.400–15). Ktesippos' ox-hoof further proves, albeit sarcastically, the thesis that "gifts" can demean and wound.

Beetling brows signify a violation of etiquette, of Homeric "ceremonial interaction." The darkly looking interactant nonverbally signifies a breach in acknowledged manners. Akhilleus nonverbally menaces Agamemnon by his nasty mien and then tries to browbeat him out of his startling threat to seize personally the hero's prize. In the same way, Zeus (alone of the gods) so threatens both Ares and Hera when they act up in the *Iliad*. The nonverbal behavior marks a superior's displeasure at an inferior's breach of accepted decorum; the superior thus tries to police the unruly subordinate by "face."

Odysseus emits seven of the nine scowling looks in the *Odyssey* (ὑπόδρα ἰδών). Euryalos on Skheria, Iros, and Melantho (twice) receive such looks for their unprovoked and unsanctioned insults. After beggar Odysseus maliciously prods them, Antinoos and Eurymakhos, from their superior rank, thus signal their displeasure at a perceived caitiff. Inferiors' craven requests for mercy meet the lowered brow. Only once, after revelation, does the now openly aristocratic Odysseus thus glare at a group: the suitors, of course, treated as one body in their wrongs. They and their retinue are the object of two-thirds of his nasty looks, all of which transmit affronted "face."[18] One rarely glares secretly or dares to do so openly at an acknowledged superior. So Odysseus disguised as beggar must control his gaze intensity and brow among the suitors, until he chooses to reveal himself as rightful lord of the premises. Thus, his dark looks at saucy Melantho either arrogate a beggar's equal status to a servant-woman or leak his uncontrollable anger as a loyal guest at a misbehaving and ungrateful maidservant. That the servants' sins are worse than the suitors' is clear from their demeaning style of punishment—hanging, torture, genital mutilation, and so forth. Children, when angry at their siblings, are adept at glare production and control—until parents turn their backs and more damaging symbolic speech can be mobilized.

The multivalent nod can silently convey to privileged confederates a prearranged signal for action in a hostile encounter: Odysseus so signals to his

---

18. Holoka 1983, 6–7, 11, provides the essential facts about this significant gesture. See 8.165; 18.14, 337; 19.70; 17.459; 18.388; 22.60, 320; 22.34.

sailors to row hard *now,* the Phoenician pirate so signals to baby Eumaios' kidnapper-nurse to leave *now,* and Odysseus arranges with Telemakhos that this gesture will be the signal for sequestering weapons (12.194, 15.463–64, 16.283). A superior person also thus signals with his brow the moment for a subordinate's agreed-on act. Odysseus wants his crew to loosen his bonds when he audits the Sirens' song, Athene wants mortal Odysseus to come out of Eumaios' hut, and Telemakhos telegraphs his servant Eumaios to prepare for final battle.[19] The head-nod signals a superior's assent or refusal (κατανεύω, ἀνανεύω). Greeks famously express alignment by raising and lowering the chin and eloquent eyebrows. The instrumentality of the communicative nodding brow is grammatically conveyed by the dative case (ὀφρύσι νευστάζων). The simultaneous and separate raising of the chin and brow signifies emphatic "no," ὄχι, and perhaps constitutes the best-known ancient and modern Greek ethnogest, or ethnic differentiator, in symbolic communication. Odysseus silently prohibits his sailors from grieving aloud as they prepare to leave Kyklops' island by thus "nodding up" to each. The same gesture from the covert king articulates and punctuates the crisis in the bow contest. He nods up to deflect Telemakhos, about to string the mighty bow and derail their devious stratagem (ἀνανεύω, 9.468, 21.129).[20] On the contrary, to depress the chin, κατανεύω, conveys formal and actionable assent, all one ever hopes for or needs from laconic and ever distant Zeus. Thus, also, Autolykos affirms an offer of birth-gifts, and Menelaos the gift of his daughter's hand to Akhilleus' son (*Il.* 1.514, 524; *Od.* 13.133, 24.335, 4.6 only).

Odysseus' manners are themselves offensive (by any standard) in the Kyklops' cave and on Ithaka. He enters the cave without permission and expressly to enlarge his assets; he begs beyond need to test the wooers' mannerly limits at Ithaka. He poses as chief defender of the established social order and the rules of Zeus, however, a paragon of gentlemanly manipulation. Therefore, he is better remembered as the victim of Polyphemos' inhospitality, Phaiakian Euryalos' rude athletic challenge, and the suitors' relentless misbehavior (see chapter 10; *Od.* 9.229, 266–71; 14.56–58; 7.159–66; 8.158–64; 17.483–87; and passim ad nauseam for the suitors).

---

19. 12.194, 16.164, 17.330, 21.431: νεύω simplex. The brows are mentioned eight times. The other four references involve moments of weeping. Only women, the weepy crew of the hero, and "good guys" cry tears in the *Odyssey,* so far as I remember. For other expressive eyebrows, see *H. Hermes* 27–29, Aesch. *Cho.* 284.

20. Other examples of the refusal gesture (noticed by Stanford) are found at *Il.* 6.311 (statue of Athene to Trojan Theano); 16.250, 252, (Zeus to Akhilleus); and 22.205 (Akhilleus to the other Akhaians). Lattimore 1951 reasonably "translates" the first upward nod of the statue from the Greek gesture into English body language as Athene "turned her head *away* from her."

Heroic Etiquette 79

The house of Odysseus is widely famous for generous hospitality (14.62–67; 15.280–81, 489–91; 19.240, 314–16). This constant giving to others has lasting consequences: Odysseus "owns" debts from gift recipients and houseguests, prior to his departure and during the suitors' lengthy and voracious suit. Eumaios, the beggar (19.240), and others warmly and significantly recollect Odysseus' paternal generosity and openhandedness. When the suitors abuse it and do not reciprocate in kind, their indemnity must be doubled. Penelope cannot stop the suitors' wasting of resources, nor can socially immature Telemakhos figure out how to terminate their wastrel ways. He has no leverage, as he knows (cf. 17.75–83, 397–400). Their expostulations, however, serve notice to the suitors and the audience of the sacrilegious offenses of the "guests."

The suitors show "negative reciprocity," taking much and giving nothing or very little (and some not their own) in return. They thus prove themselves undeserving of chiefdom or even of heroic mercy. They are unfit to rule or to take, because they do not know how to give. They pervert the protocols of prestation and reciprocity (thematic in the poem) so far as to threaten to enslave and mutilate the beggar, already identified as one protected by Zeus. Besotted with anticipation, proprietary Antinoos refers to Odysseus' table as his own, directly to the face of disguised Odysseus, who subtly contradicts him.[21]

Penelope's mooching suitors consistently and outrageously violate exacting laws of host-guest relationships. They consume another's household stores rather than give suitable wooers' gifts, as she tells the roisterers (16.430–33, 18.275–80). They are rude to hosts and overbearing to visitors (22.414–16). We miss Homer's broad humor if we don't observe the social comedy of the suitors' acting as if they rule this roost. Any decent guest knows better than to outstay his welcome. The injustice of their eternal partying is multiplied by their stinginess toward the beggar. Such unheroic greed is doubly disgraceful with another's wealth, as Telemakhos pointedly remarks (17.397–404). The suitors supply the Homeric textbook case of boorish verbal and nonverbal behaviors (cf. chapter 10).

4. Departures

Leave-taking expects equally prominent displays. The greeting and the farewell bracket a period of increased joint access. An expectation of long,

---

21. 20.380–83; cf. 14.56–58, 283–84, 389; 17.155, 483–87; 17.447 (ἐμῆς ἀπάνευθε τραπέζης, "away from my table"), 456–57 (ἀλλοτρίοισι παρήμενος, "sitting next to others"). See Donlan 1982a, 1–4, 7–9.

uninterrupted separation provokes more expansive leave-taking. Telemakhos is barraged with gifts in Pylos and Sparta (3.346–55; 4.590, 612–19; 15.113–17). Aiolos provides Odysseus a grand banquet, a fabulous going-away present (the bag of the breezes), and a fond farewell—the first time. When Odysseus returns, his host is disconcerted and displeased (10.14, 18–22, 64–75). Tears, feigned or genuine, spring out at departure (2.371–72, 376; 4.703–5; 11.5). Friendly Akhilleus stalks off in energetic, kinesthetic pride for his son; sullen Aias turns on his heel away from Odysseus without a word (11.539, 563). Both men, by proxemic adjustment and minimal verbal communication, convey overwhelmed, ultraverbal states of mind.

When Odysseus leaves Skheria, the disappointment of Nausikaa and Alkinoos is patent, but the civil host observes all niceties: gifts (described in detail and stowed away), food, grandiose after-dinner speeches, substantial escort from the palace, and even the swift, magical ship and sailors who transport the hero home (8.424–32; 13.7–48, cf. 15.99–132; 13.63–65; cf. 4.301; 20.361). The muteness of Nausikaa's fare-thee-well is prescribed by both gender and age etiquette that easily override host-guest public expressions of regret (8.457–62). Her female voicelessness is all the more poignant because of her full heart. Nausikaa has violated virginal formalities of gendered public "civil inattention" at the beach. There, the rules of hierarchy, propriety, and public order had to be temporarily and partially suspended (cf. 6.211, 222), but she fully realizes their return in full force when she is back under the watchful eyes of her family, especially her mother, and the town (6.186–210, 260–89). Indeed, Homer highlights her age-induced breaches of gendered decorum, her froward anticipations of hospitality rituals, suitable only to the patriarch and the married matron at home. Her adolescent sentiments and raging hormones are well suspicioned by her father before the bizarre seaside encounter and by her mother, Arete, after. We hear the "clean laundry and let's have a wedding" theme played (7.233–38; Austin 1991, 238). But back at the Skherian ranch, Nausikaa can only manage a moment's private colloquy with the mysterious arrival (8.457–68). Fortunately, he is more eloquent than the usual masked man of American Western movies; unfortunately, he is even less "available" for her fantasy-life.

Another side to comic Homer is the parody of heroic farewells in the *Odyssey*. Several hosts are oppressive in their hospitality. Telemakhos can barely escape garrulous and generous Nestor and takes pains—just this side of downright boorishness—never to "stop in again" as he has been invited and expected to do (15.200–201). Menelaos is yet more egregious. Telemakhos wants to pursue his father-finding quest, but Menelaos, who, like Nestor, now lives in and on nostalgia and reminiscence, wants him to party on, at least eleven or twelve days more. Telemakhos politely responds that even another *year* would be pleasant, but . . . "duty calls." Telemakhos is so much in a hurry that, to avoid lengthy departure ceremonies, he unheroically nudges and kicks his companion Pisistratos awake from sweet sleep before day, so they can leave while it is yet dark. His more experienced traveling companion politely reminds him that the prehistoric roads are bad (and the chariot doesn't have headlights). Furthermore, a decent guest must receive gifts before departure or he brutally offends his host. At daybreak, obtuse Menelaos continues to suggest a joint tour of Hellas, with partying everywhere and profitable stopovers, if Telemakhos collects all his ξενίη.[22] Homer deflates Menelaos by his original inability to identify Telemakhos by body badges and build (whereas Helen does), by his windy speeches, and by interactional deafness to urgent verbal and nonverbal pleas. Finally, Telemakhos experiences the Atreid's inability to interpret an obvious omen—divine nonverbal communication of a sort that deserves more attention. Helen again comes to the rescue with quick-witted hermeneutics. Μερμερίζειν twice characterizes the master's muttering confusion. While he ponders, Helen explains. The lonely, unhappy host sensitively portrays a pathetic war veteran who has lost emotional, mental, and social elasticity. Telemakhos and Pisistratos, almost set free, are yet once more delayed. Menelaos runs out in front of their horses to offer a libation, "one for the Bronze Age road." In claustrophobic desperation, the youngsters nearly run down the windbag.[23]

Nearly all scenes of departure impede Odysseus too. The antihospitality of the Kikones, the Kyklops, the Laistrygonians, and Skylla is obvious enough. But the debilitating food of the Lotus Eaters, the sexual enticements, perpetual goodies, and sonic song-traps of Kirke and the Sirens, and the unbending warm embraces of Kalypso retard progress. The man wants to get back to his life, not freeze-dry it. Aiolos promptly responds with the right stuff the first time, but here and on Thrinakia, Odysseus' crew spoils the hero's prestatory progress. This catalog of layovers leaves out only Skheria. Here Alkinoos' generous offers of bride and kingdom parallel Menelaos' in amusingly solicitous overkill and failure to take the traveler's lucid point (9.267–71; 11.356–61; 13.41, 215–16).

Odysseus keeps asking for prompt conveyance home, while Alkinoos

---

22. Autolykos appreciated grandson Odysseus' insatiable, childlike, and entrepreneurial gift-lust (19.460).
23. 4.93–99; 4.587–92, 597–99; 15.44–55, 78–85; 4.117–45; 15.160–77, 145–53. G. Rose 1971 brilliantly anatomizes characterization in scenes of departure. Goffman 1971, chap. 3, 79 n. 20 (cf. Youssouf et al. 1976) notes that animal ethologists find scant parallels to the ubiquitous human "good-bye."

offers his daughter, food, games, gifts, narrative entertainment, and dialogue galore. Odysseus ostentatiously watches the sun set, wanting nothing more than to hasten it down on his last day in "paradise."[24] This nonverbal behavior is inadequate, as were Odysseus' tears at the banquet, which at least led Alkinoos to some alteration in the entertainment. Odysseus' exasperation at kindly detainment leads to an outburst: πέμπετέ με, the somewhat rude imperative of a man delayed too long—ten to twenty years and counting. Now that he is "in [notional] sight of" his destination, he wants to jump-start the final step. Still, Alkinoos will not be budged from honorific departure rites: group potation, divine libation, prayer, a speech from the guest, and a pompous parade out the front door with attendants (*Od.* 7.151–52; 8.30; 13.28–41; 7.313–15; 8.37–39, 100–103, 389–97, 424–25; 13.24–28). The ship is launched, finally.

After the voyage, Odysseus, awakening alone from another heroic sleep (or trance),[25] worries whether Alkinoos' sailors have double-crossed him. Did they take his triple treasure when they left him comatose on the beach—wherever it and he may be? The poet voices his hero's justified doubts about escaping one more set of friendly clutches. The landfall turns out to be Ithaka. Homer both admires and satirizes Odysseus' ever suspicious nature and greed.[26]

---

24. This pointed gaze is the ancient nonverbal behavior equivalent to plainly "peeking" at your wristwatch to signal impatience to depart. On the beach on Aiaia, Odysseus perpetually looks far out to sea, straining for sight of his homeland (1.58–59, 5.82–84).

25. His comas had already landed him in trouble, once after leaving Aiolos and next on Thrinakia. Mythologists recall Gilgamesh's unfortunate catnaps in the land of Dilmun.

26. 13.135–216; cf. the poet's textual mouthpiece(?), Athene, soon (13.291–99).

Chapter 5
Leaking Heroic Sentiment: "Face" and "Tone"

1. Leakage

The body anticipates, participates in, and echoes all real-world, face-to-face communication, but Western traditions oscillate between glorifying and denigrating this sometimes undependable, always visible, permeable prison of the (otherwise) invisible spirit. Voiced words seem the most accurate source of information from another; they suggest a direct passage to the soul. The negative term "*non*verbal" reflects this devaluation for gestural, vocal yet nonverbal, and postural methods of communication.

Yet we performers, interactants in life and literature, intentionally and unintentionally employ body language and cannot stop sending messages. Our daily dramatic performances include facial and other displays for seven types of affect: fear, surprise, anger, disgust, happiness, sadness, and interest. When Athene strokes Odysseus' arm, for instance, she expresses both concern and reassuring, but parental, superiority (13.287–88, cf. 5.181, 4.610). Parental touching communicates strong affect throughout Homeric epic. This ordinary intercourse, verbal and nonverbal in interactive confirmation, also unintentionally leaks truths about persons through their bodies, vocal apparatus, and posture—inadvertent admissions that belie words.[1] This chapter examines unintentional communication of attitude, not least, respect and disrespect.

Appearance is generally taken for reality in the *Iliad,* except when characters become alert to potential dissonance. Akhilleus alleges hatred for those who say one thing while another is hidden inside (9.312–13). In his sometimes ingenuous world, a hero masquerading in tattered beggar's disguise would seem absurd, a cause of dishonor, and no hero at all. Men are taken at "face value" until proven otherwise. The *Odyssey* is quite opposite. No alert

---

1. Paul Ekman and Erving Goffman have created the empirical study of unintended self-disclosure and the art of unmasking deceptive clues; see the bibliography for representative titles. Ekman seems to have coined the term *leakage* for this phenomenon. The modern American political leak to the media, in contrast, is entirely intentional and largely verbal.

audience can doubt Homer's realization of the body's wide communicative resources for transmitting information, misinformation, and disinformation.

Build, δέμας, imposes on or fails to impress others. It is the objective, physical person, distinguished from perceived appearance or εἶδός, and reports the perceptible person, as opposed to the θυμός and φρένες (the internal—the "inward self" and "sense" or "passion") or the ἔργα and αὐδή ("acts" and "voice"). Appearances can deceive, however, and so can sounds. Smaller Aias boastfully alleges his awareness that gods "leak" their presence; they are ἀρίγνωτοι, ("easy to recognize"), by nonverbal traits and physique (*Il.* 13.71–72). Apollo's careful disguising as the human Agenor and annoyed Odysseus' whining at Athene's successful deceptions on Ithaka suggest otherwise (*Il.* 21.600, *Od.* 13.299–301, 312–13). The gods can turn their "presence" up or down nonverbally, be visible and/or audible or not, betray presence by nonverbal metamorphosis into another gender or genus (*Od.* 13.288–90, 22.210, 1.320, 3.371–73, 22.239–40), or admit identity outright and explicitly (*Il.* 22.9–10, *Od.* 13.299–303). The gods choose their times to "leak" identity. Their epiphanies provide them with Olympian delight at humanity's sudden surprise or dismay at divine disguise. Such responses are betrayed by their human pawns, notably, Akhilleus, Odysseus, Metaneira, and Ankhises.[2]

Odysseus, on the human level, consciously manipulates his body as suppliant, vagrant, and beggar with limited rights of approach and speech. Athene has altered body badges of age and object-adaptors of class and status. Athene metamorphoses Odysseus, leaving him still human but marginally so—in a crucially different disguise that alters his presumed age (the body badges of baldness, flabby muscles, and old and wrinkly skin), object-adaptors (tattered rags and a battered hobo's bag instead of *xenia*), and grooming (we see the converse of his scruffiness here when Athene smartens him up so that the ladies Nausikaa and Penelope admire his presence). Like all individuals and groups whose utterance, and even presence, is socially blocked, he necessarily and purposely develops the rich resources of bodily expression to articulate sentiments that for him are publicly unvoiceable. Such devious modes of communication are in no way secondary to or derivative from ordinary speech. Rather, body language eloquently expresses situation, sentiment, *and* repressed verbal speech. Iros' trembling, leakage of fear,

---

2. *H. Dem.* 268–80, *H. Aphr.* 171–83. See H.J. Rose 1956 and Clay 1974. *H. Dem.* mentions size and stature (μέγεθος καὶ εἶδός), radiance, and smell of clothes as nonverbal signs of immortals. Their ability to vary body badges, humanly nonvariable appearances, sets them most apart. Kirke so transforms her swine. Vergil notes distinctive gait, complexion, odor, and clothes (*Aen.* 1.314–20, 5.647–49).

and the suitors' sudden pallor are paradigmatic of unrepressible "leakage." But maintenance of immobile "face," not expression of interior feeling, is Odysseus' prime δόλος (19.209–12). He literally does not blink: ὀφθαλμοὶ δ' ὡς εἰ κέρα ἕστασαν ἠὲ σίδηρος / ἀτρέμας ἐν βλεφάροισι.

Honesty and duplicity both employ and are betrayed by nonverbal behavior. Through the face, voice, hands, and legs and feet, actions and tone sometimes reveal what words mean to conceal. Nonverbal feedback to an audience sometimes subverts or contradicts an intended, explicit but duplicitous message. Deceptions both dissimulate facts, such as Odysseus' identity or Telemakhos's inability to bend the bow, and simulate fictions, such as Polyphemos' initial, seemingly friendly encouragement of his captive audience or Penelope's seeming encouragement of the suitors' presentation of *hedna*. Communicated consideration and respect in these instances is entirely deceptive, as the narrator explicitly or implicitly makes clear.

Kyklops openly disdains duplicity and deception. He sees no double meanings (except at 9.369–70), and confident in his brawn, he makes loud noises—dropping wood, whistling, screaming to rattle rocks, groaning, and shouting to his fellow monsters. He usually acts suddenly, without extensive reflection, and violently—grabbing men and slapping out their brains, gulping wine mindlessly, and hurling mountain peaks in his King Kong–like anger. He comports himself crudely—sprawling in sleep, slumping in his cups, vomiting his raw cannibal-meat dinner, and writhing in pain. Thus, his body talks for him and back to him. Meanwhile, it keys Odysseus' every move. Some of this body chatter humorously underlines his monstrous size, force, and threat. The giant size of everything connected with him reflects the ogres of wondertales. All his equipment and Bunyanesque appetites demonstrate his lack of heroic self-control, his uncivilized ways (his Nowhereland is at once a colonial paradise, an anti-Greek universe, and a dystopia), and his inability to manipulate communication skills (verbal *and* nonverbal)— unlike Odysseus. He is fooled by Odysseus' pseudoname, "Nobody," as he is fooled by Odysseus' pseudogame: the gentlemanly "prestation of the wine" trick and the tactics of the "hidden crewmen escape" trick. Like an animal of limited cunning (which he is), Kyklops can act and react but cannot well remember, plan, or deceive, the ultimate strategic skill of the *Odyssey*. The low brute is all "leakage." He reveals his intentions and vomits his raw food. He respects neither gods of Olympos nor men, he says so loudly, and he is proud of it (9.273–78). His is the limited case of unwitting self-revelation, while Odysseus represents the other extreme, witting self-occlusion.

Other characters are marginally or much better than Polyphemos at hiding true sentiments and emitting false ones. "One of the more powerful behaviors of deception," alter-adaptors (movements and positions taken toward interactants), are utilized in many channels (visual, oral, tactile, olfactory) in transmitting affection and respect or their opposites—for instance, in opening and closing encounters.[3] Sincere and simulated affection and disaffection are displayed by Telemakhos and Penelope, Eumaios and Melantho/ios, the suitors, and other hosts through facework, sympathy, reciprocity, and dominance and submission patterns.

When the hero is disguised as Aithon the vagrant, he offers the extended example of simulated deference. Odysseus the pseudobeggar treats Iros as his social equal and Eumaios as his peer or better. He takes notable pains to "greet up" to Telemakhos, the suitors, and Penelope. They are indubitably superiors, and he attempts to express deference, to ingratiate himself, and to create social bonds. Such conscious somatic behaviors are crucial for any scam or deceptive scheme, because if the interactant has a hunch of insincerity—based on a present phoney gesture or any "leaked" expression of scornful superiority—or perceives absence of expected honor due to a higher-up, suspicions will lead to further tests and perhaps to punishment for detected fraud. From this vantage, Odysseus' rare leakage—the unmeant cue to sentiment or identity—is dramatically interesting because it arouses audience fears for the hero: will the suitors realize too soon that he is not what he seems to be?[4] Self-contained Odysseus constantly defers revenge (e.g., 17.238) and defies others' expectations, but he does so within the socially acknowledged parameters of his imputed identity. His signature act is the strategic deception: simulated helplessness and nonidentity managed on both the verbal and nonverbal levels. He even *pretends* to "leak" damaging information to disarm Nausikaa, Polyphemos, Eumaios, and Penelope's hopefuls. He falsely leaks sexual interest in Nausikaa (Athene's doing, really), fear to one-eyed Polyphemos and the shortsighted suitors (e.g., 18.55–59), and alternately misery and calm to Penelope (e.g., 19.167–68, 209–12). He feigns inability to discern whether Nausikaa is a goddess,

---

3. See chap. 4. Poyatos 1986, 505–11, includes not only greeting and parting rituals but also rituals of aggression, protection, grooming, comforting, ratifying, etc.

4. When Odysseus does not flinch after Antinoos hits him, an interesting issues emerges. How can we decide whether the reason is the smart hero's need to preserve the secrecy of his true heroic identity or whether Homer subtly communicates his hero's somewhat discrepant leakage of self-control (by heroic nonreaction). Here Odysseus fails to conform fully to the "profile" of decrepit, presumably vulnerable vagrant. Certainly when Odysseus girds up to fight Iros, the suitors' explicit observations on his impressive musculature contradict Athene's disguise for an old and flabby man (cf. Page 1955, 88–91). An oral epic tradition is pulled apart here by competing pressures: reveal the heroic warrior and conceal the returned husband until the "nick of time." Murnaghan 1987 discusses modes and meanings of Homeric disguise; pp. 84–85 examine the demi-semirevelation with Iros.

whether Polyphemos can be trusted after eating humans, whether Eumaios will see through his indirect request for a mantle, whether the suitors will be punished, and whether he has any strength left in his old limbs (22.281–84).

The counterpoint between the suitors' verbally and nonverbally expressed public anger at Penelope's tergiversation and Fabian tactics—their incautious self-revelation in a false sense of security—and Aithon/Odysseus' dissimulated, contained, and concealed private fury in his *thymos* is highlighted when the hero beds down in the forecourt, apart from all others, the night before the sagittarian contest. His rest is no rest while the promiscuous maids cheerfully chortle and scatter to the beds of their fornicating, out-of-place lovers.

Odysseus' body twists and turns (ἑλίσσετο ἔνθα καὶ ἔνθα, 20.24, 28), a leakage of anxiety permitted in his imagined isolation, but an unintended revelation to Athene (who appears nearby) and to us, the audience. His furious heart barks like a bitch ready to fight for her pups.[5] He strikes his breast and scolds his passions, which are now beyond control. In short, his autonomic nervous system (κραδίη) is acting up. Elsewhere in Homer, only women, and men in the slough of similar despondency over the death of Patroklos or Hektor, commit this extreme degree of symbolic violence on themselves. Here, this behavior is not a part of ceremonious death ritual or a sort of interpersonal communication, because Odysseus has good reason to think that no one sees him (although Athene and we do). However, the affect display leaks Odysseus' wrought-up state to the sympathetic unknown observer and to Homer's audience. The self-styled hero of endurance and *metis* (20.20) not only talks to himself but gestures to and on himself.[6] Only alone and now, after a long and difficult day, can he let down his false "front" and release (on himself) his suppressed urge to retaliate physically, his need for

---

5. G. Rose 1979 analyzes Homer's imagery to show how Odyssean the perceptive dog Argos is (222–23) and how like a ferocious hunting dog or watchdog Odysseus is. "The dog is his trademark" for the nonce (225). Rams are speechless, as Polyphemos the zoologist notes (9.456–57), and dogs and hearts cannot verbalize, of course; but a *barking* heart, by metaphor and "personification," confers explicit human meaning and affect on bestial "paralinguistic" expression.

6. A similar moment of nonverbal "talking to oneself" can be discerned when he awakes alone, he knows not where (13.197–200): he springs upright, groans, slaps his thighs with open palms in surprise and frustration, like Ariadne deserted by all companions, and only then starts to speak words—still to himself. Thus, the poet conceives a nonverbal soliloquy. It serves no "practical" purpose for the abandoned wanderer but very forcefully communicates his frustration to the audience and supplies a capital joke, since the hypersuspicious hero is—as Homer slyly notes—just where he would like to be, on his own home island, but he cannot recognize it and therefore does not know it (ἔσιδε πατρίδα γαῖαν).

kinetic expression. Even *his* notorious restraint can barely contain his fury after so many affronts to his both assumed and real dignities.

Penelope's meretricious verbal messages and seductive behaviors wheedle wealth from her wooers—so successfully that her son wrongly suspects that she intends to filch his family property and betray his patrimony (13.379–81, 18.274–83, 15.19–23). Yet her apparent vacillation about remarriage, poor-mouthing of her beauty and charm, and labile emotional states (grief, joy: 17.38–42, 18.163[?], 19.589–90) manage to keep order in Ithaka for four years and to play the suitors against each other. Her tenacious cunning and patience in fulfilling her duties to her husband's house (e.g., the *dolos* of the shroud, 2.89–110, 19.138–56, 24.128–48) explain and lay a foundation for her subsequent caution in the bed-trick scene.[7] Her best weapon is face-work, female guile and deception. She, most like Odysseus in every way and this one especially, leaks very little "give-away" nonverbal behavior to her publics (son, maids, and suitors). In the privacy of her room, however, she drops her "face," weeps copiously, and falls to the floor, and she also laughs a little laugh (4.716–20, 21.356–58). Here, hidden affect obtains expressive outlet, secret from prying eyes but revelatory to privileged audiences, that is, goddesses and the listener/reader. Both husband and wife control their bodies as communicative *and* noncommunicative instruments so as to deceive enemies and reassure friends, as chapters 9 and 11 further demonstrate.

2. "Face"

We detect unintended messages and intended false messages, or deception, both in-awareness and out-of-awareness. The face anchors personal identity, dignity, and perceivable mood. It is our major nonverbal liar, although every part of the body participates in face-work. Microdisplays of emotion on the face, such as lip biting, blanching, a trembling chin, and/or gaze avoidance can leak true affect when speakers' conscious posture—expression or "face"—intend or send messages quite different from their words. Senders may quickly squelch transmissions of hostility, fear, or ambivalence when they become aware of them on their face or in their stance. They may even deny socially unacceptable behavior that gains remark, such as others' observations and assertions of angry expression or sarcastic tone. But both clues

---

7. νόος δέ οἱ ἄλλα μενοινᾷ is a Penelopean formula and a spiritual trademark of her bifurcated social roles and personal emotions (2.92, 13.81, 18.283). Like Odysseus, she has developed profit-making cleverness to a remarkable degree. Cf. 2.118; Marquardt 1985; Levy 1963.

and denials shape the subsequent transaction, collaborative or antagonistic (Ekman and Friesen 1969b, 98–99).

Face-work participates in both ritualistic moments and moments of intense emotion, with in-awareness or out-of-awareness affect display. For instance, greeting and parting visibly use all parts of the face except the peripheral ears. Smiles and frowns, controlled or spontaneous, punctuate words and other, less prominent body language. The many variations of kisses and embraces may be nonreciprocal or symmetrical. Arched eyebrows, spitting, kissing, frowns, and tongue protrusions communicate, politely and impolitely, conversational feedback and response.

Conventional words are particularly embedded in meaningful facial metatalk. The pragmatics of epic utterance encompass many expressive social acts. These glosses, conventions of nuanced nonverbal social performance, include, most obviously, frowns and smiles. Clumsy Agamemnon grins while propitiating Odysseus (after one of his trademark, unsuitable critiques of battlefield valor), and this leakage helps him save "face." Odysseus, in his lack of concern for a Trojan enemy, derisively leaks a smile at doomed Dolon. Akhilleus, as prize-master, unexpectedly but charitably smiles at blustering young Antilokhos, who threatens to fight one and all for his rightful trophy. Antilokhos reveals much of his young self as he triumphantly smiles while carrying off boodle.[8]

Homer uses the gazing eye and avoidance of eye contact in attention-focusing protocols. Eurykleia tries to catch Penelope's eye, Telemakhos eludes Eumaios' eye, and gazes are avoided and turned away by Aias and Odysseus (19.476–77, 16.477, 11.563, 5.158[?], 20.385). Eumaios stares rudely to convey disapproval of rude Melanthios; in profoundest sorrow, Odysseus and Eurykleia cover their faces to prevent leakage through eye contact. Others, "looking darkly," quickly convey a gazer's disapproval of the action of an inferior or supposed peer—for instance, Odysseus' look, as beggar, at Melantho (17.239, 8.83–93 and 521–31, 19.361, 18.337 or 8.165). Locked-on gaze simulates or suggests sexual penetration in mixed-gender encounters; between competing men, it simulates lethal, weaponlike penetration and remains dangerous on the mean streets of America.[9]

Two clear, deictic signals are the semiautomatic disapproving head-shake (usually "leakage") and the intentional head-nod (signal of assent or nega-

---

8. *Il.* 4.356–61; 10.400; 23.553–57, 786; Firth 1972, 22–25; Levine 1984, on *Od.* 20–23; Martin 1989, 10–20, 71, 96.

9. An unrepentant killer explains that his victim had looked him in the eye too long. In the *Philadelphia Inquirer* of 13 December 1992, p. C1 and 8, Andre Johnson says, "The dude challenged us with his eyes. . . . If our eyes meet [too long], the dude's looking for trouble."

tion; cf. chapter 4). Since the face is our most versatile and therefore our chief channel of nonverbal message-sending and receiving, its movement easily attracts attention. The body's language speaks when the verbal channel is stopped up, too dangerous to use, or too removed from subsequent deniability, or when emotion is too sudden to control or repress. Three times, as tension grows in Ithaka, the sons of Laertes "shake their heads silently" at outrageous treatment: ἀκέων κίνησε κάρη, κακὰ βυσσοδομεύων (17.465, 491; 20.184). Odysseus thus leaks his anger (to us), when Antinoos throws his footstool; Telemakhos, when Antinoos taunts and abuses his disguised father so far that even other suitors find him intolerable (κερτομίαι, taunts elsewhere; τὰ χερείονα νικᾷ, 18.404); and finally Odysseus again, when Melanthios officiously instructs Odysseus to move off. The first half of the formulaic line describes relative passivity with leakage; the second half, "planning evil in their hearts," provides the contrasting active, but secret, complement to the visible bodily microresponse. The head's emotional expression declares a resounding, if silent and even unawares, "no" to the circumambient partying and abuse. The most telling "leak" in the poem responds to the divine "speech" of the bowstring's twang: the angry and raucous suitors suddenly blanch (21.410-13). Their fear drains their faces.

3. Paralinguistics or "Tone"

"It's not what you say but how you say it," "say it as if you mean it," and "you don't sound sincere" are three examples of aural sensitivity to the delicate vocal apparatus: phonation or nonlexemic intonation, pace, pitch, loudness, and other sonic variables. These variables separate the segments of controlled noise flow, they color the words, and they sometimes make them slippery by intention. Any communicative oral effect not composed of language segments or phonemes constitutes paralinguistic behavior.[10] Paralinguistic phenomena can lubricate dangerous, abrasive, or unwelcome speech. Alternatively, it can spoil superficially attractive statements by recipients' perception of irony, sarcasm, persiflage, or mockery. Phonation also betrays otherwise successfully suppressed emotional states, as when a sudden sob reveals a hidden sorrow.

Human and divine phonation differ. Plebeian goddesses—Ino, Kirke, and Kalypso—express themselves with human voice—*aude,* or intelligible hu-

---

10. E.g., *shouting* challenges or taunts (9.473-74), whistling, whining, using a sarcastic tone (8.158, 179; 17.394), or clearing the throat; cf. chap. 1. Clapping, stomping the foot, finger tapping, and thigh slapping, examples of *strepistics,* provide an additional nonvocal but sonant avenue of human expression.

man speech and vocabulary.¹¹ These inferior divinities live on earth, more or less, and share mortal phonic qualities. Four times, omniscient Homer provides fragments of a human-divine, bilingual Rosetta stone.¹² Our interest here is paralinguistic, not lexical. High divinities speak differently and therefore must modulate their voices from the usual divine ὄπα and ὀμφή, perhaps changing frequency and speed, to synchronize communication and converse with mortals.¹³

The figurative use of *aude* for Odysseus' bowstring (21.411) climaxes a phonic Gestalt: it suggests divine epiphany, but also explicit and intelligible human meaning. The bowstring plainly "said": "Lethal pain has arrived." Ὄπα, Clay (1974) determines, refers to "timbre, especially a clear or shrill tone" of singers (divine and human) or of an orator (*Il.* 3.221). These are generic or biological distinctions, so to speak, not indications of inherited status, personal esteem, momentary mood, or rank inside a social realm. In our limited Homeric sampling, gods refrain from paralinguistic "alternants": hisses, clucks, grunts, exhalations, coughs, and sniffs. At least the muses did not vouchsafe their earthly medium Homer any information about them.

Examples of attention to paralinguistic sound in the *Odyssey* include half-human Polyphemos, who cheerfully whistles and later vomits in his stupor. In anguish, he shouts and groans (πολλῇ δὲ 'ροίζῳ, ὁ δ' ἐρεύγετο οἰνοβαρείων, σμερδαλέον δὲ μέγ' ᾤμωξεν, 9.315, 374, 395, 506). The lascivious, carefree maids are characterized by their exchanging glances and giggles; Iros, smashed up while boxing and in animal pain, bleats like a sheep; Eumaios glares at and speaks harshly (νείκεσι) to rude Melanthios; the suitors laugh themselves "to death" and later scream in pain when their heads are crushed (18.320; 18.98; 17.238–46; 20.346, 374; στόνος, 22.308). Examples of phonic vehemence and violence are easily multiplied.

Homer explicitly refers to "tone" less often than a modern audience expects.¹⁴ Every society prefers to observe certain forms of body language.

---

11. Clay 1972 discusses *dionymy*; Clay 1974, 131, quotes Khrysippos, who defined *aude* as intelligible speech but noted "wheeping, whistling, wailing, and bleating" as other stomatic communications (see p. 135 for *opa*).

12. *Il.* 1.403–4, 2.813–14, 14.290–91, 20.74; cf. *Od.* 10.305, 12.61. Once, a horse briefly abandons whinnying to speak as humans do (*Il.* 19.407, 418; cf. 17.426–40).

13. *Od.* 2.297; Athene formulaically changes five times into human δέμας καὶ αὐδή. Xenophanes expresses a similar Ionian curiosity and multicultural liberality about the speech of gods of horses and cattle.

14. Clay 1974, 130–31, reports epic's rich vocabulary for "the production of sounds" and the relative absence of modern critics' attention to it. Modern authors often notice "larynx effects," such as whispers and huskiness, but Homer mentions little of this. He brings heads near heads for whispering, to avoid being overheard and to indicate trust (e.g., 4.69–70 = 17.592, 16.338). Modern professions have conscious and unconscious styles and patterns: the brisk

92 Sardonic Smile

Europeans and Americans lean toward facial expression to determine "face," but other societies prefer to judge by feet and hands. Are the Homeric poems reflecting some particular Hellenic historical reality in this or devaluing characteristics of the voice beyond the words as a channel of *epic* communication? The means to answer this reasonable query are no longer available. The response of historical linguistics would not affect, in any case, the ubiquitous importance of body language in the epics. Hellenic historiography and biography often report the same gestures and facial expressions as Homer, whether this be literary reflex or accurate report. Since the epics are the distillate of a long oral tradition, we can reasonably expect them correctly to record slow-changing, standard ethnogests.

"Leakage," then, informs one character of another's verbally suppressed emotional state or disguised intent. The *Odyssey* presents great variety of personal strategies of self-revelation and deception. We observe the games people play, verbal and nonverbal. Study of heroic interchanges demands attention to Homer's presentation of characters' intended and unintended cues and messages. When information surfaces that means more to *us* in our privileged position as audience than to the other characters, as with Odysseus' steadiness in the ballistic scenes or his crowding of the suitors' table as beggar, this cannot be described as "leakage" vis-à-vis his interlocutors, but as literary irony. Chapters 9 and 11 examine disguise, clues to deception, unmasking techniques, and recognition in further detail.

---

policeman, the unctuous undertaker, the hurried radio newsreporter, the methodical but slow license clerk, or the crisply authoritative professor (known to us only in innocent youth); cf. Crystal 1975, 167. We can probably detect traces of ancient equivalents in Aristophanes' comedies, like the government official in *Lysistrata* or the crowd of officious walk-ons in *Aves*. Chap. 11 examines Penelope's peculiarly private laugh.

Chapter 6

"Standing Tall": Posture, Elevation, and Deference

The word *courtesy* provides the etymological origin of the curtsy, a complex and difficult gesture of elevational respect, self-lowering learned through intensive posture-training. Kowtowing, head sinking, hand raising, bowing, crawling, prostration, and formal kneeling provide alternative symbolic expressions that acknowledge inferiority.[1] Courtesy as a system of nonverbal and verbal behaviors varies in frequency and degree of expression as a function of the fixity of class distinctions. Heroic "smooth operators" minimize extravagant dominance displays of elevation and priority among their touchy peers and near peers. Touchy Agamemnon and the brusque suitors of Penelope offer Homer's intended paradigms of "faulty interaction"—nearly pathological inability to "do the right thing" at the right time under many circumstances. Arrival and reception, the hospitality of creation and closure that fill the *Odyssey*, require some pattern for establishing relative status—superior, inferior, or equal. Gestures and postures expressive of equality can be discerned, such as balanced gift-exchange (actually rare in Homeric hexameter) or those embraces in which each side is equally implicated (e.g., 16.214–15, 21.222–25, 23.296; not 16.20–22, 22.498–500). One can duel with gifts, with proxemics, and with greeting formulae or can accept another as an equal. Every interchange is a potential challenge and contest. Courtesy itself offers another arena for displaying superior or inferior wit, will, and wealth.[2]

1. Posture

Postures and positions of respect communicate relative rank. They are further articulated by structural arrangements of interior space and furniture, such as thrones and the "head-of-the-table" position (3.406–9, 7.162, 8.469). The summit of a hierarchy is likely to be furthest from the entrance,

---
1. Firth 1969, 201, supplies theory and comparative data for this paragraph and the next.
2. Donlan 1989, 6, 14–15; also Donlan 1971, 111, on Agamemnon's progressively lessened authority in the *Iliad*; the same diminution can be plotted for the suitors in the *Odyssey*.

elevated, centrally located on either axis, and most opulently accoutered. Again, Nestor, Menelaos, and Alkinoos and Arete, as well as Olympian Zeus in state, provide evidence. When Odysseus the suppliant is raised from the ashes at the periphery, then seated at the table right next to Alkinoos, his high status is made public by the proxemic arrangement and displacement of a prince (7.170–71, 190; cf. 3.39). This nonverbal act of noble propriety establishes a debt, creates and publishes the shipwrecked man's local privilege, and re-creates his spirit. It furthermore structures his future relations with Phaiakians as emphatically as winged words can convey. The body, a powerful instrument of social communication, is read by all who can observe. The stranger needs to manipulate his body (nonverbal communication) to establish his place, physical and social, in the endless negotiations of status warriors (see section 3).

Homer employs postural cues to suggest the psychological state of his characters and to sketch the social matrix of their interactions. Postures are essential to every culture's communication system. Consider sitting on chairs, for an example. In Pylos and Sparta, princely Pisistratos and Eteoneos rise and come forward to welcome strangers. Telemakhos on foot approaches the rulers Nestor and Menelaos. They are seated (3.41–46, 469; 4.50–51). Later, Odysseus penetrates a palace on foot when he approaches the seated dyarchs Arete and Alkinoos to grasp a knee in formal supplication. To symbolize his lowly status more affectively, he then retreats to the hearth and lowers his body to the ground in the ashes (7.135–54).

This complex performance provides many types of nonverbal messages: the approach to close quarters (proxemics); the making of the first move and the pausing for reply (turn taking, chronemics); the knee-grasp (emblem); and the lowering of the body, first before the queen to supplicate, then in the hearth's ashes to symbolize lack of status (posture, alter-adaptor).[3] All these symbolic movements are carefully plotted and controlled, like the hero's riskier, hands-off approach to Nausikaa, as if she might be divine, but in reality because an unmarried, unguarded woman is too hot to handle.

One clear measure of the poet's esteem for characters is precisely this allotted measure of self-control. *The more thoughtless, uncontrolled, or uncontrollable a character's nonverbal behavior, as reported by Homer, the less admirable the person displaying it.* Some slack postures convey for Homer a lack of deference and an insouciant or disrespectful demeanor. Such colorful

---

3. When Odysseus wreaks havoc at home, his frightened menials not only supplicate according to heroic etiquette but, being nonheroic, also cringe and beg obsequiously as they do so (Leodes, Phemios, and Medon: 22.310–80). Different nonverbal behavior appropriately characterizes different status groups.

English lexemes as "sprawl, straggle, or slouch" similarly communicate disapproval of certain lax body positions. Casual postures and endless lounging, shouting at the table, and relaxed courtyard gaming convey the suitors' habitual disrespect for the mistress of the Ithacan house.[4]

2. Elevation

Odysseus reduces himself to the low level of supplication before a monarch on Phaiakia, then grovels in ashes. Back on Ithaka, he sits in abject ethological surrender before savage sheep dogs and crouches small in defenseless fear before suitor-Fuehrer Eurymakhos (7.142–45, 153–61; 14.30–31; 18.394–96). The lowered body visibly conveys humility when unheroic Eurylokhos on Aiaia or heroic Odysseus kneels to beg a favor, places himself both far from the table and low near the floor at entry, and extends his hand for begging (cf. 6.142–43 with 7.142; 10.264; 17.339, 365–67). Odysseus' body later expresses self-confidence and status arrogation or dignity, when he rises upright in response to Alkinoos' invitational hand and when he leaps on the threshold to strike down enemies (7.168–69, 22.1–2). The body transmits an image of self-evaluation and the will in concrete form: here, "standing tall" marks elevated social recognition. The body not only emits but also receives messages from others. Comrades pat backs, grasp hands, embrace, and kiss heads in loving recognition.

Similarly the defeated and disoriented beggar Iros slumps against the wall, propped up against it, not entirely in control of his muscular system (18.102–3). The bobbing bodies and pathetic death twitches of Odysseus' shipboard companions, the suitors, and maids, however little we hold them responsible for their autonomic activity, humorously convey in a brutal society like theirs (and ours) this limit of corporal autonomy and self-possession, in brief, of controlled presentation of self—face-work or demeanor.[5]

Shifts in posture, or displacements, signal major shifts in internal attitude or signify change in the structure of any communicative event. Ekhenoos ("Thoughtful"), the wise old man of Skheria, urges Alkinoos to raise the unknown suppliant. Then the ruler makes contact and leads him by the communicative hand. Penelope invites the standing and therefore respectful stranger to sit and to do so next to her on a fleecy *diphros* as a sign of

---
4. ὁμαδέω, "to make a din," characterizes only the suitors (1.365, 17.360; 18.88–103). See also 16.107–11; 17.605–6; 18.40–41, 349–50, 395–400; 20.284–86, 345–49, 373–74; 21.285, 367.

5. 12.254–57, 418; 22.17, 84–88, 471–73. Gasping fish similes in the *Odyssey* connote total nonverbal helplessness before powerful foes (12.251–55, 22.384–89).

unprecedented social access and acceptance. Compare the suitors' negotiations at "arm's length" or further. Odysseus sits comfortably on his lowly stool when he strings the bow with aplomb and dexterously shoots the first arrow. When he finally stands up and discards his rags to signal restored, confident power, both gestures and postures contribute to revealing his true identity. Thus, his self-elevation (on the raised *oudos*) assists the meting out of royal revenge and the re-reversal of his status (7.155–68; αὐτόθεν ἐκ δίφροιο καθήμενος, 21.420; ἆλτο, 22.1–2).

Relative elevation signifies relative status. Humans can take position cross-legged on the ground, may fold halfway on their rumps in a chair or crouching, can lie down, or can stand on their feet. Such postures constitute some Homeric "moves" in suppliant abasement, litigation, the formal courtesy of rising for a peer or superior, or the informal expression of feelings.[6] The transitions of bodily elevation also nonverbally communicate alterations of relations or attitudes. For instance, when one rises by sharply bounding up, Homer indicates determined purpose or change of mood/role. Telemakhos bounds up to greet ignored new arrivals, the suitors so rise to enjoy a new diversion, Philoitios bounds up to carry out his revealed master's command, newly stripped Odysseus bounds to the threshold, and Penelope bounds out of bed when told her husband is home.[7]

To sit *or* stand constitutes higher rank as situations dictate. Movement, change of position, or displacement of self honors the interactant. We stand for judges, shift to stiff attention for officers or the flag, and bow for royalty, while we remain seated or standing (nonmovement) for a friend or child. Inferiors and especially the powerless rise from seats, and guests come to a standing halt before hosts or crouch before a person of eminent status, as foreigner Odysseus does before Queen Arete—but as the suitors do not (4.22; 7.142, 153). Rising, that is nonsitting, shows graciousness to an equal (1.118–20, 3.32–35, 16.41–45). A commanding position that still displays full respect to peers is to stand, as Telemakhos does in the assembly when he speaks with the significant object the scepter, as Thrasymedes does at Pylos when he sacrifices a bull to the gods, as Telemakhos the host does to greet his guest, and as any hero does to answer a challenge (2.36–37, 268, 278; 3.210, 448; 17.73; but cf. 4.42; 343). The Homeric orator stands; a person engaged

---

6. For Hades' courtroom, see 11.571; cf. *Il.* 18.503–5. See Penelope's sorrow and grief on the floor at 4.717–19. Cf. Menelaos' collapse on the sand at 4.539 and Odysseus' at 5.82, 151–58. In the performance of grief or ritual mourning, the traumatized person or paid mourner stops, drops to the ground, and rolls about (4.541, 718; 10.499; *Il.* 22.414, 24.165), the grandest example of all being Akhilleus' unparalleled grieving for Patroklos. Cf. the survey of Sittl 1890, Alexiou 1974, and Danforth's 1982 modern comparanda and photographs.

7. 1.118–20, 18.40, 21.388, 22.1–2, 23.32–33. The topics of who sits and stands, when, and for whom provide the rubrics of a valuable Homeric dissertation.

in prayer to the gods stands with arms outstretched. Judges sit as a mark of honor; *basileis* receiving guests can remain seated (as does Nestor before Telemakhos' arrival). The gods sit in conclave, but rise to honor Zeus' arrival. Elevation and its modifications, high or low, confirm hierarchy. Thus, in book 23, as master and mistress jockey for position, Odysseus first sits—as does Penelope. After, however, Odysseus has unwittingly betrayed himself to his wife and Penelope wants to convey her recognition and signal his renewed equal or even superior status, she rises from her equal seat and runs to him, kissing his (still seated) head (23.164, 207). Parties of equal status stand up together to greet and to part. Companions in dining and play sit together. Husband and wife lie down together at night in Troy, Sparta, Aiolia, and Ithaka.[8]

The nonelevation of Agamemnon in the awkward stop-and-start "reconciliation" scenes of *Iliad* 19.54–276 poses no less a crux than Akhilleus' long-deferred acceptance of his offers of reparation. Agamemnon spoke αὐτόθεν ἐξ ἕδρης, οὐδ' ἐν μέσσοισιν ἀναστάς, "right there from his seat, and not getting himself up amongst them."[9] Akhilleus for his part wants compensation on his own terms at his own time, when Agamemnon has suffered enough to compensate him for his public disgrace and humiliation (Van Wees 1992, 133 n. 141) and so rejects immediate delivery of the goods. Practical Odysseus interferes with gastric platitudes. If one believes that Agamemnon stays seated (19.77) to show his more exalted status, then his ex cathedra apology and further commands again reveal that he has not relin-

---

8. For standing, see 2.224–25; 9.527; *Il.* 1.450. For sitting, see *Od.* 2.240; 4.628, 659; cf. 674, 17.177; *Il.* 18.503–5 (sitting judges, standing litigants); *Od.* 11.568–70 (some litigants also sit); 2.14; 3.32, 406; 4.51; 5.3. The warriors or "citizens" in assemblies sit to distinguish the speaker from the listeners. See Kirk 1985–93, 1: 145, with parallels. For mutual elevation, see 1.120–21, 3.34–35, 15.150; 1.26, 108; 7.169, 17.530. For bedtime, see 4.304–5, 10.8–12, 23.296.

9. Donlan 1971 and Van Wees 1992, 131 clarify the many *basileutic* status issues. M. Edwards 1991, 243–45, reviews the suggestions about the chief *basileus*' inertia: Agamemnon is sitting because of his wound (unlikely since the damage was to his lower arm, below the elbow, and he is well enough to slaughter a sacrificial boar: 11.251–53, 19.266); sitting to convey still superior political status and military rank; or standing in place when he speaks, a possibility that might otherwise emphasize ungracious unwillingness to meet Akhilleus halfway. Clay 1995 explores this Iliadic gestural and semiotic crisis. She notes the nonverbal (elevational) implications of Odysseus' pointed and vital demand that Agamemnon take suitable oaths *standing* among the Akhaians (19.175).

Odyssey 13.56 presents the unique parallel verse, when the Skherians, while seated, pour a libation to the gods for Odysseus' protection: αὐτόθεν ἐξ ἑδρέων. This libation, like others performed while seated (Sittl 1890 has no entry on libation activities), seems to show that the Iliadic occurrence of the phrase does not mean "there in place [but *up*] *out* of their seats." Immediately after the Skherian libation, in the same verse, Odysseus does rise to offer the mortal queen a special toast: αὐτόθεν ἐξ ἑδρέων. ἀνὰ δ' ἵστατο δῖος Ὀδυσσεύς. Both verses thus contain the seated-standing antithesis, although employing it in different ways.

quished one whit his need to express his supreme power visibly and to compel acceptance of his uniquely *basileuteros* status. This inflexibility certainly suits his curiously angular character. Sitting signals his regal superiority just as it does for Zeus, Hera, and Apollo among the gods and for Nestor, Alkinoos, and the suitors among humans. But unlike the rest of them, Agamemnon can never relax his status warfare.[10]

So Agamemnon says (9.160) Καί μοι ὑποστήσω, "Let him stand down below me." His tactless (and therefore unrepeated) recapitulation of instructions to the departing ambassadors summarizes his anomalous hierarchical expectations in a postural metaphor. His unwillingness to displace himself in *any* direction, up or down, expresses Hellenic "intuitions" or conventions that approach, removal, or abasement suggest deference.

To cause someone to be seated (καθίζω) signals respect for that guest. So, in the type-scene of formulaic reception, Telemakhos honors Athene in Mentes' disguise, Nestor's family honors Telemakhos, Kalypso honors Hermes, and Penelope honors the vagrant.[11] Contrariwise, the humble servant, the isolated, unrecognized stranger, and the outcast must take the trouble to seat themselves (4.136; 17.334, 339, 466–7; 21.243), usually on humbler forms of furniture. One might call this mere etiquette, if etiquette were ever merely "mere."[12]

3. Nonverbal Forms of Deference

We read interlocutors' bodies for external signs of deference or disdain and for expressive hints about invisible emotions. Homer and oral poetics eschew explicit psychological analysis but provide clear visual and oral indications of mood and intention.

---

10. For divine displacement, see 1.532–33, 15.84–86. *H. Ap.* 2–13 notably surveys sit or stand elevation protocols: some spring out of chairs to honor, some stay seated to show rank, one supplies a throne for the dynamic young god, and then all return to their seats. For human displacement, see 3.412–13, 416; 7.159–62.

11. 1.130, 3.416, 5.86, 19.97. At Penelope's, the honor granted the beggar of seat near the hero's spouse must appear wildly eccentric for those who reject the Harsh hypothesis even in its milder forms (Amory, Russo). If Penelope does not intuit/suspect/realize the beggar's true identity, however, why does she order a chair for an unknown vagrant male? What would the suitors say or do?

12. Familiar to us, sitting on chairs and thrones has been a posture distinctive to Western civilization for five thousand years. Originally, sitting signaled social superiority. Hewes 1957 discusses alternatives to chairs, such as the deep squat, cross-legged and straight-legged floor sitting (for the former, see Nestor's picnic festival at 3.37–41), the Nilotic one-leg stance, etc. Houston 1975 discusses the articulated Homeric vocabulary for seating instruments and its careful employ.

Rules of conduct in Homer are honored in both the observance and the breach. Helen and Menelaos embody punctilious hosting. They observe all obligations to their friend's son and graciously exceed Telemakhos' every expectation.[13] The Kyklops and the suitors are equally discredited by violations and sardonic perversions of hospitality, or *xenia*, the Homeric touchstone of personal morality. To threaten or maltreat the submissive stranger-guest disconfirms pretensions to status and divine favor. The guest owes deference, but the god-fearing host owes honor and respect, for the guest may be a god (7.159–66, 9.266–71, 17.483–87). Ceremonies are profaned when even the little salutations and offerings due a visitor or a suppliant—even, or especially, a beggar—are denied or inverted, as when the suitors' guest-gifts become assault weapons.[14] Indeed, the suitors ostentatiously stint on status rituals for all Laertids and their retainers as well as the beggar to demonstrate disrespect. This "dissing" is the conscious inverse of honoring (18.288–89, 1.368–82, 20.345–46, 21.330–33). Even the suitors' grudging observances of hostly decorum insinuate sardonic disregard by modifications of tone, pacing, and hyperbolic description (17.393–408, 18.245–49, 20.293–300).

Symmetrical and asymmetrical deference punctuate the *Odyssey*. We can identify deference maneuvers based on age, status, territory, and gender. Younger Telemakhos generally allows his numerous elders to structure their encounters with him—except once, when he rudely avoids reentering old Nestor's presence to escape his aged prattle. So, we mark respect for elders in Eumaios' reception of the older beggar and in the first stage of Odysseus' treatment of Laertes, his initial engagement (24.242–55, prior to the cutting to the quick with hard words). As a repeatedly landed, suddenly "penniless" stranger, Odysseus waits for various local residents—for example, Nausikaa, then Eumaios, then the suitors, and finally Penelope—to "call the shots."

The alien defers to the enhanced status conveyed by territorial prerogatives. Hostly interlocutors deserve respect. When unequals meet without territorial claims (e.g., on a battlefield or in a neutral athletic venue), both parties have deference obligations as serious as the demonstrations of mutual

---

13. Goffman [1956] 1967b analyzes the "ceremonial idioms" of different American social groups. Odysseus suits his behavior to the gender, status, and age of every interactant; cf. the meetings with Nausikaa, Athene as little Skherian girl, Athene as male shepherd, Athene as goddess, Eumaios, Telemakhos, Penelope, Eurykleia, etc.

14. Their words and gestures convey negative deference, ritual contempt. For instance, the Kyklops and some suitors not only deny guest-gifts and alms but mock the institution of Zeus by the so-called "gifts" of promising to eat Mr. Nobody last and by hurling at him the hoof of a sacrificed ox (9.369–70, 20.296).

esteem found when knowing equals confront each other in heroic households. Odysseus knows the deference style appropriate for all encounters—including competitions—and leaves it to others (e.g., the Phaiakian loudmouth Euryalos) to disrupt and abuse the hallowed rituals of social interaction. Meanwhile, he shows mannerly restraint by contrast. Indeed, Odysseus demonstrates an anthropologist's reserve and observational tact (1.3): πολλῶν δ' ἀνθρώπων ἴδεν ἄστεα καὶ νόον ἔγνω, "he observed the cities and got to know the worldviews of many men."

The *Odyssey* is "among those exemplary epics . . . , a key to the principles of social conduct," especially in its presentations of rites of incorporation for strangers. The stranger has "no place within the system, no status save that of stranger (. . . status of being statusless)." Host and *guest* are entirely unequal on any occasion in a given location, but they alternate give-and-take roles, at least hypothetically. The system implies equality by turns, with hostility suspended or avoided. As guest, Odysseus/Aithon receives hospitality and gives honor by doing so and by returning suitable deference. Nameless on Skheria and many-named on Ithaka at Eumaios' pigsty and at the manse, his alleged (former) status makes him "guest-worthy," "hostable," even honorable in the giving and gaining of hospitality. Yet he may ever revert from guest to (protectionless) stranger, if he abrogates by any jot or tittle the Homeric code of *xenia*.[15]

As *beggar,* not guest, Aithon/Odysseus renounces honor. He cannot gain honor or pay it in the role of Iros' surrogate. If the beggar aspires to guest status and behaves accordingly, his insistence implies an impermissable threat to the honor that he has established for his host(s). A beggar implicitly presents a different claim from a guest, one that confers honor on the almsgiver because of no expectation of return. His Zeus-legitimated claims as beggar permit no *right* as guest. Thus, the suitors object with some justice to the stranger's progressive arrogation of privilege, from liminal scraps-eater to semisuitor in the final *agon*. Assertion of guest-right (*xenia*) denies a statusless status, as it presents a claim with an implicit offer (to repay hospitality later).

Possessors have only a diffuse obligation to the possessionless mendicant. Pitt-Rivers distinguishes Andalusian habitual, local, shameless beggars (sleeve-tuggers, moral blackmailers, often female or crippled) from a gruff and manly, rural but transient proletariat. These latter men wander seasonally for honorable jobs, scouring the Andalusian countryside to request work

---

15. Pitt-Rivers 1977 94, 97. Pitt-Rivers' article is most suggestive on this central issue of the *Odyssey*. Van Wees 1992, 228–37, discusses "the hospitality racket."

or, if none be offered, momentary, onetime charity in the form of food for their further journeys. They are indigent but not unwilling to work. We can recognize, through a lens darkly, pari passu two and a half millennia earlier, Iros as in the first class and Aithon/Odysseus as pretending to the second but operating momentarily—to gain entrée—as if in the first. Homer has elided, perhaps, the unreciprocal "endomendicant" with the potentially reciprocating "exomendicant."[16]

When a host refuses a local mendicant, the community understands the act as the rebuffing of a nuisance, but if a host refuses a stranger, the community's repute suffers. Telemakhos' scandalized embarrassment at (the as-yet-unknown stranger) Mentes' standing unrecognized in the doorway reflects a sentiment of damaged honor for Ithaka as well as for the Laertid name. To refuse the stranger is to lose a patron's honor as well as the community's. The stranger must be incorporated, fed so as to become a guest. As guest, the stranger must be protected within the domestic sanctuary, perhaps even to the community's farthest borderlands. While particulars among the codes of hospitality differ among human communities, this law remains quite constant.

The host must honor a guest. The host's obligation requires physical protection, verbal honor, and nonverbal granting of precedence and fine consumable objects, that is, food. The host's best hospitality earns the host the gratitude that is the host's due. Alkinoos performs properly after a prod. Humble Eumaios and Telemakhos provide as best they can. The suitors, however, as de iure guests but de facto hosts, fail on both counts. As guests, they insult their nominal host, Telemakhos, usurp his role(s) as provider of food and honor, and interfere with his duty to protect *all* guests.

The suitors begrudge their very host commensality, and some resent giving the accepted mendicant even scraps. They attack both. As presumptive hosts, they formally follow formalities of greeting when Telemakhos returns to his manse (17.65–66), but they soon dishonor him (17.375–79, 406–8), mistreating him as de facto "guest" as well as threatening the licensed beggar. The beggar is eventually identified by both sides as Telemakhos' guest, now a stranger due hospitality. Aithon/Odysseus shifts from nominal beggar to insistent guest, insistent to his fellow guests about his (limited) rights as another guest. He is beggar (*ptochos*) to the suitors, deserving no more than freely given alms, but guest (*xeinos*) to Telemakhos, then to Penelope. The suitors are right to think that beggars have no rights to participation in

---

16. Pitt-Rivers 1977, 102–4, does not remark Odysseus' manipulation of these two different statuses.

sociable interchange beyond food-gifts, but they are wrong to imply that more fortunate people, hosts or not, have no obligations to beggars. As guests of *their* host, Telemakhos, the suitors have further obligations to their fellow guest. But that shared status is intolerable to them. Telemakhos is manipulating these two sets of roles to reduce their illegitimately usurped authority. We are confronting a symbolic system that is coherent and—like any system—open to and for exploitation, manipulation, and perversion.

Guests as well as hosts might infringe the social law of hospitality. To insult the host or claim superiority, to usurp the role of host, or to refuse what is offered are all acts in which the guest questions the host's honor. But the guest's sole obligation is precisely to uphold and extend their benefactor's honor. Odysseus tries to avoid arrogation of status and participation in Skherian competitions as careful guest; and on Ithaka, he accepts whatever is offered—as long as *something* is offered by Eumaios or the suitors (who are pretending elevation to the status of hosts and owners and are thereby, as guests, denying Telemakhos his due honor).

Hosts in some cultures offer to share their wives with guests. To refuse or interfere with this offer is as offensive as it would be to attempt such a sexual act without invitation. But this is precisely the outrage that the suitors attempt.[17] Odysseus' polite refusal to compete in the (bride?) contests as guest on Skheria should be recalled when he surprisingly requests a chance to try his strength (*not* as suitor) on Ithaka. The reversal seems conscious on the poet's part and would be palpable to an audience finely attuned to guest-host mutual obligations. On Skheria, Odysseus underlines his limited status as accepted suppliant. As honorless beggar on Ithaka, the "presentation of self" that the suitors accept, the request to compete is prima facie absurd. As honorable stranger and guest of good birth for the house of Penelope and Telemakhos, a status the Laertids have acknowledged for the stranger, participation remains exceptional, but not impossible. So the polite *xeinos* must request permission and does so. The request is granted by the appropriate parties, the Laertid mistress and heir presumptive. Why? The dangerous tactic not only honors further the guest but also dishonors further the unwanted, objectionable, and objecting other "guests." "Killing two birds with one arrow" is good deference economics. That the bizarre outlander is considered an honored guest by the proper hosts is clear from Laertid references to him as *xeinos,* a term with which they never grace the suitors (19.309, 325–28, 350, 509, 560, 589[!]; 21.331–35, 349).

---

17. Pitt-Rivers 1977, 109–10; van Gennep [1908] 1960, 30, 35, on the ethnography.

Homer emphasizes Penelope's gendered circumspection (περίφρων, ἐχέ-φρων; like Odysseus, ἀγχίφρων), a virtue especially suited to women's limited proxemic mobility. Her perfect womanly discretion controls situations where the substantive rules of male society (law, morality, and religious custom) are precarious and unstable. Her maintenance of a limited freedom and her gendered barricades against remarriage depend on manipulating her space, deportment, appearance, and dress. She exploits male displays of deference and wealth as they compete for her favor. Her nonverbal comportment (maintaining her "distance," not sitting with the suitors, keeping chaperones close by, *kredemnon*) complements nicely her verbal jousting (promise of spousal decision after shroud production, lament for lost beauty, late report of spousal remarriage instructions). These deferential female tactics maintain her desired isolation, dignity, and right of (non)choice.[18]

A polite listener remains patiently quiet, both verbally and kinesically, but good listeners everywhere monitor, cue, pace, and censor speakers continuously by paralinguistic, facial, and body responses. When we nod, smile, mutter "un huh," or move in or away, we signal to the speaker attitudes of attention, agreement, and desire to respond or their opposites. The beggar Odysseus, however, has lost the right to react, except with patient gratitude. He must patiently hear, observe, and endure whatever interlocutors choose to speak or communicate with condescending phonation, posture, and body motions. He can never in character "stand tall." His reduced elevation, silence, response only on demand, and humble postures and placement convey deference. Once anchored on the gateway *oudos*, however, the beggar Odysseus' strategy turns from doorsill deference and lowdown passivity to penetration, aggravating uppityness, and emergence to heroic elevation: ἆλτο δ' ἐπὶ μέγαν οὐδόν (22.2).

---

18. Goffman [1956] 1967b, 55, 59; Sealey 1990, chap. 6, "The Women of Homer," esp. 122; Katz 1991.

Chapter 7

Heroic Proxemics: Social Space and Distance

1. Read This First

The "triple structure of communication" consists of nonverbal, paralinguistic, and verbal modes of transmitting intent, reaction, affect, and attitude.[1] Body language communicates both in-awareness and out-of-awareness. Some types are especially liable to manipulation below consciously intended or perceived levels—for instance, the human use of space, proxemics, an underappreciated element of semiotic activity. The subject of "nonverbal behavior,"[2] intended and unintended body messages, rewards closer attention from students of ancient life, letters, and art. Distant and fragmented messages from antiquity—literary, sculpted, and painted texts—provide our only data for reconstructing face-to-face interaction. The symbolic, nonverbal acts of individuals, groups, and cultures and the investigation of their gestures, postures, verboids, and other phonation to convey status, dominance (honor and humiliation), affect, emotion, and thought demand a corner of "literary anthropology."[3]

The body transmits formal and informal micromomentary or extended cues through many channels. The mind receives and then adjusts to and

---

1. Poyatos 1983, 346 presents the triple system in imaginative literature. Dissertations describe the pinching of secretaries' buttocks in commercial offices: Goffman [1956] 1967b, 74 n. 19. Film and videotape enable frame-by-frame descriptions of American bourgeois rituals at children's parties: Kendon 1973. Bremmer and Roodenburg 1991 collect historical examples; e.g., Bremmer, pp. 15–35, reviews "walking, sitting, and standing in ancient Greek culture."
2. Ekman 1981, 270 finds no better phrase than *nonverbal behavior,* a "terrible term." He excludes vocal nonverbal behavior and proxemics from nonverbal deception—his field of study here—but wrongly in my opinion.
3. Does the semiotic code of Homer exist only in his text and not reflect actual social practice of any era? Nods and hugs surely reflect Bronze Age and Iron Age repertoires. No argument suggests that people were once less nonverbal rather than more so. Odysseus' many smiles, however, both imitate behaviors of real people and code his uniquely elaborated, and admired, self-possession. Furthermore, they seem to reflect an appreciation of irony developed during the last phase of oral elaboration; cf. Levine 1984, 1. Perhaps the text alone owns *some* puzzling nonverbal behavior, such as the suitors' hysterical laughing fit (coding divine blindness) or Penelope's goose-slaughter vision (coding intuition or emotional ambivalence).

returns verbal and nonverbal responses. Experts in interpretation, subconsciously alert to such signals, all of us read nonverbal texts as reinforcing or contradicting explicit words. Words, in fact, convey only 10 percent of expressed emotion in daily encounters, while tone carries 35 percent, and facial expression, gesture, and posture present the majority, 55 percent. Narratives in all cultures, oral and written precipitates of experience (however channeled through various media [see chapters 1 and 2] and filtered through time and "genius"), emphasize, amplify, italicize, ironize, and undermine performative words and instrumental deeds by the same means as interactants, although not in the same proportions. Gestures, postures, and their ilk are certainly reported in written texts more rarely than they are experienced in daily life, but they are the more, not the less, important for that reason when they are mentioned.

Comparatively, across social strata and cultures, one can inventory ethological universals (e.g., species-constant smiles and frowns) and culturally arbitrary semiotics, that is, ethnogests, such as head-nods, slouchers and ramrod types, and the varying body and adaptor codes of different genders, age-groups, and classes. Elements that surely vary by societies are the distances, orientations, and elevations at which different cultures and subcultures transact their business.[4]

Gesture and posture may be the most obvious segments of our large field, but body-talk comprehends two lesser-known but equally significant categories of nonverbal behavior: chronemics and proxemics, human uses of time and position to structure communicative events. Formal rank and informal sentiment are easily and necessarily conveyed by relative distance and by turn-taking protocols, by relative elevation and by (temporal) pause and interactional pace.[5]

Proxemics examines "social and personal space and man's perception of it" in different cultures. As many as 20 percent of the words in a concise

---

4. Ekman and Friesen 1972, 356 discuss "arbitrariness" for hand gestures with references to their earlier publications, especially the taxonomic classic of 1969b. Hall 1966 laid the groundwork for discussions of distance regulation, crowding and isolation, and for cross-cultural studies of interaction and urban planning.

5. Hosts speak first to guests, as Telemakhos to Mentes, Nestor's son and Menelaos to Telemakhos, Eumaios to Odysseus disguised as a vagrant, and Penelope to the wayfarer (on the chronemics, see 1.122–24, 3.43, 4.60, 14.37, 19.103; cf. 19.415; and see the appendix). Indeed, inexperienced Telemakhos breaches turn-taking decorum by speaking at the table to his sidekick *before* his Spartan host addresses him, even though he employs respectful paralinguistic whispers at the intimate distance (4.71–77). But the experienced host, Menelaos, graciously picks up the conversational ball. Superiors entrain interactants to their interactional rhythms, volumes, and pace.

English dictionary refer to space and spatial relationships; in life, closeness to others and distance from others convey many crucial attitudes and reactions (Hall 1966, 1, 93). Physical proximity has social causes and psychological consequences. Ethologists report that every animal species has a sense of territoriality, territory claimed and defended against intruders. The *Iliad* and the *Odyssey*, privileged reflections of some social order,[6] not surprisingly play with this sense of space, an "instinct," and its perversions, transgressions, and reestablishment on the personal, familial, and communal levels. Humans depend on close-range receptors, particularly smell and touch (taste is least important in social relations). People in states of fear, anger, or sexual excitement transmit specific odors that others interpret out-of-awareness (Hall 1966, 45–50). Every culture has olfactory boundaries as well as touch boundaries, beyond which we register trespass. Somatic characteristics that produce responses in others include our thermal, dermal, and chemical stimuli. Haptic and olfactory stimuli produce strong and immediate reactions.

The progress of the human species in controlling the immediate environment has partly resulted from highly developed "distance receptors," sight and hearing. These sweep up information from a long range. The Hellenic sensory world (touch, smell) and gestures and postures, ancient and modern, differ from the Euro-American experience. Sometimes these differences are patent: Priam, Odysseus, and Laertes roll in the dirt in mourning, and Hecuba bares a breast to supplicate her son; we don't. Most examples of nonverbal behavior in Greek literature, however, are common to both them and us or are comprehensible or seem so with a little explication. Exceptions would include the misunderstandings of seated greeting and gifting protocols discussed in chapters 4 and 6.[7]

The phrase "personal space" provides current jargon for one aspect of territoriality, a facet of animal ethology. Everyone manages a personal "body-buffer zone," a characteristic and regular distance that we employ

---

6. This is not the place to examine the vexed issue of the historicity of the Homeric poems, particularly the accuracy with which they reflect the society of a specific historical moment. The studies of Finley, Snodgrass, Redfield, Qviller, I. Morris, and Van Wees have resulted in a legitimate *aporia*, acknowledging such factors as archaizing, idealizing, and modernizing tendencies as well as flat anachronism, interpolation, and incomprehension. This book attempts to show coherence and consistency in systems of communication, especially nonverbal, which tend to change slowly in any case.

7. Nonverbal behaviors, especially emblems and speech regulators, can easily be misunderstood. Those familiar with contemporary Greeks recall negative vertical head-nods and palm-hiding good-bye waves; cf. D. Morris et al. 1979, 161–68, 241–46. Hall 1966, chap. 8, "The Language of Space," applies proxemic observations to a few paragraphs of Butler, Twain, and other modern writers.

108   *Sardonic Smile*

when approaching another woman, man, child, animal, or object, and that we maintain when approached, stepping back if necessary. The human ego, the social persona, extends beyond mere skin to an invisible and usually inviolable body-envelope, the parameters of which vary by culture and class.

Few *neutral* gestures, postures, positions, or social distances appear in everyday life, and *none* appear in literature, least of all in Homer. Every movement or alteration of the thousand or so cataloged postures communicates—in-awareness or out-of-awareness, crudely or subtly—respect or disrespect for the interactant. Social distance and body position, especially in the vertical plane (e.g., as in chapter 6, standing tall, hovering over, crouching, and groveling), emphatically signal status and/or disposition.

Anthropologist Edward Hall postulates four chief social distances between communicating individuals, moving from greater to lesser: public, social, personal, and intimate.[8] The *Odyssey* presents self-exiled Laertes off one (far) end of this calibrated social-distance scale, totally out of touch and even out of earshot of the outrageous goings-on in town. Then we locate the stigmatized, marginal and *publicly* distanced beggar; the presumptuously self-invited and self-important suitors infringing the host's prerogatives in the *social* distance; the *personal* closeness of mother and son or mistress and maids; and the ultimate *intimate* distance of body contact between the revealed Odysseus and the traumatized Telemakhos, hugging closely and weeping in waves, and eventually between Penelope and Odysseus, in the bed with the olive-stump post (16.213–16; 23.205–8, 295–96). They have at last relinquished the precarious body-envelopes that insulated them from all those who would violate, penetrate, or swallow them up. These spatial relationships recapitulate Hall's discrimination of four meaningful proxemic levels. In his typically "externalized" manner, Homer conveys (what we call) psychological motivation and situation by describing physical position and distance, posture, and body tonus.[9]

Proxemics, however, even if we limit the study to two-way exchanges, further includes all the following: *distance,* along with its actual and potential modifications (far to near); *posture* (stiff to relaxed) and *elevation* of the body (standing, seated, or abased); *precedence* (serial order); and *orientation*

---

8. See the useful charts of proxemic perception-distances extending from 0 to 30 feet in Hall 1966, 196–97. The four proxemic zones, starting from the distant and measured in English feet, are defined as identifiable persons to 10 feet, 10 feet to 4 feet, 4 feet to 1.5 feet, and 1.5 feet to 0 feet.

9. Hall 1966, 113–29. Succulent Nausikaa cajoles father by coming into his face, the "intimate distance" (μάλ' ἄγχι, 6.56, hapax). Hellwig's 1964 study concerns characters' conscious discussions of space and time.

(frontal, oblique, or dorsal).[10] This chapter sketches literary proxemics,[11] studying how the *Odyssey* presents heroes manipulating and experiencing space, consciously and unconsciously. Homerists have yet to exploit this "hidden dimension" of Homer's art, one found with explicit indications on every page.

The *Odyssey* deploys space and control of delimited territory as a semiotic code that shapes its plot. Every reader recalls the excluded hero's disguised approach and cautious entry into his own perimeter, farmyard, and marital space. His false outerness (physical appearance, object-adaptors, assumed role, "perches") enables him to achieve physical innerness, but step-by-step, slowly, by stages, first enduring and overcoming self-appointed gatekeepers like the goatherd Melanthios, his dog Argos, and the officially sanctioned parasite Iros, he searches for appropriate entrée and an appropriate location and social niche to occupy.

The personal manipulations of space in the poem have analogues on the larger scale of Homeric topography. The superiority of the polis and of urban sophistication to the rural *agros* and labor, repeatedly asserted (e.g., 14.222), is inverted and completely perverted by the brawling, manhandling suitors. Because of their consumption of the "best pork" (14.80–82, 17.171) without *xenic* reciprocity, because of their usurpation and hostile occupation of the lord's house, the Ithakan polis has become "a place strictly to be avoided" by decent animal herders and the prepolitical agglomeration's degraded patriarch (1.189–90, 14.372). The suitors, ὕβριν ἔχοντες, evade the reciprocal obligations of *xenia* and destroy their host's wealth νήποινον, "without recompense" (1.377 = 2.142). Telemakhos' *philoi* could not do this, for he would demand compensation, τίσις, and get it in the form of honor and goods, χρήματα. That would be κέρδιον, more profitable than the nonnegotiable (ἄπρηκτον) situation that he now faces (2.70–79). From the bizarre, self-aggrandizing space perspective of the Ithakan suitors, Odysseus is out of the picture, Laertes is a self-imposed exile, Penelope is under close

---

10. Odysseus annihilates the social or personal distance between himself and his mother's shade, his son, his wife, and his father, but only when *he* chooses to identify himself as their intimate. His proxemic predominance reinforces other heroic qualities. The slack posture of drunken Polyphemos, the collapse of Iros, and the springing upright of hosts Telemakhos and Akhilleus to greet unexpected guests illustrate posture and elevation. For shift in bodily or facial orientation, recall Aias' shade stalking away from Odysseus or Eurykleia's turning her gaze toward Penelope in a vain effort to catch her mistress' eye.

11. Also known as part of comportment, postural metacommunication, symbolic speech, somatic semiosis, kinesics, and body language. Both dynamic and static nonverbal behaviors are included. Gould 1973, Pedrick 1982, Holoka 1983, and Lateiner 1989, 1992a, and 1992b offer studies focused on one or another aspect.

house arrest (and a deadline), Telemakhos is persona non grata, and Aithon the beggar is an undesirable alien. Eurymakhos tries to redirect this beggar from the town, where all agree begging is best (17.18, 227; 18.1–2, 363), to working for him on his farmland in the country (18.357–61), a transparent claim of birth status and territorial privilege—ironic in the extreme considering to whom the interloper and squatter speaks.[12]

The reader should grasp firmly that nonverbal behavior of literary characters can be in-awareness or out-of-awareness *for them*. When Nausikaa stands her ground as salty, naked Odysseus comes nigh, he explicitly considers at what speed to approach her; how close to come; at which posture elevation, with what words, and with which tone of voice to speak to her; and whether to touch her nubile knees in supplication, a ritualized in-awareness gesture (6.141–47, esp. 141–44):

στῆ δ' ἄντα σχομένη· ὁ δὲ μερμήριξεν Ὀδυσσεύς,
ἢ γούνων λίσσοιτο λαβὼν εὐώπιδα κούρην,
ἢ αὔτως ἐπέεσσιν ἀποσταδὰ μειλιχίοισι
λίσσοιτο. . . .

She held her ground standing face-to-face with him;
   Odysseus pondered whether
To supplicate the lovely-faced girl by clasping her knees
Or keeping his distance to beseech her with reassuring words. . . .

He is "priming himself" for the task at hand and consciously calculating the most effective communicative strategy.

Heroes and villains often visibly exhibit sentiments unawares, however. Odysseus' sole sardonic smile communicates power and confidence to us, directed by Homer to notice it, although it is ignored by the dyssemic suitors—inadequate signal-interpreters. Most visible trembling, an exhibition of fear, seizes Iros to the amusement of many. The established bum of Ithaka has found to his (conscious) dismay that he has to support his abusive,

---

12. See A.T. Edwards 1993, 46, 49, 51–52, 72–73; Edwards' article is a stimulating analysis of "ethical geography" that imports more theory and ideology than the Homeric text easily bears. Roisman 1990b examines concepts of advantage in Homer. Fisher 1992, 151–84, considers thoughtless insult, intended humiliation, and malicious mischief and injury. Lateiner 1992b addresses some of the same territorial issues from a psychological and anthropological angle. Lateiner 1993 discusses some of the same issues connecting territory to status in an article that appeared simultaneously with A.T. Edwards'. A.T. Edwards 1993, 73 n. 97, misstates Odysseus' riches-to-rags fables, following the capitalist cliché rather than the inverted order more appropriate for an unstable, aristocratic society.

surly words and ugly tone (choppy rhythm, 18.10; cf. πανθυμαδὸν ὀρκιόωντο, 18.33) by fighting the new freeloader (18.4, 8–9, 26–31, 33, 41). The clownish bully is dragged forward by the servants (76, 89), closer to his opponent, and into the informal ring of men. This impermanent nonverbal, proxemic structure creates an arena, an audience, and, perforce, two gladiators. Iros' nonverbal leakage of fear and his transparent proxemic aversion provide more malicious joy to the playboy princelets. Later, the postmatch stupor and physical paralysis of Iros produce renewed laughter and *kledonic* (unintentionally ominous) toasts to disguised Odysseus (100, 102–3, 111).

Nonverbal behavior overrides contrary verbal messages for observers and is generally more reliable.[13] Iros' prefight blustering words—his deceptive "front"—are easily decoded with the aid of his subsequent unintended, unaware body-talk, or "leakage." In this pair of examples, the first, Odysseus' needy supplication of the princess "at a distance," involves in-awareness proxemic nonverbal behavior. The second, Iros' emotional collapse and postfight physical paralysis, exhibits out-of-awareness psychophysical symptoms and proxemic nonverbal behavior (trembling, raised hands, then kicking and "bleating," depressed elevation, motionlessness, and nonresistance to being dragged out of play and propped up outside). His original approach, threat, and raised "dukes" exhibit inclination and symbolic speech; his final stillness shows a quite distinct instrumental inability to function further in the social arena. Status is constantly being renegotiated in Homer, and the vulnerable body always provides legal tender. Its position, orientation, and elevation relative to other bodies communicate attitude and intention.

Proxemics can be intended or unintended, regardless of whether the interactants are aware of its effects. For examples of intentional body language, recall Menelaos' paternal stroking of Telemakhos' arm, Melanthios' kick of the vagabond, or Odysseus' aggressive stance facing Iros. For unintended acts, recall the suitors' hysterical laughter or the Kyklops' sharp bellow of pain. Proxemic examples of both types include all space-contracting or space-expanding greeting and parting protocols, treaty-making movements, standing, sitting, and supplicating (e.g., *Il.* 1.245–46, 19.77; *Od.* 22.310, 342, 365).

Unintended behaviors again divide into controllable and noncontrollable. The puny companions' scuttling off to dark corners in fear at Kyklops' cave or Odysseus' incessant but stoppable tossing in the night before slaughter can be compared to Odysseus' uncontrollable shudder at Kalypso's revela-

---

13. Ekman 1981, 270, and elsewhere, argues the superior reliability (for the observer) of nonverbal channels.

tions about his itinerary or Polyphemos' slack-jawed, drunken, stuporous sprawl. Borderline cases would include Kyklops' later ceaseless groaning, a paralinguistic alternant.[14]

Conscious and voluntary gestures and postures provide the most frequent types of nonverbal behavior in Homer.[15] For instance, secular and sacred ceremonies with spatial rituals, such as Khryses and Akhilleus' departing to pray privately, appear everywhere in Homer, as indeed in all ancient literature. They provide norms of proxemic behavior and spatial contexts for stressed individuals in crisis. Such reported nonverbal behavior frequently is socially functional, integrating public and private concerns and pressures (e.g., secular feasts and divine supplications). At other times, a group's sentiments and behavior are embodied in an expressive individual and his movements; for example, synecdochic Antinoos' duplicitous smile and unwanted touch represent all the suitors' mocking condescension (2.302, 323). Nevertheless, Homer frequently allocates one gesture to one person or group, others to others. For instance, only suitors bite their lips, while only the Laertids Odysseus and Telemakhos ever abort the self-revelatory "dead giveaway" of tears.[16] The attentive detail that Homer allots to proxemic interactions of Telemakhos, Odysseus, and Penelope while they deal with friends and enemies borders on the clinical.[17]

Homer occasionally describes the different proxemic tendencies of crowds as well as of individual heroes. "Bunching up" activity reduces heroic stature in the *Iliad* and the *Odyssey*. The anonymous suitors, for example, cluster around or behind the more active peers while they lark about in games, at the seating arrangements at the table, and during the contest with the bow. The young men form a ring for the mock-heroic beggar-boxers (17.65, 18.41).

Later, locked into unwanted battle, their huddling together alive is echoed by the imprisoned wicked maids' guilt-ridden movements (22.270, 446–47). The suitors' undisciplined scattering exhibits a common group-fear reflex.

---

14. See Youssouf et al. 1976, 815, on acceptable social forms; Poyatos 1986, 478, 493, on noncontrollable expressive systems.

15. Vergil and modern fiction writers, in contrast, devote more attention to involuntary self-revelation (Lateiner 1992a, Newbold 1992). Also, in modern fiction, gesture and gesticulation are often idiolects, unique neurotic symptoms, such as Melville's psychologizing of Captain Ahab in *Moby Dick* or Herman Wouk's Captain Queeg in *The Caine Mutiny*.

16. E.g., the hidden or aborted tears of Odysseus with Argos and Penelope; Telemakhos with the suitors (17.305, 19.211; 17.490–91). For the heroic record, Odysseus does weep unashamedly and openly three times while on Ithaka alone: with his son, wife, and father.

17. See Combellack 1946/47, 210, for clinical claims made in Homer's behalf. Lateiner 1987, 108–12, categorizes Homeric nonverbal behavior; Lateiner 1989, lip and tooth behaviors; Lateiner 1992a, the vocabulary and descriptions of aphonia and emotional paralysis.

The free *basileis,* even worse, are described in ways elsewhere applied to slave women. Their voluntary proxemic behavior echoes that of the saucy serving women, who are lowest on the social scale (17.34, 22.497–98). The poet equates the two groups as contemptible lawbreakers, incompetents, and nearly less than human adversaries, when he describes the eventual penning-in of both gendered groups, the slaughter of the men and the lined-up execution of the women. He even produces parallel descriptions of bodies piled together and stacked like fish in a heap—no respect for these dead (22.299; 22.136–38, 460; 22.381–83, 470–72; 22.389, 450).

Sprawled postures convey unintended or freely chosen vulnerability. Such group behaviors are denigrated. Agamemnon's ambushed and enfeebled henchmen resemble the deactivated Kyklops (11.419, 9.371–74, cf. 22.17). The suitors frequently loll about at games, drink, eat food, and chatter.

Men thronging together in small compass (e.g., 16.641, 21.607, 22.12, 24.662) suggest unautonomous henchmen, children, or flocks. The dead souls swarm around Odysseus and Minos (11.42, 570, 632), and the anxious Trojans in the *Iliad* crowd around Priam—both figures of presumed salvation or authority. Undifferentiated groups of people queue up for minor privileges, showing acceptance of the concept of *serial order:* dead queens for blood, the other shades in their quest for blood, and the suitors for the bow contest. One might say the suitors' lineup for trying the bow equates them to the honor-deprived dead, the boring world that Akhilleus describes (11.233, 21.141). This egalitarian, if unheroic, proxemic method for deciding and exhibiting turn-taking hierarchy (chronemics) conveys a (localized) absence of invidious distinction and a dearth of inherent prestige, visible and acknowledged forms of social priority.

2. Case Studies: Proxemic "Movers and Shakers"

Let us observe three suggestive examples, which show three disenfranchised persons manipulating contested space: tender Telemakhos, still mocked and disparaged because of his unproven youth and labile "face," a proto-*basileus* with minimal proxemic privilege in his own house; Odysseus, stigmatized and ostracized for his status as social outcast, a wandering beggar on the margin of the community; and seemingly passive Penelope, disadvantaged by her sex and confronted in her very home by a horde of invasive princelets. Telemakhos, Penelope, and Odysseus face exclusion by age, gender, and rank, yet they discover how to break down, maintain, or erect socially sanctioned proxemic barriers to further their power and personal interests. Odysseus' approaches to the boisterous suitors, the immobilized queen, and the

114 *Sardonic Smile*

long-unused and spatially isolated bow violate parochial rules. He ap-*proxim*ates the rank of *basileus* by appropriating their exclusive, dominated spatial domain. The *basileis* lose the prize not only by inferior warrior skills but also by inferior nonverbal, including proxemic, manipulative skills.

Seating positions of host, invited and welcome "guests," and unexpected *xenoi* signal tacitly negotiated relative status. Abroad, Telemakhos meets courtesy and the treatment due a noble's son. At home, Telemakhos holds an ironic position: a segregated seat of honor in the great hall amidst his dishonor. The *megaron* functions as an arena for status warfare, in which kinship and factional ties are nonverbally expressed, announced, shifted, and manipulated.[18]

3. Telemakhos the Deferential Adolescent

At *Odyssey* 3.22–24, young Telemakhos and his mature friend Mentor disembark at Pylos. In the distance, they see a ritual feast in progress. Telemakhos has manifested teenaged anxieties and timidity already in books 1 and 2. Now he appears paralyzed at the thought of meeting impressive grown-ups. So he says:

Μέντορ, πῶς τ'ἄρ' ἴω, πῶς τ'ἄρ προσπτύξομαι αὐτόν;
οὐδέ τί πω μύθοισι πεπείρημαι πυκινοῖσιν·
αἰδὼς δ'αὖ νέον ἄνδρα γεραίτερον ἐξερέεσθαι.

Mentor, how should I approach them? How should I greet him?
Never yet have I had experience with carefully chosen words;
I'm embarrassed as a young man to start interrogating an older man.

Adolescent Telemakhos alleges that he is not yet familiar with nonverbal, distant-approach protocols for friendly encounters, social distance salutation procedures, rules of verbal turn taking, and age-based (here, adult) etiquette, including even the right words. The initiation and termination of

---
18. Late-night departures from the manse of male *basileis* and nightly closing of the house's doors exemplify temporary, temporal segregation by sex and social relationship, a temporary modification of (permanent) spatial separation (18.427–28). The locking-up of the servant-women in the *Odyssey* provides another example (21.235–39), this time proxemic and gendered.

social encounters abroad have not been part of his enforced, extended childhood. No dad has shown him how to assert his place or obtain ξενίη.[19]

At home, the Homeric hero controls his own space. Nestor, Menelaos, and anomalous Alkinoos admit and entertain visitors in the *Odyssey*'s first quarter. In his hut-home away from home in *Iliad* 9 and 24, Akhilleus welcomes, receives, feeds, and directs Akhaian and Trojan visitors. The power of the male housemaster is conveyed verbally by greetings and invitations to enter, approach, bathe, eat, speak, sleep, and so forth; and nonverbally by extended arms and hands, toasting goblets, glowering looks, sudden movements, tears, awkward silences (zero-grade act, chronemics), and frightening and threatening tones of voice.[20]

As we have seen in chapter 6, greeting and parting procedures offer standards of nonverbal respect and disrespect throughout the concatenated narratives of the *Odyssey*'s first half. Away from home, Telemakhos encounters heroic politeness in space management. His repeated approaches and welcomes, ratified by proxemic nearness to head men at the table, mark nonverbal honor and precedence. Homer develops a Telemakhian paradigm of "honor at entrance." The stylized proxemic and other nonverbal rituals of greeting and parting present many gradations of emotional response and diplomatic expressions.[21]

As in early modern Poland, Homeric visits to provincial gentry were sufficient inducement for elaborate welcomes, feasts, and hunts.

> Servants would sit on the roof . . . watching the road. . . . Crossing thresholds . . . gave occasion to more fussing . . . hugging and kissing. . . . The entire household would [entertain . . .] the guest . . . for many weeks. It was easy to come for a visit, but very difficult to leave.

---

19. His recent unintentional breakdown into expressive (nonverbal) tears in the Ithakan assembly belied his brave face, his social front and public persona of the scion of the leading local *basileus* (2.80–83). Emotional arousal often produces both leakage of true feeling and clues that a deception is being practiced; cf. Ekman 1981, 271. Chap. 8 of this book describes youthful Telemakhos' nonverbal behavior, including inappropriate leakage, such as his laugh at 21.101–5; cf. Olson 1994, 371.

20. Lady Penelope arrogates several male proxemic prerogatives of invitation and *xenie*, *faute de mari*. Kalypso and Kirke assume privilege by divine right (as goddesses). Swineherd Eumaios knows and carefully executes the rituals of guest welcoming on his hog farm in the hills (14.33–120.).

21. Penelope plans signal proxemic honor in her mansion for the vagrant who once befriended her long-lost husband: a seat next to her princely son at the next day's banquet (19.321; cf. 97, where he is invited to sit near her regal presence). In both cases, commensal and conversational seating (reduced elevation and distance from the host) signify enhanced status. Firth 1973, 308 (on proxemics), details "bodily symbols of greeting and parting."

> The host would protest and try to delay . . . sometimes . . . taking the wheels off [the visitor's] carriage.[22]

Telemakhos provides this precious opportunity to relieve deadly boredom in a world of few distractions. Palace life appears highly ritualized on public and private occasions. Telemakhos' hesitation to return home via Nestor's hospitable domicile is perfectly understandable. His evasion causes Nestor's son great anxiety.

Nonchalant suitors disbelieve in Telemakhos' journey—his escape. In book 2, Leokritos the suitor doubts such a distancing ploy will ever happen. He thinks Telemakhos will "sit a long while" in Ithaka. The suitors treat his intentions toward them as merry prattle (2.255–56, 323–26). Telemakhos steals away from de facto jailers. His visits to friendly strangers parallel Odysseus'; like his father, he faces detention and temptation, since Helen's ephemeral anodyne is parallel in place- and time-deadening effect and disengaging result to Kirke's potion, the delight of the Lotus, and the Sirens' song. Menelaos cannot offer eternal life to his guest, but he promises perpetual feasting, dazzling entertainment, and a year of distraction. Helen is old enough to be Telemakhos' mother (cf. 4.143–45, 235–36; 15.125–29; she is Penelope's cousin), but she thematically parallels Kirke and Kalypso as an overpowering, self-serving, sexual sorceress. Both Odysseus and Telemakhos tarry too long as a result of pleasures and pressures that alone they cannot evade or deny (Apthorp 1980, 12–13, 21).

The travel narratives reveal much about Telemakhos' growing expertise in social relations and space management. Neither Nestor nor Menelaos can clarify his father's whereabouts. Nonverbal components draw a clear contrast between the elder generation's two festivities. At Pylos, the hosts rise quickly and easily to greet and considerately seat the strangers at the head of their large, informal feast for 4,500 "guests," their loyal warrior clans (3.34–41). Social proprieties and hospitality rules are effortlessly observed. Appropriate conduct like this—*aidos,* sensitivity to others' situations—is generally a hallmark of Telemakhos' host/guest behaviors also (3.14, 24; 15.64–66, 87–91, 155–59).

At wealthier and powerful Sparta, however, three gaffes spoil wedding festivities and hint at the discontented accommodation of self-serving Helen and resigned, distressed Menelaos. The King is "celebrating" both the legitimate marriage of his bastard, but honored, son Megapenthes, "Big Sorrow," and the immanent departure for marriage of his legitimate daughter, Her-

---

22. Bogucka 1991, 193, explains how Polish pomp and ritualized gesture expressed emotion.

mione.²³ Henchperson Eteoneos breaches proxemic duties to convey honor at entrance to strangers. He gauchely leaves likely guests standing outside the door. This ghastly breach of decorum echoes Telemakhos' shame in book 1 and preechoes the misdeeds of Alkinoos, Polyphemos, and the suitors. In a poetic tradition rich in gracious hospitality, and for which *xenia* is a touchstone of nobility and social know-how, Eteoneos' confusion indicates the house divided, a vertical (status) anarchy reflecting the horizontal (gendered) disunion between husband and wife.²⁴ The apparent absence of the lord's wife from the wedding of her husband's bastard son marks serious marital dislocation, unorthodox domestic heroics at the least (4.120–21, zero-degree proxemics). Leaving guests at the door to dawdle about indicates nonverbally disruption of normal patterns of greeting, patterns exemplified not only in the Spartan treatment of Telemakhos but also in its contrast to "spontaneously" courteous Nestor (1.113, with West ad loc.; 3.34–74). Menelaos sorely feels the insult given his visitor (μέγ' ὀχθήσας) and chastises the thoughtless nonverbal impropriety (νήπιος, νήπια, 4.30–31).

Telemakhos develops more surely than anyone else in Greek literature. The *Bildungsroman* aspects turn him from a νέος παῖς, a listener, to a ἥβη, a doer (cf. 4.665, 668). The adolescent's earlier vain efforts to jockey for position in Ithaka produce fiasco before the 108 usurpers. His nonverbal behavior and rhetoric have all been abortive. On his travels, he gains self-assurance from courteous reception. Treated as an adult, he becomes one. When the narrative abandons him in Sparta (book 4), he is requesting leave and portable gifts from Menelaos—not horses but κειμήλιον (compact, "bankable" wealth, 4.594–610)—a formulation that draws sad Menelaos' smile and intimate-distance arm stroking for the boy's true-to-blood Odyssean skills in capital accumulation.

When the narrative returns to him (book 15), Telemakhos, not Pisistratos, dominates decision making with a wake-up kick at his intimate (bedmate) peer. He imperatively urges obtuse Menelaos to allow him exit (ἤδη νῦν μ' ἀποπέμπετε . . . / ἤδη γάρ μοι θυμὸς ἐέλδεται οἴκαδ' ἱκέσθαι, 15.44–47, 88, 64–66). He has the wit and temerity to ask for *xenia* different from that

---

23. 4.12. See Schmiel 1972 and Dimock 1989, 46. Schmiel specifies halting the noble guest at the door; consider also Telemakhos' inappropriate comparison of Spartan splendor to Zeus' own palace, and Menelaos' faux pas about Odysseus' homecoming (4.181–86). Telemakhos then weeps, behavior that plugs the conversational flow.

24. 4.20–24. If he recalls a previous princely guest, Paris, the noble gatekeeper Eteoneos may hesitate about where his duty lies. He might well recall problems with a lavishly welcomed guest. Paris had violently abused *xenia* when he departed with his host's lady. At 1.106–14 and 17.328–29, 342, the point about the suitors ignoring guests seems to be their unwillingness to share the *burdens* of authority while enjoying its "perks."

offered, he packs up the priceless guest-gift, and he nearly drives over his dallying host. Telemakhos' manners change radically, shifting from those of stymied child to those of determined hero. So even the formalized minuet pattern of heroic arrival and departure help to show him attaining adult stature. In the first quarter, he has difficulty leaving home. In the third quarter, he easily foils those trying to exclude him from return. In the fourth quarter, at home, he proves his heroic strength as well as his determination.[25]

Telemakhos needs ratification of his theoretically elevated status as master of the battered, imploding house. He envisions the bow contest as a means to that placement (21.113–17),[26] when his life itself is no longer secure and a goddess has taunted him with his mother's unreliability (15.19–20; cf. 13.308, 336; 16.303–4). Millennia of commentators, and recently Marilyn A. Katz (1991, 55–58), wish to explain distrust of Penelope as a result of the Klytaimnestre pattern of the "forceful villainess" in oral traditional poetry. Such speculations, as usual, cannot be disproved, and distrust of women affines is certainly thematic in Greek literature. But I would defer all explanations based on external pressures until we have exhausted explanations that suit plot and character. Rational Penelope has serious village rumor to fear (19.527), her own interests to guard, the intelligence to calculate them, and a father and son and brothers to protect and back them up (15.16–17). Rational, but inexperienced, Telemakhos cannot know which of several rational scenarios his mother will follow; exasperation with her varying strategies often frames his explosive, intemperate utterances (e.g., 1.346–61, 21.344–55, 23.96–103).

The house should protect the heir, but in this one case, the insults and "practical jokes" of the *basileis* (ἀτάσθαλα μηχανόωνται, 3.207; cf. 17.588, 20.170) regularly humiliate him by verbal contradiction and nonverbal displacement to the sidelines. Eventually, he is chivied out of his own house and encouraged by his matron-goddess to leave the premises "for his own protection" (book 4). Later yet, he emphasizes his family's exclusive right to the household, whatever the status of the current spouse: "This house is not public property but Odysseus', and he got it for me," (οὔ τοι δήμιός ἐστιν / οἶκος ὅδ' ἀλλ' Ὀδυσῆος, ἐμοὶ δ' ἐκτήσατο κεῖνος, 20.264–65).

Telemakhos has a house (*oikos*) but not yet a household (*oikia*) with curtilage and collectivity of human and animal life. His mother, under mas-

---

25. Shewan 1926/27, 31–34; Scott 1917/18, 424; Clarke 1963, 139–43; G. Rose 1971, 514.

26. The contest apparently also offers him a mode of desexualizing and objectifying his mother. Only here is the (ultrapatriarchal, Athenian) legal option of "mother under a mature son's tutelage" mentioned.

ter's orders, now protects it, while perhaps a serving-woman will do so after she is gone, before a wife is in place. Finally, his wedded wife will have the responsibility (11.178, 15.25–26, cf. 23.355). Helen, referring to the future, prayed-for event of marriage, offers him a robe for the bride-to-be (15.126–27), but—gridlock again—Telemakhos cannot woo his rightful wife until his patrimony is secured. And he cannot secure his tenuous patrimony until his mother steps aside.

Telemakhos, neither warrior nor housemaster, uneasily coexists with the *basileis* in the male domain. His mother's authority and prestige cast long shadows on his capacity as adult male. By apparently ordering her out of the male domain when she asserts authority, he attempts to demonstrate his gendered-role plan for her both to her and to the suitors. He needs to establish his own (male) space. She is an ally, probably, against the suitors, but she is an "enemy" of his own independent status in a marginal phase between child and grown-up (age) and between unimportant boy and *aristos* male (gendered social status). In his world, the orders that he lays on his mother are given both for the suitors to overhear and for his mother to hear.

Ordering his mother to leave the *megaron* proxemically claims symbolic space for him as master of the house and may suggest his further expulsion of her from the premises, a possibility that is actively canvassed, although rejected. His uneasy relation to the suitors appears proxemically by his being a part of, and yet apart from, the commensal males and their songs, dances, games, unmannerly hubbub, and established routes to public status (competition in games and gifts, exhortations, taunting the boy and the beggar, ordering food service, etc.).

4. Odysseus the Misfit Beggar

The beggar's body resembles his mind: polytropic, as the punk Iros and the suitors also discover and then (if not cowering) exclaim. Deceiving doubleness and tripleness, polytropicity, complement and nonverbally confirm the hero's sinister and dextrous verbal skills (see chap. 9). Cool, chagrined Penelope will not acknowledge him as her husband in either better or worse Athenefied form. She wants neither beggarman nor demon but her flesh-and-blood, bed-building bedmate. Neither his soul nor his body are reanchored and rooted—until the bed trick is sprung and snaps in the foolish male.

The heroic standard of proxemic politesse is repeatedly shattered wherever Odysseus arrives and is received in his fabulous reported travels. Recall the too cool or too hot welcomes in the lands of Kyklops, the Laistrygonians, Kirke, and the Sirens. We behold the attitudinal flip-flop of Aiolos and continuing uncertainty in Phaiakia. Admittedly, Kyklops, as host, is provoked into not following proxemic protocols toward his visitors, who, unasked, help themselves to his "house" and stores. But indications are that he would have balked at Odysseus' requests regardless. Kyklops' efforts to prevent Odysseus' egress, to display power by closing the cave's entrance, and to consume his visitors create a feeling of spatial helplessness, lack of mobility and turf-control, even childhood claustrophobia.

Later, and parallel in many nonverbal respects (not least, posturing and clowning), the homesteading suitors first deny the beggar entry, and later, after he kills the first of them, intend to deny him exit. Then only, they find out that they, the putative jailers, not Odysseus, are themselves jailed and confined. Inversions of power coded as inversions of space control articulate much of the *Odyssey*'s narrative.[27] Beggar and lord, Odysseus, in carefully constructed sequence, passes through Hall's four proxemic, or social, distances: public (nonacquainted) beggar, social guest of Eumaios, personal friend of Penelope, and, revealed at last as Odysseus, Penelope's husband and intimate bedmate.

Nearly universal proxemic protocols and rituals of beggaring are on display in Ithaka (books 17–21). Odysseus, with his "imputed defects,"[28] originally keeps his proper public distance at the mansion's threshold (17.261, 339–40, 466; 18.17, 110), even when eating (17.466–67). He comes in with cajoling words and a parallel gesture—the defenseless, extended open hand suitable for charity. He navigates hungrily around the circle of entitled companions of the table at the pseudopersonal distance of a beggar's reach (17.365–67, 450; cf. the displaced and orphaned beggar boy of *Il.* 22.492–97). He keeps his elevation low, even speaking from a sitting position (17.466).

Once, Odysseus "de-bases" himself, deelevates precipitously, in fact falls to an undignified crouch to avoid being hit, rather than defend himself—as a hero expectably would (18.395).[29] Generally, the newcomer knows the beg-

---

27. 9.240–44, 313–14, 416–19; 17.375–78, 460–61; 22.27–28. Newbold 1981 discusses space in late epic; for Apuleius' deployment of space to enhance the *Metamorphoses*, see Seelinger 1986. G. Rose 1969 describes Homeric hospitality and its Phaiakian exceptions—no one but the lucky Skherians and the unlucky suitors are described as ὑπερφίαλοι, "recklessly disregarding others' rights" (6.274, Nausikaa's observation); Gutglueck 1988.

28. He requests a "scanty portion" from the princes (17.362; cf. 15.312 with Stanford ad 17.12); he rubs or leans his shoulder on the middle-distanced doorpost (17.221, 340), part of a poor man's status-free fidgeting, really a lack of interest in maintaining respectable postures, that is, heroic dignity. Goffman 1963 brilliantly microanalyzes social stigmata.

29. He requests humble reward for good news (εὐαγγέλιον, 14.152–54). He accepts offers and handouts of food, clothing, and even weapons and travel (16.78–81, 17.354–58, 19.309–11). Such generosity puts heroes and even beggars in debt to heroic and banausic benefactors

gar's requirement of unbashful—if limited—assertiveness (cf. 14.512; 17.347, 578), but he violates proper beggar's proxemics (distance maintenance) when he contracts the suitors' personal space and persistently importunes the ironically punctilious suitor Antinoos (17.446–47). The tramp of stigmatized status has penetrated the noble's privileged spatial envelope and stretched unacceptably time-taking permission between classes (a chronemic indication). The dissonance in Odysseus' self-presentation of pathetic vagrant in daily life angers the haughty suitor but provides amusing irony to the audience, faced with a doubled character: beggar and king.

Odysseus forages for a beggar's banquet in the *megaron*. He encounters both suitors' gestures of pseudohospitality and nonverbal rejections caused by his invasion of their perimeter of proxemic privilege. Note, particularly, Antinoos' footstool pitch; Eurymakhos' repetition of this violent, nonverbal abuse; and Ktesippos' nasty third toss, an ox-hoof. These responses themselves are carefully graded by Homer, successively less successful yet more outrageous: the first hits Odysseus but does not shake him; the second misses Odysseus and hits an innocent, bystanding waiter; the vain third hits nothing but a wall.[30]

The literally liminal doorsill of the *megaron* serves as Odysseus' base of operations, as he plots how to reestablish his territorial, proxemic rights. He takes a marginal position on the οὐδός, the threshold of the *megaron*, from book 17, line 339, to book 22—intermittently yet insistently inserting himself into the endless party despite the suitors' condescending and fierce protest about the invasion of "their" space. It is reserved for acknowledged aristocrats like themselves.[31] He progressively gains a toehold in the great hall's feast as a parasite and lamplighter (18.317–44), another foothold later near the hot spot (hearth) of Penelope, and, penultimately, a precarious placement in the supposedly exclusive bow contest.[32]

---

who have a surplus to distribute (see Donlan 1982a, 8–9). The announcement of the different archery prize available to the stranger marks acknowledgment (for both Penelope and the suitors) of his different status (21.338–42). Eumaios and Penelope both sketch aspects of the prestation system of owed debts (14.124–32, 19.309–11).

30. 17.462–65, 18.396, 20.296–302. I will examine frequent, "progressive" triadic actions in the *Odyssey* in a separate paper. Woodhouse 1930, 79, lists "triplicities"; Shelmerdine 1969 sketches a similar, subtle phenomenon, Homer's practice of varying a motif by presenting successive stages of a single type-scene (such as feasting) at different points in the text.

31. Eumaios bluntly states that their behavior is unjust, indecent, unseemly, irreverent, and wasteful (14.80–95); cf. the beggar's view as "outside observer" (16.105–11).

32. 19.506, 20.258, 21.289. Russo delineated a proxemic analysis of the *Odyssey* in a 1985 abstract, partly summarized in his 1992 commentary ad 18.33 (but not found in the earlier Italian edition). Russo posits zones of marginal, moderate, accepted, and privileged importance, a kind of affective equivalent to Hall's four proxemic zones.

122 *Sardonic Smile*

Thresholds mark moments of danger, passages through uncertainty to new status, stylized liminal space and stop-time in biological and regularized communal rites of passage. The threshold is dramatized and ironized in many scenes of danger in the *Odyssey*. Athene/Mentes at the manor *oudos*, Odysseus before seeking the suppliant's privileges on Skheria, Kyklops' massive entryway, Odysseus' farewell address to Arete and departure, and his arrival at Kirke's palace offer examples of *oudos*-based events (1.104, 7.135, 9.240–44, 13.63, 10.310). *In* and *out* are two of the most powerful words in any language, symbolizing participation or exclusion/isolation.

The most significant threshold of all is that in Odysseus' own house. As beggar, he does not at first cross the threshold but stays outside. Then he sits (lowered elevation) on the threshold, holding the social margin, which is realized by the physical edge, a line of separation. The threshold provides a "home base" of safety, a ritualized zone of security and escape for the weak. Later, Odysseus sits just inside the ambiguous threshold, next to it, inching his way from liminality to territorial claim, a transition from outsider into master. In the challenge and counterchallenge of Eurymakhos and Aithon, the beggar steps on many toes. He avers that, were Odysseus to return, the doors, although wide, would suddenly narrow down for the man fleeing through them out the forecourt. This incorrect (!; see 22.44–78) prophecy, uniquely fantastic, plays on the human sense of entrapment and imprisonment as well as on the role of the doorway as a mechanism of social control (18.384–86). Finally, as avenging lord, Odysseus looses his arrows from atop the doorway, a symbol of the master's gatekeeping power and a proxemic marker of possession for the eccentric social player. It is capacious enough for two beggars where the wide doors meet. Odysseus now reaggregates himself to the community and the house, asserting membership and ownership in a spectacularly lethal manner.[33]

Odysseus transits the doorsill pass and reincorporates himself in the locale where he once was born. Spatial passage from outside to within symbolizes the change in, and enhancement of, his social status, much as van Gennep argues for all life-crisis, *rite de passage* ceremonies. Instead of ritualized participation and stable, shared traditions, however, Odysseus faces an anomalous, unique, life-threatening situation: his father self-exiled to the countryside from Ithaka town; his wife wooed as if a widow and self-isolated upstairs in her apartment; his son threatened with physical expulsion,

---

33. See 18.10, 32; 17.339, cf. 18.17; 17.413, 466, and 18.110; 17.339–40, 20.258–60, 22.1–2 and 72, 76. See also 18.17, 385; 22.203. See Segal 1967, 337–40, who also refers to the rituals of the restorative baths (330–31) and purifications, such as exorcism through fire (336). Russo ad 18.33, based on van Gennep [1908] 1960, esp. 19–22, 25.

disinheritance, and assassination; and his own very existence as *basileus* on earth and his zero-grade role as beggar in Ithaka treated as problematical, even by his wife, son, and father (19.315; 15.268; 1.166, 215–18; 24.289, note the wan, formulaic ἐμὸν παῖδ', εἴ ποτ' ἔην γε). The threshold of the main door—a traditional focus of sanctity and proprietary ritual—thus can signify for the hero either exclusion or control, depending on context.[34]

In Ithaka-town, gestures of respect, positions of deference, and the repertoire of movements that express social niceties hold the same meaning as elsewhere and before, but they are mentioned usually when honored in the breach. The audience's knowledge of the beggar's exalted true identity ironically intensifies appalled reaction to the display and disgrace of distance protocols and table etiquette. "The man of many moves" occupies only the ambivalent doorsill (he is neither in nor out) to feign respect for the suitors' alleged priority, superiority, and prerogatives in his own house (17.339). He sits on the sill, looking for entry, but abjectly begs for food from his own larder—after divine nudging from Athene (17.362, 365–66, 466; 18.110). He expects, as a man without status, to be served comestibles last and to compete last, if at all, with his "betters." These are the bodily practices of the disempowered.

Odysseus has "many moves" to make vis-à-vis those in his marginal zone (receptive Argos, challenger Iros, and the unperceptive suitors), a small space still open to the public.[35] The middle zone of social and personal space lies inside the house, where his intrusion usurps the beggar's doorsill, and where he arrogates the servants' functions of lighting the braziers (18.311–44). From this vantage point, he troubles the suitors and needs Telemakhos' intervention to protect him (18.405–9). Antinoos angrily reacts to the beggar's persistent approaches with proxemic instructions (17.446–47):

τίς δαίμων τόδε πῆμα προσήγαγε, δαιτὸς ἀνίην;
στῆθ' οὕτως ἐς μέσσον, ἐμῆς ἀπάνευθε τραπέζης.

Which nasty devil brought in to us this mischief, a party killjoy?
Stand off, in the middle, far away from my dining place.

---

34. Conversely, elusive Penelope's outrageously eccentric invitation to the beggar to sit by her privately and to chat offers access to privileged space that will be eternally denied to the suitors. The cross-gender dyadic intimacy at the sacred hearth foreshadows sexual union and climax in book 23.

35. Once beggar Odysseus leaves the sill, *he* never returns to dwell on it until, after the apocalypse, thence he slaughters the suitors (18.33, 22.2; cf. 18.343, 395; 19.1, 102; 20.1; 21.190).

The beggar has moved "too close for comfort." Melantho represents the fractious housemaids at their worst; she challenges his enhanced proxemic status (17.478, 566–67; 18.329–30, 336; 19.66–69). Odysseus eludes the suitors' attempts to evict him first from the beggar's recognized perch at the door and later from the lee of the privileged table near Amphinomos (18.395). Soon after, in *Odyssey* 19, his earlier invitation to private audience with the Queen is renewed (cf. 17.584). Sitting close, he becomes her confidant and coplotter in privileged, personal space, a position that the suitors crave but never enjoy (19.97, 209, 506, 505–99; 17.509, 529, 544; cf. Penelope's modesty at 18.184). With delicious irony, the beggar, sitting next to the queen, says that Odysseus is ἄγχι μάλ', οὐδ' ἔτι τῆλε φίλων, "very near, not at all far from friends" (19.301). Odysseus has continually gained access, proxemic prestige, and authority, a fact clear from his spatial behavior. He has progressed from nearly statusless outsider to trusted insider.

This inner space next to Penelope at the sacred hearth is a proxemic achievement and a semiotic clue at a preconscious level. Elevation and proximity—indicated by such words as *high, low, up, down, near,* and *far*—structure our reading of any situation, "real" or literary. The choreography of authority is constructed from these elements. This degree of contiguity to the queen is barely conceivable, even to a person of high status and privileged access, such as Telemakhos.[36] Contrast the touching of his body by the servant Eurykleia, which is sanctioned by differentials in status, age, and gender. She washes the poor guest, and, in the process, feels his thigh. She recognizes by touch his hunting scar, a symbol of male, teenaged initiation and a foregrounded emblem of identity. This serving-woman and nurse-maid had picked up the newborn and laid him on his grandfather's knee. She gave suck to the infant, a proxemic intimacy and a universal, paradigmatic bond of physical union (19.401, 482–83). Both her humble station before, and currently below, a guest-stranger and her prior physical intimacy with her now recognized lord impel her, confused and aphonic, to touch his

---

36. Gould 1973, 96–100, describes the protected nature of the Greek hearth and the females of the *oikos*. Henley, M. Hamilton, and Barrie Thorne 1985, 168–85 discuss gender-specific aspects of nonverbal behavior, such as touch indicating dominance, aggressive looking (leering, ogling, come-ons), dialogue initiation and turn taking, gender displays (such as voice pitch, posture, or clothing) that make sexual identity visible or salient, personal space, and "appeasement" ploys. They here refer to nonverbal behaviors of reassurance, such as smiling, head nodding, and body tension in posture. Nonverbal gender dimorphism and its asymmetrical obligations and rights in ancient literature and life deserve a separate study. These cultural cues transmit power and dominance messages.

beard as a sign of reverence. He instinctively grabs her throat, both emblematically, as a threat, and practically, to choke off any further revelation (19.393, 468, 473, 480, 505). Proxemic electricity and recognition short-circuit their desultory, if ironic, conversation about bodily similarities between the present beggar and the absent housemaster.

On Ithaka, Odysseus is liminal on several levels. First, proxemically liminal, he physically occupies the threshold after winning his first, auspicious victory against the suitor-surrogate, Iros (18.17, 110–17; 20.258). Second, socially liminal, vagrant and beggar, he is neither honored guest, acknowledged enemy, nor person of any certain identity at all. He is "betwixt and between," known by a caste status rather than by an individual past. Third, as unsanctioned competitor in a prize-contest, he stands briefly poised between the suitors' exclusion and the host's inclusion, between power and helplessness, between home and abroad, and between life and death.

No one on Ithaka, however, remains fixed, objective, or neutral; the social order is poorly balanced at the point of revolution, social and political. On arrival, Odysseus had been willing merely to share scraps with Iros at the peripheral threshold, the furthest point in the great house from the locus of *basileutic* power. But, after the bowshot, when he leaps to the threshold, the doorway's meaning is inverted. The consensual "firing line" for all the bowmen (21.124, 149; 22.2) now becomes Odysseus' checkpoint, and he is the gatekeeper, the guardian of exit and entry for the house.[37] Self-control, abnegation, the successful vagrant's skill par excellence, is reconverted to standard forms of "heroic" heroism. Henceforth, the *basileus* settles the suitors' fate, while they exhibit unheroic crowding and huddling behaviors more suited to ignoble classes.

Odysseus penetrates the house's deeper recesses slowly. He defers revelation with everyone.[38] The great house itself participates in the continuing postmassacre deceit—"resounding aloud to the thud of [dancing] footsteps" (23.146). The family has excised the former uncontrolled din. The dwelling-space of Odysseus is purged of pollution. Proper and purified heroic and orderly spaces are restored.

---

37. The loyal servant Argos the dog, similarly disgraced, now deceased, serves as a telescoped narrative of status inversion and proxemic reversal. The dog on the dung heap dies alone and excluded just at the moment when the hero penetrates the enemy's perimeter. The narrator highlights both Odysseus' emotional susceptibilities and his self-control.

38. The ultimate seal of reunion and approval is the marital coitus in the hidden, rooted bed, a nonverbal ritual or convention (θεσμός, as Homer expresses it at 23.296, hapax) at the ultimate degree of proxemic intimacy, mutual interpenetration and envelopment.

5. Penelope the Polytropic Communicator

Penelope seems to enjoy a ground-floor sitting room ("Queen's *megaron*") from which she can overhear, if not oversee, the suitors in the main social space, the *megaron* (17.492–93, 20.387–89). Hence, a reserved staircase leads to the bedchamber above and away (ὑπερῷον, 1.362 = 23.1; also 19.600–602, 21.356, 4.717–18). Lockable, private chambers, *thalamoi* (not always a bedroom), depots, pantries, and storerooms, perhaps below or further inside, are mentioned (cf. 2.337; such rooms are common in Mycenaean palace remains).

Space is somewhat segregated by gender, but Penelope can enter and leave—that is, descend to or ascend from—the *megaron* at will, mixing with men in ways unknown to respectable women in classical Athens; but she always summons and is accompanied by women chaperones. She controls her seclusion, except when her *dolos* was disclosed and she was quasi-judicially discovered in flagrante (2.94–110). The semantic nexus of proxemic terms (including *hyperoion*) connects to motifs of "inner, upper, away," and eventually to "chastity" (Nagler 1974, 77–79).

"Gendered spaces" correlate with status differences as does age-based segregation. Knowledge and power are shared out in secret and separated meetings of the *basileis*. They leave the palace, meet in seclusion, and return inside afterward (4.659–74, 16.342–408). Spatial segregation furnishes a mechanism of domination. Penelope "keeps her distance" by retreating to the women's quarters or standing near the men's area. Tactics of the habitat facilitate her determined singleness. She stays out by manipulating the system of spatial barriers, and, just so, Odysseus gets in. Social processes employ spatial segregation for the benefit of the advantaged classes. Those disadvantaged by status, gender, or age, or by a mix of such factors—those who challenge the *status quo*—require spatial know-how to survive.[39] Gendered spaces instrumentally segregate and symbolically separate the empowered from the "weaker" sex.

Territoriality—behavior by which an organism lays claim to an area and defends it, keeping others of its species out or in (Hall 1966, 7–14)—generally occurs out-of-awareness by means of unobtrusive body language, facial expression, and paralinguistic phenomena (growls, tone, and voice

---

39. Cf. gendered spaces in some children's schools, women's and men's lavatories, jail cells, and, at least in the past, at Oxford High Table. Consider religious regulations that keep women on balconies in Orthodox Jewish synagogues and prohibit Muslim women from entering a mosque and Catholic women from becoming Pope or even priests. See Nagler 1974, 77–79; Spain 1992, 5, 15.

volume; spraints, animal excrement, also mark "possession"). The suitors of Penelope are much preoccupied with maintaining group affiliation and cohesion so that one of them might gain possession of the woman, a prerequisite for establishing individual dominance and the others' submission. Telemakhos, Penelope, and (implicitly and nonverbally) the beggar Aithon question their place in the manor house, their pecking order, and their self-determined exclusive rights to plunder the family and occupy the widow's bed.

The suitors repeatedly try to make their privileges explicit. They jockey for place precisely because their position is contested. They try to shut out (proxemic exclusivity) all other comers, especially the pathetic beggar. They are right to object to his claiming privilege from two mutually exclusive identities. As present beggar, he has gained entry and access to food scraps; but as former nobleman and warrior, he claims inclusion in the contest of the bow. The suitors' closed-market strategy italicizes the precarious nature of their dubious and downright illegitimate claims. Meanwhile, they occupy another man's domicile and leer at Penelope, another man's wife. The narrator does not penetrate her motives or responses but expresses Odysseus' glee in her duping the dopey suitors into giving bride-gifts—among alter-adaptors the gendered correlate to heroic *xenia* (18.281–83). His collusive appreciation of her verbal and nonverbal finesse provides one facet of their "likemindedness," *homophrosyne*—which means grief and expense to a couple's enemies.[40]

Efforts to separate oneself from the dominant group defines the behavior of the relatively impotent (in heroic terms) Penelope, Laertes, and (to a less successful extent) Leodes. All three disapprove of the suitors and want to distance themselves from their infantile and high-handed behavior.[41] Young Telemakhos can command his mother, Penelope, to withdraw to her women's quarters because of the asymmetrical, lesser freedoms of Homeric women. Her successful manipulation of a circumscribed realm of proxemic freedom clearly elucidates her sentiments. She, when she chooses, may advance toward the men or disaffiliate herself and retreat to protected areas of the house, isolated rooms of her own. She continually asserts control of her

---

40. "All is fair in *their* love and *her* war" (Poyatos 1986, 502; Eibl-Eibesfeldt 1972, 302–3; Murnaghan 1986, 109, 113; Pedrick 1988, 94–95). See 6.180–85 and Russo ad 18.281–83, deconstructing the analysts' epistemological crux concerning Odysseus' knowledge of Penelope's motive in her charade (e.g., Fenik 1974, 120).

41. 11.187–96, 18.302, 21.145; cf. Hesiod's silver race, *Erga* 128–39: homebodies, fools, mutual insult (ὕβριν ἀτάσθαλον), bad faith, and nonsacrifice. Theoklymenos and, briefly, Amphinomos see the pressing need to dissociate themselves from such dangerous behaviors (20.364–72, 18.153–57).

space—and successfully. Penelope is proxemically symbolized by the hidden recess, the raised retreat, up and away from the hurly-burly below.[42]

Like her modern Greek counterpart, the wife and mother Penelope protects the house, its stores, scion, and honor, by segregating screens of evasions, gender ruses, and unfulfilled promises. She weaves the shroud of Laertes and later unravels it in her helpfully secluded "personal space." She sweetly persuades the noble thugs that grumbling Telemakhos is too young yet to be territorial and thereby to threaten them (4.663-68; 18.216-18, 269-71; 19.160-61; 21.105, Telemakhos plays along with the charade). This factor of proxemic concern explains her continuation of his (otherwise puzzling) enforced, overextended adolescence.

Penelope demands more gifts from the suitors, who agree to her demands, depart, then deliver the costly gifts. She invites the recently grubby stranger to a private parley. She initiates the idea of the peculiar bride contest of the bow in *her* courtyard. The vagrant encourages the execution of the plan, and she announces the contest, the rules, and the consequences (21.68-77); she watches the competition, and the prize herself speaks up at the crisis for the vagrant's turn to try the bow (21.311-42).

The only proxemic degree the disguised Odysseus has yet to enjoy with his wife is the reestablishment of intimate distance. This follows his unintended certification of his identity by his outburst and knowledge of the arrangement of intimate space and private furniture in the forbidden space of the bedroom. In the only room that the modern world names for a piece of furniture stands the fixed bed that cannot be moved out, ἐκτός. It is secured and undisplaceable, ἔμπεδον and ἐντός (23.178, 203, 190). Knowledge of it is a sure sign, μέγα σῆμα, of the husband's rightful place and space (23.188, 202, 294-99). The suitors had each prayed to share Penelope's bed, an object that serves as a common metaphor for the intimate proxemic zone in which touching and lovemaking occur (18.213, 258; 23.300).

Penelope's proxemics exploit opportunities reserved to women under the gender dimorphism of heroic Greek life. The men, beggar and suitors, deploy outside and inside, standing, sitting, stooping, and crouching. Penelope has the additional, female, vertical axis of the ground floor or the upstairs, where she may remain hidden away in her chambers. The men operate solely downstairs, on the main floor, but Penelope can rise above them at will or can

---

42. 1.362, 17.505, 18.206, 21.8. Proxemic degree zero—isolation—paradoxically represents every society's highest and lowest positions (royalty and pariah status or solitary confinement). All societies design for the outlaw involuntary dissociation from the community, jailing. In the *Odyssey*, Melanthios serves a brief term as imprisoned miscreant (22.200-201, cf. 22.126-30).

at will become visible to the suitors. She moves sometimes down and nearer to allure or reassure them, but never very near to them, never into the personal, much less the taboo intimate, distance. At times, she has considered the strain of staying at risk in Odysseus' establishment less desirable than going far away, home to her natal family as a widow or even out of Ithaka to marry a new, live husband (19.579, 531)—or so she tells the attentive guest. The modern Greeks' double-bed, *to krevati,* is still the locus of prenuptial rituals and postnuptial sanctity. No one but the married couple will even sit on it.

By the double-cross deception, the mistress of the house forces Odysseus to show his true self, surprised, hurt, and angry over furniture rearrangements and space reallocation in their bedroom. Then Penelope surrenders and collapses her closely guarded space in a proxemic and gestural submission display (23.207–8):

δακρύσασα δ' ἔπειτ' ἰθὺς δράμεν, ἀμφὶ δὲ χεῖρας
δειρῇ βάλλ' Ὀδυσῆι, κάρη δ' ἔκυσ' ἠδὲ προσηύδα·

Shedding tears she ran straight across to him, her arms
she put around his neck. She kissed his head and said: . . .

Women's deliberate misdirection through "come-hither" misleading smiles, beggars' deferential elevations and postures, and servants' reassuring distances contribute to the Laertid household's controlled public personalities. These proxemic strategies conceal more than they reveal about the family's intentions. Penelope must keep the besieging suitors out of her quarters, her bed, and her body. The physical, sexual reunion of *Odyssey* 23 is anticipated by the subtler, yet no less lucid, and carefully wrought spatial progression in books 17–19. Odysseus has advanced from distant, unknown alien to sympathizer, ally, and intimate friend (no other "guest" or "stranger" is ever called "friend" by her). Odysseus must penetrate the house to regain control of the *megaron*'s activities, his bedroom, and his mistress. He has passed through a reinitiation rite, starting as the most alien outsider and ending as the ultimate insider in Ithaka. The couple's equal aplomb and success is conveyed by deed, speech, and peripheral gesture. Their proxemic maneuvers also preserve house, home, henchmen, and appurtenances.

6. The House of Odysseus

Odysseus' *domata* exemplifies Homer's attention to proxemics. Buildings never talk and rarely move. Nevertheless, persons exist in personal space and interact differently in differently defined and owned spaces, such as caves, bedrooms, and assemblies. Habitations, work places, and political areas affect Thersites' behavior and Odysseus'. The princely houses of Nestor's Pylos and Menelaos' Sparta (θεῖος δόμος, 4.43—hapax) strike awe into those who enter them. Polyphemos appears to have absolute control of his primitive (cave-)space, gatekeeping, patrolling his lair, and enforcing savage rules. Odysseus manages to sneak out of murderous confinement, just as he sneaks into Alkinoos' *domata,* an earthly palace despite its magic guard dogs (6.300–302, 7.91–94). The house of the Laertids supplies as interesting a character as Amphinomos or Argos, the pathetic dog. I would argue that the house signifies more, since it is the locus of half the poem, the costly prize for which all strive, and a symbol of supreme social, political, and economic (i.e., heroic) achievement in Ithaka. The Ithakan big house is the source of family identity for all of Odysseus' family and of local power for all of the island and beyond. Real estate (land) and architecture (buildings), human uses of space, indirectly determine how people see themselves and others. The articulated manse—with its specialized rooms, private and public spaces, and cobwebbed *thalamos* (empty for twenty years)—and the expropriated, occupied *megaron* communicate wealth, threat, and the premeditated infraction of heroically sanctioned exclusivity.

Homer represents the world and its spaces more directly than our psychological century usually admits. Space, as an epic entity with variably penetrable boundaries, often serves as the medium for personal expression. Nowadays, Homeric directness has been evicted; Homeric perimeters have been largely annihilated. Primate territoriality, however, remains an ethological basic that is always capable of many levels of textual appreciation. Odysseus' stringent self-regulation allows an *out*cast on Ithaka to become an *in*vader. His mobile gestures and cryptic bodily surfaces enable him to exchange placelessness for the most coveted position on the island.

The "prosperous house" motif becomes somewhat disheveled in the vocal complaints of lord, lady, heir apparent, and suitors, but its nonverbal substance appears central to the conflicts (e.g., 1.386–404, 14.90–108, 16.383–86, 20.211–16). This establishment and its environs are worth fighting for. At Alkinoos' table, Odysseus states the *Leitmotif* of fair feasts in happy households. His relation of a fantasy of orderly banqueting prepares us for degenerate Cyclopean, Circean, and Ithacan versions (9.5–11).

Proxemics of the house densely texture the *Odyssey*. All senses except taste are drawn into Homeric proxemic communication: vivid touch at the intimate distance; sight, hearing, and smell at the social. Spiritual and emotional distance are concretely expressed by measurable separation in space by both actions and notable epic similes.[43] Symbolic and instrumental proxemic acts encapsulate compressed information about society and the individual's face, place, and space within it.

Even Eurykleia, Eumaios, and other attachments of the house, part of the *oikos,* serve as its loyal voices. The guard dog that pricks up its head and ears, the maid who drops Odysseus' leg and turns her head to her mistress at the unexpected (nonverbal) news, and the doors to the treasure room that bellow like a bull when Penelope opens them (17.291, 19.468–77, 21.48–49) are three nonverbal "voices" of the inarticulate house.[44]

The neglect and exclusion of Argos reveal displaced or "surrogate contempt" for his master. Dog and master are excluded from the feast and find themselves ἐν πολλῇ κόπρῳ (17.297; see Schwartz 1975, 180, 183, on the *kopros* motif). The faithful hunting dog alone, however, penetrates Odysseus' god-given disguise. The associations of home and its appurtenances give special resonance to that nuclear and most precious territory in the *Odyssey.*

Discussion of the Ithakan house requires clarity about its spatial organization and unfamiliar architectural terminology.[45] But the attitudes attached to the various areas make them significant for this chapter. The deployment of posture, elevation, innerness, closeness, and exclusion in the house determine their interest.

---

43. For example, his sailors gather around Odysseus as calves around their mother cow, and Penelope embraces Odysseus as shipwrecked sailors embrace the land when they reach it (10.410–18, 23.233–46).

44. In fact, another "reverse [sexual] simile" (cf. H. Foley 1978) has Penelope penetrate her husband's house's inmost recess (θαλαμόνδε ... ἔσχατον, 21.8–9; 21.46–50). She removes the protective (chastity) belt (cf. *Il.* 14.214), inserts the key, and thrusts it in the hole, face-to-face. The doors shriek and give way to her determined intent.

45. I have no solution to various archaeological and philological problems of ancient standing associated with Homeric architecture, such as the meanings of *megaron,* the layout of the farmhouse rooms, the height of the stony and/or wooden thresholds, the nature of the *orsothyre,* and the location of the men- and women-servants' sleeping quarters (up or down, right or left of the *megaron,* etc. (4.718, 17.339–41, 22.126). Consult, for bibliography and details, Lorimer 1950, with plan on 408; Wace 1962; Drerup 1969, only 3 and 128–33; and the learned William Beck, 1955–, s.vv. δῶμα, μέγαρον: "a mixture of elements from Mycenean and geometric times." See also Fernandez-Galiano in Russo et al. 1992, 210–17, or the summary and illustration in Jones 1988a, 10–11. The palace at Pylos (thirteenth-century B.C.E.) and the House of the Columns at Mycenae have floor plans that well suit the events of the *Odyssey.* Although in size the first is too grand and the second too small, the exigencies of oral epic poetry can accommodate up- and down-sizing. Knox 1970 tabulates and analyzes the blurred Homeric vocabulary for house and palace, *oikos* and *domata.* She finds consistent usage, the former word *never* used for gods' residences, the latter often employed for gods and the magnificent dwellings of princely humans, i.e., palaces.

Ragged Odysseus' arrival home is stopped short and punctuated by his admiring, detailed description of the manse, τάδε δώματα κάλ' Ὀδυσῆος (17.261–71), which no one could scorn, as they can and do scorn its rightful owner in beggar's disguise. Odysseus' *oikos* is a "second-class palace" (Wace 1962) or a "large, rustic farmhouse" (Halverson 1985). For this reason, Telemakhos wonders at (σέβας μ' ἔχει, 4.72–75) Spartan Menelaos' much superior, vast, and lavish establishment replete with gold, silver, bronze, amber, and ivory. Odysseus shows a similar admiration of Alkinoos' palace. He expresses again, as beggar, appreciation of the distant sight, smell (κνίση), and sound from within the Ithakan party-house. He then enters it to approach the suitors for charity (7.132–34; 17.342–50, 414, 447). The Ithakan dwelling is not consistently a fancy palace, yet this noble pile's integrity in space and time dominates the poem's second half. As the *Iliad* focuses on Akhilleus' wounded honor as warrior in camp and battle, so the *Odyssey* focuses on the honor of the house (here subsuming the clan, wife, child, servants, and stores) and so sometimes glorifies the unpretentious physical building. "Odysseus is the hero of the οἶκος" (Halverson 1985, 143–44).

From front to back on the ground floor (from *aithousa* to *prothyron, aule, prodomos, oudos,* and *megaron*), the big man's house becomes less open to public entry, more reserved. The ground floor is the scene for all social activity beyond the family and its dependents. Guests of all ranks sleep "outside" in the *aithousa,* or portico, of the courtyard (3.398–99, 4.296–305, cf. 18.101–3). In Ithaka, this area has an earthen surface. There is a midden for manure beyond the front gate (20.150, 17.297–99; cf. Stanford 1965, 2: 435–36; Wace 1962, 492–93).

The *megaron* room is the focus of the social structure of the Homeric house and the locus of the main conflicts in Ithaka (other than those in the *agore*). There, the *basileis* eat, drink, and are merry. There, too, Telemakhos seems to set up axes for the problematic bow contest. "Agglutinative grandeur"[46] makes it large enough for all the epic action.

The house is dishonored because the suitors consume its stores and livestock (16.431, 21.332, 22.36) and despoil its women, the slaves already and the mistress before long.[47] The *oikos* is uniquely personified as the victim of

---

46. Wace's fine phrase 1962, 489; Fernandez-Galiano in Russo et al. 1992, 210–17. See 19.573; 21.100, 124. At Pylos, the palace *megaron* remains measure 42 x 37 feet, and at Mycenae, they measure 42 x 39 feet—for whatever mere "reality" is worth in the analysis of oral epic with its "homeostatic tendencies"; cf. I. Morris 1986, 86–87.

47. Anyone distressed by Odysseus' lack of "Christian charity" in killing every last suitor fails to appreciate the shame and stains already inflicted on his honor. Such critics bring to mind

the suitors' intolerable depradations (1.250, 1.248 = 16.125, 19.133), as nearly shattered like a ship in a storm (2.48–49), wounded (23.9), ravaged (1.378, 22.36), and destroyed (1.377). These metaphors characterize the *oikos* as more than a building and even more than the collective physical objects and locale of the Laertid family. The suitors have nullified Telemakhos' and Penelope's scarcest resource, private space, but Odysseus trumps their violation with his own intrusion, by means of a subtle spatial-status joker card, nonnegotiable beggary. He undercuts the ground they walk on. He has the weapon of the weak, a visible, invincibly low status.

7. Conclusions

Proxemics enrich the coherence and color of the *Odyssey*. Individuals communicate with the position and distance of their bodies, and they do not fail to use closeness and "farness" to help express what they want to "say" or hide. Human beings require these bodily messages to understand each other. In addition to their explicit words, reported thoughts, and nonsymbolic, instrumental deeds (like chewing on raw flesh or poking out an eye), Homeric bodies constantly emit heroic and unheroic proxemic messages by their position, distances, and orientation.[48]

Homer's reported nonverbal behavior reinforces or undercuts his characters' words. On Phaiakia, Odysseus underlines his explicit claims by proxemics and gestures that augment his words, known in the jargon as "illustrators."[49] These speech-related, "redundant" proxemic behaviors appear when he remains at a distance from maiden Nausikaa in a socially unsanctioned encounter to reinforce his verbally expressed respect for the gender-tabooed, untouchable creature (6.143–47), and when he stoops *and* embraces the knees of Queen Arete while he verbally begs protection. Further, we note "self-priming," self-effacing postures and positions when he tries to disappear, look small, excuse himself, and sit out the Phaiakian "macho"

---

the Persians (Hdt. 1.4.2) who thought the Persian Wars too great a consequence for mere rape of women.

48. Orientation usually concerns the facing or nonfacing relationship of one person's head and/or body to another's, but it may also denote direction of gaze toward an object, which can nonverbally communicate immediate concerns to "third parties." Homeric examples include the assemblies' focus on each speaker's possession of the "floor-giving" scepter; the companions' fixed attention to the sleeping Odysseus' bag with Aiolos' precious gift, after meaningful glances at each other; and Telemakhos' locked-on gaze at Odysseus, waiting for the (nonverbal) signal (2.38, 80; 10.37, 44; 20.385–86, 21.431).

49. Ekman and Friesen 1972, 357–58, employ this term for fist shaking, finger pointing, etc. Homer refers to comparable illustrators, such as knee clasping, dark looks, and Odysseus' accelerated advance to the discus competition on Skheria.

134   *Sardonic Smile*

displays at the contests and when he finally competes only last (deferential chronemics) in the games. When Odysseus requests conversation at the personal distance in the Otherworld, Aias silently walks away from him. Not only is this silence[50] more expressive than any abrasive words could be, but reorientation (turning his back) and increasing the social distance send the message in yet another channel. Later, on Ithaka, denied his beggar's portion, Odysseus, with scornful words and body-talk, draws away and turns his back on beetle-browed Antinoos. That dastard's footstool hits him on the back without shaking him. Zero movement (nonwithdrawal) signifies hidden heroic strength (11.563–65, 17.453–64).

Much body-talk could be called redundant if communication were entirely a matter of logic. Do we have somatic repetition, or is the vocal expression to be considered the "echo"? Communication requires redundancy, however, so we might better view the two channels' "overlap" as complementary *and even explanatory* with respect to symbolic systems. Odysseus needs to employ all channels to achieve his difficult goals. "Subversive" or contradictory messages in postures and proxemic adjustments have produced subtler effects than verbal raillery could have. Odysseus' aggressive begging, comprising words, postures, and close proximity (414, 447, 450, 453, 466), proxemically pushes Antinoos to violence, although it superficially suggests that the vagrant is entirely at the aristocrat's untender mercy (17.413–62). Iros' cowering, his shaking flesh, and the force that the menservants apply to drag him toward his opponent betray his real sentiments. Although he raises his fists in the ritualized "squaring off" gesture that usually indicates readiness to slug it out, the ring-enforced personal distance of the bout undermines and ironizes any alleged willingness (18.76–89). He then falls in the dust, the formulaic verse echoing the death throes of animals downed and the dropped elevation of better warriors. He is dragged away from the laughing princelings as a sign of proxemic dishonor (18.98; cf. *Il.* 6.453, 16.469, 18.101–7), an exile, no longer πτωχῶν κοίρανος, "big-man of beggars."

Homer "reports" proxemics—distance, elevation, and orientation—to describe *and explain* interpersonal relations. Proxemic data, a subset of

---

50. More than once, Telemakhos lapses into awkward but communicative silences—communicative both to other characters and to the more knowledgeable, external audiences. Menelaos too finds himself groping for words (4.116–20 with 137–39). Besslich 1966 and Poyatos 1981 explore the "semanticity of silence." Thus, both generally nonloquacious heroes are characterized by their nonverbal, half-unconscious table manners as well as by their diplomatic, chosen words. See 3.469, cf. 3.389; 4.51. Silence can also convey passive assent as well as dissent: see 2.240; cf. 17.465; 20.320; 21.386 (formulaic, gendered voicelessness; see Fernandez-Galliano in Russo et al. 1992, ad loc.).

nonverbal behavior, constitute a separate channel of textual information parallel to speech but not necessarily running in the same direction. Proxemic acts sometime support—but sometimes contradict—words. Contrast meanings and intentions in Menelaos' words and candid hand stroking for Telemakhos with Kirke's treacherous words and enchanting food for the sailors or Antinoos' touch of spurious friendship (4.609–14, 10.230–43, 2.301–5).

Human communicative systems generally observe the principle of nonexclusivity, but in literature as in life, actions prevail over words in cases of contradiction. Sometimes proxemic acts by themselves substitute for words, sometimes they constitute the primary but not the sole message. Odysseus' wordless approach of the royal Skherian hearth, Melanthios' nasty kick of the wanderer, and Odysseus' post-bull's-eye seizure of the doorsill may exemplify these possibilities. Body-talk contrasting to speech, perceived as irony in the palmary case of the sartorial disguise of Odysseus, humble in speech but incongruently forward in proxemics, is probably as common as complementary messages. The mute messages of the body communicate sentiment while preserving deniability.

When liar Odysseus describes to Penelope his Cretan hospitality as Aithon for Odysseus, he drives her to sobbing by describing himself (present) as absent. Homer touchingly notes that the wife was κλαιούσης ἑὸν ἄνδρα παρήμενον, "crying for her man sitting right beside her" (19.209). For the audience, proxemics here poignantly contradicts the fable being told, and of course Penelope's grief adds to our pleasure. Here, the action has meaning that the deceived Penelope cannot know, for she still supposes (or so we suppose) that the beggar is anyone but Odysseus. This spectrum of proxemic usage is congruent to "real life." Territorial integrity and trespass or violation provide both themes and metaphors for exclusion, welcome, penetration, and possession.[51]

Hellenic bodily expressions, including proxemics, sometimes resemble and sometimes differ from modern European, feudal Japanese, or American versions (ethnogests). The entire body (face, head, trunk, and limbs) is saturated with, and constantly emits, psychological and social meanings. These are often coded in positions of arrogated rank and in movements of approval and disapproval in openly stratified societies. The *Odyssey* exhibits nonverbal behavior in every scene and on every page. Hierarchy and lineage are asserted, preserved, and transmitted. Homer shows rather than tells audiences what people want or dislike and how they feel. The canonical text

---

51. Further studies will isolate Homeric vocabulary of heroic proxemics, its relative frequency in various books of the *Iliad,* the *Odyssey,* and *Homeric Hymns,* and habits varying by gender, age-group, and social class.

enabled Hellenic society to remember how to perform. Reading the face's expressions and the position and movements of the limbs as cognizable text, Hellenes communicated much that our psychological century allots to novelistic psychological analysis.

The pervasive contribution of spatial semiotics—proxemics—to heroic characterization and plot has invited our attention. Audiences have always been aware of characteristic, often formulaic gestures. Homer's nonverbal behaviors, such as nods, beetling brows, and rituals of supplication (for example, bended knees), and his notice of social meanings of space suggest not the analyst Wilamowitz' notorious "patchwork poetry" (a choice 1884 quotation appears in Katz 1991, 96) but a complex and consistent presentation of character, plot, and narrative "clues." Homer invites audiences to note clues of deception but occludes the obvious signs from stumbling suitors. They miss even obvious hints and fumble the manipulation of proxemic protocols.[52]

The presentation of self to others, verbally and nonverbally, creates social personality. Consequently, the "Bible of the Greeks"—with its pervasive contrasts of true and false messages of voice and body, deception and revelation—constructs, maintains, and rips away the necessary and varied faces and gestures that *all* people exhibit. Posture and proximity, proxemics, are equally telling (Winkler 1990, 133–37; du Boulay 1976).

The topography of social position creates a nonverbal rhetoric of status and heroism. The prepositions and adverbs *before, in front of, above, close to,* and even *"in the middle"* situate the privileged party. *Behind, in back of, below, far from,* and *at the edge* describe the proxemically disadvantaged. Human space—"proper distance"—is assimilated to cultural hierarchies and values. Proxemic assertion conveys both topographical place and rank. The spatial signifier (precedence, elevation, and zones of inviolability) encodes social meaning. The *Odyssey* inscribes important messages and feelings in location and distance.

---

52. 18.74: the suitors notice the interloper's powerful limbs, proving that they are not totally blind. 17.481–87 and 18.403–4 show them staring at equivalent windows of opportunity, but the suitors, despite glimmers of light, fail to see through them. Their failures to understand are just as pleasurable to audiences as Laertid perceptivity.

Part 3
Nonverbal Characterization in the *Odyssey*

Chapter 8
Youth: The Boy-Man's Body-Talk

Standard behaviors are transmitted across generations. Infants learn through biological and ethological mechanisms (sucking, smiling, imprinting "faces"). As children grow and gain self-control, they assimilate social behaviors (shaking hands firmly, meeting a guest's gaze, answering adults' dumb questions). Parental or pseudoparental guidance also appears for various Homeric life-stages. Both poems refer to generational bonding as well as conflict: infant Akhilleus with baby-sitter Phoenix, Astyanax with his parents, Nausikaa and Telemakhos with their parents, Pisistratos with his father Nestor, old heroes and heroines with Telemakhos, precipitous but deferential Diomedes, Hekabe and Priam with their son Hektor, and even pseudomotherly Athene with her protégé Odysseus. Role-reversed Odysseus, the returned son, re-creates his physically decrepit and severely isolated father.

The body-talk of youth includes "spontaneous" and ceremonious gestures. Homer enjoys picturing the impetuosity of youngsters. Father Odysseus says of Nausikaa to mother Arete: αἰεὶ γάρ τε νεώτεροι ἀφραδέουσιν (7.294), "Younger people are always somewhat less careful." Audiences respond delightedly to vomiting infant Akhilleus, baby Astyanax's instinctual backpedaling fear, teenaged Odysseus' accident and wound while on his first hunt, Telemakhos' curtailing of his mother's expression of concern in his first-time traveler's hurry, Pisistratos' young and eager response to guests espied on the beach, Nausikaa's sudden whim to leave her house, and her imprudent young suitor's thoughtless insult at the public games of the royal guest. In the comic interludes of the *Iliad's* games, the vehemently angry chariot-race driver Antilokhos expostulates at the loss of a prize and its attendant honor. He threatens to attack Akhilleus himself (*Il.* 23.587–90). Antilokhos eventually apologizes. His formulaic references to the hasty thoughts and lightweight minds of youth are nonetheless true despite their conventional language. The relative inexperience of youth can lead to deep wounding as well as gaffes, crossed signals, embarrassed pauses, and the elders' controlled amusement. The next step depends on the authority figure's "take" of the situation. Compare insecure Agamemnon in *Iliad* 1 with Akhilleus in 23.

Instinctive, ritualized, and personal behaviors of the young carry precise messages to peers and elders. These faces, postures, and gestures are not always adequate communications by themselves, but they are never otiose. They often allow inferences about motives not yet or ever made explicit. We can make the familiar text again unfamiliar, attending to unheroic, but sensible, children. Athene, disguised as a girl-child, informs Odysseus: ῥεῖα δ' ἀρίγνωτ' ἐστὶ καὶ ἂν πάϊς ἡγήσαιτο / νήπιος (6.300–301), "Even a silly little child could guide you easily to well-known things."[1] Thus, we see new generations join life's well-organized parade and make it orderly and bearable.

"Natural" Hellenic composure produces youngsters of great dignity as well as awkwardness. The poised princess Nausikaa stands her ground at the shore, and the proletarian sons of bondsman Dolios appear with equal aplomb near the poem's close (24.387–411). They welcome the lord both verbally and with a gesture—the mysterious "pledge" or "toast," δεικανόωντο—and they clasp his hand, but they do not presume to kiss him as their father did.[2]

Every culture and subculture teaches its young how to tell the truth—and how to deceive. Many youthful and mature recreations depend on bluffing and feinting (e.g., Halloween costumes, "Go fish," poker, chess, "cowboys and Indians," thumbwrestling), as do real-life business, academic, and mili-

---

1. The thematic epithet *nepios* appears twenty-seven times in the *Odyssey*, where it is applied to Telemakhos, Odysseus' companions, the suitors, and various others. The term, generic for children and fools, signifies qualities of social and cognitive disconnectedness opposite to those of the cautious and aware hero. See the 1976 Harvard Ph.D. dissertation of S.T. Edmunds, published as *Homeric Nepios* in New York in 1990.

2. 24.410; cf. 18.111 with Russo ad loc., 15.150; see also Bremmer in Bremmer and Roodenburg 1991, on "quiet and noisy" strides and stances of commanders. The aged, polyprogenitive servant and his sons are stopped in their tracks by Odysseus' amazing return. When they recover themselves, fond or fearful Dolios, Laertes' age-mate and helper, opens his arms, runs up to Odysseus, takes his master's wrist, and kisses it. As father of the gratuitously abusive lackeys Melantho and Melanthios, Dolios perhaps realizes that his family's survival depends on extravagant deference displays. Around Odysseus quietly cluster the farmer's sons. The distinction between father's and sons' greeting finds partial explanation in Dolios' prior acquaintance with their common master.

Tribal societies often display more nuanced and stylized etiquette, defined by age as well as social gradations, than our pseudoegalitarian, industrialized contemporaries. Odysseus is master for all, but he is also very senior to the boy-servants. They do not yet possess the right of intimate-distance embrace and kiss. Age as well as prior (non)relationship keep them at "their distance." They do not enjoy equal access or right of affect display. Sexual protocols, furthermore, more strongly control expressions of physical affection between persons of virile years, regardless of sex.

tary wheeling and dealings. "Mere" words and gestures, large and small, transmit affect and character, so the wary interactant subconsciously calibrates *every* observed behavior. The *Odyssey* immerses characters and audiences in this urgent need to decode simultaneous, but not always congruent, signals.

Telemakhos presents the limiting case, the dangers of growing up amid macho thugs who wish to seize your mother and your inheritance. Public and private contacts with acquainted and unacquainted others teach youngsters the range and working of norms that regulate interactions. The rules that "go without saying" never prevent clever exceptions, such as the manipulation of norms by people with inside information and the desire to manage protocols for personal advantage. Telemakhos reads signals and parries thrusts intermittently from the beginning. On the one hand, he intemperately and pathetically bursts into pitiful tears in public assembly, but on the other, he knows how to draw back from unctuous Antinoos' hypocritical smile and pseudoparental intimacy of stroking and hand-holding (2.80–81, 301–2, 321).

Gestures bind human wills through bodies. Symbolic acts produce real results. The "dumb" insolence of reluctant Akhaian troops at Troy in *Iliad* 2 and the proud swagger of young Phaiakian and Ithaka-area nobles put across, as they are meant to, serious messages about intent and status arrogation.[3] Gestures and facial expressions, then, perform his social communications (guest welcome, parent comfort, invitations to fight) and reveal his hidden emotions (frown, smile, alacritous spring toward guests or the axes). Gestures articulate, emphasize, and ironize his jockeying for social acceptance and dominance. If we read all of Homer's languages, attentive to these signals, we realize, beyond a series of anecdotes, a four-dimensional text and an exemplary, if nearly fatal, heroic education of one young man in $τιμή$ (honor) management.

Semiegalitarian, but always accumulating respect, the heroes in Ithaka possess limited power to coerce. As we re-create the coherent society that Homer and his cocreative audience took for granted, our social archaeology discovers a world of competitive giving, insult and amends in status manipulation, and validating ceremonies of welcome, entertainment, and departure. Once-*nepios* Telemakhos, impatient and clumsy (1.297, 4.818, 11.449, 19.530 [earlier days]; cf. the sham at 21.102–5, 131–32), becomes a masterful master of ceremonies.

---

3. The culture of heroic epic has a complete repertoire of gestures, a *langue*. From this pool, Telemakhos has to choose his particular *parole*. Social context (age, gender, birth) as well as idiosyncratic responses narrow his choices.

Management of honor, power, and authority includes abusive taunts like "senseless, unformed" *nepios,* symbolic acts like gifting "give and take," body language like deference elevations, distances, and accommodating gestures. In Ithaka, there is face-saving and face-losing, status advance and creative degradation. The beggar moves up and the suitors down when they botch their original authority advantages. In the *Iliad,* Akhilleus eventually wins every verbal and nonverbal contest against Agamemnon (Donlan 1993, 160). Just so, in the *Odyssey,* Odysseus as beggar and Telemakhos as returned householder, with self-restraint and deceptive behaviors usually deemed unheroic, lead their enemies into violation of divinely sanctioned law and fatal errors. They publicly deconstruct their own "front" in quarreling and lose face to inferiors.

The traditional audience senses irony because of foreknowledge of the plot and familiarity with ten thousand formulae of Hellenic one-upmanship and powerlessness, both verbal vaunt and nonverbal taunt. Telemakhos' story functions as a "gateway" to the *Odyssey,* a first round of authority and deference confrontations: *xenie* issues, power conflicts, and status gambits, such as dueling with gifts and meat. Telemakhos failed to win every early battle with the suitors, even though they are "Paris"-types of luxury and lechery. At first, he acts like the confused and noisy "fatherless child" that he fears he is (1.208–19). The crybaby, scepter-hurling boy without an estate slowly learns big-man gesture and big talk.[4] Later (in books 4–16), he performs as a maturing, but still overtalkative, boy trying to run with the men. His prudence, perseverence (the root *tl-* of *tlemon* echoes in his name, regardless of true etymology), and improved "dissing" skills in the second half, however, present him as his father's true son, a dissimulator of stalls, tricks, and evasive tactics before Menelaos, expectant Nestor, his mother, and, the final test, the suitors—and an effective simulator of the even more arcane heroic deceptive gestures of humility and weakness. Finally, he has become carefully circumspect, a self-contained minihero—a prudent echo of his quiet superhero dad.

Characterization of Telemakhos benefits from the traditional oral-formulaic medium, as Richard Martin has argued (1993, 228–39). His epithets and speech frames, his rhetorical strategies, and the narrative's use of him as a focalizing figure to filter the flow of the plot show us an Odyssean hero in embryo, *in nuce.* My topic in this chapter is Telemakhos' effort to establish himself in adult Ithakan society. Starting from a position of high

---

4. *Mythos* is the "marked term" as Martin 1989, 27–29, explains. See 1.358–59, cf. *Il.* 6.490–93; *Od.* 11.352–53; 21.353.

birth-status but personal insignificance and symbolic nonbeing, he asserts his social and personal assets to achieve honor and position through the symbolic systems of Homeric warriors. I show that body language and nonverbal behaviors are essential elements for understanding young Telemakhos' characterization and heroic social stratification in the subtle and nuanced text of Homer's *Odyssey*. My evidence will be mined from narrative and speech in the Homeric texts, verses that explicitly describe gestures, postures, and vocal, nonverbal (paralinguistic) features of his face-to-face interaction.

There are five important social contexts for Telemakhos.

1. At first, he remains home alone, nearly helpless with his enemies (books 1–2).
2. Then he travels abroad to query the heroes of yore (books 3–4, 15).
3. He returns to highland Ithaka and his faithful swineherd Eumaios (books 15–16).
4. After his father's self-revelation, the partners in cahoots plot against the suitors. Telemakhos returns to the "urban aggregate" to reassure Penelope but does not inform his mother about the counterattack (books 16–17).
5. Finally, Telemakhos protects the stranger, administers the bow contest, and stands by his father in the suitor-slaughter, *mnesterophonia*. He stands by to collaborate in the male-bonding, female-bashing berating of Penelope (books 17–23) and the mop-up of disaffected relatives of the defunct *basileis* (book 24).

1. Home Alone

Telemakhos offers charming examples of adolescent lethargy, haste, and anxiety. He everywhere provokes his elders' candid and not-always-kind responses. The prominent comic side of Odysseus has obscured his son's humorous contretemps. Our natural sympathies with his family and with his personal social dilemmas obscure amusing aspects of his discomposed face, scrapes in woman-control, and abortive attempts at social self-definition. The developmentally delayed and often disconcerted youth systematically misconceives what he can achieve or get away with. He is crossing the social (not physical) border between adolescent dependent and adult warrior. Whereas Odysseus' instability is registered by his appearance before and after baths (to Helen, Nausikaa, and Penelope, 4.244–58; 6.242–43; 23.115–16, 154–63) and before and after Athene's anamorphoses of him into someone unprepossessing, ἀεικέλιος (13.398–402, 430–38; 16.173–

76, 456–57), Telemakhos' gauche preactions and reactions get him into another kind of hot water.

Like many younger teenagers, Telemakhos appropriates authority first from an occupied and awestruck parent: control of bard and selection of story on the home-entertainment system (1.345–49). He rudely "bosses around" mother and maid before taking on peers and elders. The signifying formula "mine is the power" provides a probe, a test, rather than stating an established fact. Only powerless or insecure males use it in Homer.[5] He climbs into the Ithakan ring on his mother's head.

Telemakhos is given a "hard time." Beseeching the suitors to depart his domain—first privately, then publicly in the agora, with unmanly, nonverbal tears—he gets nowhere in books 1–2.[6] He is an impeded host. His "front" is repeatedly and purposely damaged by the suitors. *Front* is constituted by the *setting* in which people perform their social roles, their *appearance* with personal props included, and their *manner:* demeanor, expression, and gestures. The "guests" seize his setting, mock his presence among them and his approach, and smile at and stroke him as if he were a child—to keep him a child (e.g., 2.301–36). They "get a rise" from him and fluster his hostly attempts at managing hospitality. Dispensing ξεινία is a prominent form of authority, house control. Telemakhos, however, must interrupt his own daydreams to welcome the ignored guest-at-the-door, Mentes. He immediately—and improperly, since he has not yet fed him—bombards him/ Her with self-pitying complaints. He offers hospitality to Pisistratos if he should visit and refuge to Theoklymenos, and he apologizes for not accommodating the beggar better. He has a big bag of excuses.

We meet a new "man" when he returns to his house after his travels. Despite objections and minatory obstacles, with a single nod and three verses, he orders victuals to be delivered to the mendicant and insists on

---

5. 1.353–59, 2.372–73, 15.46, 20.262–67, 21.368–77. Moralizing twaddle about the later interpolation of Telemakhos' rude outbursts has little basis in the text. It inadequately depends on Aristarkhos' report that some ancient manuscripts lacked the verses describing Telemakhos' rudeness (cf. St. West ad 1.356–59 in Heubeck et al. 1988–92, vol. 1). Telemakhos suitably violates Homeric rules of parental address (cf. the families of Nestor, Aiolos, and Alkinoos), precisely because this character (a) has never seen other princely households, (b) has not experienced a father's example, and (c) needs an argument, however bad, to inject himself into power. Ask my children if logic is necessary to engage parents in their exotic ego-building exercises!

6. "Hazing," a term of male-bonding, brutalizing, peer-group social incorporation, is too kind a name for the cutting suitors' bullying and destructive actions. They are not initiating mother's boy into their *Männerbund,* elders' peer group, but trying, with a united "front," to dispose of this impediment to the capture of his still sexy mother and the clan's considerable belongings. Goffman 1959, 22–30, explains the developed concept of "front" found later in this chapter.

owner's rights of house regulation (1.120–43; 15.195–98; 15.280–81, cf. 15.509–19; 16.69–89; 17.10–15; 22.344–53, 369–75). Not only as a snotty son but also in a campaign of self-assertion, Telemakhos sometimes talks in loco parentis of and to his mother. Participation in the bow contest puts him in his father's sandals to exclude outsiders and to fight for family "front." Now he puts up rather than shuts up, in the crude phrase of American gambling.

Telemakhos' repute—when he gets one—constitutes his social identity, his real self in a sadistic "shame" culture. What other people say about you makes you who you are (Jones 1988b, 500–505, following Redfield 1975, 32–34). His *kleos* comes into being by public speech, assertion on the home front, and travel to wealthy princes, who bless and indirectly tutor him with benevolent assessments of physique, manners, and bloodline, as well as with prestigious gifts (3.120–25, 313–28; 4.140–54; 4.158–60, 17.354–55; 4.611–19, 15.104–31). He comes to understand what he must do in order to claim Odysseus' κλέος and κτήματα (15.86–91).

Telemakhos is the unhero. He begins as a big baby, timid and choked up, self-pitying and lost among the big boys who studiously ignore or insolently patronize the estate's heir. Although he can welcome a guest with his right hand and get bossy toward his mother (1.120–24, 356–59), he "chickens out" when chiding the suitors, slipping from threats of stark eviction to cajoling and to feeble acceptance of unheroic majoritarianism (cf. 1.274–75 and 373–80). He has been "trapped into making implicit identity–claims that he cannot fulfill." This situation invites and obtains public humiliation. He admits to a trusted guest his inadequacy in driving out the suitors, not very culpable in our eyes. More damning, he cannot even approach and address his father's friend Nestor without the miracle of divine Athene's prodding.[7] Compared to his age-mate and well-fathered foil Pisistratos, he lacks interpersonal skills, self-confidence, and heroic aggressiveness (3.36–37, 226–30; 4.70–75, 155–67; 15.54–55). Maintaining and increasing honor requires quick anger, competitive taunting, deference demands, and others' display of deference granted. Consider those superior status-warriors Zeus and Akhilleus.

His older, non-Ithakan allies later try to jump-start his heroic engine. He hears the adventures of Odysseus in the passive voice, so he can realize the potential for local leadership that Nestor, Helen, and Menelaos discern in him (Clarke 1963, 139–40). The suitors try to compel Penelope's and Telem-

---

7. 2.58–60, 3.14–28, 75–77; cf. chap. 4. See Goffman 1967a, 107, for the quote; Scott 1917/18, 423, for a witty summary.

akhos' consent to their so far nonviolent siege and woo operations (2.130–31, 110, 127–28). But violent threats are their trademark.

Telemakhos himself cannot strong-arm his mother into departure or marriage, so he makes a virtue of necessity and claims filial piety. Or he truly respects his mother's right to oscillate between staying and departing. Actually, his comments about her future—like hers—are not consistent (cf. 1.249–50 and 20.334–43 with 2.124–26 and 18.270, 19.533, 21.103–5). Her indecisive, patient game in a no-win situation is clearly not the one he would have chosen.

Telemakhos spends considerable time "licking his wounds," admitted and lovingly delineated, to those he regards as friends or teammates (including the sympathetic vagabond). His early refrain, until his father's self-revelation, is his frustration in attempts at establishing possession, rank, and authority. And though Penelope, Eumaios, the vagrant, and even Amphimedon—the other admitted, sometimes loquacious failures on Ithaka—experience different losses, "their talk about their talk is quite similar" (Goffman 1959, 176).

Telemakhos clearly would be better off economically and politically if he had his father's death certificate (1.166) and if his mother were married and out of "his" house (19.533–34, 20.341–42). His filial grief is less than his personal alarm for life and property (1.243–44, 250–51).

His griping at the gods and excuses for inaction (1.234, 244) do not impress Mentes/Athene. Athene—visiting goddess disguised as elder, male acquaintance—eggs on buffeted Telemakhos. She sardonically asks if he/she has interrupted a "wedding feast," perhaps the chilliest joke in this antic epic. Her age-based point follows: οὐδέ τί σε χρὴ / νηπιάας ὀχέειν, ἐπεὶ οὐκέτι τηλίκος ἐσσί, "You can't indulge anymore in excuses of youth." When Athene speaks, the audience listens—and Telemakhos appreciates the paternal (1.308) note.

Athene suggests two drastic alternatives, one of them unexpectedly heroic for a sole child: Telemakhos should expel the suitors with public support and send Penelope packing—back to her father, Ikarios, for remarriage—or, seemingly more "do-able," take a trip, discover whether his father is alive (and, if so, hold out). If Odysseus is dead, Telemakhos should erect a monument, give his mother away in marriage,[8] and massacre the suitors by fraud

---

8. As he perhaps then (as male chief of household) can do, by custom, regardless of her wishes; but cf. 18.270. "Homer" seems unclear as to which man "gives her away"; see 2.52–54, 113–14; 4.769–71; 23.135–36. This problem is related to the no-longer-vexed question of dowry versus bride gifts frequently raised by the term *hedna*. See 2.196; cf. St. West in Heubeck et al. 1988–92, 1:59 and n. 17, also ad 1.275; Perysinakis 1991. For the bridal paradigm,

or open force (1.274–97). Athene concludes that he must surmount the Homeric "*nepios* complex." He must coerce deference and enforce respect, like any other self-respecting Homeric male.[9]

Telemakhos is not fully Telemakhos, heroic son of heroic Odysseus, unless and until other warriors acknowledge this "chosen" personal and social identity. Telemakhos is known by name and patronymic but ignored for lack of heroic fame (ἀκλεής). Telemakhos lives in social limbo. Like Odysseus in Polyphemos' cave, he remains a "Nobody" until he acquires honor and so becomes a significant somebody. He is an absent presence.[10]

Telemakhos' coming-of-age involves economic, political, and sexual indeterminacy as well. He is the confident hero's biological child, his wily parents' genetic heir, their "literary" and social parallel, and their putative political replacement. His diffidence sometimes fades before his thinly veiled willingness to accept the "fact" of his father's death. He expresses reasonable doubts about the vagrant's later identity claims (1.235–42, 16.194–200).

2. Kleos

Telemakhos is the prehero. As Austin argues, he is *pepnumenos* as praised heralds and advisers are, undeceitful and insightful, with the candor of the young. The quality is essentially positive but is characteristic of the yet-too-young and the preheroic, potential but not actualized, noble peers.[11] Telemakhos knows and shows courtesy and deference to his elders; he has promise but still needs guidance. The pre-Odysseus negotiates passage through his own set of temptations, dangers, and travels. Smaller-scale offers and threats

---

consult Penelope at 18.275–80. Penelope is to marry the man who produces the best boodle, the biggest offer (20.335, 15.16–18, 16.76–77, 19.529).

9. Although slimy Antinoos wrongly blames Penelope rather than his pals for Telemakhos' loss of *oikos* capital, he has a point based in Penelope's stalling strategies (βίοτόν τε τεὸν καὶ κτήματ᾽ ἔδονται, 2.123–26). Athene later goads the boy by the bogus threat of Mom's stealing his toys (15.19–23). However cynical this "blame the (female) victim" ploy is, certainly Telemakhos has not been invested by her (if she could) or by the demos with the authority he urgently requires. Mother nowhere shows confidence in his ability to keep the importunate suitors at bay. Telemakhos vents frustration with Mentes. He reports that Penelope's strategy is "neither to refuse loathesome marriage nor bring fulfillment to the matter" (1.249–50 = 16.126–27), i.e., marry one of the *aristoi*. This possibility he clearly and even cheerfully envisions, as his mother realizes. It offers a solution to the statusless impasse (20.341–42, 19.533). As Katz 1991, 7, says, the Laertids are enveloped in uncertainty: sociological (Penelope), geographical (Odysseus), and chronological (Telemakhos).

10. Penelope's frequent talk of her own social death (18.201–4, 251–53; 19.313–15) conversely provides a present absence. Similarly, in Ithaka, Odysseus/Aithon becomes another kind of "Nobody" as long as he parades as vagrant.

11. Austin 1975, 76–80; cf. Heubeck ad 1.207–13. Menelaos, Athene, Odysseus, and Penelope supply pertinent remarks at 4.204, 3.52, 18.125, and 19.350–52.

(Menelaos' touring package, the bumpkin suitors' ambush) enable emergence into manhood. The *Telemacheia,* books 1–4, presages Odysseus' outlandish adventures in books 5–13. His danger-seeking rite of passage reminds us of Odysseus' teenaged (ἡβήσας) journey for first-kill on Parnassos and confirmation gifts (19.406–12). His public and private words, gestures, and acts reveal the Odyssean glimmer. His "form, gestures and speech . . . [provide] a physical imitation of Odysseus" and "unlooses . . . a flood of memories of his father" (Austin 1975, 79) in his elders, when he tours the nearby Peloponnese. The resemblance is thematic—yet also essential in persuading us that Telemakhos deserves his inheritance, since merit and birth as decisive factors tremble in unstable balance. Athene/Mentes notes the uncannily similar head and eyes (1.208); Nestor appreciates the wondrous correspondence to father in speech and expressed thought; and sensitive Helen wonders at (σέβας) the similarity of build, the "spitting image" (3.122–25, 4.141–46). Menelaos gets even more specific, focusing on Telemakhos' feet, hands, gaze, head, and hair (4.148–50). Visible appearance warrants character. He is *pepnumenos* when about to speak, a Homeric epithet—yet also a cue for the young *aristos.*

The *Odyssey* is a world of zero-sum games. Many characters enter such contests during the travels and back on Ithaka, often with death and/or mutilation for the losers. This applies to Odysseus and the Kyklops, to Telemakhos and the suitors, and even to Odysseus the beggar and his "competition," Iros and Melantho/ios. Jocular death threats from the bullying gentry—fighting words, fighting tones, and fighting postures—have to be taken seriously.

Mother Penelope, where the action is, runs the toughest game. Like the casinos in Reno, she tries to manage a "Heads, I win; Tails, you lose" operation. Either she remains mistress of Odysseus' palace and estates or she marries some wealthy, highly sexed young lord. This frighteningly successful manipulation adequately accounts for much of the universal male distrust expressed toward her. From her point of view, however, the dilemma is dire and unwinnable: either way she betrays someone: husband, if she leaves; son, if she stays.

Telemakhos knowingly pursues precarious interests through unusual ploys (cf. 2.76–79) and various temporary alliances. His strategic interactions involve calculations with and against his mother, his "guests," his terrified and silenced demos, his hosts away from home, and even his nursemaid. These individuals help and hinder him (Mentor and Eurymakhos), appear to help or hinder him (Nestor and Eurykleia), and, most insidiously, appear to help him while actually hindering him (Menelaos and Antinoos).

The teams do not wear clearly distinguishing uniforms. Tense confrontations include expression games we have discussed above, such as manners, smiles, tones of voice, protocols of greeting, and food sharing. Such verbal and nonverbal communications with various degrees of disclosure engage all sides in impression management (Goffman 1969, 1–7).

Telemakhos learns to control, manage, and dissemble information. After too candidly offering to the suitors in public assembly Mentes' choice number one, he succeeds in departing in secret (from mother as well as enemies, 2.70; 4.707–10, 638–40). Before local *padroni*, he must inhibit "leakage" (giving away facts) and deception clues (giving away the fact that he wants to mislead his interlocutors). He suppresses truth in part by holding his voice and eyes steady, but mainly by not sharing his plans. He is still too much the novice to fabricate credible stories and engineer nonverbal expressions of (feigned) satisfaction, but later, after his return from Sparta, he shows improvement in these "impression-management" skills.

Abroad, Telemakhos has intermittent divine assistance. Disguised as family friend Mentor, Athene accompanies him to the mainland. The youth does not immediately obtain all the desired information. The goddess in drag at Pylos prays for his success, but the same ultramundane power does not make it happen forthwith.[12] Nestor, in his forgivable ignorance, had spoken the ironic, "god's honest" truth of her matronage: "I hope that grey-eyed Athene would love you as she once loved Odysseus" (εἰ γάρ σ' ὥς ἐθέλοι φιλέειν γλαυκῶπις Ἀθήνη, 3.218–19). He also hones adult skills for detecting fabrications of word, manner, and mien. He cannot, any more than we (but cf. Odysseus, 19.209–12), inhibit all signs that warn interactants of deceptive ploys, but as the epic progresses, his bluffs and feints, simulations and dissimulations, become more effective, more Odyssean.

In Sparta, (chronemic) turn taking in talk is unbearably awkward. Every speech dies in its tracks. Menelaos cannot proceed after driving Telemakhos to tears, so Helen intervenes to extricate him (4.113–46); Pisistratos adroitly "covers" Telemakhos' silence by alleging youthful bashfulness (4.156–67). Inadvertent clumsiness portrays Telemakhos' late progress in the niceties of heroic visits. He muffs nonverbal silence (too long), verbal compliment (sacrilegious comparison), and paralinguistic turn taking.[13] In fact, Pisistratos

---

12. Note the most imperfect imperfect of 3.62: καὶ αὐτὴ πάντα τελεύτα, worse than "a pious fraud" (Stanford ad loc.).

13. Schmiel 1972 specifies three gaffes: keeping the guest at the door, Telemakhos' awkward comparison of Spartan splendor to Zeus' own palace, and Menelaos' faux pas that makes Telemakhos weep and cover his face (like his father). The Homeric gesture seems meant to check conversational flow.

must talk for two on the first day. The mutual (verbal) chafing of Helen and Menelaos deconstructs alibis and foregrounds poorly suppressed domestic strife. The Trojan War ironically did not end; the principals carry it on just above the surface, verbally with implicit contradiction and sarcastic thrusts, nonverbally by mind-altering drugs and *xenia*—gift competition: δῶρόν τοι καὶ ἐγώ, says Helen, "tailgating" her husband's generosity (4.220–34, 15.125). The husband-wife paradigm and inserted tales at Sparta offer another connubial foil and several warnings about Ithakan outcomes.

Telemakhos' gestures and bearing—his feet, hands, glance, head and hair, moans and tears of lament, and retreat behind his cloak—reveal paternity to Spartan Helen and Menelaos (4.113–17, 149–54; cf. Odysseus at 8.84–93, 531–34). Bashful Telemakhos' journey correlates to Odysseus', but every heroic achievement is smaller: he develops from near inability even to greet friendly Nestor to a deviser of false pretexts for escaping that kind man's honeyed clutches, from awkward whisperer in Sparta to effective manipulator of nonverbal and verbal etiquette, including that Laertid concern, extraction of valuable and plentiful guest-gifts.

Helen is Penelope's cousin, double and opposite. Both lament the destructive danger of beauty and its loss (*Il.* 6.343–49; *Od.* 18.251–52, 19.124–25). Both discern identity hidden beneath Odyssean disguises. Helen alone penetrated Odysseus' mutilation and disguise at Troy; she bathed and anointed him herself so as to entice him into confession: καὶ τότε δή μοι πάντα νόον κατέλεξεν Ἀχαιῶν.[14] Helen even more quickly identifies Telemakhos as the current visitor. Helen kens the omen that Menelaos cannot. Perspicacious Helen should prepare us for cousin Penelope. Both are conspicuous for effective self-grooming and chemical or conversational gambits that lull male acuity. Both always act so that, no matter what happens, "the outcome will be the best possible one for her."[15]

Little can alleviate the painful, dreadful living death of Menelaos (4.35), the unworthy survivor. Helen's detoxifying sorcery, so powerful that one would, as in Lotus-land, carry on cheerfully even if one saw a *brother* or son butchered (4.221–28), only displaces grief. It cannot heal the twenty-year wound of her sexual treachery or reverse the more recent murder of the king's brother. Nevertheless, passive Menelaos will not help Telemakhos,

---

14. 4.244–66. Intimate ablutions are performed sometimes by menials (4.47–50, 19.317), sometimes by princesses (Polykaste at 3.464–69). We cannot therefore anachronistically adjudge all ablutionary scenes as sexually seductive, but Helen certainly suggests such thoughts.

15. This is Laurel Bowman's acute observation, made by electronic mail on the Classics network in September 1992. Ambivalent expression and deniability provide a woman's shield.

although Nestor and Pisistratos hint he could (4.161–67; Bergren 1981; Dimock 1989, 49, 52).

Telemakhos is the first human in the *Odyssey* to act decisively. What he does, arrange his journey and leave, is ordained by a thinly disguised goddess. The achievement hardly advances Odysseus' immediate return. The stated goal of the mission is to discover whether Odysseus is alive (1.289); Athene already knows. She sends the youth on a safe wild-goose chase (books 2–4), away from home, his tearful mother, and the joshing suitors. She takes him in a direction seemingly opposite to his father's. He hears from Menelaos that Odysseus is—or at least was—alive, and he remains unsure whether to believe it. He obtains no assurance that what was once true is still true. A period of dead time for the deuteragonist ensues, useful for the suitors' preparation of ambush (books 4 and 15). This assassination subplot justifies Telemakhos' alteration from legitimate desire to have the suitors depart to righteous desire to kill them all, revenge just like his father's. His two basic patterns—voyage and revenge—thus coincide, on a smaller scale, with his father's:

1. withdrawal (from the assembly and Ithaka), travel and adventure in palaces, fairy-tale receptions, threats to life evaded, and return;
2. surprise reappearance, abuse by usurpers in his own house, hardening of resolve, agonistic demonstration of bow control (possession and use), and revenge by *mnesterophonia,* mass slaughter. Like father, like son, in structure and themes.[16]

One puzzling nonverbal action is Telemakhos' entrusting of his accepted suppliant Theoklymenos to his worst enemy, Eurymakhos, on return from Pylos.[17] This maladroit, apparent violation of suppliant procedures stymies scholiasts, Analysts, and even unitarians. The alert young man here, however, "turns the tables" on the parasitic suitors by taking economic advantage for once of another's house and supplies. He intends to force hospitality duties on one of the company that is seizing his stores. He is dueling with hospitality. Theoklymenos, his guest, however, rushes to discover a more propitious omen, a falcon on the right, to ensure his own protection from unscrupulous hosts. Outflanked, Telemakhos reverses himself. Now he sends the asylum-seeker to a more expectable destination, to his loyal friend

---

16. Delebecque 1980, 11, 41–42; G. Rose 1967, 393. Olson 1992a refutes Delebecque's "iron law" of epic time moving inexorably forward, calculating only a ten-day absence, more in line with Menelaos' explicit offer.
17. 15.508–43; see Austin 1969, 58–59, referring to Whitman [1958] 1965, 341 n. 13.

Peiraios' house. This ominous and humorous incident provides the opening salvo in the reinversion of hierarchy and hospitality.

3. Back at the Ranch

In books 17–22, Telemakhos is graduated from childish, inadequate, and open self-protective mechanisms to Odyssean ruses and fully adult duplicitous and aggressive strategies. He promotes the contest of the bow, really the auction of his mother's body (21.106–10), in an ingenious and ironic "disguise," his former self. The stage director assumes the guise of witless child, as if unaware of the game's fateful consequences. He even forces father Odysseus' hand, by ordering the contest to be held forthwith (21.111–12). Instead of waiting once more for father's signal, suddenly the young *basileus* impatiently gives it to his ever cautious father (Austin 1969, 62; contra Woodhouse 1930, 112–15). The follower has become the leader.

Telemakhos' return to Ithaka, specifically to the safe-house steading of the pig-drover Eumaios, includes interaction with an elder dependent and a stranger. Unlike on his way out, when strangers (at least kings) petrified him, he now advances confidently with loud footsteps toward a known retainer (16.6). The dogs recognize and fawn over him (rather than attack). Odysseus correctly interprets these two nonverbal indications of identity. The unknown stranger does not discomfit the maturing princeling on arrival. Odysseus rises and yields his seat and place of honor, an appropriate display of deference, but Telemakhos controverts the wordlessly respectful act and kindly commands him to stay put, indicating that Homeric rank trumps age (16.44–5). This proxemic and elevational deference-exchange conveys mutual respect, social recognition, and generous esteem (16.41–48, cf. 7.170–71).

Only after a full meal does the host-by-rank Telemakhos courteously ask Eumaios the homeland of the unknown *xeinos*. The nonactivity of silence while sharing food,[18] the stillness of the Ithakan environment away from the always noisy suitors, marks the momentary absence of anxiety and competition in an epoch of disturbance and political instability.

Eumaios advocates helping the stranger, but Telemakhos alleges that he cannot entertain him at home. He will affirm support and send nonverbal warrants of his goodwill—clothes, weapons, and passage out, or provisions into the hills. Alone, however, he cannot control numerous suitors' *hybris*,

---

18. The greater, paralyzed de-elevation and stillness of Laertes on hearing of his grandson's departure—abstention from food, drink, and work (16.143–45)—resembles that of frozen Niobe (*Il.* 24.602–17). Lateiner 1992a examines sudden epic silences.

their arrogant assaults on other men's self-respect. This conversation through proxy protects Telemakhos and the guest from direct rudeness in his denial of hospitality. Telemakhos' explicit refusal to entertain the stranger at home, as a hero should, provokes the vagabond's bold retort that *he* would fight even a multitude in this impasse; that death is preferable to seeing guests abused, servant-women manhandled, and stores consumed (105–11). Now they address each other face-to-face. Other than this outburst and proxemic expressions of respect for the young master, Odysseus exhibits his usual reticence about information, one facet of several pseudo-Cretan, nondecodable personae.

Athene's sudden, secret arrival alters the situation. Telemakhos senses nothing, but Odysseus and the dogs see her. They do not bark (16.160–62). She beckons to the elder by nod and instructs Odysseus to reveal himself to Telemakhos. She transforms the decrepit beggar back to powerful hero with her magic wand for more persuasive (since nonverbal) recognition. Telemakhos, however, expresses understandable fear by looking away from the miracle, much as Aineias in the glow of Aphrodite's epiphany. He requests grace and offers gifts to his divine (?) *xeinos* (16.179–85, *H.Aphr.* 180–84). Odysseus identifies himself verbally by name and nonverbally by kissing his only son only now, after twenty years' absence, and by pouring out tears, the first time the unyielding man melts on Ithaka (16.190–91; cf. 17.305, 19.211–12, 24.234). Telemakhos, true to blood on both sides of his family, cannily doubts this novel, assumed identity. So he should, given the changes in humanly unchangeable "badges," senility to radiant virility, and from the object-adapting rags to riches (16.196–200). Athene's plot is humorously foiled for the nonce. Odysseus patiently explains the anamorphosis as just another miracle of Athene's, with platitudes about divine puppeteering (16.207–12).

Telemakhos' familiar family hesitancy, which serves Odysseus, Telemakhos, and Penelope well, has provoked the exasperated hero. That man hides behind so many masks that he can no longer persuade anyone that the mask is ever off. He testily says, "No other Odysseus will ever arrive here for you" (οὐ μὲν γάρ τοι ἔτ' ἄλλος ἐλεύσεται ἐνθάδ' Ὀδυσσεύς, 204). Then the men embrace; one gesture leads to another. Now in postural and emotional congruence, they shed tears together. Due partly to a *nonverbal feedback loop* (mutual and self-enhancement of moods), they fall into phase with extended shriek and shrill moaning. One nonverbal component is bound to the other. They have cued and entrained each other. Their nonverbal behavior provides not only feedback for emotional rapport but advance notice of self-expression. The mutual embrace of long-lost father and son opens the sequence for "reunion" tears. Telemakhos' letting down of his manly guard in the presence of family closes the internal emotional feedback loop—hugs to moans to tears—and coaxes his father's fragile sense of trust into limited flower.[19]

In summary, returning from Sparta, Telemakhos predicts and avoids necessary delay with Nestor, gives all orders (nods and words) to his waiting ship's crewmen, and accepts the fugitive Theoklymenos' verbal and nonverbal requests for asylum. All these signs convey growing self-confidence and poise (nonverbal messages of self-possession). He stomps to Eumaios' hut, courteously refuses excessive deference, and vacillates only momentarily at the traumatic revelation of his father's supernatural presence. He reasonably questions his father's plan to slaughter an enemy band fifty-four times their number (16.6, 44, 192–95, 243). The prolonged journey has made a second, or at least second-class, Odysseus of the former ninety-pound weakling (Scott 1917/18, 425; Clarke 1963, 133 n. 9, 138–39).

The comparatively well-policed nobility of the *Iliad* is polemically trashed for a world of endurance and sly expediency, polytropic cunning. The very root of boldness in the *Iliad*, τλ- as in τλήμων, signifies its opposite, endurance, in the *Odyssey* (e.g., 5.222). In this world, sadist and victim, fraud and dupe, or grifter and sucker endlessly play musical chairs. Manipulators themselves get hoisted by their disguises and feigned roles.

Telemakhos and his parents exhibit wiliness, constancy, and emotional breakdowns. Odysseus has been forgotten by his people, as the presumably authoritative narrator Athene notes (5.11). He is unknown to his son and the world (1.216, 235–36) and has been repeatedly presumed dead by his stymaster, son, and wife (14.68, 90, 137, 167; 1.235–38 and 413; 2.46; 19.257–58, 313). His physical absence from Ithaka dominates the entire poem, in and out of Ithaka—even when he is actually present there. His potential presence is denied, foreclosed, silenced, and derided—even when he sits next to his son on the edge of the suitors or opposite his wife.[20]

Critics interested primarily in character allege that Telemakhos matures psychologically, but one might better formulate the very real change as a dawning awareness that he must forcibly or fraudulently occupy new social niches, or inhabit institutional arenas, to become the (social) person he wants to be. After failure to become—by mere words—presumptive lord of the

---

19. Telemakhos' later clever questions about his father's previous mode of maritime transport shows that Laertid skepticism has not perished from the blood.
20. Pucci 1987, 14, 17–18, 46–53, intertextually reads the *Iliad* and the *Odyssey* so that they continuously define each other and redefine themselves.

manor and persuasive orator (books 1–2), he is gentled and pushed by heroic advisors to become the worthy successor of a heroic, wandering father (books 3–4). He acquires the knack of forestalling traps, either pleasurable and kind or mean and murderous (Helen and Menelaos, Nestor, and the suitors' ambuscade in books 15–16). Telemakhos aligns his public body and its gestures with new social roles. His gestures become quieter, as they are reduced to nods, stares, and smiles—except when he feigns his former noisy immaturity and an almost Aristophanic ungainliness of word and manner. Homer points to the contrast by referring to his new, controlled (and deceptive) demeanor as a "divine grace" (2.12 = 17.63).

Telemakhos' coming of age leads others to expect from him appropriate social roles, for instance, *kleos* acquisition and *xenia* distributions, nonverbal tokens of esteem. Theoklymenos and the vagrant approach him to request protection. He accepts the suppliants, heroic manhood's task; yet he shunts them both away from his manse, rationally fearing incapacity to keep them safe, as he is obligated to.

In book 20, however, he verbally arrogates hostly privilege (ξεινόδοκος μὲν ἐγών, 18.164) and nonverbally provokes the suitors by means of his suppliant visitor. Beggar Odysseus becomes his own son's nonverbal instrument of social progress. He tells the vagrant to sit among the suitors and drink at table; he will—as host—ward off jeering insults and blows. He commands the suitors to control spirit and hands, or they must fight him and will perhaps be killed (20.262–67, 305–9). *Xeinia* manipulation is the currency and game by which he negotiates promotion of his adult status and demotion of his unwanted visitors' guest status.[21]

His adult status, more than the body "badge" of a beard, has been repeatedly denied by the suitors and himself (books 1–3, even 16.71). He becomes adult, that is, he begins to "act adult," in part, by hearing that he is adult and has no choice. As in sensory and emotional feedback loops, we come to be what we pretend to be (Cic. *de Orat.* 2.189, 191; cited by Holoka 1992, 239). It helps when others—Athene, the vagrant, and his mother—tell him he is "man enough" (1.206–7 and 296–197; 16.100, 260–61; 18.216–20). Repetition of claims to maturity makes it more believable, makes it happen, a common parental technique. This grown-up status becomes evident, once Athene (in part, a personification and externalized sense of adult behavior)

---

21. Murnaghan 1987, 105–7; Katz 1991, 126. Four times, he asserts birthright arrogance in words to four audiences (2.313–14 [at 16.69–72 he backslides], 18.229–30, 19.19, 20.309–10), but his latent heroic qualities appear most clearly in nonverbal behaviors: quiet signals to servants and strategic body placement.

156   *Sardonic Smile*

impels him to return with all deliberate speed to accept the suppliant prophet, slyly to avoid the suitors' ambush or *lochos,* to accept the vagrant as *xeinos,* and to conspire with his Autolycan father (1.89, where μένος = "piss and vinegar"; 1.271, 15.8–13, 16.78–89).

Formulae apply to both Laertid males and to none others. For example, the nonverbal "follow in Athene's footsteps" formula and the verbal "I'd like to stay a year, but . . . " self-exculpation for departure formula both suggest transgenerational identity and people skills (2.406, 3.30, 5.193, 7.38; 4.595, 11.356). Paradoxically, Telemakhos' assuming the disguise of an adolescent proves his manhood. No adolescent would or could perform that fraud. By successfully simulating incompetence at playing the adult (e.g., 21.131–35), he becomes a competent adult. He pretends *not* to be what he has truly become. This is role-playing with a vengeance, as Erving Goffman might have said.

4. Father and Son

The narrative articulates the growing menace that the young man faces. In the *megaron,* suitors had first ignored and then teased him. In the *agore,* they laugh at his exasperation and fecklessness; they taunt his acts and mimic his syntax. After he leaves, they plan murder. Antinoos begins to take the verbal menaces of the near-*hebe basileus* seriously: ἄρξει καὶ προτέρω κακὸν ἐμμέναι (4.667–68).

Having heard his father's cunning praised by Nestor, Helen, and Menelaos, Telemakhos chooses to emulate *dolos,* to "keep his distance," to protect himself by deceptive nonverbal behaviors, and to evade his exemplary mother's uncomfortable questions before and after his voyage. After his father reveals himself in the swineherd's highland hut, Telemakhos returns downtown to manipulate "the facade of despair." Back in Ithaka town, he enters the charade with immense zest. In the fourth quarter of the epic, he continues to speak and to act as a resourceless adolescent, allowing the suitors to rile him up and deceive themselves. Indeed, he seduces them into taunting and browbeating him at heightened levels of iniquity.[22]

---

22. Austin 1969, 54 n. 2; Wilamowitz-Moellendorf 1927, 106, characteristically dismisses character development from Homer's text. Telemakhos just follows orders, *Verhaltungsmassregeln.* The analysts looked no further than the consistency of inconsistency, but Telemakhos now has excellent reasons for mimicking former indecisiveness. He now merely pretends, for instance, inability to string the bow, since we are authoritatively told that he is perfectly capable of doing so. However, if we momentarily read Telemakhos' story as *Bildungsroman,* we decode a rough, gritty culture that believes in edification through creative humiliation. Laughter here, as in Herodotos, Sophokles, and Plato, perhaps in literature in

Telemakhos' political inheritance is fragile. His grandfather is infirm and has opted out, his father has been absent, and his own youth handicaps him, even though vestiges of Laertid respect remain (nonverbal place yielding: 1.114; 2.14, 416–17). A *basileus* owns more, gets more, and should give more. Underclass, proto-Marxist gripes of the crew leaving Aiolos' island oddly echo Akhilleus, the frontline "grunt," on the subject of unfair division of labor and spoils (10.37–45; *Il.* 9.319–33). Odysseus' troops repeatedly succumb to oral temptation, brief and mind-numbing gratifications (lotus, Kirke's drinks, and forbidden steaks), as do the young draft dodgers (?) back home at their banquets.[23]

Odysseus defers taking pleasure and giving information, however: food on Aiaia and Thrinakia, sex with Kirke, and identity exposure. Meanwhile, he obsessively accumulates *khremata*. Student Telemakhos defers several offered gifts (but takes the most valuable, 15.114). He fails further deferral tests both with the bow and at his parents' mutual recognition scene.[24]

As Telemakhos becomes more assertive, Penelope can consider remarriage to be more legitimate. Oddly, as Katz points out, she can also play the public role of housemistress more freely *because* Telemakhos assumes the (male) role of *kyrios*. A new housemaster changes the rules of female proxemics. Now she can appear less timidly among visitors and welcome the stranger as *xeinos* (19.253–54). As with Arete, a body-adaptor—recognized clothing—furnishes the opening. She offers him potent privileges of esteem: a bath with female assistants, clothes, a bed, a high place at the feast (proxemics), protection, and even male prerogatives of prestation, that is, offensive weapons (a javelin, a sword, and *the* bow) and a "'ticket' wherever he desires."[25]

Telemakhos feigns a youth's respect for the older suitors by urging them to show their superior skills and by yielding place order (chronemics, turn taking) in the preliminaries to the bow contest. He has advanced from public

---

general, is rarely funny. Winning is only half the thrill of life. Degrading the competition and helpless others is the other half.

23. P. Rose 1992, 130. His Freudian observations (123–34) strike me as the ahistorical, nonfalsifiable psychologizing that he criticizes so well (e.g., 135), but they are darn clever, nonetheless.

24. First, Odysseus must nod to him to desist; in the later, quieter scene, the father must "cool out" the angry son. He is still a second-class simulacrum of his father: his ability to string the bow, just barely and on the fourth try, dimly echoes heroic mettle and shows superiority to the suitors who cannot do it at all, but his father still draws it easily and while sitting (21.128, 152–54, 245–47, 407–9 ['ρηϊδίως]). The test requires instrumental act, but the symbolic value of their tactful gestural communication deserves notice.

25. 8.403–6; 17.550; 19.310, 322–28; 21.339–42. Katz 1991, 140–43 (cf. 151), instances 19.313 (cf. 7.317) as proof that conveyance is excluded, but 21.341 suggests otherwise, strengthened by Telemakhos' earlier words at 16.80–81.

tears, angry and impotent scepter dashing, and confusion about approach etiquette at Pylos in books 2–3 to an assumed acceptance of the suitors' social order.

Telemakhos trades with *xeinia* to incorporate allies into his group. Potential or actual rivalry is transformed into pseudokinship—as Alkinoos explicitly analyzes it (8.546–47). In "the male world of challenge and riposte," Telemakhos learns to boast, threaten, bluff, and intimidate—that is, to compete. His assumed role empowers him; he becomes what he pretends to be, the preserver and successor of his father (Katz 1991, 150, 159).

Now he exerts *kyrieia* at the manse. He sets out the axes, calls the shots, silences his mother, threatens Eumaios, and leads the suitors to the fatal moment, their lethal unrestrained hilarity—the Hellenic nonverbal sign of letting your guard down (21.376). He extends *xeinia* to the beggar, he protects him from harm, he orders the decisive contest, and he expels his mother out of sight into women's work. He claims authority to dispose of the bow as weapon, token of patriarchy, prize, or even free gift. He alleges control over all household servants (17.342–45, 397–400; 18.61–65; 20.304–8; 21.344–53, 369–75). This claim is not empty talk. The claim persists as reality unless someone challenges it and successfully supersedes it.

5. Whose Is the Power?

Telemakhos is "not yet fully actualized" as *kyrios,* male authority, head of household; so his claims and Penelope's sometimes clash as they jostle for dominance. He is eager, he says to Agelaos (not truly but in an entirely plausible lie, 20.341–42), to marry her off as she wishes and with gifts galore (ἄσπετα δῶρα). Her presence impinges on his available authority in an abnormal situation.

In the suitors' bantering and baiting games, discriminating heroic norms of nonverbal sociability, they continue to observe basic forms of proxemic bounds and verbal politesse for inferiors (e.g., 2.323–36, 20.284–320). Mean and outrageous statements to outsiders and staged fistfights for food largesse promote cohesion among these licensed peers. Assault and battery reveal their moral inadequacy. The youth and old beggar, perceived as defenseless, are expected to absorb jeers and sneers, to "grin and bear it." Effective put-downs are performative utterances. Like fists in the ribs, taunts hurt like proverbial sticks and stones rather than describing something in words or merely committing someone to future policy. Such hurting words are sanctioned in the competitive world of heroes.

As Goffman (1969, 116) says, "mere words aren't mere any more but have full weight." Verbal dueling tests the interlocutors' tempers and allows the powerful to show off. Will Telemakhos "crack" and cry or lash out pathetically at the derisory taunts of Eurymakhos, Antinoos, and Ktesippos? Can Telemakhos get the leading suitors to transgress their own rules? Beggar Odysseus, by witholding expected deference, can and does provoke the suitors to quarrel among themselves, for instance, after Antinoos starts throwing furniture at him. This loss of temper, a flagrant breach of nonverbal decorum, reduces his status as leader among the other suitors. And it also spoils their collective "front." Upset, angry, and irregular syntax and spoken curses confirm this upshot (17.460–88): ὑπερφιάλως νεμέσησαν· / 'Αντίνο', / . . . οὐλομεν', "Furiously upset, they reproached him, 'Antinoos, . . . you damned idiot.'" Antinoos, the son of Eupeithes, "Persuasive," has a most ironic patronymic.

No less significant here is what Telemakhos does *not* do. Precisely like his father, immediately before and after him, and with the identical verse (17.465, 491; 20.184), in the face of insult and injury, Telemakhos does not cry out in rage or let a tear fall—which would be nonverbal leakage, tones and signs of impotence. He only shakes his head in ominous silence—a sign that the suitors fail to read but that Homer thrusts into our attention (17.465, 491; 20.184): ἀλλ' ἀκέων κίνησε κάρη, κακὰ βυσσοδομεύων.

Confrontation based on personal status has failed to produce results, but later, standing on heroic principle (i.e., exploiting the symbolic systems of his epoch), the youth assertively protects the pseudobeggar, at once his (known) real father and, like his mother, a dependent of the household in need of protection from threatening suitors. Moving from periphery to center, again like his advancing father (cf. chapters 7 and 9), he witholds deference, pulls rank, and takes effective control. He nearly strings the bow and wins the contest, until a nod up from his father stops him (21.125–30). The suitors become more impressed, despite themselves, by his leadership skills and freshly assertive style. His decisive move is to insist on the beggar's turn at the bow. And here his youthful impetuosity and murderous verbal candor defuse a hostile and threateningly violent situation. The suitors laugh at his blunt and seemingly worthless death wish for them and let go of their determination to keep the beggar from the bow (21.368–77).

Odysseus bolsters Telemakhos' status as a host possessing *xeinoi* by explicitly remaining a stranger when he first pierces the axes and then even when he perforates Antinoos' body (21.424–25, 22.27–30). Only after winning the announced contest and beginning the crypto-bride contest by killing the first suitor in his assumed guise of Telemakhos' *xeinos* does he announce his true identity as *kyrios* and his concordant *kyrieia* (22.35-38).

We now conclude this survey of Homeric young folk's interactions and body language: Telemakhos develops from timid and deferential lad to resolute man in the course of the epic. Not only is his position unstable and tenuous to begin with (in terms of family status, peers, and political and economic limbo), but Homeric "political" power by nature is precarious and ever subject to individual initiative. Telemakhos learns to discern *kairos,* the right moment, starting with Athene/Mentes' epiphany. Here his candor dies and his resolve begins to be taken. He mirrors Athene/Mentes' movements here, then his father's craft in the final battles.[26]

He learns to replace youth's ingenuous frankness by polite and needful adult mendacity. He shows reticence with Nestor about his interest in Orestes, he excuses himself from Menelaos' hospitality (3.195-209, 4.595-99, 15.91) with a "story" about his impatient comrades, and he divulges to his mother everything about his journey except the one essential fact: that Odysseus is home (17.107-49).

Where he ineffectually complained to strangers or the demos before, he now giggles, pretends embarrassment, sneezes at the "wrong moment," bluffs, and, *seemingly* inept, encourages the bow contest—an event promising fatal consequences to his *oikos*. The nonverbal behaviors guarantee his sincerity, since they appear to be uncontrollable, risible leakages. His deceptive intent is clarified by his apparent self-criticism (21.102-5): "Alas, Zeus has taken out my brains (ἄφρονα). . . . I laugh and rejoice in my fool's heart [at the thought of my sensible mother's departure]."

Failing to succeed by confrontation, Telemakhos develops the Autolycan mode of his grandfather, father, and mother: chicanery of deed and word and drastic, even clownish nonverbal gest and expression, when deceptive. After he returns, he physically remains the young man with his first beard. Back in Ithaca, however, the callow youth starts to exploit the "fact" of youth; the child recently ignorant of his own father comes to behave much like him (1.216 and 16.274-305, 18.227-32, 21.102-5) in his project to kill the suitors or be killed (2.332-36). His body and adaptors have not changed, but spiritually he has learned the Odyssean lesson of interiorizing, patience, and deceptive nonverbal behavior that suggests compliance if not complaisance.

Telemakhos has traded in the idle and wasteful ways of himself, the

---

26. Finley 1978, 84, 88, 93. Austin 1969 well describes Telemakhos' *Bildung* in evasive maneuvers.

suitors, and Menelaos (1.270, 296–97; 2.303–5, 18.427–28; 4.587–99), but Homer slyly retains embarrassing elements of his youthful indiscretion. Back at the manse, he still giggles of turn, provokes suitors' mirth, sneezes in crisis, nearly botches Odysseus' master plan by stringing the bow, forgets his father's instructions, and speaks sharply to his mother (21.105, 20.345–47, 17.541–42, 21.127, 22.153–55, 23.97–103).

Like Odysseus the stigmatized beggar, Telemakhos employs language and body language to project an *un*dignified self-image. He is incapable both of Akhilleus' dangerous boasts and manipulative rhetoric—praise and insults—and of Odysseus' flair for elaborate Cretan fables of impressive hardships survived. Telemakhos, however, has learned to hold his ground and to compete differently, by siding with the resistance, in an openly hostile environment.

One infrequently lemmatized facet of Telemakhos' patriarchal socialization is the lesson of women's undependability. Eurykleia, the most faithful maidservant of literature, must be threatened or silenced by both Telemakhos and, later, Odysseus (2.372–76, 19.480–82). Both men fear Penelope's possible misuse of information that might destroy their well-laid machinations. On his return, Telemakhos remains evasive with his mother. Their relationship shows significant strain. When she politely requests itinerary and summary, she is encouraged to freshen up her face and pray, an order that stupifies her at first—no winged words fly out—and that is mentioned with indirect, but unmistakable, annoyance later (17.46–51, 57, 101–6). Telemakhos, when he answers her at *his* chosen time, promises the truth but delivers a consciously truncated story that denies her knowledge of her husband's presence on Ithaka and his imminent arrival home.[27] His partial trust obediently reflects Odysseus' usual small dollop, Athene's advice, and Odysseus' own command (13.254; 13.336, 403; 16.303–4).

The culminating nonverbal sign of Telemakhos' heroic maturity is his readiness, psychological and physical, to string the hero's lethal bow (21.125–35), a validation of lineage and of worthiness to assume his father's place, but a grievous problem for the plot. Odysseus gestures "no" (raising his chin up) to stop him in the nick of time, but more interesting for study of interpersonal dynamics is Telemakhos' canny apology to the suitors for even trying. He calls himself *nepios*-like, too young and feeble to defend himself against insults: ἄκικυς, νεώτερός εἰμι—the former adjective used elsewhere

---

27. 17.108–49. The adverbial element in ἀληθείην καταλέξω suggested to Lattimore "the whole true story"; see also Shewan 1926/27, 35–37. Cf. Odysseus' request for a *cata*log of suitors at 16.235.

162 *Sardonic Smile*

only when Kyklops describes unimpressive Odysseus (9.515). His very self-effacement is a deceptive performance that demonstrates self-confidence to us and his father. He disarmingly says just what the suitors want to hear (21.131–33; recalling 2.60–62, 16.71–72; cf. *Il.* 24.368–69):

ὦ πόποι, ἦ καὶ ἔπειτα κακός τ' ἔσομαι καὶ ἄκικυς
ἠὲ νεώτερός εἰμι καὶ οὔ πω χερσὶ πέποιθα
ἄνδρ' ἀπαμύνασθαι, ὅτε τις πρότερος χαλεπήνῃ.

Gosh, before and in the future I will be a coward and a weakling;
too young still and not yet confident and able
to defend myself against quarreling bullies who push me around.

His protective cover—for us, an ironic pretence—reflects his former reality. His plans are no longer transparent; he is gameworthy in dissembling and can pursue long-term interests. The self-insults promote his team's viability and protect its strategy. He denigrates himself to the lowest level of weakness to save his life and estate. He has absorbed and demonstrated his father's "gamey" heroism, not that uncircuitous boldness of, say, Akhilleus.

6. Conclusions

Social personality damage and damage repair permeates the verbal and nonverbal cut-and-thrust of the *Odyssey*. Pig-drover Eumaios grows grander precisely as the tribal *basileis* shrink. He lords over his own domain as host, protector, and dispenser of hospitality more effectively than they preside over theirs. Nonverbal behavior in literature permits Homer to express ego violation that has visible or aural components, and of these there is no shortage. Clearly prolonged malaise and disorientation in Ithaka lead to open assaults against Telemakhos, Penelope, Laertes, and Odysseus/Aithon. The suitors' self-estimation and social assumptions become increasingly questionable as they are provocatively questioned (see chapter 10).[28]

---

28. *Body-boundary anxiety*, the fear of violation, invasion, or deformation of the flesh—alive or dead—provides a concept for rational and irrational concerns about mutilation, engulfment, disintegration, rape, and transformation. These intense, nightmarish physical sufferings and violations excite the secure listener with reminders of our fragile, permeable, and vulnerable somatic state. The social person faces similarly threatening assaults in a warrior society. The spirit has its own thin envelope, an ego territory or selfhood with boundaries that are equally or more brittle, frail, and frangible than the body's. In the *Iliad*, we encounter gawky Thersites, humiliated and abused, if not entirely stilled, after his deference denials. Briseis' social roles as female captive include passive trafficked merchandise but also and more actively lover and mourner.

Does Homer highlight Telemakhos' development of fake-out skills? Does the narrator recognize and plot progress in back-channel nonverbal communication and suppression of self-disclosure? This youngster, like his father, Odysseus, learns to wear a "face" suited and deployed to offer minimal true information. Homer "discerns" both men dropping nonverbal hints that belie for the audience the real dearth of dependable data transmitted to the hapless suitors. For us, the Laertid face is not a "stone face" but an infinitely and explicitly expressive one—for what it chooses to express. Odysseus fabricates lies and "faces" for Polyphemos and then for Athene, Eumaios, the suitors, Penelope, and Laertes.[29]

Deceit proves heroic manhood in the *Odyssey*. To preserve family integrity and personal independence of social competitors' constraints justifies "information management." Aristotle (*Poet.* 24.1460a18–19) terms Odysseus the best teacher of all lying rhetors. The lies of Odysseus, Penelope, and Telemakhos disarm the suitors' anxiety that they might do them harm. The "stranger's stratagem" of acknowledged inferiority well serves the duplicitous needs of young, unallied Telemakhos.

After Athene empowers him with fatherly advice (1.253–54, 269–77, 307–8), he henceforth takes a stronger line with his mother and the suitors, learns quickly the grown-ups' protocols in Pylos and Sparta, and returns to Ithaka with enhanced survival skills for the cruel world and *charis* from Athene. His new stride and "front," or presence, causes the cowed, somewhat neutral populace to gaze with new respect at him, while the annoyed suitors try (unsuccessfully) to suppress his initiatives with pretended goodwill (17.61–67). Nonverbal behaviors convey both his change in "front" and their various responses.[30]

His deception ploys, when he returns to the "overgrown baby" persona, remain flawed. The choppy verses in which he sardonically compliments Antinoos for hypocritical paternal solicitude shows both bitter irony and an adolescent's testing of uncertain bravery. The entire speech (17.397–404) vacillates between sarcastic praise for nonexistent decency and blunt, frustrated fury, as Russo (ad loc.) notes.

---

29. Most 1989a, 131–33, following Walcot 1977 and Trahman 1952. The last emphasizes the profuse variety of Cretan lies, their bogus detail, and the nice fit of each lie to its listener.

30. Millar and Carmichael 1954, 61–62. Russo ad loc. points out that this enhancement service of Athene makes Telemakhos more Odysseus-like. Eckert 1964 believes, with much ingenuity, that Telemakhos' entire history mimics Greek male initiation rituals: separation from child-nurturing women, older male mentor Mentor, night journey, hero tales retold, death threats and survival, marvelous vision (Athene's lamp, 19.35–46), and first kills.

> . . . πατὴρ ὣς κήδεαι υἷος, . . .
> δός οἱ ἑλών· οὔ τοι φθονέω· κέλομαι γὰρ ἐγώ γε.
> μήτ' οὖν μητέρ' ἐμὴν ἄζευ τό γε μήτε τιν' ἄλλον.

> How fatherly is your manner in caring for me.
> Take and give. I do not begrudge you. I even urge you.
> And don't show respect in this for my mother or anyone else.

Telemakhos transits from flustered, helpless, and powerless son to enterprising *aristos* and *basileus*.[31] He has learned Hellenic male discernment and discretion, delicate cognitive social skills that the myopic suitors conspicuously and fatally lack. He has learned to control the small muscles of his face and to suppress leakage in posture, limbs, and affect expression (20.384); he has comprehended that flaunting weakness can camouflage strength.

Telemakhos has experienced a counter-cultural education of body and emotions. Like a caged monkey in a crazed scientific experimenter's laboratory, he is pushed to retaliate, go insane, or die. Isolated, emotionally deprived in a man's world, and tortured by snide keepers, the perpetual boy has experienced social deprivation and devastation. We see the Ithakan scene through his eyes. He prudently chooses to leave his torture chamber. Through hearing tales of his father's achievements, through learning to talk with receptive *basileis* elsewhere, the alternately garrulous and morose quasi-orphan learns to listen to internal cues and to ignore destructive cues from copresent desecrators and competitors.

Until and even after Odysseus returns, we share Telemakhos' frustration and sense of shame. He constructs personal ties, body idioms, and ways of "coping" (Buck 1984, 122–23, 145–48). Ratificatory rituals choreographed by elderly heroes, proprioceptive feedback (Athene[?] and/or growing self-confidence), and a developing sense of self and social position allow him to act his age and lineage.[32] He learns an acceptable heroic self: how to entertain friends and inferiors and how to intimidate peers and enemies. In nonverbal terms, he learns to wink as well as blink, to feint as well as fumble, and to send leading and misleading messages about fight as well as flight.

---

31. At Sparta, he is treated as a man and redefines, with Athene's prodding (15.7–26), his expectations of himself. Athene advises him to return to his possessions, not to trust his mother (who will be loyal to any new husband!), to run the house, to marry, and to beware the suitors' hit squad.

32. After repeating "mine is the power" often enough, both the words and the concomitant gestures and proxemics, he (and others) begin to believe it and to act on it without saying so.

On a more abstract level of literary ethnopoetics, what are Telemakhos, Odysseus, and Penelope? A set of textual actions, characters in a story, a set of ethnic narrative conventions, or linguistic functions—only this and nothing more? Inside the epos, what is Telemakhos to Odysseus or Penelope, or Penelope to Odysseus? Are they memories, hopes for the future, properties of the past, or desired daydreams for dissipating the present—an image in each other's minds? This boy, this man, and this woman try to maintain something that trumps lotus, the Sirens, anodyne tears, and Kirke's and Helen's potions. To each other, they are faint points of orientation in a world of loosened coordinates (οὐ γὰρ ἴδμεν ὅπῃ ζόφος οὐδ' ὅπῃ ἠώς, 10.190–92).

Spatial disorientation, as so often, is a topographical analogue to social disorientation or disorganization. Oaf Polyphemos denies Odysseus' Zeus-guarded privilege in his Platonically isolated cave; the crew negates Odysseus' communally won position and power repeatedly and unto their deaths; and the suitors, in the midst of a vacuum of esteem, will not distinguish their property from Odysseus'. The extended disarray of Ithakan order leads the imperceptient townsman or ill-informed passerby to surmise that the commandeered party is a joyous wedding feast;[33] thus, both the beginning and the end frame a story of bluff and deception (1.225–29, cf. 23.141–52) and encourage the audience to beware their own hoodwinking. The *Odyssey* and the *Iliad*, however, deal not only with mere character and its flaws or even with individual development but with social constraints, cultural contradictions, and issues of social ambiguity. These epics' pride of place reflects this profound meditation on social values.

Competition and potential exploitation color every Homeric relationship, including that between father and son. Children usually seek sustainable selves in a protected environment. Telemakhos lacks such an asylum—he lives in a jungle of murderous jocks. Trust is a dried crust among the Ithaka suitors. Repair, maintenance, and mutual recognition of claims fade before infringement, merciless importunity, exclusion, and hideous transgression. In this hard school of familiar strangers and strange familiars, he masters skills of status manipulation: undercutting repartee, nonverbal and deniable implications, comeback gambits, and assertive postures. He is well known and yet increasingly unfamiliar to his torturers. As the poem progresses, his heretofore latent—rather, suppressed—hostility explores new, undiscreditable, and heroic outlets in both language and body language.

The communicative Homeric body sparkles in the nonverbal channel of

---

33. In fact, "the guests are not guests but pirates, and the hosts their prisoners" (Austin 1975, 163).

the speech-laden text (nearly one-third appears as *oratio recta*). Every player in the *Odyssey* profits and suffers from his or her own and others' gestures and postures of "dissing," respect and status manipulation. The insider turned out, Telemakhos, features among important players who struggle for social dominance and status. Adolescent males represent a permanently mocked and seriously disadvantaged group, as my sixteen-year-old son, Ulysses, often reminds me. Intermittently adult Telemakhos and equally interesting Nausikaa, two important secondary characters, offer age-based nonverbal behavior of youth. Like Odysseus, we must regretfully leave behind Telemakhos' teenaged female equivalent, Nausikaa. She requires separate study,[34] as do elderly Nestor, Eurykleia, and Laertes, since gendered as well as age-based nonverbal behavior very much interests Homer and his audiences. Males and females, youngsters and oldsters, and powerless peripherals and empowered protagonists like Odysseus, Penelope, and the suitors manipulate bodies, postures, and gestures to express emotion, intention, and situation.

---

34. Geneviève Hoffman, *La jeune fille, le pouvoir et la mort* (Paris, 1992), 65–75, 88–98, offers useful observations.

Chapter 9

Status: Odysseus' Body and the Beggar's Stigma

1. Odysseus and His Body

Odysseus' multiple personalities screen him from ill will and harm. Telling any truth to Polyphemos had been a big mistake at the beginning. Subsequent narratives on Skheria and Ithaka fend off and defuse potential complications, such as marriage and remaining cold or forever incognito in the hills. Past achievement and suffering also purchase sympathy and material assistance. Every tale of the Mediterranean flotsam and autobiographically creative Cretan advances Odysseus' hidden agendas. He fashions novel narratives for heroic types (sly ways to obtain coats, 14.459–512). He employs tactful omission—for example, giving no graphic report to Arete of his naked state when approaching the queen's virgin daughter or of treacherous Eriphyle's hateful crimes (7.290–96, 11.326–27). He indirectly claims seemingly gentle disposition (ἀγανοφροσύνη, 11.203—hapax). Beggar's rags protect him better than weapons in vulnerable isolation among the suitors. The lying that is central to his life enables his entry into the last sanctuary.[1]

Projecting their society's hostility toward women onto the shade of Agamemnon and untouchable Athene, Homer's Odysseus and Telemakhos redirect responsibility for their shared mistrust of Penelope (11.178–79, 441–43; 15.20–23; Doherty 1991, 159–61). Agamemnon's phobic vilification of women (11.422–56) does not advance the plot but neatly displaces the narrator Odysseus' anxiety onto an authoritative voice from the Great Beyond. Self-serving tales about inhospitable Laistrygonian women, asexual Kyklops, Aiolian incest, and two too-friendly nymphets, Kirke and Kalypso,[2] create diversions for and distance from the somewhat friendly Phaiakians, especially the daddy-daughter duo eager to marry the new male in town. Polite spousal refusal by narrative proxy (Kirke and Kalypso), set in

---

1. Herzfeld 1985; Most 1989a, 129–33; Newton 1991.
2. Kyklops and Kalypso, aside from near anagrammatic identity and inhuman diets, reside in dangerous, noncivilized caves, symbolically parallel, orally and vaginally dentated nightmares. Skylla trumps both for bared Homeric teeth; cf. Lateiner 1989.

other lands and earlier days, clarifies Odysseus' determined intent to remain monogamous. Penelope's goose and eagle dream similarly and more transparently projects her hopes and fears of rescue into the unchallengeable and ever deniable world of nocturnal transmissions.

Nonverbal behaviors promote Homeric *progressive definition,* the gradual revelation of personality by expressive, unmediated gestures and "vocal[ic]s beyond the lexicon." Growls, chattering teeth, and moans tell as much as heroic word and deed (Poyatos 1992b). From the motions, noise, and static of real life, every author, actor, and griot selects his characters' "necessary" movements and thoughts and reduces the channels of activity reported, a compression reversed when the hearer or reader mentally re-amplifies each personality from a text. Picture an hourglass set on its side, with the neck representing the performed or written text. The successful poet is precisely the one who evokes a whole person from a purr, a human from a humm, a noble from a nod.

Manipulative narration, telling tales to advance one's interests, identifies a type-scene, a theme, a technique of social advancement, and a moral issue of the *Odyssey.* Different tellers before Kurosawa's *Rashomon* offered conflicting versions of a single event. The implied reader is left to ponder each internal narrator's trustworthiness, be she Athene, Arete, or Penelope. Athene, Telemakhos, Nestor, Menelaos, Zeus, Phemios, and the shade of the dog-eyed, "kingliest" leader of men himself, Agamemnon, all report the *nostos* of Agamemnon. Agamemnon's queen plots a homecoming disaster that "pre-echoes," or projects, a less successful end of Telemakhos' and Odysseus' journeys.[3] Misdirection or, better, multidirection without authorial omniscience, increases suspense, the need for deception, and irony—not to mention prudential reflection by the audience(s) inside *and* outside the tale. Will Odysseus and Telemakhos emulate Agamemnon and be bushwhacked, "luckier" Menelaos and ponder endlessly the horror of past and present women, or Orestes and stealthily punish crime in Ithaka (Olson 1990, 57, 63, 70; Katz 1991, 42–45)? As it happens, not at all by chance, the answer is none of the above.

Heroic nonverbal behaviors require several bodies for Odysseus (16.202–5).

---

3. Furthermore, since Akhilleus and Aias died at Troy, Menelaos returned home to nothingness, or to worse than death, to living forever. Here on earth and in Elysion (another debt to his Zeus-connected spouse: 4.561–70), he has to endure the luxury of endless creature comforts along with the memory and absence of his murdered brother and the presence of his coeternal, somewhat impossible wife. He is no prize himself, as Homer makes clear by his numerous gaffes. The humor of mortals' gaining this eternity, their fondest wish, is a Hellenic favorite (cf. Eos' desire for Tithonos in the *H. Aphrod.*).

1. The real-time, over-forty, scarred and waterlogged Trojan War veteran, not too tall and not too handsome, as Polyphemos notes (9.513–15).
2. The first of two reconfigurations by Athene: an enhanced sublime transfiguration, better than human, or "godlike," at least to an infatuated teenaged girl (6.237) and a frightened teenaged boy (16.178–79). They reasonably infer supernatural interference on sighting the suddenly hyacinthine hunk (6.240–43, 16.192–200).
3. The third, another creation by Athene, but now a disfigurement: worse than average, decrepit, belly-driven, and comical. This *de*based body communicates the status of *un*based, unhoused, and taboo-laden beggar.

Odysseus' nonverbal "badge" of hair (a relatively unalterable physiological aspect) has noteworthy manipulative potential for a goddess. Like dress, one's hair condition everywhere expresses social pretensions, allegiance, and status. Alteration conveys changes in societal status or biological phase. Cutting hair or letting it grow long provide examples of ceremonial mutilation, social initiation (e.g., among Spartan troops, Buddhist or Christian monks, and American military recruits), and symbolic separation (e.g., among anchorites, Nazarites, Laconizing Athenians, and hippies). Social outcasts and sidelined elderly persons deviate from social hair norms.[4] As hair-impaired, postmature elder and rank-deprived beggar, Odysseus acquires, bears, and takes advantage of biologically and socially stigmatized status.

Homer repeatedly notes the condition of Odysseus' head and hair: the hero is both a shipwrecked sailor covered with scurf of sea brine (5.455, 6.226) and a handsome hero, artfully "dressed" by Athene in curly, flowing, hyacinthine locks (6.231 = 23.158; cf. Kalypso, 7.246 = 255). His auburn, xanthous hair is "ruined" again by the same goddess for good disguise (13.399 = 431); but his beard, disguised in senile gray(?), returns to cyanean black (16.176) when his son is meant to acknowledge him. (Athene's plan, however, here falls afoul of characteristic Laertid suspiciousness.) Once again, if only briefly, healthy, colored hair and, of course, new clothes denote the hero's renewed vitality and honorable access to society. Baldness, on the contrary, denotes aged incapacity, as needling Eurymakhos unnecessarily comments.[5] The suitor tries to control the misfit at the party by pointed abuse, with an insult directed at the guest's unvirile "looks."

---
4. Hallpike 1969 summarizes anthropologists' discussions.

5. 18.353–55; he seems to pun, contrasting ἠβαιαί, "few [hairs]," with ἥβη, "vigorous manhood." See 8.136, 16.174. We lack a study of Homeric puns; Louden 1992 offers a start.

The beggar's body is itself variable, *polytropos,* as the punk Iros and the suitors abruptly discover and, if not cowering, exclaim. Deceiving doubleness and tripleness, polytropicity, complement and confirm nonverbally the hero's sinister and dextrous verbal skills. Cool, chagrined Penelope won't acknowledge his identity in either Athenefied form, older or younger, as her current husband. She married a person, not a walking scar or a god in a wig. To reanchor and root his soul and body, she springs the bed trick and snaps him back into an acceptable self and a historical social context.

By Ogygia's shore, Odysseus adopts Akhilleus' self-imposed isolation and tearful postures of mourning (5.151–53; cf. *Il.* 1.349–51; 23.59–61, 125–26). Akhilleus lost interest in the killing business of life, but sly Odysseus needs Kalypso's pity and cooperation to regain control of his. Heroic tears are never condemned, and no one sheds them more frequently than Odysseus (Waern 1985, 223). His body language and orientation speak volumes (immobility, isolation, looking away, tears, collapsed elevation, and posture). Kirke and Kalypso need more pressuring than nonverbal and merely human persuasion; thus, Hermes makes his mission of mercy with *moly.* Odysseus is not so much patient or explicitly introspective as able, when necessary, to wait out the opposition, to defer, and to endure insult (κήδε' ἀνασχέσθαι, τετλάμεναι, σιωπῇ / πάσχειν ἄλγεα, 13.306–10, thus, he deserves the telltale passive sense of his name, "Pained" rather than "Painer"). He knows how to manipulate "zero-speech," silence, and speech gaps, hesitation, and lags (6.141–48, 7.153–54); his stillness is particularly ominous (17.462–65; Arend 1933, 113, cited by Pucci 1987, 72; Poyatos 1992b).

On Phaiakia and Ithaka, everywhere perhaps, instability of status stalks the landscape and scars the faces. Halitherses and Mentor are silenced by public threat of fines and humiliating insults, Nausikaa rightly fears for her virgin reputation (as precious as life itself in modern Muslim as well as ancient societies), and Laodamas loses his seat of honor and Euryalos part of his public esteem for taunting the stranger. Odysseus, though cautious, loses his temper at intimations of subheroic occupations (Polyphemos, Euryalos, Eurylokhos, and Eurymakhos). Eumaios and Eurykleia, once free and both of royal stock, suddenly became bondspeople. Odysseus' lies about former royal rank and wealth are purveyed and accepted by some as true, so they are at least plausible fabrications. The myth of imperial Troy assaulted, seized, and sacked emblematizes the transit from glory to grief: conquest, loss, and death; for others, displacement, slavery, and suffering. The resonant, extended simile of 8.523–31, describing Odysseus' visceral pain as he audits Demodokos' third song of the Trojan Police Action—at his own request—foregrounds nonverbal behavior. His tears are compared to those of a captive woman whose dying husband lies gasping before her. She throws herself around him and shrieks her grief, while enemy men pound her back with spear-butts and lead her away to a slave's life. Her gesture and posture externalize the castaway's emotional state, in a dramatic and graphic portrait of flattening grief. The narrative eschews, if it knows it, the later novel's psychological analysis. The inversion of gendered nonverbal behavior for Odysseus' and Penelope's extended similes (cf. 23.233–39; Newton 1991; Foley 1978, 7) suggests their transcendence of societal norms at moments of critical emotion, a shared bisexual vulnerability expressed by hands, body, voice, and face.

2. Kyklops' Clown

Odysseus' least heroic role is the clumsy clown, a stigmatized presence that disarms potential threats by its antiheroic ineptitude. In the Kyklops' cave, every body and every thing is magnified and parvified, including stature, boulders and beams, voice, other sounds, and toxicity of wine (9.296, 332, 241 and 481, 257 and 395, 235, 209). Tiny Odysseus keeps his distance from the overgrown, overviolent, over-the-brim (ὑπερ-φίαλος), hulking ogre. A clown by nature occupies a separate space, vulnerable but death-free. This claustrophobic theater has no unlocked exits. The anonymous, acquisitive man extemporizes a "command performance." His antics gain a pathetic prize (death delayed) from a scornful audience of one (369–70, 273). The beggar has a modest and Zeus-guarded dignity, greater than the clown's.[6]

Odysseus pretends powerlessness and hopelessness as he offers the milk-drinking anthropophage his power-wine. He reveals his deceitful alias, "Nobody," apparently under the ogre's duress. In reality, as later with the beggar Iros, he is constructing a misleading defense that protects his limited space (9.413–14 and 18.8, 17) from encroachment and readies him for offense.

The ogre-entertainer maintains a sassy, plucky candor in asking for gifts due. A clown feigns powerlessness, but the rascal has license to humiliate his audience of betters. His resources are unheroic, but his derring-do is efficacious against Polyphemos the Kyklops ("Big Talk the Round Eye").[7]

Isolated, Polyphemos—even before, but especially after, imbibing wine—

---

6. Austin 1983, 4–7; Hainsworth ad 1.134, in Heubeck et al. 1988–92, vol. 1.

7. Mondi 1983, 34 and 37, rejects the "eye" etymology. His folkloric essay discovers the monstrous brood's origin in Near Eastern mythical forces of nature and in Hesiod's older portrait, where they are craftspersons and builders. He argues that the Homeric poem displaces one of these idyllic idiots into an ogre folktale. The Homeric theme of hospitality violated has been elaborated in a pre-existing *Schlaraffenland*-setting under thematic pressures.

does not control his orifices. His own burps, vomit, and belches and the animal dung spread like a rug in his cave, reject Hellenic subjection of, or inattention to, the body's excreta. His recalcitrant digestive system is monstrously funny. His deeds and gestures invert the norm and offer a zero-grade portrait of Greek politesse and etiquette. The lout believes he manages the theater; by misusing Zeus' libation and the Zeus-protected stranger, he becomes the victim, the center-ring object of audience consumer satisfaction. No longer does he control the lights, and he loses his own. He ends up blind; he has lost control of his environment and, moreover, the meaning of his words. A simple statement of fact about his tiny tormentor ("Nobody is killing me") is true but amusingly opaque to his peaceful, non-"cannibalistic" fellows.[8]

Odysseus has no need to visit Kyklops for supplies—Goat Island sufficed. And he still has *geras*, honorable loot, from the Trojan booty and the Kikones' land. Yet he rejects his men's sound, if unheroic (κέρδιον, 9.228), advice to take the cheese and run. He does not vainly hope for fancier fare, since it is obvious that the savage has none, but his heroic hunger for *philotimia* needs frequent and regular satisfaction. Long ago, he went to his grandfather's house for "glorious gifts" (19.413). Fighting hostiles or *xenia*-formation (loot grabbing or exchanging) at close intervals is expected and valued by the heroic ideology. This costly desire leads to the instructive tale of the hero's total humiliation and self-abnegation. He becomes a comical, toadying servant. Surviving by cleverness or *metis*, he becomes unheroically anonymous, "Nobody," *Outis*. His nonverbal behavior starkly shifts from impetuous heroic self-assertion to humble self-abasement. Fast or slow death in Polyphemos' cave, either without heroic boldness or with unfamed and therefore empty heroism, has only one viable alternative: shit-eating grins (if I may). So, now a more responsible commanding "officer," he accepts the need for self-effacing endurance in the face of outrage (9.175), triage of his

---

8. Kyklops' nonverbal behavior is highly marked. He alone whistles (ῥοῖζος, 9.315) and isolates himself from all others (proxemics, 189). He indulges in sudden, sharp actions, such as springing up, snatching things, slapping men against the ground, and smashing objects (311, 344, 235, 458). Like a modern sociopath, he does not bother to control posture; he slumps and sprawls (371) in reckless disregard (ἀφραδίῃσιν, 361). In drunken stupor, he vomits, lolls his head, and after the ophthalmotomy, he emits a huge cry, frantically shouts and groans, and hurls a mountain peak, partly in aimless frustration, partly hoping wildly to damage his enemy with more than words and paralinguistics (372–74, 395, 398–99, 415 and 506, 482 and 538). Kyklops' nonverbal behavior prefigures that of Iros and the suitors: affect display and noise, in particular. He and they indeed caricature the respectable characteristics of great *anaktes* in both poems. Odysseus is the exception that proves the rule, and the *Odyssey*'s rule is not friendly to "the ruling class."

(here) innocent crew, and quiet and ignominious victimization—for the moment, for self-preservation, and to secure the escape of some men.[9]

Kyklops inverts and perverts the host-guest relationship: "instead of inviting his guests to eat, he eats his guests." This tale of violation revels in reversals of nonverbal codes and *xenia* etiquette, decencies of the banquet, and rules of food consumption in general (carefully described and prepared in books 1, 3–4, and 7–8).[10] Kyklops insults his visitors by word and deed, ignores their suppliance, grabs men bodily, offers nothing, impolitely asks for a name (ὄνομα) before hosting, greedily accepts the visitors' gift (wine) and demands more, occludes departure (by murder, boulders, and bodily interposition), and forgivably throws a mountain peak at the departing strangers who have blinded him (9.250–54, 266 and 207, 275, 289, 353–56, 416–17, 481).[11]

Odysseus is the first to violate heroic protocols in Kyklops' cave. He enters the abode uninvited, helps himself to food in the host's absence (9.231–32), and yet later congratulates himself for vindicating the heroic code of hospitality. He claims to restore Zeus' moral order but in fact exacts "a very personal revenge to restore a very personal honor." Zeus' reactions speak for themselves; he permits his brother Poseidon extensive revenge (9.552–55, 13.141–45). While Friedrich's (1991, 26–28) sharp contrast of the early, presumptuous adventurer of book 9 to the matured, chastened justice of the peace and executor of Zeus' will in Ithaka seems too pat and comfortably moralistic, we agree that Odysseus commits wrong at Polyphemos' and "deserves" setback. The situation is parallel to that later on Ithaka, where uninvited suitors help themselves, no permission is granted, and the host is

---

9. Friedrich 1987a, 126, 129. On Thrinakia, per contra, Odysseus shows prudence, his men imprudent boneheadedness: *atasthalie* (1.7, 11.110–15); cf. Friedrich 1987b, 397. His three verbal warnings and two (nonverbal) sleeps (resulting in the loss of Aiolos' bag of winds and the cattle of Helios) exculpate him, providing the alibi that justifies his unique survival, which is so necessary to Homer's next plot, the husband who returns in disguise. The narratologists ask why does Odysseus at the court of Skheria tell a story that makes him look rude, poor as a commander, and stupidly informative (name revelation). A possible motive for Odysseus' telling the self-denigrating Kyklops story to the royal family is his desire to appear a less than perfect candidate for son-in-law to Alkinoos and spouse to the suddenly sexual Skherian princess.

10. Friedrich 1987a, 128. ξείν-words appear five times in five lines: 9.267–71. Skheria and Kyklops-land display striking polarities of hospitality at the beginning and end of the fantastic voyage. They are opposite but parallel loci of danger; Webber 1989, 3, 11.

11. At his penultimate destination, for contrast, *aristos* Alkinoos takes Odysseus by the hand to acknowledge suppliance, then displaces his favorite son from his seat of honor to favor Odysseus in a chair next to himself. He properly allows the suppliant to wash, eat, and drink before Arete asks his name. He promises transport home seven times and delivers it. He obtains gifts galore from the *basileis* for his *xeinos* (7.168–81, 238, 192–93; 13.10–15, 70–81).

mocked and jeered—both Telemakhos and the master in disguise, Odysseus as (once again) nameless suppliant.

Odysseus' endurance, *tlemosyne,* wakes up long enough to suppress his heroic "heart," *megaletor thymos,* in the cave of Polyphemos. The adjustment enables escape. Although he could have harvested food on the deserted and therefore unthreatening Goat Island or sneakily seized cheese enough from the cave itself before Kyklops returned (9.224–27), he wants a heroic guest's *geras,* a host's freely given gifts of honor and tokens of acknowledged esteem. *Philotimia* maroons him; heroic gestures are meaningless in a tomb, as he realizes almost too late (9.298–305). Here, old heroic *amechanie* requires new heroic *metis.* Trickery suggests to him self-abasement, denial of honor and glory, even renunciation of his very name.[12] Thus, he carries out his smarmy garçon facade: he is no ὄνομα κλυτόν (9.364) but only the clever "Nobody," *Outis.* Thus, he flourishes in Kyklops' face the appearance of stupidity, the protocols of feigned subservience (waiting to serve, to speak, etc.), and the stigma of doomed slave-meat.

Odysseus' "most splendid stratagem" for one-upmanship constitutes also "the extreme humiliation" of his person and ὄνομα κλυτόν. Full vengeance requires the abandon of prudence and endurance, an announcement of identity. Once free, he taunts the ogre, asserts his true identity (in one of only four times in which he does so in the epic), and mocks an Olympian god, much as dopey Kyklops had.[13] Carried away by unwisely *mega thymos,* he foolishly brings on grief and disaster. The gain—not inconsiderable although not bottom-line *kerdion*—is the reclaiming of glorious name and swaggering, vaunting and taunting, or heroic game. The prudent oarsmen cannot restrain this ego-rebuilding "heroism" (9.492–501), his restoration of verbal and nonverbal identity. Of course, they pay the price, an irony not lost on Iliadic Thersites or Akhilleus.[14]

To restore violated esteem and honor, Odysseus addresses three tasks: first, to escape the cave; second, to reaffirm his heroic *alke;* and third, to

---

12. Brown 1966, 195, refers to Sir James Frazer, *The Golden Bough* (1911–15) 2:318–34, for the power of the name. For other intimations of name magic, Brown compares 19.260, 597, and 23.19. See also Friedrich 1991, 22.

13. 9.475–79, 502–5, 523–25. This odd moral equivalency constitutes one of many elements in book 9, some of them amusingly spotlighted by Page repeatedly, that suggest, even to unitarians, a difficult welding of a giant-killer to a disguised husband folktale. From this vantage, one can argue that the foolish revelation of name is a necessity of the plot, since nearly every event before landing on Ithaka is a consequence of Poseidon's stalking.

14. Stanford ad loc. cites Arist. *Rhet.* 2.3, 1380b22–25, discussing 9.504, the necessity to identify oneself fully for heroic full satisfaction after insult to the social person (identity, status, and body). Cf. Podlecki 1969 and Friedrich 1987a, 130–31.

assert his own identity and flaunt his enemy's helplessness in defeat. *Iliad* 21 provides adequate parallels for unthinking, spontaneous, and impetuous "ego displays." There, Akhilleus too exhibits second-thought survival ploys, excessive slaughter, and jolly vaunting (e.g., 21.17–20, 120, 184–99, 222–26 246–83, 299–304; cf. 22.371, 395–404).

Interaction with the lawless ogre—the deceptive flattery, the potent gift of Maroneian wine, the outwitting log in the unwitting eye, and the sheep-transporter stratagem—produces the first desideratum, escape. The ferocious postparting speeches—heroically essential, if rationally foolish—provide the latter two. Reminding implicitly monocular Kyklops of Zeus' policy toward strangers is not enough (474–79). Taunting the nonocular ogre jeopardizes the escape, as the chorus of fear-crazed sailors sagely points out. Further, revealing his full name (502–5) enables the humiliated and damaged monster to repeat it with magical precision and therefore to curse effectively his no-longer anonymous tormentor. Finally, Odysseus' *eukhos* adds insult for Poseidon to the injury of son Polyphemos and finally annoys Uncle Zeus (523–25, 552–55).[15] The errors are credible, exhibitions of pain and pride that prepare us for his later mistake playing hide-and-seek *semata* with Penelope and their bed frame.

3. Contact and Tact

"Tact . . . is merely the play of light on the surface of a culture's submerged ideology: . . . superficial appearances depend . . . upon profound structural tensions." Odysseus shows "exquisite tact" in the tidy series of four Cretan lies, each role fitted to his interlocutor's gender, education, social and economic situation, and peculiarities.[16]

His body language and turn taking in a new environment and his reports of former gestures and postures fit his four various, all once privileged, Cretan personae. First, a paternal and demanding killer-henchman-castaway appears to the "young shepherd" Athene in his close approach and hint of menace (13.226, 270; recall the nightmarish kidnapping of the teenaged prince in *H. Dion.* 3–12). Second, as now coequal unfortunate vagabond and self-reliant individual, but once rich man's bastard child, he cozies up to fallen prince (true?) Eumaios. He greedily eats and retails earlier Egyptian

---

15. Brown 1966, 194, 201; Austin 1983; Friedrich 1991, 23.
16. Trahman 1952, 41; and Most 1989a, 127, 132–33, who cites Arist. *Poet.* 24.1460a18–19, on *Od.* 19: δεδίδαχεν δὲ μάλιστα Ὅμηρος καὶ τοὺς ἄλλους ψευδῆ λέγειν ὡς δεῖ. ἔστι δὲ τοῦτο παραλογισμός . . . παράδειγμα δὲ τοῦτο ἐκ τῶν Νίπτρων, "Homer has taught the rest [of authors] how one ought to tell lies, that is, by frauds (encouraging inferences)—for example in the Washing scene."

and Thesprotian supplications, earlier unheroic weeping resulting in protection, and clothing granted (14.110, 279-80, 318-20). Third, a mendicant supplicates *aristos* Antinoos with arm outstretched at close proximity (too close!). He alleges his own former labile prosperity and generosity as a nobleman with ten thousand retainers (!; intended as a provocative lie). He refers to earlier sanctioned alms-giving of his own and others' violent impulses and unsanctioned commodifications of the body (17.365-67, 414, 420, 447, 442 = slavery). Fourth, the wanderer lets Penelope the queen take first turn at talk (chronemic order) but insists that he is a quondam prince, divinely descended from Minos and Deukalion (19.103, 178-84).

Odysseus trades sighs and secrets with Athene and Eumaios. Their mutual confessions elicit noble, self-serving histories behind improbable and self-seeking fronts. The shared dependency of disenfranchised mortals invites gradual, guarded disclosure, stories that always allow deniability or expanding detail while invoking noble blood and remarkable ingenuity. They never put foot into mouth by falsifiable claims, although their convenient utility is patent to skilled, lie-detecting, incredulous internal audiences (14.122-32, 166-68, 363-65; 16.192-200; 19.203, 215, 309-14). No one gets flustered telling the tales, and nothing is jeopardized—as long as the audience cooperates. The tellers' tact and attention invites manly and womanly sympathies and generosity. Beyond this unruffled front, we hear lies that show tact with respect to tact. Internal narrators do not paint themselves or their interlocutors into a corner. They hint at deserving a better fate and mutually hope for mutual rewards (14.144-47, 395-400, 509-17). The former nobles at the pigsty "dine like kings," as they indeed are, on lavish and choice portions.

Odysseus indeed "always made his many lies like to truth" (19.203). The thrice explicitly Cretan adventurer insistently claims connection with Idomeneus: either he murdered that man's son, was his co-commander, or even calls him brother (13.259, 14.237, 19.181). Idomeneus *is* Trojan War glory and Crete; Crete is rich, flat, and fertile—everything Ithaka is not. The beggar claims heroic identity, *kleos,* by association.[17]

Cretan Odysseus is marginal on Ithaka and yet intent on becoming upwardly mobile. He rejects inherited social inferiority, even if his birth is stigmatized as illegitimate. At last, perhaps at least, he is no worse than Aithon, the younger, therefore less significant, son (13.265, 14.202, 19.184).

---

17. The Cretan connection deserves fuller examination. Vidal-Naquet 1986 remarks that there is more geographical truth in the untrue cover stories (cf. 3.291-96) than in all the *apologoi.* West in Heubeck et al. 1988, vol. 1: 43, discusses Zenodotos' report of Telemakhos' journeying to Crete and Idomeneus rather than to Sparta, perhaps an alternate version developed by Cretan singers for parochial audiences.

His lies "are a retelling of the truth under color of lying." He lies in saying that he was a *Cretan* warrior, a captain, a courageous son of a prince, and a husband proud of a wife from a rich family. He lies in saying that he was deprived of his proper *Cretan* wealth and property by insolent (ὑπέρθυμοι) young aristocrats (14.209–13, 230–34; Redfield [1967] 1973, 148–49). Except for the word *Cretan,* all this is true. His truths sound like lies: to Eumaios (14.362–65), because they contain promises of Odysseus "too good to be true"; to us, because there are too many Cretan stories while there can be only one (non-Cretan) truth. However, there never were truer lies than these from the man on the margin. Like his body language, his verbal language "leaks" the truth to careful observers in the narrative (Eumaios and Penelope) and to the privileged poet and audience.

Odysseus' disguises are penetrable and in fact are often nearly or really penetrated. His semicovert tears and head ducking into his cloak at Phaiakia nonverbally attract verbal inquiries about his identity. His risky disclosures to Eumaios and Penelope assert that Odysseus νεῖται, "is now returning" (14.152, 19.300–302). Eumaios' admiring report of the "stranger's" ability at θέλγειν (a magical word used mainly by or about Odysseus; e.g., 17.514, 521), Eumaios' nearly scandalous and extravagant hospitality, and Eurykleia's fond leg fondling of her baby's clone suggest Odysseus' agitated ambivalence about continued disguise and his dear ones' justified suspicions. The suitor Amphimedon implies that Eumaios was already privy to the plot when the herder and the vagrant sallied forth and down from the hills (24.150–56). Eumaios' switch in menu from paltry piglets to lavish boar steaks (14.80–81, 419) marks covert, nonverbal acknowledgment of his guest's identity or—at the least—appreciation of a "great lie," a major status advance by a speech act.[18]

Odysseus the *basileus* presents himself as an anonymous, unwashed, hungry beggar. Nearly no one asks him his name, because it does not matter; he is again "Nobody," again an efficacious dis-guise for excluded hero rather than

---

18. Roisman 1990a, 216–19, 228, suggests that Eumaios—no dumber than Penelope, Eurykleia, and Philoitios (19.358–59, 380–81; 20.194, 204)—recognizes Odysseus long before he openly acknowledges that awareness in words. Consideration, generous portions, and ambiguous utterances convey tacit acceptance of the pseudostranger's stratagem. Newton 1991 notes Eumaios' explicit (exaggerated?) disbelief in the stories (14.166–67, 363). This attractive, but subtle and inexplicit, piece of characterization and plotting finds as few supporters as Harsh's controversial thesis concerning the moment of Penelope's recognition. I like both, since double deceptions run riot in Hellenic suspense narratives and since the supporting cast is given more credit, by this reading, and its own victories over a less than perfect hero. Both problems of recognition seem curiously insoluble at the moment, but the confidence of the naysayers rests on numbers of critics, not on the text.

licensed suppliant. With Penelope, he adopts a convenient name, Aithon. His narrative "cover," the false story told to Eumaios, presents a long tale of marauding, shipwreck, enslavement, and escape (14.192–359). Life on the edge (topographical, economic, and social) is the lot of both the guest's false beggar persona and the host swineherd. Yet it also applies to the real ruler. The pretense of beggar, or marginal man, oddly suits the former reality of the king, another marginal role at the opposite end of the social spectrum, one who dwells a cut above the hustle and bustle rather than participates in it. "High and low are interchangeable" in myth and in scapegoat rituals (often based on myth; Bremmer 1983, 304); king and criminal/vagrant/stranger share communal significance that fits both the imputed role of Odysseus and his real one.[19]

Disguise and hierarchy thematize the *Odyssey*, as Douglas Stewart realized in his unjustly neglected study.[20] Each encounter of the hero receives its own proper lie but, later, its own proper clue. The herder hears a story of disempowerment and hardship but salvation in porcine intimacy, Antinoos of previous wealth but present misfortune in the *megaron,* the nurse of a misleading rejection of contact with young servant-women and a child's scar at the fireplace, the wife of a proper banquet once enjoyed with Odysseus but also of an identified erotic but violent talisman. The suitors are confronted with the old slob, a passive emblem of demotion and failure. They ignore *their* coded clue: vagrant, windblown (ἄρπυιαι, 14.371) wanderer Odysseus' increasing immobility in the face of their verbal threats and nonverbal attacks. The townspeople likewise later hear the sham merry music, intended to suggest (to the suggestible) Penelope's long-delayed marriage. Indeed, ironically, it does convey this happy message, a true one, but it disguises the equally true (and more important) slaughter of the suitors on a holy day (23.144–51; cf. the suitors' similar misapprehension at 4.767–71).

Feigned narratives are performative speech, not only a speech act that states "facts" or persuades, but a stream of words whose performance achieves some end by simple occurrence, if the falseness remains undiscovered. Odysseus' Cretan lies make him into a noble Cretan "for all practical purposes." His later constatation that he is an Ithakan possesses

---

19. In fact, Homeric *basileis* have notably little pomp and fewer insignia. Government for or by the people functions at a minimum, aristocrats perform menial tasks, little vocabulary of class distinction exists, kings have rank but no office and few duties. Military discipline at Troy is conspicuously absent from both sides. See Geddes 1984, 19, 23, 35, based on Calhoun 1934. On warfare, see Van Wees 1986 and 1988, with helpful bibliography.

20. This scholar is never mentioned, for instance, in bibliophobic Dimock 1989, Griffin 1977 and 1980, Pucci 1987 (cf. 90–91), or even Winkler 1990. Bibliophiliac Katz' 1991 book justly acknowledges the book. Murnaghan 1986 focuses on this very theme.

more truth value for us because (a) readers want to believe something someone says sometime and (b) the narrator of the whole poem himself validates certain asseverations. However, Odysseus' Skherian *apologoi* are not always truthful or omniscient, nor always accurate and correct, even when (or if) he tries to be straightforward. The will of the gods is nothing transparent.[21] Characters within the narrative, moreover, tell us that ruse-dependent beggars and hungry bards recite stories and concoct lies from self-interest and for pleasure (8.479–83, 11.337–41, 364–69, 14.122–32, 22.346–48; Phemios is another autodidact), so perhaps Odysseus' "real" identity remains veiled after all.

Odysseus' "manyness" is replicated by Athene's gusto for anamorphosis and playful games. Gullible Telemakhos and audiences yearn for stability, for at least one recognizable, if transient, reality. A good poet will not give it to them, ever. Others relax their guard mistakenly—for example, Telemakhos with Mentes/Mentor/Athene. Alkinoos (11.363–69) ironically praises Odysseus' apparent candor, similar to the art of an *aoidos*. Mistress and stage manager Athene distills forever Hellenic "heterophany" in abundant praise of convertible Odysseus (13.291–300; Clay 1974, 129–36). She personifies indeterminate utterance, shape, and deed in her so-called Pylian bird epiphany (3.371–85, cf. 13.312–13, 22.239–40; Pucci 1987).

Telemakhos twice fails to discern the real god Athene and thinks he sees a god when he does not (Odysseus), in books 3 and 16. Human failure, not childish fault, mistakes divine disguisings (cf. 7.199–210). The miraculous phenomenal changes indeed betoken a god. Even professors would make the same mistake. The scared child is grudgingly persuaded by the words of Odysseus—partly again, like Penelope (see chapter 11), because of a dearth of choices. If, on the one hand, heroic Odysseus is a god, he had better accept the god's lie. If, on the other hand, the stranger's reality conforms to the shape-shifter's assurances (he has never since infancy seen his father), he can accede to the peculiar truth. Discretion cannot help much here, beyond assent. Innocent candor becomes suspicious in situations permeated with deceit. The truth is disguised, now by a godlike form, later by the humble one. Penelope also benefits from "immortal" improvements (18.190–96). The disguise offers some kind of truth, since Odysseus is a larger-than-life

---

21. Friedrich 1987b, 385–87. Among the hero's mistakes, note the unjustified (as it turned out, anyway) mistrust of Ino, the attribution of storm activity to the wrong god (proving the narrator's superior knowledge), and the calculated but nearly catastrophic entrusting of his body to (female, therefore) impulsive Eurykleia (5.355–64, 5.284–85 and 303, 5.382 and 408, 19.389–92).

father. There is no other Odysseus to come (Pucci 1987, 94–99). The young Laertid prudently embraces the revenant Laertid.

4. Adornment and Disenhancement

Display of the body and adornment through clean and expensive clothes communicate public status and also private affect. Nestor's scepter, fine clothes, precious tableware, and jewelry constitute emblems of office and badges of exalted rank (3.412; cf. 4.131–32; 6.26–29; 7.173; 18.293–300). When he properly supplicates Arete, Odysseus' clothes unexpectedly and improperly reveal Nausikaa to have been his benefactress (7.233–38), one of several strategic errors in the imperfect hero's plans. The clothes give him away, but the fault is not fatal. Back on Ithaka, the foul grooming and patchy rags and wallet of Odysseus garbed as Cretan beggar clearly and persuasively convey lowly status. Students of nonverbal behavior refer to auto-contact grooming and postural body movements as *self-adaptors,* while clothes and other communicatively manipulated objects are termed *body-adaptors.* All adaptors serve to persuade and deceive others about our status, mood, loyalties, and intent. "Clothes make the man." Odysseus gets good mileage from his masquerades.

Homeric Athene shamelessly and supernaturally manipulates a third category of visible speech: "body badges," the normally unadjustable indicators of sex, age, and physical fitness.[22] She alters both Odysseus' clothes and his "real" physical characteristics: he is now younger and clothed to attract Nausikaa; now older, initially to deceive and reassure both Laertid loyalists and the suitors; now younger once more to enlighten and overawe the males and, finally, to attract lonely Penelope (6.242–45; 13.397–402, 430–36; 16.174–76; 18.67–74; 22.1–3; 23.155–63). Goddess Athene can instantly change her own or another's ordinarily unalterable "body badges" to communicate aged decrepitude or simple youth. The formula "resembling a wretched beggar and old man," πτωχῷ λευγαλέῳ ἐναλίγκιον ἠδὲ γέροντι (16.273), appears four times and conveys a similar devaluing for contemptible social status and disempowered advanced age.[23] The zero hero at zero hour at ground zero deceptively sports white hair, shriveled skin, bleary eyes, bent posture, and a halting gait, proofs of sexual sterility and physical vulnerability (cf. Demeter in disguise at Eleusis, *H. Dem.* 2.101–2, 275–76).

---

22. The analyst Page mocks these major fairy-tale transformations of Odysseus' permanent features (1955, 88–91), a narrative fact otherwise largely ignored or contradicted by the "realistic" poet from books 16 to 24.

23. Falkner 1989 surveys Homeric agedness and its formulae, e.g., ἐπὶ γήραος οὐδῷ.

These unthreatening qualities reassure the tough and randy, but suspicious, wooing companions.

Odysseus' hair appears neat or shaggy, his eyes bright or dim, his stature straight or stooped, his face smooth or wrinkled, and his entire skin glowing or dull—depending on ephemeral needs. In general, skin appearance is often perceived out-of-awareness by others, as a revelatory external signal, a surface or screen between internal and hidden moods, drives, or desires for power and visible and external social norms, expectations, and status. Lying, cheating, concealing, deceiving, and duping actively exercise the body and the tongue. Blushing, blanching, and sweating are dermal "dead giveaways."[24]

Consider the nonverbal messages that heroes and beggars wear or carry. First to be noticed, of course, are the hero's body-adaptors: military gear, defensive and offensive; elegant and impressive fabrics and colors; fancy jewelry; a clean and groomed body; and, often, "speaking tools," or accompanying lackeys. The beggar embodies the absence or opposite of such appurtenances, with his ragged clothes, wallet and supportive staff and his absence of weapons, a commanding scepter, and companions. The accessories, such as they are, signify degradation and powerlessness. Body decoration (cosmetics and jewelry) and clothing express and enact feelings, status, and ritual occasion. The ministrations of females and slaves to rulers and their visitors—for instance, the bathing and dressing of heroic guests—remove the visitors' rank sweat and alien impurities, but they more urgently mark the guests' baptism, or legitimated entry, into the host's protected community—regardless of whether they have lost their luggage and gewgaw souvenirs, as Odysseus has. The rules and social cohesion of the local group are reaffirmed. The guest's acceptability and temporary integration are made visible.

The body's ornament and condition thus facilitate social intercourse. Odysseus' taboo nakedness before Nausikaa suggests sexual irregularity. Furthermore, the absence of nonverbal sartorial signals inhibits initiation or even the possibility of normal verbal interchange. Typical "archaic" lessons of feminine deportment have not prepared Nausikaa's companions for suddenly encountering salty, naked men with their jingling genitals at the beach. Odysseus' social personality and adornment is at the zero-grade (or subzero if one counts the ridiculous "leafy branch," 6.129). He has no social context, no signals that he can reassuringly send. Even *he* hesitates here. His words,

---

24. Consult Ekman 1992, e.g., 142–43, who adds pupil dilation, blinking, gaze avoidance, expression duration, etc.

"safe distance," and ad hoc comportment serve as his only credentials (chapter 7 further discusses this proxemic passage). In contrast, later, among the suitors, he has a full, if false, set of body-adaptors and beggar behaviors that reassure the parasites. His clothes give him a helpful history and social matrix. The suitors know what to do with such a person, even if they do not often do it. Negative adornment, a repellent presence, less than zero, initially completes a passive role, one that alms-givers *can* comfortably adjust to.[25]

Odysseus' disguise as a homeless, hungry, and aged beggar represents *negative display,* a diminution of ego and identity that substantively advances his projected plot of survival and succession. His social stigma has a richly symbolic function. It announces global deprivation of family, wealth, estate, friends, and even many remaining years. His falsification affirms, for the reader, his wily character and divine endorsements, while it emits to the nondecoding, oblivious suitors a comforting, status-affirming message quite opposite to the deadly truth.[26]

Greek words for "beg" and "beggar" (πτώσσω, πτωχός) derive from the potent nonverbal signifiers "to cower, shrink, skulk, and cringe."[27] Such nonverbal behavior in Homer describes hares, locusts, small birds, and a few derelict and unproductive men. If we ask a natural question, why this disguise of beggar for Odysseus seemed best to Homer's Athene, our answer incorporates this recognized low extremity of weak, demeaned, and victim status. The word and the appearance constitute a stark and simple package: shabby clothes; an aged "look"; and a homeless, unattended, hopeless, and helpless vagrant, without local resources or effective protection. This amalgam of feebly positive and strongly negative qualities, opposed to the generic and powerful war hero, least troubles the suitors and permits the stigmatized misfit initial access to house and hearth.[28] No less important than the strate-

---

25. At the other extreme of deceptive adornment behaviors, when Hera deceives Zeus in *Iliad* 14 to seduce him from battle, her extravagant preparations, toilette, and dress-up bemuse and devastate her suggestible consort. She washes, anoints, and dresses her body, combs her hair, and adorns her face with earrings and the seductive veil. Visual and olfactory stimulants, more than her verbal lies, distract him from the killing business to that intimate, chiefly nonverbal act, sexual copulation (14.159–353).

26. O'Hanlon 1983 discusses comparable contemporary display behaviors among New Guinea's tribes. Poyatos 1986, 512–16, examines body-adaptors; Block 1985, 4, examines the *Odyssey* itself. Nagler 1974, 44–77, extracts veiled Homeric veil assocations.

27. Ebeling 1880, s.vv. πτώσσω, πτωχός. The rare and ugly initial consonant cluster may have kinesthetic and synesthetic force. One spits out the sound. Cf. πτήσσω, "crouch, cower"; πτοέω, "scare"; πτύω, "spit out," clearly onomatopoetic for a mouth's gesture at *Il.* 23.697 and *Od.* 18.97–99.

28. Helen reports that Odysseus practiced this hobo scam of his already before, to penetrate Troy (4.246–51). A plebeian folkloric complex of Odyssean masquerade tales may have existed

gic problem and trickster Gestalt is the moral potential of the beggar in the *Odyssey*. We mean the narrowly, but unambiguously and divinely "privileged," status of the vagrant beggar in Homeric Greece: violation of his Zeus-protected rights (positively, to receive food and shelter, and negatively, not to be harmed or abused) multiplies the suitors' already flagrant sins (17.483–87). This stigma protects. This chapter examines Odysseus' manipulation of inferiority so as to stake out territory and protection.

Laertes also consciously, but more transparently, represents depressed feelings and affective status by squalid togs. Homer reports that he wore a scratchy cap to increase his misery (24.226–31), a prehistoric awareness of *sensory feedback loops,* the psychological mechanism by which one reinforces in oneself what one intends to communicate to others. Penelope also connects her appearance to affective state (18.180–81, 251; 19.124–25).

5. The Beggar's Concealment, Deception, and Leakage

In contrast to thickly planted visual or external descriptors of Odysseus as a pathetic person, Homer maintains Odysseus' (secret) dignity by *not* ascribing to him certain involuntary nonverbal behaviors of the unempowered. Unlike the established panhandler Iros, who foreshadows the suitors in many bumptious particulars, Odysseus does not tremble, grow pale, writhe in anxiety, twitch, huddle in fear, panic, groan, gasp, or swoon.[29] Therefore, the inner-versus-outer, affect-versus-effect, and appearance-versus-action contrast between hero and villain is forcefully maintained for the collusive audience. Nonverbal behavior both establishes the hero's pathetic but impassive disguise and stamps the various villains' clumsiness at domineering and suppressing unwitting revelations.

Body language also promotes appreciation of dramatic irony in the imbalance of power. From our critical and informed vantage, Odysseus' not flinching when hit, his sardonic smile, and his disapproving head-shake remind audiences of his real identity. Heroic stolidity itself would leak useful warnings to the suitors if they could read nonverbal behavior as well as you can—with Homer's help (cf. 17.235, 238, 463–64; 22.302; 17.465; 20.184).

His stillness is a menacing, inappropriate impassivity for mendicants, an ambivalent tolerance of abuse, and a narratological sop to his affronted dignity. Among many interesting types of demonstrative, intended nonverbal

---

as part of the "shifty lad" cycle in the ocean of Hellenic story. Cf. Stanford 1963, 8–14, with the rich notes on 247–48.

29. See 18.77, 88, 98–99; cf.22.42–43, 68, 84, 88, 270, 299, 309, 330; and Levine 1982b.

behavior, the *Odyssey* pervasively portrays the consciously concealed behavior of this rogue invert. Odysseus' self-control, his in-awareness avoidance of "leakage," unusually replaces out-of-awareness, devil-may-care, nonverbal expressions of heroic character. Akhilleus' supposed candor would endanger Odysseus' isolated perch and stigmatized persona.

Like the rest of us, epic characters, even Akhilleus, cannot always openly express sentiments, at least in certain publics. Concealing passion and feigning detachment is required, but the omniscient poet allows the audience to penetrate nonverbal and verbal facades. Contradiction between social act and private emotion builds literary suspense and heightens ironies. Ancient epic develops this bifurcation, exploited further by tragedy and comedy, where speech and visible act diverge obviously on the stage's two channels (eye and ear). Odysseus' wrinkled physique and ragged clothing, his meek and beggarly demeanor, his respectful distance from the suitors' high table and his *not* taking a chair (contrast his behavior on Skheria, at Kirke's, and Kalypso's), his outstretched hand, his wheedling tone, his not hitting back like a hero when assaulted, and so forth are public, visible and audible, self-denying nonverbal behaviors (e.g., 13.398–402, 430–38; 17.337–40, 356–57, 365–66, 447, 465–66). These appearances and actions contrast starkly with heroic and lordly plans for justice and capital punishment, shared with audiences by interior monologue, description of barking thoughts, and private restlessness. The thoughts, aggressive panhandling, and suppressed gestures and postures "leak" the beggar's real intentions.

Odysseus in vagrant's character draws back at Antinoos' words, but the ballistic footstool does not budge his targeted and struck body (17.453, 464). He crouches for protection, in suitable fear of Eurymakhos' outrageous missile, remaining submissive but safe. He easily avoids Ktesippos' ox-hoof, then smiles his only sardonic smile, a private release of anger (18.395–96, 20.302).[30] Melanthios' savage kick, Iros' punch to the shoulder, and Antinoos' insistent verbal browbeating (17.234, 18.95–96, 21.312) have no effect on the social nonentity. This largely nonverbal, steadfast stillness affects sympathetic audiences. The miscreants cannot expel or even budge disguised Odysseus, anchored to his newly recovered house. Penelope's tears encounter similar stillness: his eyes stay dry before a friendly witness, despite

---

30. The rictus falls between a smile and a suppressed snarl. μείδησε δὲ θυμον / σαρδόνιον μάλα τοῖον conveys intensity by the adverb, extraordinariness by the enjambment, and controlled malice by the unique adjective. See Levine 1982a and 1984 on facial expressions of pleasure. Self-lowering to convey inferiority and for protection against seemingly more powerful creatures like Eurymakhos appeared twice earlier, in his supplication of Arete and in his (ethologically prudent) sitting in the dirt when Eumaios' shepherd dogs attacked (7.142, 153; 14.31).

his inner pity and shared grief. The poet explains that the dangerous situation compelled this unnatural control of nonverbal behavior. Self-abnegation of the soul's instant messenger service, the body (19.209–12, cf. 17.304–5), partly fails when Odysseus perceives Argos' foul and final situation, secretly weeps, and covertly wipes away tears. Nonactions and effortless and calm actions transmit self-confident power and control. Others weep, gesticulate wildly, or scold extravagantly, but Odysseus keeps silent, smiles "to himself" (20.301), and strings the bow (21.409) "without strain," that is, without extraneous motions or unnecessary and futile affect displays—such nonverbal behavior as grunting, panting, or sweating. Stillness paradoxically betrays heroic identity to cognoscenti. Lower forms of human life flinch, squeal, fumble, and blink.[31]

Odysseus must conceal creditable facts and reveal, or pass for, what he is not. Dissimulation complements simulation. He manipulates stigma symbols, negative social information, and also accepts prestige or status symbols, positive claims that raise his stature. The deceit and indeterminacy that permeate human relations permeate the *Odyssey*. The ratty clothes, emblems of degradation, illustrate the first, while generous food from Eumaios and Telemakhos and Eurynome's humble help with a blanket communicate the second, emblems of social (and personal) recognition (17.343–44, 20.4). His disidentifiers provide a successful "cover" among banqueteers, just because the notion prevails there that no Homeric hero could willingly stomach so degraded a role. Only the geriatric dog Argos immediately recognizes the scruffy stranger. He is impervious to human (though not canine) status markers and so escapes "the problematic exchanges of human communication"—for example, language, bodily appearance, and social definition by identifying clothes and appurtenances.[32]

Odysseus as vagrant beggar becomes remarkably immobile. He never leaves the nest until the suitors are disposed of. He needs some needling to beg, he allows himself to be struck by a projectile or leans slightly aside, and he keeps silent and still in the face of rude taunts, jeers, even physical attack (17.11, 578; φρεσὶ δ' ἔσχετο, 17.238). In part, his assumed cover of inferior

---

31. He gestures emblematically with his hand at her throat to intimate a throttling of Eurykleia. Here he urgently needs to forestall verbal catastrophe brought on by his own mistake (19.480). Other nonverbal improprieties include the aforementioned borrowed clothes before Skheria's queen, entering the larder without invitation chez Polyphemos, taunting the defeated monster (a "crowing" tone is a palmary example of hybris in classical Athens: Dem. 54.9), and (purposely) crowding the suitors at the table.

32. Goldhill 1988, 18 offers a charming plea for more open-minded Homeric critics. Odysseus is vulnerable to subhuman and superhuman unmasking. What would have happened if Argos had not died in timely fashion and had started whining?

status explains this nonretaliatory passivity, but, nearly as important, his strategic territorial imperative overrides any momentary (tactical) desire to establish superior dignity. The wanderer is reestablishing roots, while the suitors, by their behavior, are eradicating claim to consideration. Being there, home, is supreme for Odysseus. His stillness and silence convey intense disapproval to the audience. His nearly inhuman suppression of emotional affect and his calibration of face and body before inferior males' provocations herald a different heroism. His cloaked and concealed human inclination, after twenty years absence, to weep for his dog, extend sympathy to his wife, and reveal himself to his decrepit father reflects a less forthright heroism, controlled endurance, or, perhaps, frozen emotions.

Odysseus has renounced heroic self-assertion and learned survival skills of disguise and distrust after extended bluffing, suffering, and hard buffeting. He comes to relish the role of "empty envelope." Many stops along the way exhibit the varied "p's and q's" of the host-guest relationship. Being socially peripheral becomes his central occupation and identity; when the nomad reaches his home island, isolation and insulation have become the core of his personality. His social ascent begins at the very bottom, as nameless dependent to a slave, Eumaios. Fiendish and unnatural distrust has permanently displaced relating openly to others, even to his son, wife, and father. Their loyalty has every ratification and reassurance, heroic, divine, and psychological, that Homeric bards could invent. Odysseus, however, has been reduced to a set of negative defenses and evasive identities, "a walking set of contingency plans," always surveying his own gestures and postures to ensure that they reveal little or no truth. He hesitates at every entrance (at the beach on Skheria, at Arete's palace, at Polyphemos' cave, at Kirke's villa, at Eumaios' hut, and before his own gate). He defers credence and commitment to Leukothea, Athene, and Penelope, to loyal serving-men and serving-women. Penelope's congruent female behaviors draw his smile and inner approval, but the testing continues (Goldhill 1988, 10–11).

He sometimes seems perversely comfortable experiencing social inferiority and powerlessness in his own realm, with Eumaios, Penelope, and the suitors. He appears more at ease in displaying insincere gratitude or subservient behaviors than in revealing himself as the limited hero named Odysseus. This last personality he cannot shuffle off. Penelope asks for background information, "just checking," asserting (proverbially) that her guest cannot lack family or local roots, be inhumanly impenetrable, or be "born from stone or oak," the stigmata of noncommunicative objects. His dissembling answer soon dissolves her in tears. *His* eyes stay dry, Homer says, as if they were "horn or iron—his trick."[33] He softens up enough to provide *a* name, however duplicitous, the first and only step out of Cretan anonymity since his arrival in Ithaka—not counting his responses to Athene's prods (19.183). Thus, he *is* hard, crusted over in deceit, out of touch with trusting others and being himself, name and all. The clinician would have to determine whether he is a psychopathic liar (charming, remorseless, egocentric, and incapable of love or shame) or just a natural liar (confident, remorseful, and talented in otherness; cf. Ekman 1992, 56–58). He is lost, still at home in a trance of subterfuges and fugues of otherness. Penelope must finally shock him out of the habit before he can fully return as her husband Odysseus.[34]

6. Nobody Again

Each adopted persona and its conciliatory moves meet success. The suitors do not cleverly unmask the pretender, despite justified suspicions. The loutish, unmannered bullies suspect loiterer's inertia but are faced by polytropic dynamism. The languages of the tongue and small muscles reduce and disarm potential impatience or ire. The integrated lies all suit the actor's appearance as well as the requests that he is performing. Odysseus' *hypokrisis* matches *rhesis:* together, they make him unrejectable. He has checkmated objections to his presence and preserved stigmatized, but handy, autonomy as a vagrant beggar.

The topography of the hero graphs a social rhetoric. Place and change of place mark his status and heroism. Location, elevation, and distance from hearth and forbidden space (at the table, in the *thalamos,* or on the doorsill) communicate objective status and subjective feelings in the *Odyssey.*

Odysseus gains esteem by degrees, even among the suitors, just as physical progress moves him slowly, inward and upward. At first, the *aristoi* are

---

33. 19.162–63, 211–12; 16.191. Lachrymose Penelope cries herself to sleep every night and young Telemakhos is teary-eyed: 2.80–81, 4.113–16, 153–54. Some readers deny personality deficiencies to Odysseus; for them, all of the hero's disguises respond acceptably to murderous circumstances. This psychological analysis fails to account for his unnecessary games with Penelope and the nearly fatal and still puzzling deception of miserable Laertes *after* the dead suitors are stacked up. Some critics interpret this last mask as formulaic reflex; others as primitive psychotherapy, a slow and gentle return to "normal" for the elderly; others yet as the uncontrollable psychopathic cruelty of the masked man.

34. Stewart 1976, 75–83, 107–8, eloquently describes this logjam, although he ignores Penelope's similar situation and equally frozen response. Play made with naming in this epic (false names, postponed names, negatived, etymologized, and revealed and revealing names) justifies attention; for a start, consult Sulzberger 1926; Dimock 1956; Stanford 1965, vol. 2: xxii; Louden 1992.

willing to sacrifice Telemakhos' "guest" to the mercies of a local bully and to ship the remains to the overseas ogre Ekhetos. Later, they offer the nuisance faraway farmwork, a nonnoble occupation removed from the freeloaders' feast. Instead he does work in the manse, arousing Melantho's vituperation (18.317–44, 19.65–67). The consuming idleness of the suitors could not be more complete. Eventually, they fear the beggar might be able to do just what they cannot, string and shoot the bow in the *megaron* itself. On the threshold, his body is liminal, but his mind games are subliminal, purposely provoking maids and suitors to revile him in self-condemning outbursts (13.336, 19.45 and 18.346–48, 20.284–86, with Russo ad loc.), true to his name Odysseus, "Abuser" or "Abused." By threat and force with the lower orders, by insidious requests of the upper crust, he penetrates the feasting sanctum, ascends the stairs to Penelope's hideaway, and mounts the executioner's raised doorsill.

The beggar's "front" requires intensely dramatic realization. Odysseus' performance is supernaturally aided by Athene's superficial gerontification, by decrepit clothes (13.434–38, 14.512, 17.24), and by other body-adaptors (staff and wallet). The postures, gestures, proxemics, and expression are Odysseus' own fraudulent confections. His highly visible, tattered nonverbal product is supported by the beggar's (verbal) cant that ordinarily reaffirms the caste system.

He tries to confide collegially in Iros, "putting out feelers" to share the plentiful leavings. He pretends to want to relax and momentarily discard his beggar's ceremonial deference, so, although not teammates, they can pause for awhile their humble poses. We find honor among thieves and suitors but no ésprit de corps in Iros. Guarded disclosure, an insinuating strategy, does not work.[35]

Odysseus plays a "discrepant role" as beggar. He plays well the unfamiliar routine of victim. He must overcommunicate poverty, resourcelessness, and so forth, while he undercommunicates divine aid, muscle power, and other "destructive information." His spectacularly false guise of disempowerment paradoxically enables him to spy on and test man and woman in Ithaka as long as he can remain passive (13.307–10, 402–3; cf. 11.433–34, 441–56).

---

35. On beggars' routines, Goffman 1969, 41, refers to the classic study of H. Mayhew, *London Labour and the London Poor,* 2 vols. (London, 1861–62; reprinted frequently). Pseudo-Aithon cautions hostess Penelope about the risks to her of his drowning in drunken tears, subtly refers to her husband's extensive wealth, and shows good humor to servants when he is in his unwashed state (δακρυπλώειν, 19.122 hapax; 19.293–95, 383–85, 327). All these confidences fit his persona of varied experience. The routines fit a strategy of upward mobility.

His psychic alienation from himself further empowers him to impersonate others.

Odysseus the vagrant and Penelope the unmoveable house-guardian share guarded displays of mutual familiarity (names, events, words of endearment [19.253], precious objects), signs of an anchored past in a stormy present. Their *homophrosynic* (like-minded) strategizing structures this false relationship as it did their separate identities within the conjugal unit twenty years ago. Consistent wariness, ability to melt "tactfully" from view, serves smart predators as well as survivalist prey. All four Laertids (by blood or marriage) possess age- and gender-specific cloaks of reassuring threatlessness. Rarely invisible, they disappear at will and appear again to pose no concerns to the poachers.

7. Social Stigmata

A beggar is stigmatized by the urgent needs of his belly. Odysseus' repeated abuse of his insistent digestive organ while begging (7.216-21; 15.344-45; 17.286-89, 470-74) both acknowledges economic and social inferiority and lays claim on the common humanity and advantaged situation of superiors. The wanderer has a divinely secured place and an acknowledged call on others in ordered societies (17.419-23).[36] As he has license to accost others and exploit his poverty in highly bounded settings, so the approached possessor of resources can ignore, decline, or meet the request. Brusque humiliation of an alms-seeker without charity, however, is as inappropriate today as it was in the eras that were the setting of this tale and the time of its tellers. The prosperous accosted individual, after helping, may banter, chaff, or sometimes gently mock the anonymous beggar, but he should not both deny him and throw bones at his head. Such behavior is explicitly evaluated as inhumane insult, *hybris* punishable by gods.

Homer's Alkinoos, Eumaios, Odysseus, and even a suitor theologize the etiquette of helping the helpless by reference to Zeus Xenios, protector of aliens, suppliants, and beggars. This mythical sermonizing underlines the serious infraction attached to harming unthreatening strangers (7.164-65;

---

36. Goffman 1963, passim, analyzes the stigmatized individual's "special discrepancy between virtual and actual social identity" (2-3), and Goffman 1966, chap. 8, discusses such "focused interaction," civil inattention (ignoring the bum on a bench or nose picking by your spouse), and rituals between unacquainted persons. Millicent Fenwick, *Vogue's Book of Etiquette* (New York, 1969), 554, prescribes recent, if no longer current, strategies with beggars; Goody 1972, 42-43, describes mendicants' manipulative techniques. Chr. P. Jones 1987 explores physical stigmata, such as tatooing (not branding), as punitive degradation rather than decorative touches (143).

9.266–71; 14.56–58, 402–6; 17.475, 483–87). Polyphemos' reception of Outis the stranger paradigmatically inverts the norms. The encounter produces a travesty of Greek manners and religious values that the suitors nicely, point by point, echo.[37]

The nonverbal behaviors and rituals of begging are carefully detailed at the manse. Odysseus requests the leavings of others, socially devalued objects (17.362); he rubs or leans his shoulder on the doorpost (17.221, 340), part of a poor man's status-free fidgeting and lack of interest in maintaining posture, that is, heroic dignity. He keeps his proper social distance at the threshold (17.261, 339–40, 464; 18.17, 110), even when eating (17.466–67); he extends an open hand for charity and navigates hungrily around the circle of entitled table companions (17.365–67, 450; cf. *Il.* 24.531–33). He crouches to avoid being hit, rather than defending himself (18.395); he humbly requests reward (14.152–54) and subserviently receives offers of handouts of food, clothing, and even weapons and travel, which put him in debt and in thrall to benefactors (14.80, 109–13; 16.78–81; 17.356; 19.309–11; 21.338–42). Generally, he knows the beggar's requirement of unbashful, although circumscribed, assertiveness (cf. 14.512, 17.578), but with regard to proxemics and chronemics, he violates proper, nonverbal begging behavior of both distance maintenance, when he closes in, and temporal permission, when he persistently importunes the preposterously punctilious suitor Antinoos (17.446–47). The tramp has penetrated the noble's spatial envelope and stretched, beyond the breaking point, time-taking permission between classes. He carefully disattends to his own acknowledged weaknesses.

Stigmatized Odysseus lives on the frontier between acutely delimited acceptance and massive menace to his life and limbs. He hears that he ought to be grateful for scraps (17.450–52, 20.293–300). The local lords insult disqualified interactants at will with hostile bravado. Iros, the paradigm of bullying besieger of the house, apes and clowns as the suitor's mascot while he imitates (and foreshadows) his betters' swaggering and inobservant behavior. Iros ingratiatingly plays to the hilt the stigmatized clownish role of spoiled identity (Goffman 1963), a licensed worm that confirms the suitors' (false) sense of moral and social superiority.

Odysseus tries to placate fellow beggar Iros. He offers him a deal he

---

37. The suppliant sharply differs from the vagrant or beggar in status and request. Each has distinguishable "rights," but a common needy helplessness characterizes both King Priam in Akhilleus' tent and Iros in Odysseus' house. Odysseus at Polyphemos' cave provides a peculiar test case. The little fellow demands help as suppliant but also proudly requests heroic *xenia*, gifts for warrior-heroes, clearly an affiliation of equals. The hero outside heroic milieux gets neither. His obliviousness to Polyphemos' indifference to heroic protocols soon becomes dangerously apparent, as Heubeck explains ad 9.259–71.

should not refuse, a chance to share scraps. Thus, the poets of the *Odyssey* grant to heroes humane sympathies. Homer suggests once more, from a removed and reticent point of view, Akhilleus' explicit ideology of the irreplaceable value of life, an Iliadic and Odyssean isomorphism of the human situation for hero, beggar, slave, and peasant—for everyman (*Il.* 9.318–20, *Od.* 11.488–91). Iros, however, has gained phantom and circumscribed acceptance as the "honorable guests'" official parasite (Goffman 1963, 122); his marginal but privileged situation (so long as he knows his place and keeps his distance) seems too precarious to share.

The suitors and the dastardly doublet of cynical sibling servants Melanthios/Melantho show conventional signs of disrespect for social misfits. They verbally abuse and curse, they nonverbally threaten, and they kick and assault by footstool, ox-hoof, and torches (17.231–35, 249, 409–10, 462; 18.396). They humiliate and manhandle "their" token beggar Iros, they threaten without warrant bodily mutilation and nonburial for Odysseus incognito (17.447–49, 477–80; 18.9–10 [76, 101, for Iros], 84–87, 116). They continually taunt and insult hungry vagrants with harsh sounds and scolding words, paralinguistic indicators (17.215–16; 18.326–36, 389–93; 19.66–69; 21.288–310; 22.27–30).

Honoring the peaceful guest or suppliant (nonverbally) with food and kindness indexes social order in the Homeric world. Odysseus' conversations with Eumaios imply that nonverbal ill-treatment of beggars was common enough in heroic times. High-living Antinoos ironically complains about too many freeloaders. Andromakhe pathetically prophesies Astyanax' orphaned and pummeled beggarhood, insults endured while wandering for scraps (17.278–84, 375–79; *Il.* 23.490–99). Violating the rules of supplication or the table of friendship marks numerous immoral men. The paradigm of Homeric *xenic* treachery is Aigisthos, who first feasted, then murdered the misguided King Agamemnon (4.535, 11.409–15; cf. a host, 21.24–30; a guest, 295–301).

Nevertheless, or perhaps therefore, Athene impels the stigmatized elderly agent provocateur to trouble the feast. Even a beggar's small respect is lost if he pesters and gestures too long or too loudly. His place is to take, not give—except for verbal and nonverbal deference. His very absence of dignity and his obvious bad luck protect him from some injuries but not from insults that excessive forwardness invites. Odysseus exploits a limited, but real, reciprocity of accostability. Odysseus wants to "get a rise" from the "hyper" suitors; his success in getting them to mistreat him and to violate Homeric manners further seals their fate.

Beggars employ "formalized" speech in their stigmatized role. In fact, the coercive power that we sense when a polite panhandler accosts us has less to do with fear than with the performative force of a beggar's depersonalized, restricted communication. His tone, syntax, and gestures are nearly invariant, ancient or modern. The situation and the request offer few responses. When Odysseus asks for a handout, he demands a handout. The suitors cannot argue against such a request, because the dance-steps of this encounter are fixed. The approached nobles cannot say "no"; when some of them do so or stoop to bargaining (!), they have violated obvious appropriate manners and spoiled their own presumed "front." Their oafish greed makes them no better than subhuman Kyklops.

The testing of the suitors' generosity is a "pop quiz" but is the easiest one ever set. Their failure to treat the beggar by the rules of Zeus (17.483–87, 494) shows that they are not heroes, and also that they are not equal to Eumaios, now an enslaved pig-drover. Odysseus' lowly, *lowest* status as social "nobody" is simultaneously divine, timeless, placeless, even faceless, and yet all the more sacred. His stigma offers others no real choice. His requestal, respectful gestures are the opening moves in Zeus-sanctioned ritual, the traditional authority of which, and the response to which, cannot be denied. The nastiest suitors rightly suspect the stories of the interloping beggar, but for fatally wrong reasons. By the time he sheds enough pretense to ask for permission to string the bow, their claims to any social superiority seem hypocritical and shabby. Their fear is patent.[38]

Back on Ithaka, Odysseus bears highly visible blemishes, sartorial and bodily signs of few assets, advanced age, and low status. He openly claims former equality among aristocrats (17.419–24), and he repents of nothing; but his stigmatized body, accoutrements, and lack of resources disqualify him from welcome at the endless party. He is accused of being a tramp or hobo, an intentional loafer, not merely an unfortunate soul (18.357–64). His identity, whether spoiled by circumstances or character, has been stigmatized and certified as negligible by the "normal," norm-setting suitors, those who decree the status quo for the nonce. His age and his "nobody" rank deform him, exclude him from in-group activities. The suitors continually remind him to act his role (as butt), to be ashamed of his crippled situation and vagrancy, and to be grateful for little (e.g., 18.354–64, 21.288–92). The suitors want to shape, broadcast, and confirm the stranger's discredited social identity, then have him tacitly and explicitly conform to that beggared

---

38. Since Odysseus' "stylized speech" and speech acts as beggar occur within oral heroic poetry, a relatively fixed form of oral (and nonverbal?) expression, we expect in his various venues similar or identical "beggar's cant," requests and explanation of his "hard luck." We are not disappointed (see his concocted Cretan tales following 13.256, 14.199, 17.415, 19.172, and 24.303). The paragraphs above draw on Bloch's 1974 discussion of ritual as a form of power.

image. The hungry man, however, ruled by bossy Belly (18.53–54), cannot remain reticent, as the vagrant himself is told by allies and reminds others (17.347, 473–74; 19.73–74). He furthermore claims he has nothing to hide (14.192–98).

Odysseus' stigmas place his "situation on his sleeve"; he appears to exert no control over his circumstances. "Beggars can't be choosers" is no recent formulation. The arts of impression management seem unavailable, leaving the vagrant geezer entirely vulnerable. The suspicious Greek environment is tuned to detect verbal and nonverbal bluffing. It is relentless in censure and ridicule of the weak and unempowered (remember the suitors' raucous handling of Theoklymenos, Iros, and Telemakhos at, e.g., 2.230–38, 321–36, 20.358–83, cf. 19.370–73). Odysseus' simulation requires not only constant exertion to act feebly but even more effort to disregard savage insults. The hero from youth was moulded to lash back at such slights. Given the elaborate disguise, the final switch back to hero requires thorough re-guise or de-disguise.[39]

8. A Sardonic Smile

. . . ἔρριψε βοὸς πόδα . . .
κείμενον ἐκ κανέοιο λαβών· ὁ δ' ἀλεύατ' Ὀδυσσεὺς
ἦκα παρακλίνας κεφαλήν, μείδησε δὲ θυμῷ
σαρδάνιον μάλα τοῖον· ὁ δ' εὔδμητον βάλε τοῖχον.

. . . he threw the ox-hoof . . .
Taking it from a basket; Odysseus evaded it
Easily, tilting aside his head. But he smiled bitterly,
A scornful smile, indeed. The hoof hit the house's hard wall.

One sardonic smile (20.299–302) glints from the epic; therefore, no comparisons are possible with the text's five other smiles. Upbeat, cheerful, supportive facework enlivens condescending Menelaos, Kalypso, Athene, newly refathered Telemakhos, and Odysseus, after Telemakhos' tantrum at his mother's hesitation. The five others all follow line-initial ὣς φάτο and precede the connective δέ. Warm looks confirm, or facially express, what has

---

39. Homer reports that Odysseus stripped off deceptor rags at the moment of truth (γυμνώθη: 22.1, 488); but, as an uncomfortable, but precise, Stanford comments (since later he must explain some notable rags apparently still on the hero's back), the stripping must have been incomplete. The conflict, I suggest, is between mythic disguise and ritual resumption of heroic persona. Zero-grade object-adaptors, tabula rasa, *corpus rasum*, are ritually and psychologically appropriate, if not sartorially realistic.

already been said. The smiles supply supportive "redundance" for important messages. Otherwise they ensure nuclear-family complicity in excluding third parties from secrets.

The sardonic smile responding to assault and battery, to intended humiliation, is different. Δέ in 20.301 falls after the caesura and weighs in as a balancing adversative. Focus shifts back and forth thrice in three consecutive lines marked by contrasting δέ: from the suitor's weapon to its handicapped target, from the visible head to the socially invisible affect, and from the passive smile to the active weapon's trajectory and destination. Ktesippos grabs and throws the hoof (a), but Odysseus evades it (b); effortlessly tilting aside his head from the object, (a), while smiling to himself (b); surely quite an angry and bitter smile (b), but the objective ox-hoof still hits the immoveable wall (a). Each line provides "split-screen," binocular focus.

The puzzling bitter smile, privately experienced, the menace of Odysseus' "ominous silence"—the smile ignored, suppressed in its meaning, or pasted there deceptively—titles this book. Precisely because I cannot explain Homer's unique sardonic smile to my own satisfaction, this emblem of insoluble faery knot suitably beckons further study of nonverbal expressions of emotion and personality. The sardonic smile spotlights Odysseus' doubleness and the *Odyssey*'s intense evasiveness, second thoughts and aborted violence. The scornful smile epitomizes interior-exterior dichotomies and oblique defenses. Odysseus has a range of smiles, but this poisonous one (visible or not) textually ironizes his reflexive and passive self-defense. The smile conveys indestructible self-confidence and power lurking in abeyance. "The father's quiet is stronger than his son's loud outrage—the poet manages even this contrast in addition to everything else he is doing."[40]

The multivalent sardonic smile responds to an unprovoked attack. Ktesippos' throw caps three incidents of assault and ballistic battery. The attack does not answer any activity of the beggar. The sardonic smile indicates a perverse satisfaction with thrice-repeated, god-provoking, outrageous behavior (17.462–91, 18.394–404, 20.367–70). The facial gesture emphasizes the latent power of the self-possessed hero. Its duplicity corre-

---

40. Fenik 1974, 180–86; Levine 1984. Russo ad loc. translates *thymoi* (dat.) as "inwardly" or "with bitter resolve." An inward smile, like an inwardly barking heart, presents an uncomfortable paradox. But the noisy bitch image occurs in a simile that licenses the illogicality. The angry smile describes Odysseus' reaction, extreme self-control of no retaliation but the "leakage" of heroic fury, a pre-echo of his less restrained self-revelation at hearing that his bed has been moved. Both the adjective *sardonic* (in etymology and semantics) and the adverbial dative pose insoluble problems. Stanford ad loc. believes it to be a visible gesture. The verbal phrase "sardonic smile" and the symbolic act that it represents, both clear enough at first hearing/reading, become more occluded the more one attempts to grasp their specific point.

sponds to the sardonic suitor's, when he calls the servile portion, insult for anyone, a "guest-gift." The economy of the Greek epic appears on the formulaic level, in Milman Parry's terms, and also in the astonishing functionality of minor patterns and body-talk, such as this triplet. The smile is ambivalent and deniable, like Penelope's elusive and "uncharacteristic" laugh (18.163; Russo ad loc.).[41]

Silence and stillness are defined only by contrasting sound and movement. Nonactivity becomes a signifying zero-sign, a "filled pause"—if preceeded and followed by words and acts. The silence of Odysseus after Ktesippos' ballistic aggression is itself aggressive, as the scornful smile shows and as we know.

9. Objects

A brief review of significant things reveals how traffic in material goods shapes Odysseus' status and standing. What Austin (1975, 127, 129) divines of words and gestures is also true of things:

> There are no wasted words or gestures in Homer, since every gesture reveals something else. An outward gesture reveals an inward attitude, an inward attitude will express itself in an outward gesture . . . [E]ven the slightest shift in posture . . . reveals character . . . [T]he danger is not of reading too much into Homer, but of reading too little.

There are no wasted objects in the epics.

Gifts and material goods articulate symbolic structures, a fact well demonstrated by Griffin (1980) for the *Iliad*. Odysseus asseverates that loyal Ithakans will proffer him more respect and love in proportion to the more gifts, *dora* and *geras*, that he imports (αἰδοιότερος καὶ φίλτερος, . . . πλειοτέρῃ σὺν χειρί, 11.359–60). No event or reason questions his logic. Inquisitive

---

41. The divine story of Hephaistos, suitor Ares, and Aphrodite, a seemingly irrelevant interlude, serves the narrative in at least these three other ways also. It parallels the human situation of Odysseus, the suitors, and Penelope. It foreshadows the victory of outnumbered brains over sex-hungry brawn. Furthermore, the included cautionary tale of book 8 prompts a worsted Skherian bully to set things right. The local poet, by his Olympian drama, sends an oblique message to Euryalos about making material as well as verbal amends for misbehavior (8.402). Braswell 1982, 132–37, discusses Demodokos' tactful efficiency in transmitting hints about social healing. Newton 1987 describes Hephaistos' similarities to Odysseus: an unhappy love, weak legs, and a dangerously beautiful wife (see 18.192–4, 245–49, and 19.54 = 17.37 for Aphrodite comparisons). Only these two beds are described in detail and fouled with spider webs in the epics (16.35 = 8.280). Is this formulaic pressure or a skillful suggestion of parallel action?

and acquisitive, Odysseus unstoppably seeks presents (9.224–29). Maron's wine, Arete's robe, tunic, and coffer, Euryalos' sword, and the Phaiakian clothing, gold cup, tripods, and cauldrons will be heaped higher, Zeus avers, than Troy could ever have afforded him (5.35–40; cf.8.403–5, 424–31; 13.10–15). And like father, like son; Telemakhos leaves Sparta with Menelaos' divinely crafted cup, a king's gift several times over in the past, the most valuable metalware the ultrarich monarch owns (κάλλιστον καὶ τιμηέστατον, 15.113–19).

Compliments, deference in facial demeanor and headwork, and self-effacing postures are coded verbal, expressional, and postural modes of recognizing interactants as worthy. Similarly, "[g]ifts are compliments made tangible, memorials of esteem and friendship" (Austin 1975, 159). They are earned by Odysseus' tact and tales on Skheria and Ithaka. They are gently proferred. Garbage and furniture hurled by the suitors signify the converse: animal-house insults made tangible, memorials of disesteem and hostility, violence parallel to humiliating words, abusive airs of superiority, and self-assertive displays for dominance. These travesties of hospitality occur because timid Telemakhos, vacillating Penelope, despairing Laertes, and even the tick-bit hound, each in his or her own way, feels forced to abdicate responsibility and retires to quiet corners not contaminated by bungling goons.

The menials Eumaios and Eurykleia "retain some vestige of order" and conserve and husband animal and household resources, while their paralyzed or outstrategized masters retreat (Austin 1975, 165). Unpretentious Eurykleia expresses her wishful theme, ironically when Telemakhos is assuming power: αἲ γὰρ δή ποτε, τέκνον, ἐπιφροσύνας ἀνέλοιο / οἴκου κήδεσθαι καὶ κτήματα πάντα φυλάσσειν (19.22–23), "If only, child, you might show such adroit responsibility in caring for the household and protect *all* its holdings." Telemakhos has not been well positioned to control gift traffic. The beggar, moreover, well-disposed to Laertids by old ties (lies), has no gift to give, only attractive but incredible forecasts (14.161–70; 16.100–104; 19.300–307, 555–58, 584–87).

Objects identify class and character. Angry Priam abuses his remaining sons as liars, dancers, and "thieves of their own people's lambs and kids" (*Il.* 24.260–62)—verbal, gestural, and objectual identifiers. So the suitors are engaged: they lie to Penelope and Telemakhos, dance and play the day away, and rustle by commanded proxies the *basileus'* flocks and females (16.435–39, 2.400–404, 1.420–22, 2.55–65, etc.) As with Herzfeld's picture of modern Cretan *semasia*, manhood's meaning is found in cattle thieving and macho posturing. Thieving is the inverse of prestation. Instead of civilizing agreement confirmed by respectful exchange, one observes the jungle's law—the hawk's law of the claw in Hesiod's archaic Greek terms—where brute force pleases itself with insult, patent rape, and vaunting seizure from neighbors' capital. In both extremes, however, human relations gain concrete expression through objects, nonverbal tokens of (dis)esteem.

Where analysts once observed clumsy *Einlagen* and bric-a-brac, unitarians again disclose meaningful physical manifestations of plot development. Objects define people, in our world and in the poems. A house, clothes, and an automobile reveal, as they are meant to, personality. The stages of Odysseus' territorial progress into his house are punctuated by descriptions of significant objects, each emphasized by admiration or praise of their artisan. As the mendicant approaches the manse, he lauds as a quondam commander its solidity and defensibility. When he enters the domicile, the once strong and still prescient dog at the gate draws a hunter's praise and speculation. At the *megaron*'s threshold, he leans against a column shaped from a single cypress tree that the narrator praises (*pars pro toto*) for the conceptual and constructive skills of its careful crafter: "which once the carpenter / expertly smoothed and trued to his line," ὅν ποτε τέκτων / ξέσσεν ἐπισταμένως καὶ ἐπὶ στάθμην ἴθυνε (17.340–41). This formulaic line elsewhere (four times) applies to Odysseus' similar constructive achievements: shaping his raft and building his bed. The formula also describes one more significant liminal object, the threshold of the master's inviolate treasury, the storage room that guards the poem's most significant object. This is yet another locked-up analogue of Penelope, a μνῆμα of long ago, an untouched, yet deadly, beauty—namely, the backstrung strongbow.[42]

The bow, hidden in its shining case, is like Penelope, protected by her shining clothes, veil, and domicile. She and it have been left behind in Ithaka for use only there, a prize indefinitely inaccessible but now at long last to be set out before hungry suitors. Superficially beautiful and *kleos*-granting trophies, the woman and the bow ultimately become high-strung agents of death (17.38–40, 73, 59–62). She holds it on her knees, where it provokes her tears, and later also those of Eumaios and Philoitios, abused as fools for their pain (21.56–57, 82–83; 85, 95). Their failure to draw the bow shames the suitors, as they well realize. Note the heap of words that indicate sunken status: αἰσχυνόμενοι, κακώτερος, χείρονες, ἀμύμων, ἐλέγχεα (21.285–87,

---

42. 17.265–68, 296–300, 340–41 with 22.8, 5.245, 23.197, 21.40–45; Austin 1975, 168–71 pulls this *Gestalt* together. The word *ithyne*, "directed, aimed," here applied to "truing" a threshold, verbally anticipates Odysseus' later aim of a lethal arrow at Antinoos at 22.8. The action nonverbally implicates, as do *xes-* words ("smooth"), long-pondered and carefully drawn plans and their execution.

305–9, 322–29). The very idea of the beggar's attempt disgraces them. The contest loses its noble character and becomes stigmatized as a free-for-all. Odysseus' most careful inspection of the decisive object reveals no damage, no pollution at all. He tests the lovely evil every which way for worm-rot. He takes every precaution and no chances (21.55–57, 82–83, 393–400). He tests everyone and everything. The bow has remained intact, untouched, and responsive to his touch.

The murderous bow is also emblematic of Odysseus: long lost from Ithakan activity or even sight, a proper *xeinion* from a proper host, Iphitos, himself later an abused and murdered *xenos*. At once a symbol of friendship and an instrument of enmity, its essence is pain and penetration—death. It suddenly awakes from deep and distant obscurity to focus all attention and determine sex rights to Penelope and property rights to a vast estate. He who manipulates it manipulates the mistress. The unique bow is Odysseus' distinctive personal attribute as hunter and master, his objectual correlate, the sign and tool by which he pivots from beggar to master. In mirroring mode, the unique spiderwebbed bed is spinning Penelope's objectual pivot from presumptive, commanding widow to reestablished, obedient wife. At one and the same time, from different perspectives, the instrumental bow provides symbolic expression of the husband, the wife, the family, the house, and the situation of impotent obscurity masking lethal potential.

10. Conclusions

Annoyingly obtrusive Odysseus employs visible, social handicaps to approach, comment on, and make requests of the suitors. His final asking—the bow—ought to be precluded by his apparent social identity and its "imputed defects." His true social stigmata are his objectlessness and familial baselessness and his presumed attendant powerlessness. As soon as he departs from accepted mascot performances and requests a try, both Penelope and the suitors explicitly assert his social deviance (21.285 = 17.481; 21.309–10, 317, 323, 329, 339–42). The once and future wife confirms that the beggar's prize would necessarily be different. The insecure wooers still express justified fear of losing "face," here their recognized elite privilege and status.

Begging for elite privilege makes nonsense of the social system. The clowns are not fools in this realization. Attempting to string the bow falls beyond the boundary of this stigmatized interloper's tolerable behavior. Penelope's offer of different gifts, a kind of consolation prize, should the vagrant be successful acknowledges the social eccentricity of his request. Odysseus' verbal and nonverbal behavior here conflict with each other: he demands consideration in words, while his appearance and its "implied biography" deserve little or none. Odysseus is told to resume his expected role—or else.[43] At this moment, his inability to continue to manage a counterfeited social identity infuriates the blustering nobility. The suitors noisily try to police the scene by well-justified cautionary tales and coercive threats. Disclosure at this critical moment would be lethal, but Homer's "disguised husband" folktale plot, Telemakhos' boyish impatience, and Penelope's folkloric bride contest do not permit turning back.

No moment in the *Odyssey* creates more hair-raising pleasure for me than the *seated* beggar's slow but easy flexing and stringing of the mighty bow, his testing twang that nonverbally announces victory number one and suggests number two, his perfect shot through the ax-heads. His brief speech, still in guise of guest-friend, about the suitors' dishonor to *Telemakhos'* house follows. Then—in a "loud" proxemic shift—he rises to an *elevated* position,[44] strips off his stigmatized body-adaptors, and takes an assertive, oppositional, and heroic orientation before aiming at and killing Antinoos. All these nonverbal behaviors assert identity and possession. The angry, still benighted suitors comically misinterpret this last symbolic as well as instrumental act as an error: νήπιοι οὐκ ἐνόησαν. Now Odysseus first nonverbally reveals himself as a peer, indeed a superior. His unprecedentedly *open* dark-browed look at them marks his basileutic social privilege of condemning their breaches in decorum. Then he addresses them with the insulting (and rare) vocative "dogs." Finally, he verbally identifies the premises as his own: house, servants, and wife (22.34–38, 60).

The situation demands that the suitors rapidly, comically, and drastically shift their ground and claims. They try to recognize new status and new relations. Eurymakhos' urgent effort to appease Odysseus, the restored hero of the household, utterly fails, but his unique speed in acknowledging the new, awkward situation characterizes an able and agile interlocutor. His "double-take" tries to take back all the previous cuts and snubs to the seemingly powerless outlander and reveals a becoming, if impossibly sudden, moral reassessment. Duplicitous deference to the new princely identity assumed by the stranger(?) offers an example of inadequate and poorly timed

---

43. Goffman 1963 analyzes forms of excessively unequal intercourse (8, 12, 43–45, 49, 93, 110, 122, 130, 142).
44. He is standing instead of sitting, and only here the threshold seems raised; see Stanford addenda ad 22.126–27.

(an aspect of chronemics) revisionist manners.[45] The change is maybe too little and certainly too late. In a minute's peripeteia, the beggar has moved from condemned, outcast murderer, easily and righteously consigned to the vultures, to lawful lord of the people and the *oikos,* wronged in house, woman, servants, cattle, and land. In even the suitors' eyes, he stands most deserving of reparation (τίμη: cattle, bronze, gold) and honorable, social restitution. The confession restores a proper hierarchy on the cognitive and moral level, but much blood yet needs to be spilled to satisfy the heroics of the Laertid household and the teen-age blood-lust latent in all audiences.

11. Epilogue: Odysseus Who?

The weird beggar becomes increasingly impudent, no longer menial, as he responds to Amphinomos, Eurymakhos, Antinoos, and Ktesippos' gratuitous nonverbal and verbal abuse. Indeed, despite his own foreknowledge and a strategy shared with Telemakhos (13.306–10, 16.274–80), he starts to lose control of his much vaunted, resolute endurance. Powerful immobility yields to inappropriate aggression and alacrity, for example, when he travels around the table, manages the torchlight, and requests and examines the bow (17.446–62; 19.44–45, 66–71; 21.393–95).

Similarly, Telemakhos' responses increase in intensity and open hostility. He maintains silence when Antinoos assaults his father, just shaking his head; after Eurymakhos' mischief, he blurts out pent-up anger verbally; after Ktesippos' unprovoked belligerence, he threatens death itself (17.489, 18.406–9, 20.304–8). The intensification and triplicity emphasizes both the suitors' *hybris* and the inherent difficulty of heroic restraint. Telemakhos emerges more and more into the limelight and runs the carny show in book 21, lines 106–12: "Hit the target, win a wife."

Odysseus' official role as suitors' housepet is strained. Indeed, his repeated claims to *former* nobility and royalty are essential for him to play an openly double role: displaced gentry of yore and currently hard-up vagrant. For the first-time reader, and not only for him or her, it is curious how long (in narrative time, not "real" time for the reader) Odysseus wears the uncomfortable mask. Poetics of narrative deferral mirror the hero's strategics of deferral. His performed, demeaned character has already been strained to the breaking point in interchanges with leading suitors, but Homer maintains

---

45. 21.404–22.68. See Schiffrin 1977, 682, 687, on conversational shifts. At 22.45, Eurymakhos still has understandable doubts about the vagrant's sudden change: εἰ μὲν δὴ 'Οδυσεὺς 'Ἰθακήσιος εἰλήλουθας . . . , "If in very truth, as you say . . ."; cf. Denniston 1966, 345.

the charade to the last possible moment. Premature heroic boast would conflict with Odysseus' successful ploy. When he later handles the bow expertly, when he successfully strings it, and at last when his pluck tests it, his identity has been nonverbally revealed. The suitors' affect, pale faces, confirms this reading nonverbally. In a reflex of the "eat first, identify yourself later" pattern, Odysseus kills first (Antinoos), then clarifies his true(?) identity.

Who, finally, is Odysseus? Readers, always encouraged to think they know more than the characters imprisoned in a story, sympathize with Telemakhos' impatience at Penelope's refusal or failure to acknowledge the stranger as her estranged husband. Her calibrated resistance is validated by the bed trick, but should she have ever given in? Is he the same Odysseus? What constitutes *the same* Odysseus? Do his identifying traits and apparent and seductive beauty, scar, and cleaned-up appearance finger him? Does the heroic murder of the suitors (easy accomplishment for any god, as Penelope notes), his knowledge of the bed's immovability (easy information for any god to know), and failure to remain calm when lied to prove he is the "real" Odysseus (23.155–63, 73–77, 94–95, 174–76, 63–67, 184–204, 181–83)?

What is distinctive and specific about me, you, or him? Odysseus, wanting recognition, stops offering signs about himself. After twenty years, Penelope has every motive to and interest in accepting this man as her husband. Not only that; how can she refuse the man(?) who has some odd power watching over him and who has obtained her son and nurse for allies? Consequently, she does accept him, once she has stripped him of self-assured cockiness.[46] As always, she makes the best of impossible situations. After all, she had publicly agreed to marry the bow champion.

The silence of Penelope opposite Odysseus conveys radical uncertainty, and its duration (an aspect of chronemics, the only qualifier of affect now easily available) conveys how deep it is. Their mutual stillness communicates profound paralysis, the dynamic balance of powerful, *homophrosynic* forces that here have stymied one another. Silence and stillness in position (proxemic zero-sign) here and elsewhere complement speech. They are not redundant; in fact, they can be argued to equal or surpass the verbal message. The semiotics of narrative distinguishes voluntary from forced silences, reciprocal turn-taking pauses from univocal interruptions.[47] Odysseus' stillnesses in

---

[46]. Pucci 1987, 89–94, asks good characterological questions of a slippery text.

[47]. The last term indicates interruptions by others, such as "cutting in," intrusive laughter, or complete aphonia. For example, the surprising Odyssean formulaic response of "no winged words" requires attention (1.345, 21.386, 20.346); cf. Combellack 1950/51, 21–22; Poyatos 1981, 7, 11–13, 20; Lateiner 1992a.

his own house are voluntary pauses between ten years of travel and the coming massacre, between necessary, competitive deconstruction and marital reconstruction, between journeys out and further journeying inland.

Does Penelope know this man, at best a middle-aged, trench-hardened war veteran? Is a husband absent for twenty years, killing for ten of them and wiving and swiving for eight sufficiently the same person as the man she married? As is so often true in real life, yes and no. In a narrative about the interplay of psychic identity and social roles, we are induced, like Penelope perhaps, but with less pressure and less excuse, to accept as spouse[48] the polytropic favorite of the pantotropic goddess. If we take Penelope's final ruse seriously as probative of one male's identity, we can argue that not the body, the manners, or the cunning consciousness makes Odysseus Odysseus but rather Penelope's imprinted memory of touchy pride and her goads of male frailty.

Odysseus' props come to possess him, not only (literally) his superficial clothes and complexion, but also his convenient and elusive identities. By every disguise that congeals on him, he loses some nondisguised, original trait or feature. Perhaps Homer suggests that we all confide too much in the existence of personality "essences." In any case, the wedding march plays for the true groom or the new groom. The blessed event includes its own torchlit procession and "first night" lovemaking "in the old bed's firm place" (23.296).

"Retroactivation" (*Nachträglichkeit*) suffuses the *Odyssey*.[49] Earlier scenes gain pungency when later events trigger reconsideration of an earlier one. Odysseus' arrival on Ithaka mirrors (reflects and reverses) arrival on Skheria; Odysseus' initial Ithakan conversation with Athene mirrors that with Nausikaa; and Odysseus' tall tales told to Eumaios, the suitors, and Penelope mirror those even taller ones told to Alkinoos and his table guests. Doublets, triplets, and quadruplets reflect composition by theme, catenary construction, and the momentum of popular oral tradition. Penelope recapitulates the evidence for the hero that every woman is *vagina dentata* as well as potential spousal perfection. So he stays wary. The next morning, however, he directs her back to her room and the surviving servant-women, into secluded patriarchal silence (23.364–65).

---

48. Daniel Vigne's film, *Le retour de Martin Guerre* (1982), Janet Lewis' novel, *The Wife of Martin Guerre* (San Francisco, 1941), and N.Z. Davis' historical study, *The Return of Martin Guerre* (Cambridge, 1983) explore a similar historical conundrum from sixteenth-century France. The American cinematic remake, *Sommersby* (1992), sets the same problem in post–Civil War America.

49. Pucci 1987, 86; the analyst Fenik's 1974 book, part 2, esp. "anticipatory doublets," preechoes deconstructionist criticism.

Chapter 10

The Suitors' Take: Manners and Power in Ithaka

1. Introduction

The suitors' behaviors present a coherent pattern that is offensive to heroic decency. The give-and-take procedures of those men of acknowledged stature are notable for violation of rules, intentional insult, and nonverbal humiliation of the host. The method of this chapter borrows from the human sciences of social psychology, historical anthropology, and comparative economics. Categories of nonverbal behavior, of social order and face-to-face interaction, and models of distributive reciprocity, including patterns of gift-exchange, provide students of antiquity with tools for analyzing practices and habits that structure all communities. Heroic power, prestige, and their creative deformations employ scowls and sneers more than swords to establish dominance.[1]

This chapter explores institutions of ubiquitous influence (religious, economic, political, and social) and personal interactions among the suitors and between them and the Laertids. This exploration of elite ideology, of "what goes without saying," describes quotidian values with which all comply complaint-free. Those in power "extort the essential while seeming to demand the insignificant." This chapter will foreground lesser phenomena,

---

1. A growing consensus holds "that the institutions and modes of thought [and social interaction] in the poems were ultimately derived from the world in which Homer and his audience lived" (I. Morris 1986, 82; pace Kirk, Finley, et al.) Reflections of real life in *some* contemporary period, more than a settled date for any particular institution or cultural artifact, are important for my belief that oral epic gains its immediacy from observing everyday behaviors. Lacking archaeological, contemporary artistic, and historical evidence, our generalizations about heroic human behavior depend on one fixed literary version of a once fluid, cocreative oral tradition. Non-Homeric comparative data from Greece and elsewhere exist for *Realien* (helmets, goblets, ships and trade routes, "palaces"). Material goods thus allow more historically verifiable interpretation. I. Morris 1986, 81–83, and Van Wees 1992, 1–58, describe the methodological issues. Dead features of the past continually perish in "collective presentation," such as traditional oral epic; "epic distance" accounts for archaizing, exaggerated, and invented elements (I. Morris 1986, 89).

small gestures and apparently offhand comments, in a carefully plotted text. "One of [the *Odyssey's*] . . . central themes . . . is the contrast between those who notice tokens and put together meanings and those who do not."[2]

The depth and "psychology" of Odyssean characters, including Penelope and Telemakhos, have provoked revisionist debate, but this dispute has not affected the evaluation of the less-articulated suitors. They are obvious villains. Hungry and thirsty, they are lazy consumers, lustful, increasingly murderous, and bullying toward their social inferiors. No one has fully dissected their carefully plotted, but clumsily executed, attempts to seize power.[3]

This chapter provides social context, a pattern of mannerly expectation that enables appreciation for the suitors' comedy of manners. Maladroit face-to-face encounters and awkward gestures require comparison to the adroit players. A sociopsychological critique of egregious "manners" develops from inside the Homeric value system. "To the manner born," the suitors nevertheless stumble frequently. The social bunglers exemplify every flaw in the heroic system. Their *kakoxeinia,* faulty and inverted management of rules of heroic reciprocity, and their *dyssemia,* faulty and "out-of-sync" nonverbal behaviors, invite Homer's close attention and his audience's amusement. Manners often reveal morals. Courtesy and deficiencies in etiquette produce communicative reactions of pleasure or indignation.[4] Zeus is usually invoked in the *Odyssey* as *xenios* and *hiketesios.* The god of guests/strangers and god of suppliants amounts to the god of just dealings, *dikaios.*[5]

Embarrassment is an efficacious means of social organization. Odysseus, in his roles as beggar, guest, father, and *philos,* needs to express alignment or disalignment to events in Ithaca by small behaviors. He can remain "composed," ignore slights, become flustered, withdraw from the presence of tormentors, or develop screens behind which to hide his reactions from

---

2. Bourdieu 1977, 95. Austin 1975, 128–29, bravely challenges minimalist and analyst critics while chiding the myopic suitors.

3. Woodhouse 1930, 200, 204; Donlan 1982b; Levine 1982b, 1983a offer helpful observations. Paris in the background, the culturally embedded Trojan War myth, and Polyphemos in this poem provide "anticipatory doublets," preechoes of the theme of legitimacy trampled, deference deferred, and hospitality violated. See too Van Wees 1992, 44–48, 228–37, on "the hospitality racket."

4. Hohendahl-Zoetelief 1980 surveys inner and outer "right attitudes," more in the *Iliad* than in the *Odyssey.* The author usefully points out aberrations from heroic norms, but problems of definition and method vitiate the study. Simpson 1992 describes Homeric hospitality as an index of morals.

5. 7.162–65; 9.269–71; 13.213; 14.56–58, 158, 284; 16.422; 17.484. The first two epithets provide the concrete embodiment or example of the third quality or principle: "observant of custom and social rule, civilized" (LSJ, 9th ed., s.v. δίκαιος).

others—players and audiences (Goffman 1967a: "Embarrassment and Social Organization," 102). He could be poised or easily enraged and lash back. The plot in the banquet hall develops the theme of deception under intense pressure.

The symposiastic suitors face the same situation and choices in moments of social awkwardness. Their own little system teeters on the verge of collapse. The cleavage that results from attacking the vagrant, the quarrels attendant on the plan to murder Telemakhos, and Amphinomos' various gestures of compromise (as the "good suitor") toward Telemakhos and his guest suggest incipient disunion, growing conflict, and problems of discipline. Antinoos pretends to be cognizant of the rules of decorum and embarrassment, yet encounters with the beggar discredit this self and the communal self-presentation of the suitors as gracious nobles or *basileis*. Attempts to embarrass thus embarrass the embarrassers. Audiences enjoy discomfitted villains.

Then, embarrassment spreads in widening circles. In "destroying another's image, he destroys his own" (Goffman 1967a, 106). The seemingly generic beggar presents a familiar social face that the suitors are comfortable with: a new, grateful Iros. His self-imputed poverty and isolation strip from him any insulation that networks and loyal friends provide. He has nowhere to turn, and his world is shrunk to the dimensions that the suitors will afford him, namely, a role of universal, unquestioning deference. While they josh Telemakhos, pretending not to mean what they really do mean, their threatening banter with the beggar is instantly serious, an attempt to force him to play the only role that they have allowed or assigned him. His counterproposals, however, assault their expectations, as he manipulates their lingering attachment to the known roles of vagrants. They proffer trial by taunts to both the socially marked beggar and the unprotected, unassimilated son.

Similarly, men of Skheria police Nausikaa by taunts and even (in her head) threat of taunts. She should not converse with or be followed, however distantly, by a man (6.273–99, cf. 6.304–7), because (a) she is a postpubescent, nubile female and (b) her gendered, grown-up personality (wife and mother) is still unsettled. Her "stream of conduct" must continually project a self acceptable to her relatives, community elders, and male acquaintanceship—the pool of spouses. Embarrassment is especially effective in controlling conflicts with a component of gender.

In modern American face-to-face interactions, it has been estimated that 55 percent of emotional meaning is conveyed through a steady stream of facial expressions, postures, and gestures; 38 percent through tone of voice and other paralinguistic phenomena; and only 7 percent through explicit words.⁶ Furthermore, nonverbal behavior, a facet of all immediate encounters, is continuous and unavoidable: face-to-face, one cannot *not* communicate with face and body. The suitors exhibit double *dyssemia*, faulty active and passive nonverbal behavior. They inappropriately use time, space, postures, and gesture to communicate; and they incorrectly read others' cues and comments. Their abuse of (intended) conventional symbols—such as Antinoos' "comforting" touching of Telemakhos; Ktesippos' "guest-gift"; the suitors' blatantly phoney, friendly tones and gestures; and their "leakage" of (unintended) emotive symptoms, such as lip biting and laughter⁷— convey heroic gaucheness, or social unworthiness for the marital, military, and political roles to which they aspire (cf. chapter 5). These semiotic behaviors communicate instability and inadequacy, interactions parallel to various faerylanders, from subcivilized and hard Kyklopes to the dancing and effete, supercivilized, and soft Phaiakians, with their warm baths, downy beds, and large wardrobes.⁸

Nonverbal behaviors universally organize, regulate, and punctuate social encounters between equals and unequals and between families and strangers. Telemakhos arrives openly and plainly at the beach at Pylos and at the palace in Sparta as a stranger. There, as part of his reception, he encounters proper peer-greetings. The royal family rises to greet a visitor of apparent equality— identifiable, one imagines, by his gait, clothes, and bearing. The hosts lay out their best: baths, clothes, food, wine, and so forth. When Odysseus enters the Phaiakian palace, first invisible, then low near the ground, unidentifiable as an equal and unannounced, his sudden and humble approach, borrowed clothes, and lowering of position (7.139–54, at Arete's knees and in the ashes of the fireplace) nonverbally betoken a different social persona. His avoidance of the usual series and sequence of guesting motifs (a significant absence) patently admits and acknowledges his lack of any status in that social order. He has calculated that it is best not to demand any.⁹ His ges-

---

6. Nowicki and Duke 1992, 7, based on the work of Albert Mehrabian, discusses American patterns of communication. No evidence suggests that ancient Greeks were *less* expressive than contemporary Americans. Roughly 10 percent of the American juvenile population experiences problems transmitting and receiving nonverbal signals. Conversation occupies approximately forty minutes per day in "real life"—no more (ibid., 19)

7. We register conscious and ungovernable aspects of others' bodily expression ("leakage") to read motives and check covertly the reality of others' attempts to present themselves in the most favorable light (social "face" and face-work).

8. Dickie 1983, 257–62, extracts for Homer the moral significance of luxurious and enervated lifestyle (θρυπτικός).

9. 3.12–74, 4.1–75, 7.142–53; G. Rose 1969; Scheflen 1972, 2, 23. M. Edwards 1992, 304–8, examines Homeric reception type-scenes.

tures, postures, and skulking proxemics manipulate his superiors' responses. Beggars, it turns out, can be choosers.

2. *Basileis* Behavior: Greeting, Eating, Gifts, and Territory

Rank and hierarchy, ubiquitous in the animal kingdom, organize all known societies. To flourish in any group, individuals must convey suitable self-image, negotiate self-interest, manipulate flexible rules, short-circuit competing parties, ingratiate themselves with higher-ups effectively enough to request favors, signal superiority to obtuse subordinates, and align status with presumed equals. Asymmetrical encounters, or exchanges between social unequals, endorse and confirm unequal status. As traveler, suppliant, and hobo, Odysseus generally can only take, not give. Generic Homeric princes like Diomedes promise full reciprocity, should current interactants ever arrive as guests (*Il.* 6.224–25). Self-lowering in encounters, which consists of granting respect, prestige, and power to interactants, positions the initiator to receive a favor or gift.[10] Parties can choose to express equal or lower status, regardless of other indexes of status ranking. Thus, at Eumaios' steading, *aristos* Telemakhos refuses to stand (or sit) on ceremony with the drover and the beggar (16.42–53).

Territoriality, animal establishment and maintenance of keeping competitors out or in, generally occurs out-of-awareness by means of unobtrusive body language, facial expression, and paralinguistic phenomena (such as pace, tone, and voice volume). Penelope's suitors are much preoccupied with maintaining group affiliation and cohesion (games, feasts, and cult), while they hope to gain possession of the palace and to establish domination and submission in their own ad hoc social order. They expend much energy policing "outsiders" by threats, proxemics, and ploys that embarrass. Telemakhos, Penelope, and (implicitly and nonverbally as well as progressively more openly) the beggar Odysseus question the suitor' space, their place, and their self-determined, exclusive rights to consume the family's stores and occupy the widow's bed. The suitors repeatedly need to make their privileges explicit and to disrespect verbally and impede nonverbally all interlopers,

---

10. Irvine 1974, 169, 175–76. In situations of prestation like the potlatch, admitting one's inferiority can save much wealth. See Crane 1992, 17, on "symbolic performance of wealth" and voluntary abasement; Gould 1991, 6–19, on "the logic of the gift" and its explanatory power in the *Histories* of Herodotos. Its nonverbal compulsory dynamic should be clear in Homer as well, from Agamemnon's abortive offers in the *Iliad* to Penelope's gift to Odysseus: the golden brooch *ekphrasis* (περόνη χρυσοῖο, 19.226).

even the rightful heir and the pathetic beggar (1.387, 402). Intended rudeness italicizes the precarious nature of their dubious claims and downright illegitimate occupation.

The suitors' partying in the manor house furthermore presents "ritual profanation" of the Laertid clan's stage for social encounters, their "front region." By treating someone else's *megaron* as their private dining-space and playroom, despite explicit territorial rejections, the four-year guests both establish the territory as their own and diminish the proprietors' social stature. Further, they usurp the owner's economic claims to distribute his accumulated surpluses. Their collusive plan is quite open: self-elevation by other-derogation—or murder.

Odysseus is presumed dead already (1.166). Even if he were home alive, he would be liable to be pushed aside (cf. 11.494–503 on Peleus, and the parlous situation of Laertes, no older than Nestor). His only heir, whose claim to the patrimony is preeminent by birth but contested, is being squeezed out economically and socially (1.386–404). Odysseus' wife, herself a source of economic productivity (4.125–32; 15.20–23, 125–29; 24.129–45), and the rest of his considerable estate are up for grabs. No viable organization or opposition beyond the *oikos* emerges (2.26–34, 239–41, 257–58). The heads of insular *oikoi* compete perpetually for every heroic chiefdom (16.385–86; Qviller 1981, 117, 124, 134; Donlan 1982b, 150). Eurymakhos himself notes that there are plenty of other eligible women (21.250–52), but Penelope seems to be considered the pick of the crop. Penelope's hand, it would seem, offers a veneer of legitimacy to the "throne" for the successful wooer.

Homeric epic presents ceremonies of encounter to indicate social equality and inequality (see chapter 4). Verbal and nonverbal behaviors include initiating, turn taking, and terminating encounters; favor requesting; and prestation. "Residual rules" govern all encounters, while dramatic crisis arises from their violation. Making acquaintance on the Iliadic battlefield, for instance, requires ceremonial challenge, vaunts and taunts, exchange of genealogical trees and economic boasts, and so forth.[11] In Odyssean travel encounters, host's and visitor's etiquette of arrival and reception is clear, if varied by military strength and social status. The second-class goddess Kalypso's resentful but polite reception of Olympian Hermes, for humorous instance, presents intelligence, self-control, and impeccable courtesy. She "greets up" to a superior and caves in to all his demands (5.55–148). Odys-

---

11. See Donlan 1993, 158–63; Donlan 1989, 6 (gift giving as a weapon), 14–15 (Agamemnon's and Glaucus' prestation defeats); M. Edwards 1992, 299–303 (battlefield type-scenes).

seus' disguise as beggar later on Ithaka allows him, by submissively "greeting up," to gain essential food and shelter from several hosts. Suitors bend and try to break every rule to check his advance, but they find their acts botched and their expectations stymied. They, like us, depend on others knowing their place.

Ithaka and its neighbors present no organized state and king, only estates and *aristoi, basileis,* and the rest of the nonelite, Ithakan adult male demos (cf. 2.239, 4.652). Homer does not portray a baronial aristocracy or idle potentates.[12] The many insular *basileis,* or chiefs, however rich, usually work with their hands. They stand in perpetual danger of replacement (18.365–75, 16.424–30) and jostle unceasingly for social dominance in a society of many chiefs. The categories for gaining esteem and eminence are the size of each household, its wealth and resources, the number of the chief's retainers, the chief's skill in forging profitable marriages and foreign guest-friendships, and the chief's leadership in foraging for booty in others' territories (e.g. 19.282–86, 294; Odysseus and Iphitos at 21.34–36).

The self-selected subgroup of *basileis* who have come to woo Penelope show determined indifference to the entire ceremonious system of heroic exchange. They reject the norms of suitorhood, the well-known *mnesteron dike* of giving gifts, arranging feasts (18.275; 1.132–34, 225–29, 365), and maintaining the peer values practiced at Pylos, Sparta, and Phaiakia. They assail and revile the lower ranges of society. Alkinoos has prepared us to judge their conduct: ξεῖνός θ'ἱκέτης τε, 8.546–47, "Anyone with any brains considers both guest *and* supplicant as good as a brother." The consistent rituals of ancient Homeric society reflect other, contemporary large tribal groups where people in small political units relate in various social ways to each other: ruler, priest, teacher, patron, parent, mate, and so forth. Nonverbal ritualization helps to clarify whichever role one fulfills at any given moment. Nonverbal etiquette often signifies and segregates discrepant statuses (e.g., son or *basileus*). Departures from such embedded custom amount to breach of duty.

After Penelope made clear her desire to wait for her husband, Odysseus, the swains' most mannerly act would have been to leave and to sue her father

---

12. Halverson 1985, 130, 135–66, and n. 18, and Finley 1978, 91, discuss division of labor. Daily work by ordinary people receives scant attention: Odysseus (posing as a former *aristos*) boasts of skill in fire making and cooking, and later in plowing and mowing (15.320–24, 17.20–21, 18.357–75; in manuring, 17.297–99; cf. I. Morris 1986, 123). No sharp distinction among classes and their tasks colors the *Odyssey*. Therefore, one should avoid the anachronistic words *kings* and *revolution,* two frequent and misleading translations for this prepolis and prestate society.

Ikarios for her "hand" in marriage.[13] By barging in and camping out, they have only rudely manifested lust and their determination to seek status and wealth. They eat without measure and dally indefinitely. The wooers of Penelope have already usurped Odysseus' position as dispenser of Laertid capital. The suitors follow their own set of rules for winning Penelope as wife. They once shower her with gifts—but only after her reproof, when one would expect that only her father can marry her off. They establish turn-taking procedure among themselves for the bow contest and propose and accept a time-out in that contest. A modicum of honor and respect, therefore, survives among these thieves, but no regulated or regular access to desired property and political dominance. The one hundred and eight suitors (16.245–53) have commandeered a physical stage, the courtyard and banquet tables. With the tone and color of paramount lords, the assembled companions bring along their "portable territory." The suitors invert the paraphernalia of hospitality and bride contests (including epithets, formulaic verses, type-scenes, and pervasive narrative patterns of power).

Guest-friendship and the dinner table are the loci of nonverbal social skills. The feast "cues in" community values, comity and ethical excellence. The vinous banquets of Nestor, Menelaos, and even Eumaios are exemplary. The egregious Menelaos realizes that immoderate hospitality can annoy as much as too little. A guest in haste should not be detained but sent off (ἐθέλοντα δὲ πέμπειν, 15.68–79). Despite his royal domestic problems, the Spartan ruler provides an expansive version of "normative hospitality."[14] To the contrary, the narrated entertainments provided by Herakles and to Eurytion (21.26–30, 295–301—negative exemplars of host and guest themselves) lead to slaughter and mutilation. All hosts and guests, good and bad,

---

13. 2.50–54. Theoklymenos shows them the exit; Amphinomos intuits that departure would be wise but is supernaturally restrained (20.371-72, 18.153–57). No precedent or parallel to this woo-and-siege operation suggests that the suitors remain by some squatters' right. The anomalous opportunity arises from husband's twenty-year absence.

14. The Spartan scene, however, offers one explanation of Odysseus' "subsequent" caution and concern in Skheria. Conveyance *out* obsesses him; eight of his tales concern "hosts" who make one linger too long or eat one up. His narrated portraits of his mistresses Kirke and Kalypso as threatening detainers clarify Odysseus' determination to return home to his wife or pretence thereof. Phaiakian manners are exceptional, perhaps shocking by conventions of Homeric name and gift exchange, and the *apologoi* of books 9–12 supply an example of one smart but helpless guest's strategy of narrative indirection. G. Rose 1969 describes the dangers of this last stop. Most 1989b, 23, 25, 29, addresses Odysseus' "narrative situation" and the function of Odysseus' long or tall tales; Webber 1989, 11, notes that only Kyklops and Alkinoos ask for a proper name and get it. Since the first revelation proved to be disastrous, Odysseus later delays it. Brown 1966, 194–99 uncovers name magic and tabu.

present foils or "anticipatory doublets"[15] for the palmary case: the suitors' extended displays of negative hospitality, indecent table behavior, and ignominious end (1.365–71; 17.564–68; 21.26–29 [the same bow!], 295–304).

The narrative prominence of *xenie,* mutual hospitality—actual or promised reciprocity and grateful requital—reflects its role in determining this story's heroes and villains. *Charis* (χάρις, χαρίεσσα ἀμοιβή, 3.58–59), fair exchange of benefits, can sometimes lead to *tisis,* revenge or requital of injuries (1.40, 2.76, 22.218). The superficially festal banquet has become a jackals' feast. When native son Telemakhos gets shunted aside in his own house, the vocabulary of bestial voraciousness describes the act (βιβρώσκειν, 2.203).[16] The rude suitors respect no one and no institutional hierarchy, as everyone notes (e.g., 2.162–69, 14.89–95, 22.414–15, 23.65–66). The banquet tests them (cf. *Il.* 4.257–59); they fail to welcome, refuse to share, sacrifice inadequately, and raise endless ruckus (1.132–34, 4.768–75).

They have perverted the social graces, manifestations of the moral order, in their extortionate commensality and treatment of society's underdogs: children, outcasts, and women. They taunt the manor's heir, Telemakhos (with perpetual "kidding," snide sniping, and, finally, attempted murder). They have boxed in the lord's spouse, Penelope (with planted spies, activity policing, house invasion, and occupation, 2.109, 198–99, 237, 247; and with threats of virtual rape or "bride capture"). They pressure and try to entrap beggar Odysseus (with verbal and physical "joshing" or abuse and with threats of enslavement and bodily mutilation, including castration). They suggest that even recognized lords get pushed around when other *basileis* see an opportunity (2.246–51; cf. Akhilleus, 11.501–3). Their ungentle acts create domestic, social, economic, and political crisis. Their nonverbal relaxations—loitering, wenching, and gaming—validate negatively the ruling family's outrage and eventual vengeance. Their anomic behavior and their allegiance solely to their ephemeral group threaten destruction of the existing, dominant but fragile household economy and political order on Ithaka.[17]

---

15. Fenik 1974, part 2, examines the place of type-scenes in oral-traditional/formulaic artistry. Aiolos also rules a prepolis-type community with perpetual feast by day, sleep by night. This closed, incestuous world honors the vagrant well—at first; cf. Vidal-Naquet 1986, 22.

16. Mother Antikleia, answering Odysseus' query about his family holdings, shows how little the dead in the far West know what's what (11.184–87). She oddly and wrongly informs her son that her young (see Stanford ad loc.) grandson manages *basileutic* special plots (τεμένεα), controls the chief's feasts, and administers justice at the behest of all (δικασπόλον ἄνδρα). This provides us with the Homeric noblewoman's horizon of expectation for the typical, (good) eminent lord, not with Telemakhos' reality.

17. One needs to unpack nests of assumptions about Homeric marriage, because the *Odys-*

212 *Sardonic Smile*

The "negative reciprocity," or profiteering, of the suitors toward all "outsiders" and their depredations of the chieftain's persons and goods indicate social dysfunction. No assembly has met since Odysseus' departure two decades ago (2.26–28). No vestige of enduring obligations remains, no suitable network of favor and recompense. Consequently, subordinate men seek "something for nothing" while eroding the chief's wealth. Abrasive uncertainty replaces the usual leader's personal generosity (exchange and redistribution) and wisdom that regularly confirm community structure, that is, tribal solidarity.

The suitors' refusal to give and failure to repay others amount to declaring civil war. The basis of this exchange system is flouted.[18] Dispensing wealth, not hoarding it, makes a man rich in the chiefdoms of the Homeric poems. Vast wealth can only be given away. Economics are woven into all other institutions and symbolic systems. Gifts given through liberal and meaty feasts, *xenie*, marriage bids (or *hedna*), funerals, protection in time of peril, and so on produce honor and insure loyalty, support, and service (e.g.,

---

sey's marriage pattern is unclear. Some critics believe the suitors' claim that they do not endanger Telemakhos' estate and personal security. They *publicly* call for Penelope's return *home* and remarriage according to patrilocal custom (Penelope's stated plan). This outcome should give Telemakhos control of his patrilineal estate, but their lively interest in the property seems evident from the cabal's plans to dispose of the rightful heir (2.111–14, 1.275–78, 19.137–59, 21.71–77; also 4.700, 16.383–92, 22.52–53; cf. 16.385–86). Antinoos explicitly expects the *house* to go to the successful gift-bidder/groom, once no Laertid estate-avenger remains to cause anxiety. Usual procedures are to be bypassed (see 18.275–80). The suitors seem to reason that, if Penelope is successfully wooed in Odysseus' palace and Telemakhos "disappears," a "shadow of legitimacy" (in Finley's phrase [1978]) would promote her new husband's claim to the Ithakan property and political supremacy in Ithaka.

The possibility of Penelope leaving for her original home creates real dilemmas. There are at least three possibilities. If Telemakhos requests that Penelope return to her childhood home, he would face "cash-flow" problems (2.132–33), because he would need to send many δῶρα with her. Such "gifts" would not restore (nonexistent) dowry but would be needed to prevent a serious rift arising from *basileus* Ikarios' otherwise offended honor. If Ikarios himself requests his daughter's return, however, Telemakhos' precarious economic situation might be safer (cf. 2.52–54, 15.16–18), but Penelope's honor might not be. Returning home at her own behest, she might legitimate the claim of Odysseus' son and lineal successor to all family property, but she would fail in her obligation as affine to protect her son's endangered estate. In her unique circumstances, it seems that it is *her* choice whether or not to return home (20.341–44; 19.157–61). If she does and remarries, her new husband would then acquire a wife, at considerable competitive (*hedna*) cost, but not her former husband's handsome territory. The base of that territory belongs to her former husband's blood descendants, while the periphery belongs to whoever emerges as local big-man. There is no matriliny in Homer (Finley 1978, 87–91)—but Helen has "inherited" the royal line at Sparta.

18. Mauss 1967, 3, 11; Donlan 1982b, 157, 160. The purpose of a chieftain's wealth is to expend it to accumulate debts. Thus, he acquires esteem, prestige, and power. The giver "owns" a debt.

19.27–28). Surplus is exchanged for authority, influence, kinship (by marriage), and even guest-friendship, a quasi-kinship (*xenia*) by the chief. The suitors violate Zeus' law. So say Eumaios, Telemakhos, Odysseus, Penelope, even Zeus and the suitors themselves (14.89–95, 16.85–88, 17.483–87, 22.413–16, 23.63–67, 24.480–86).

The island's semianarchy reflects a semianarchy in the house. Telemakhos' problematic position, as he says, is not a public, legal issue (2.44–45) but one of personal status. Like a Sicilian don, he holds no stable hereditary office in this proto-state and stands to inherit wealth, not institutional power, at best (16.373, 19.159). Telemakhos cannot, however, currently control the financial and agricultural reserves. Food sharing, owed to family, is willingly granted to guest-friends and mendicants (*xeinoi* and *ptochoi*), but not to all and sundry, and not to unhelpful, nonremunerative, ungrateful interlopers indefinitely. Without numbers of inherited followers, virile kin, and *kleos* for warrior leadership, Telemakhos lacks credibility and leverage—personal power in heroic society. Therefore, since he cannot redistribute surplus wealth, he has no public esteem and little residual rank. He cannot prevail at home, much less rule his semi-state. His "political" power, like that of any Homeric *basileus,* can only flow from martial ability and from economic capacity for controlled generosity, that is, for redistributing Laertid surplus goods, the substantial amount of which Eumaios emphasizes (14.96–108). Shifting orbits of support and power confront the not-so-eminent youth, rather than any simple succession to primacy or king's hereditary, politically legitimated office. He must compete for place and prestige with numerous, alien rivals.[19]

The central focus of Telemakhos' emergence into manhood is his conflict with the suitors. Their *hybris* (intentional insult) and his developing skills in deflecting and turning it back on them mark the death of his vulnerable boyhood and the proof of his manhood. He appropriates his father's traits as well as his prerogatives.[20] He starts to mislead, omit, and fabricate as soon as

---

19. Donlan 1982b, 152–53, dissects the nature of Homeric "politics." See also I. Morris 1986, 98–99, for a review of recent literature on the exiguous "element of heredity." Note the irony when the scoffing suitors call Telemakhos "rather poorly allied" (κακοξεινώτερος, 20.376, hapax) because his only friends are the seemingly weak beggar and the seemingly unperspicuous prophet.

20. Telemakhos has experienced a countercultural education of body and emotions. Isolated, emotionally deprived in a man's world, and tortured by snide keepers, the perpetual boy has experienced social deprivation and devastation. We see the Ithakan scene focalized through his eyes. He prudently chooses to leave. Through hearing tales of his father's achievements and through learning to talk with *receptive basileis* elsewhere, the alternately garrulous and morose quasi-orphan learns to listen to internal cues and to ignore destructive hints from copresent

Athene/Mentes leaves. Selective reports safeguard his interests against both the suitors and his mother. He now first appropriates his father's seat at the public assembly—indeed, the first one to be held in Ithaka in 20 years (1.414–16, 2.14). Having stolen a nonverbal march by grabbing the public seat of honor, he confronts the house-hunters verbally there, and he then escapes their prison (2.255). He eludes their ambush on return. He hosts the unwelcome beggar as his guest over suitors' objections and threatens them openly.[21] He develops from abrupt adolescent to capable status warrior. He eventually controls his mother's whereabouts and decides the moment of her pseudodeparture. With Odysseus, he kills the bullies.

Telemakhos, like any adolescent boy, needs help in constructing and consolidating his adult maleness. While he focalizes much of the plot, Homer exposes his tenderness in terms of gender, age, and status. He is tested and queried by friendly males, surrogate fathers. Mentes/Athena, Nestor, Menelaos, Theoklymenos the seer, and the disguised beggar tell him once and again to stand up and fight. And his real father, once revealed, serves the same purpose. They all catalyze his maturation, which is never completed in our text and is always subject to backsliding.

Telemakhos also encounters women. His mother Penelope is a source of adolescent apprehension and exogamous threat. Helen, a paradigm of sexual infidelity, in redomesticated format seems an ironic choice of surrogate mother, but the boy will not trust his own. And the gaudy tale of Klytaimnestre's treachery is thrice rehearsed to the youth, along with "cousin" Orestes' decisive matricide and assumption of power.

But Telemakhos' enemies, not his friends, are the most consistent agents of his emerging manhood. His conflicts with the suitors, their relentless taunts and intentional insults (*hybris,*) manhandle him into manhood. His developing skills in deflecting insult and turning it back on the sources spell the death of vulnerability and the proof of manly gameworthiness. Telemakhos has his own wanderings away from, homecomings to, and revenge on the suitors in the good heroic tradition (cf. 3.313–16, chapter 8). Back in Ithaka, impatient to resolve his ambiguous status, he clashes with his mother and the male

---

desecrators and competitors. Felson-Rubin 1994, 76–79, astutely examines Telemakhos on the basis of psychological and anthropological models. I regret that time did not afford me the opportunity to profit more from this book.

21. His new stride and front, or "presence," causes the cowed, somewhat neutral populace to offer him new respect, while the annoyed suitors try (unsuccessfully) to crowd him in with pretended goodwill (proxemics, 17.61–67). Nonverbal behaviors convey both his change in "front" and his interactants' various responses.

competitors. Once reunited with his father, he perfects status-manipulation skills, evidence of growing confidence and superiority to the other males.[22]

The suitors' strategy, as the *Odyssey* opens, is quite effective. Their goals are to enjoy themselves, to eliminate the basis of Telemakhos' tenuous (at best) political influence—namely, his redistributive capacity—and for one of their number to marry the "widow." Until Penelope chooses a mate, they threaten to devour the absent master's surplus. The distribution of that surplus is Telemakhos' only chance to build prestige from his slight hereditary edge and to gain personal authority in a gift-based society (2.203–5; 14.93–95, 105–8; 18.144).

Economic decline translates for Telemakhos into loss of prestige and capital. Telemakhos cannot now call on Ithakans for services, because he has not hosted them, captained overseas expeditions for booty, or even convened the demos (2.26–32). His journey in search of his father and *kleos*, an infusion of social identity, thus serves at least three purposes: it removes him from immediate danger; it temporarily freezes his continual loss of "face"; and it shows the demos that he *can* act, that he can gather companions, *hetairoi*, furnish a ship, and sail off for *xenie* (guest status and guest-gifts) and/or booty, just like his father (19.333). This demonstration impels public sentiment to shift from helplessness and/or indifference to renewed respect for the Laertid line and to favor the scion's somewhat forlorn cause (1.95, 2.257, 3.199–200, 4.611, cf. 16.371–75; Jones 1988b, 500, 505). His "youth" radically shifts from handicap to exploitable guise.

The suitors distort prestation by turning normative heroic generosity (generalized reciprocity) into personal profit (negative reciprocity). They pervert heroic reciprocity (between unequals) when they half-jokingly and half-seriously advise selling the old, accepted beggar and the newly arrived mendicant into slavery. Finally, they explicitly invert ceremonial guest-gifts so that they become insults (20.381, 105; 20.296). By dishonoring heroic conventions, they lose their chance for good repute (ἐϋκλείη, 21.331). Shame and ill

---

22. This shared male *homophrosyne*, "think-alikeness," parallels the cross-gendered *homophrosyne* of Penelope and Odysseus. The useful family trait collapses only after the suitors are disposed of, in the humorous gridlock and marital denouement of book 23. Here, neophyte hero Telemakhos insists that his mother drop her overdeveloped caution. He oversteps his nonevolving role as her son. At the same time, Odysseus smiles knowingly and tells his browbeating, female-bashing son that husband and wife have their own games and signs for mask dropping. Penelope then trumps all this male trickery, devising, and people-control. *Her* bed trick asserts universal male vulnerability—even for Ithakan heroes. The reestablishment of Odysseus as husband, lord, and master (and of Telemakhos, incidentally, as rightful heir) is achieved by a woman's deceiving and humiliating the clever hero—the final paradox of an epic about vulnerability, insult, and staying afloat in a cruel, man's world.

repute (αἶσχος λώβη τε, 18.215–25; ἀτιμίη, 13.142) are the outcome for unearned freeloading and consumption (cf. *Il.* 12.310–21) and for mistreating and allowing the mistreatment of beggars.

The suitors reward followers from another man's goods, an approved heroic custom, but, uniquely here in Homer, they do so not by raiding the unaquainted and waging battle but by exploiting the ill-guarded household of their nominal host, the Ithakan chief's estate, which is twenty times richer than any other (15.530, 17.256, 18.325; 14.98–104; 17.451–52). There is an absence of heroic leadership, that is, of ongoing reciprocated benefits and exchanges with rewards or honor (χαίροντι . . . χαίρων, 17.83) between the "natural" headman and the demos. The absence of acknowledged indebtedness on all sides appears whenever the suitors show no appreciation for the one-way flow of food and luxury and shut out local Ithakans from further communal feasting. The townspeople cannot get as good as they give; Telemakhos cannot earn their loyalty or exercise control by his stores of food and drink. Even housemaid Melantho has transferred allegiance. She repays Penelope's parental kindness and generosity with ingratitude, saucy insults, and sexual treachery.[23]

The suitors should be "duelling with gifts," the economic analogue to heroic battle, in Walter Donlan's formulation. This event we once see when Penelope descends to the *megaron* and implicitly consents to marry. The ensuing competitive gift giving suits eighth-century bride wooing as well as chieftainship seeking.[24] But this magic moment for Laertid sympathizers (and smiling Odysseus) is an enchanted anomaly (ἔρῳ δ' ἄρα θυμὸν ἔθελχθεν, 18.212) amid the suitors' quotidian routine of enjoying the big chief's material goods and seeking their own material advantage. Their behavior here, "under the influence," violates *their* norm of endless consumption. They ignore the expected norm, to sail to father Ikarios to compete in *giving* wealth, a technique of showing wealth and creating influence (2.50–55). "Giving is also a way of possessing" (Bourdieu 1977, 195). Mutually beneficial exchange of goods, women, and exactly calibrated (if often unbalanced)

---

23. παῖδα δὲ ὥς, "like her child" (18.320–36). She exemplifies, yet once more, untrustworthy female sexuality, a theme transcending class and prominent from divine conclave (1.14–15, 36, 215–16) to Agamemnon's diatribes (11.427–34, 24.193–202).

24. Compare the grandiose economic heroism of Northwest American Indian or ancient Gallic potlatch; Diodorus 5.26, from Posidonios, on Gaul; Donlan 1993. Perysinakis 1991 reviews *hedna* in Homer and discovers a coherent one-way stream of "gift bids" from the suitors to the father of the bride (298). He finds the poems internally consistent: Penelope will go to the highest bidder (16.76–77). I. Morris 1986, 105–10, also argues for bride wealth and against dowry, explaining the resistant, problematic 1.277–78 as "attracting rich *hedna*" (109, with previous *Literatur*).

respect has disappeared or, rather, degenerated into unilateral depredation. The suitors' wordy discourse employs the fiduciary currency of consensual exchange, but expropriating actions and peremptory gestures extort compliance and suggest violent capture.25 They physically consume and destroy another's wealth (φθινύθουσιν, 1.250 = 16.127, 14.95), when they should be producing and accumulating capital to lavish on others. Their very pretensions to hierarchical eminence should tell them to unhand their host's surplus. They are "loitering" (πωλεύμενοι, 2.55) chiefs with no visible braves to reward.

Penelope alludes to another example of the suitors' attrition of reciprocity. Odysseus paternally protected Antinoos' father from a local lynch mob, and the son currently fails to repay that major favor (16.424–33). Antinoos' gratuitous insult of the beggar's thematic and comedic belly draws Telemakhos' sarcastic appreciation of pseudoparental concern for his wealth: ἦ μευ καλὰ πατὴρ ὥς κήδεαι υἷος! "How well, like a father, you care for me!" Penelope condemns them for ingratitude, injustice, and interference with housework (4.682–95). Telemakhos' capital has been consumed without permission by Antinoos for over three years (17.397–402). Again, Antinoos shamelessly refers to Odysseus' once having taken Antinoos himself on his knees to feed him when he was a helpless child (16.442–44). The passing remark underlines both the hero's paternal nurture of his demos and subordinate *basileis* (cf. 2.234, 5.12; 4.687–91) and this *basileus'* inappropriate response. The passage reveals personal debts but little sense of firm institutions. Similarly, Odysseus the *basileus* exercises little discipline at home and little coercion on campaign (*Il.* 2; *Od.* 10.31–48, 428–42; 14.259–70). *Basileis* are given more loot and consumption privileges; therefore, they must spend more (9.548–51; *Il.* 1.165–68; 12.310–21; 17. 249–51; 9.39–43; 19.194–98, 309–11). *Basileis* acquire and confirm local authority by redistributing booty and locally extracted surplus. The βασιλεύτερος lord has more and therefore gives more, as Odysseus, as outside observer, reminds his "betters" (17.415–23).26 Even a boy

---

25. They endorse normal patterns of courtship and inheritance, but their abnormal occupation is condemned by Athene and Zeus, high authority indeed, and by local, interested parties (1.225–29; 14.90–95; 16.430–33, 437–49; 20.330–37; 24.457–60, 480–83). Andromakhe forecasts a gloomy situation for a young, fatherless *aristos* (*Il.* 22.487–89): his lands will be seized by fellow Trojans, even if the Akhaians depart. On prestation, see Donlan 1982b, 171, 141–42; Bourdieu 1977, 195, whose quotation in the text is ultimately based on the 1925 original of Mauss 1967.

26. Generosity exhibited to equals has less savory origins, since "legitimate" surpluses are extracted from inferiors or seized from outlanders. Poseidon and Thersites provide materialist and critical analyses of "asymmetrical reciprocity": *Il.* 21.441–57, 2.225–42; *Od.* 10.40–45

like Telemakhos knows that being "chief" is good—it produces material wealth and superior rank (1.392–93).

The Western suitors are not anomalous in vying for hero-in-chief status. Diomedes, Akhilleus, and Odysseus try to take command at Troy, whenever Agamemnon shows his characteristic foibles and weakness (*Il.* 1, 2, 9.30–56). Agamemnon, supposedly βασιλεύτατος (*Il.* 9.69), can barely cope with the troops or the *aristoi* competition. Telemakhos a fortiori cannot curb the ambitious *basileis* in the multilinear, *oikos*-based Homeric world. Unlike Agamemnon, he cannot establish any lasting debt by giving them gifts. First, the gifts are not yet his to give (despite 21.348–49; cf. 116–17); second, the *basileis* coolly seize the redistributable assets before he can master them (Qviller 1981, 118, 127–30, 143).

The suitors repeatedly mobilize themselves to restore ceremonial order. They have enjoyed excitement and stimulation without cost or reciprocity, but the precarious state of their illegal occupation and irregular consumption of Laertid stores requires continuous "small talk," expressions of group loyalty and mutual respect for their current involvement at Penelope's. They have to shore up indirectly (through metacommunication, often by body language) shared responsibility for interaction rituals and outcome. They fall "out of sync" with interlocutors. Thus, Homer italicizes their unworthiness for Odysseus' estate, house, and wife. They abuse and confuse the channels of nonverbal communication: space and touch, time, gestures and postures (ritualized and idiosyncratic), facial expression, voice (tone, pitch, and volume—all part of paralinguistics), and significant objects.[27]

The suitors institutionalize their social front of superiority by a de facto hierarchy. Their gerry-built order functions well enough until assumed rank and preeminence conflict with requests from Telemakhos, presumably the de iure owner, and from the stranger, who has no standing at all. "The impression of reality fostered by a performance is a delicate, fragile thing that can be shattered by very minor mishaps" (Goffman 1959, 56). This statement about our "routines" in everyday life is all the truer when the front is a questionable or fraudulent one. The guileful suitors, themselves imposters, usurp social status as *xeinoi* to acquire a privileged social, economic, and political eminence as spouse, consumption master, and local chief. They pretend or as-

---

(the crew's proletarian, but not entirely incorrect, suspicion), 13.259–68. These youngish suitors evidently could not or did not follow their local leader to Troy. His contribution there included twelve ships, a significant number (although meager compared to Meges' forty), but more significant for assertion of effective political power are those many *basileis* (not only Penelope's suitors) who stayed behind (*Il.* 2.625–37).

27. Lateiner 1987, 108–12, offers an imperfectly categorized Homeric list.

sume that Odysseus is dead, his possessions theirs to distribute, and his spouse available to the "best man." They impose themselves as a *team* on the house and demos, giving orders as though they were collectively the husband of Penelope.[28]

As a team with obvious coaches and directors, the wooers have insinuated themselves into the *megaron* and into control and exploitation of another man's surplus and, indeed, of all his possessions. They redefine Ithakan political reality by force and threat. They overawe potential dissenters and disturbers, such as the recalcitrant Halitherses, with violent intimations of their collective authority (2.178–93). They impose a party line on doubters within their own ranks, fainthearted Amphinomos and the conscripted Phemios and Medon (16.351–64, 22.354–60). Their conspiratorial routines promote limited camaraderie: macho, sneering riposte; persiflage; and mockery of the heir apparent and his few remaining retainers. Their abuse (σκώμματα) and high-handed invasiveness incur the labels of reckless, senseless, and indecent—ἀφραδέες and ὑβρισταί.[29] They try to elide succession to the wife of the departed warrior with succession to his barley, wine, and gold.

The *basileis* use scolding tones and threats, egg on a beggar's beating, laugh at unheroic pain, and eject an unwelcome messenger of doom (18.78, 84–87, 34–39, 98–100; 20.358–74). The suitors solemnly pledge the victorious new parasite's prospects with a nonverbal toast (18.111–23). Antinoos ineffectually strikes the beggar as his servant-clone Melanthios had. Yet both are powerless to move the new arrival by taunt or force. These class-distinct and class-shared nonverbal behaviors betoken superiority, but other symbolic nonverbal behaviors "leak" their flaccid core. Their knees (an Indo-European site of vulnerability as well as seminal power) go weak in desire for

---

28. Goffman 1959, 104–5, for his concept of *teams,* or collective front. Every society develops some legal mechanism (or a prelegal equivalent, but not this arrangement) for declaring the presumptive death of long-gone missing persons in the absence of conclusive evidence or witnesses. The Homeric poems leave this and other legal essentials in shadow. For classical Athens, moreover, the legal historian Michael Gagarin and I find nothing in the standard tomes describing relevant legal procedures: Lipsius, Harrison, or MacDowell. For contemporary Ohio law, my wife, E. Marianne Gabel, Esq., refers the curious to *Ohio Revised Code* (Anderson Publ., 1990), sec. 2121.01 *et seq.*

29. E.g., 2.282, 16.86, 17.581, 22.288, 24.282; Fisher 1992, 156–84. Mentor offers the demotic Ithakan critique at 2.235–38. Homeric epic's comic technique is parallel for the suitors and Thersites in *Iliad* 2. Odysseus, on landing on Kyklopia, Skheria, and (as yet unknown) Ithaka, first wonders formulaically whether the dwellers are *hybristai* or *dikaioi*, that is, *philoxenoi* (civilized and hospitable: 6.121 = 9.176 = 13.202; 8.575–76). The vocabulary and the anxiety link three life-threatening possibilities: insult, injustice, and inhospitality. For Skheria's pitfalls, see 6.273–74, 313; 7.15–17, 30–33, 159–60; Vidal-Naquet 1986, 33 n. 40, 37 n. 81.

Penelope, parallel in expression to the fear that later loosens the impotent maids' limbs. Their lip biting reveals frustration.[30]

Thus, the suitors have simultaneously violated moral values *and* etiquette. Their norms and their horizon of heroic manners disgrace the implicit ideology and humiliate all interactants. For instance, their athletic, gaming, and feasting protocols improperly exclude host, visitors, and mendicants (1.120, 4.625–27 = 17.167–69; also 17.375–79, 404, 446, 530–37). They resolutely ignore ground rules of the human condition. They eat and drink without limit, their health is excellent, and they never work, so their hands remain "soft and uncalloused." Their soft life of the lyre, epic storytelling, and dance freezes the fabulous "stop-time" of the holy feast-day.[31] Their idle (μαψιδίως) gluttony continues while Laertid clanspersons (or Athene) question their everyday arrangements and comportment. Cherished images of self and society are nourished by social roles they impute to each other. A new beggar seems to present just another source of "unquenchable laughter," like the clowning antics of hobbled Hephaistos on paradisiacal Olympos in *Iliad* 1. The banqueteers constitute a coherent troupe, but only for a truly captive audience.[32] Telemakhos lives in social half-existence, a survivor of his own social death.

The suitors have purposely neglected the obligation and privilege to reciprocate to men and gods (2.55–58, 4.651, 17.532–57, 18.287). They brusquely brush off the beggar as Telemakhos' *xeinos* and not theirs (20.295; 21.313, 424 [Odysseus?]). Although Telemakhos is generous with his own food, Antinoos does not share even another's (17.400–404). He offers only a ballistic footstool, "both symbol and instrument of the coercion of underlings by those in power."[33] The suitors' various truncheons provide inarticu-

---

30. 18.212–13, cf. 340–42 [γούνατα, γυῖα]; 18.410–11; 17.462–64, and 234–35. Indeed, empty kicking and twitching is a quintessential Homeric form of powerlessness (18.98–99, 22.473; cf. Fernandez-Galiano in Russo 1992, ad loc.). Andromakhe draws parallels between beggar and orphan, helplessness and ostracism from food-sharing rites (*Il.* 22.490–99).

31. χεῖρας . . . ἀτρίπτους [hapax] ἁπαλάς, 21.151—unlike the "sturdy" hand of hardworking Penelope and her husband (21.6–7, 20.299). On the inferior status of Skherian and Trojan dancers, see Fernandez-Galiano in Russo et al. 1992, ad loc.; *Od.* 8.246–51; *Il.* 24.261–62.

32. Goffman 1959, 7–9; Dickie 1983, 257; Rick Newton provided the comparison to the Olympians by electronic mail on 23 October 1992. He has studied the effects of poetry inside Homeric narrative. The suitors consume another man's estate ῥεῖα, living like the immor(t)al gods (ῥεῖα ζώοντες: 5.122, 1.160). They arrogate the privileges of another order of being. Thus, they cross the line in an unforgivable way, as the crewmen do when they eat the kine of divine Helios.

33. Thalmann 1988, 12–13, thus describes the scepter with which Odysseus beats Thersites.

late but resentful inferiors with both instrumental harm and nonverbal signs of negative reciprocity—reminders of force, battle, capture, and pain—rather than of hospitality (17.478–80). Antinoos, the creator of the social crisis, confuses "the two opposed poles of the Homeric universe" by throwing his footstool, a ballistic weapon, at the sacralized suppliant, a beggar, in the place of fellowship. Lawless (ἀθεμίστια εἰδώς) Ktesippos adds sacrilege and insult to injury by portentously referring to his missile—a food by-product—as *geras,* "chiefly due," a special *xeinion*. Such abusive "liberality" is as derisory and hubristic as the raw flesh-eating Kyklops' alleged "favor" to Odysseus of saving him for the last to be eaten.[34]

The monster's explicit *verbal* disregard of Zeus is matched by the suitors' *nonverbal* improprieties in honoring the gods. They drink more often than not without final libation, they reduce libation to an empty ritual, and they fail to sacrifice properly, even to send the savory odor, or *knise,* to the gods. They do not fulfill sacrificial promises or perform them according to custom. Thus, they do not share with the gods. Rather, they slaughter another man's cattle (echoing the Ithakan crew's polluted and inadequate ritual when they butcher the cattle of Helios).[35] Like the Kyklops, the partying princelets in Ithaka suit the paradigm of bad hospitality—they feed off hosts, not as literal cannibals, but by eating up his livestock, threatening to deliver his guest to a human butcher, and treating the stranger as the butt of cruel jokes about inhospitality. Dishonor becomes ever more prominent and honor more problematic, as is also true of the *Iliad*'s narrative trajectory.

The suitors' piety is expressed in the wrong way and at the wrong times; their social obligations are recalled by debt-holders but never repaid. "Wastage of money, energy, time, and ingenuity," conspicuous and generous distributions of one's own property that bind the donee to the donor, are all remarkably absent from their activities, except for slim scraps doled to

---

34. 20.296–97; cf. 9.189, 356, and 369–70, for vocabulary; Saïd 1979, 31–32. Fisher 1992, 151, 156–84, notes that nineteen of thirty-one occurrences of *hybris-* words in Homer apply to the suitors. Neither paradigmatically savage Kyklops Polyphemos nor his subsequent reflex, the Laistrygones, show more *humiliating* alimentary "un-manners."

35. 9.275–77; 2.395–97; 21.265–68; 12.358; Saïd 1979, 35–40, following Arend 1933 and Vidal-Naquet 1986, 23, 25: "the suitors do not sacrifice." The Ithakans have grown more isolated and insular in Odysseus' absence. They hold no assemblies and are indifferent toward neighbors. Odysseus himself violated *xenic* etiquette at the cave, entering uninvited and eating without the host present; see Newton 1983, 140; cf. Friedrich 1987, 128, contra. Normative Homeric society in general is—surprisingly—more "Cyclopean," or isolated, in its household and social structure than polis-like. There is relatively little communal cooperation or economic organization; cf. I. Morris 1986, 117–18.

Melantho/ios, Iros, and Aithon. They purposely eat Telemakhos out of house and home, while claiming to preserve it for him.[36]

Eating "is a life and death matter" in Homer. It is a most intimate act of the family and community. The suitors are feasting when we first meet them. Their ethos is immediately adumbrated by their actions—playing board games with pebbles, sitting on the hides of another man's slaughtered beasts, and preparing to enjoy commandeered wine and meat—and by their inattention and inaction. They do not see and do not welcome Athene as Mentes; even daydreaming Telemakhos does, establishing contact and protecting her from the unholy, ill-mannered uproar (ὀρυμαγδός). Yet another day or month of eating does not civilize the suitors in manners and morals but merely mirrors their ungenerous souls. "The way one eats is an index of one's morality" in the *Odyssey*. *Xenie,* by the standard forms, transforms a stranger into a guest. First, the suitors ignore Mentes; then, they try to ignore their host's son; and later, they abuse Aithon verbally, subsequently with pieces of furniture. Finally, "food itself is made a weapon" (Simpson 1992, 186 and 189), when Ktesippos throws the poorest edible bovine part at, as he notes, the guest of Telemakhos in the house of Odysseus (20.295–300).[37] Their (table) manners *are* their morals, not just a mere sign of them. Eating is their *telling* nonverbal activity.[38]

The banquet has its own formal patterns, literary (type-scene) and social (sacrifice, seating and serving ranks, prestation, generosity conveyed and acknowledged, and parting libations).[39] The leader normally gives, and the

---

36. Saïd 1979; Bourdieu 1977, 192. Penelope's independent honor being greater, the suitors' offers to and for her are more respectable. Father Ikarios, the proper recipient, sees none of it.

37. The suitors are again feasting when they are about to die. Their pollution of good companionship finds bizarre expression in the bloody mess of their meat, a reminder of the cannibal's offensive feast-day (αἱμοφόρυκτα . . . κρέα), spelled out in Theoklymenos' vision of bleeding walls and pillars fouled by a hovering mist: αἵματι δ' ἐρράδαται τοῖχοι καλαί τε μεσόδμαι / . . . κακὴ . . . ἀχλύς (20.348–57; Saïd 1979, 40).

38. Again Simpson 1992, 189. *Nomen et omen:* Antinoos = Antithought, Ktesippos' patronymic (Polythersides = Overbold), e.g., and see 7.54 for Arete = Beseeched [by Odysseus?]. An *onoma eponymon*, or telltale name, is complemented by *actio et omen*, telltale coincidences, not only meaningful, accidental utterances, *kledones*, but also the narrator's extended metaphor of feast as death (20.392–94, 21.418–30). Ἀναθήματα δαιτός, "accompaniments of the banquet," offers sardonic levity, especially with ἐψιάασθαι: there will be "entertainment," but the pleasure will be the beggar's, not the expectant princes'. The formulaic phrase appears only at 1.152 and in another echo of Odysseus at 21.430. Both occurrences accompany time-killing amusements played with pebbles in the poem's first and last moments when suitors fully command. Frequency of puns on names and events in the *Odyssey* (including the most famous and instrumental Outis or "Nobody") forces one to attend to all such undertones.

39. Saïd 1979 well describes the literary and anthropological sequences for Homeric

subordinates accept, provisions at the table. Participation indicates inclusion as a local retainer or acceptance as a guest with status. All present "stretch forth their hands," a gesture of desire, expectation, and participation as dependents or guests developing debt (1.149, 8.71; cf. 17.356, 366). Food and drink in fair shares are offered to equals at the *dais eise* (11.185) for promise of equal future returns at a peer's house, ἀμειβόμενοι κατὰ οἴκους (1.375).[40] Nonverbal signs of honor, especially at the dining table, include the special portion, the special cup and toast, the special order of drinking, and the special seat next to the host.[41] These rituals signify social bonds and degrees of consideration, because Homer uses nonverbal behavior to actualize sentiments in a physical and visual way: "la justice et l'injustice vont se dire en pain et en viands" (Saïd 1979, 21–22) [justice and injustice will declare themselves through bread and meats]. The suitors "divvy up" food, but never their own. Odysseus gets *his* fair share *only* because Telemakhos intervenes (20.279–83). Here alone in the poem does the socially normative phrase *dais eise*, "fairly shared," ironically mark the suitors' table.[42]

The suitors exhibit increasingly hostile glances, vocal tones, body positions (head-cock, muscle tautness, and posture), and movements, that is, "faces," sounds, gestures, and postures. Antinoos, the production's general manager, verbally abuses, brandishes a threatening missile, scowls fiercely, and attacks with a significantly lowly object. Other suitors echo him; they laugh nastily, imprison, occupy the house, taunt the defenseless, bite lips, and laugh and cry simultaneously (17.374, 395, 409, 450, 463; 18.35, 41, 289, 350, 388, 410; 20.346–49). When all symbolic speech fails and annoyance and anger have escalated, the suitors initiate high-handed action, acts morally unacceptable and comic: they punctuate furious emotional outbursts

---

feasts. She delineates the suitors' failures and distortions (14) in the proper parts and normal sequences of both oral-formulaic narrative and ritualized heroic etiquette.

40. Eumaios recollects a guest once well entertained who promised to do the same (14.381–85). Equal shares are also the Homeric law for equals in inheritance (14.202–13). Unequal shares may obtain in peacetime entertainment to honor special guests (15.115–27). In warfare, another kind of equity and "fair shares" emerges between overlord and warrior (4.66; *Il.* 9.318–19).

41. Chronemics and proxemics; see 4.66; 3.41, 53; 1.130–32; 3.36–39; 4.51; 7.169–71; cf. 19.321, Penelope offers anomalous placement to the (recognized?) beggar. On hospitality typescenes, see Arend 1933, on *Besuch*, 34–53; M. Edwards 1975, 61–67, 1992, 304–7; West in Heubeck et al. 1988–92, 1:90–91. Drawing on the influential work of economic anthropologists E.R. Service and Marshall D. Sahlins, Donlan 1982b describes "primitive" reciprocal gift giving and economic redistribution schemes; see also Bourdieu 1977.

42. Rigorous adherence to fair apportionment of food and booty (and the consequences of violation) are thematic in both Homeric epics. Motto and Clark 1969, 119, 124 n. 21 examines this formulaic phrase and its crucial significance. To exclude from the feast is to cast out of the community, as Andromakhe knows (*Il.* 22.492–98).

with ballistic attacks, using footstools and an ox-hoof. Ktesippos crudely and climactically misrepresents this "guest-gift," an edible(?) ox-hoof thrown at the hero's head.[43] Aside from increasing ineffectuality, these unheroic betrayals of inadequate "cool" or self-control index both haughty, really "uppity" manners[44] and shaky self-esteem. Their practice does not accord with heroic ideology for consumable goods or winning a bride. They therefore rush to reinforce new, unsecured social boundaries.

The suitors' heavy drinking poses another daily threat to minimal standards of subheroic decorum. They grumble at the beggar's allegedly equal portion (18.360–64, 20.293–95). Their ill-"disguised" hostility fails to accomplish its desired discouragement: Telemakhos and Odysseus are not cowed by bullying words and gestures.

The suitors' fragile but superficially impressive solidarity displaces and lowers the status of their ostensible hosts. They isolate the underpowered Laertid circle from the rest of the Ithakan community: Laertes far from town, Penelope upstairs in her chamber, and Telemakhos in voluntary exile, forced to flee his house and later shamefacedly to send his two guests elsewhere for their own safety (15.509–18, 540–46; 16.69–89). The companions leave occupied Laertid property only to drag themselves off to bed after another soft day.[45] They stick to their group line, the expressive status quo, with effective social discipline. The relatively benign suitor, feckless Amphinomos ("having it two ways"), briefly considers dissociation but cannot extricate himself.[46] The beggar's solemn verbal warning of trouble is italicized by an object-adaptor (the special cup) and by ritual gestures of solemn libation (18.153–55).

The suitors' presence has explicit purposes: the winning of Penelope's person and the hostile takeover of Odysseus' land and livestock. Antinoos proposes various alternatives to dispose of Telemakhos after his return with

---

43. The move is calculated to undermine further Telemakhos' authority as host. See 2.396–98, 16.292, 18.407, 21.273 and 289–90, 22.280–302; cf. Russo ad 20.299–300.

44. ὑπερφίαλοι, *hyperphialoi*, is their antiheroic epithet. Used twenty-six times in the *Odyssey*, it characterizes the suitors' behavior twenty-two times as "heedless of others" or "rash." Twice suitors thus ironically describe Telemakhos' behavior, and once each it describes isolationist Skherians and the Kyklops (4.663, 16.346; 6.274, 9.106).

45. 1.106–7, 2.395–97, 18.428. Only they have time and unheroic inclination to play board games (πεσσοῖσι ... ἕτερπον; ἐψιαάσθων, 17.530; ὥρη ... ἐψιάασθαι, 21.428–29).

46. Amphinomos' "sweet laugh," rejoicing at Telemakhos' escape from the trap (16.354), nonverbally characterizes the "good villain." Cf. Antinoos at 2.87–90, 113–15; Eurymakhos at 22.45–59, 70–78.

enhanced *kleos*.⁴⁷ He proposes that the suitors either (1) ambush and kill the boy secretly, divide his lordly possessions by lot (κατὰ μοῖραν), and give his *oikia* and mother in marriage to one of their number in the absence of effective, avenging male relatives or (2) leave the Laertid palace. Dawdling among the local Ithakans now seems precarious for the wooers with Telemakhos' *kleos* increased (16.375–82). More obviously, it seems inappropriate wooing behavior, so they should return to their own estates and make competitive bids of *hedna*, and the biggest offer should take the bride (πλεῖστα = μόρσιμος) and confer the highest status. The most giving man will be the fated spouse. Both proposals would dissolve gridlock—either (1) in a violent and immediately decisive way, or (2) in a way slower in effect but moving the situation beyond the present status quo. Both chief advisers prefer decisive confrontation. The dominant Antinoos' *Realpolitik* and murderous inclination reveals how far from common custom (δίκη) the suitors will now go.⁴⁸

3. Hoisting Suitors by Their Own Petard

The wooers explicitly recognize the beggar's penetration into their feast to be a threat to ad hoc arrangements for power, status, and wealth sharing (17.481, 18.401–5, 21.323–29). He appears an alien, déclassé novelty. An unknown beggar is marginal to any self-defined group, by definition, and often serves as a convenient outlet for internal tensions.

The beggar's actions as drifter and panhandler do not conform, however, to aristocratic ideology, to expectations based on the "Getter," Arnaios,

---

47. 16.383–92 presents a suitor's counterplot to Mentes' original solution for Telemakhos' dilemma (1.274–97): first, publicly demand that the suitors depart; then, search for your father, dead or alive, and either wait one more year (if he is alive) or kill the squatting freeloaders yourself as soon as possible (if he is dead). Athene/Mentes' advice to issue a formal, public denunciation and demand does not expect the wooers' compliance. It justifies the self-defensive violence that will then be required. She/he expects that suitors will continue to occupy ancestral Laertid property even *after* his mother's remarriage (1.292–96), although West disagrees in Heubeck et al. 1988–92, vol. 1, ad loc.

48. This statement of the dilemma unmasks Antinoos' and Eurymakhos' earlier pretence endorsing Telemakhos' acknowledged legal property rights over house and holdings (1.387–38, 391–98, 400–404), but it is vague on rulership, a topic unmentioned in 16.383–92. No elaborate institutional guarantees protect a man's status, little is "owed" to or by birth. Their realization of Telemakhos' return and their own growing unpopularity also cancels the suitors' indolent hopes of another Laertid's convenient vanishing and their own succession (2.332–36). "Don't kill without divine warrant!," Amphinomos' temporizing discretion, prevails for the nonce (16.400–402), but word of the assassination plot leaks out anyway.

nicknamed Iros, "Heavenly Hustler."[49] Haughty behaviors attempt to train a new ornamental housepet to perform welcome tricks, to monitor and police the replacement mascot (18.48–49). The social derelict stays close to the ground, squats in the *megaron* (18.395), and protects new turf. His heart is compared to a snarling bitch encountering interference from a stranger (20.14–15). The suitors Antinoos and Eurymakhos purvey improbably stern words of threat and abuse; they present packaged lectures to the sturdy poor. They specialize, however, in nonverbal paralyzing stares, glares, and lethal frowns, a significant part of what Erving Goffman (1967c, 12–13) well called "facework."[50]

The itinerant beggar, by outfacing the usual constraints, spoils their haughty "front." He begins to control events nonverbally. While not pretending to equality, he presumes an intimacy, diminishes the proper beggar's distance, and expects, as beggar and invited guest of the scion (17.339–67), his "fair share" of food and space. His submissive self-assertion exposes the presumptions of the noble parasites. Thus, Telemakhos ironically thanks Antinoos for trying to protect his food and drink from one beggar but not from scores of suitors. The suitors become increasingly outrageous in nonverbal behavior as the nonsuitor advances into "their" territory and goods. The suitors' shameful posturing is characterized only slowly, sequentially. In Homer's oral technique, their character is progressively elucidated as details accrete. Bad to begin with, their behavior and rotten ceremonies grow worse by increments, by their nonverbal acts as clearly as by their words.[51]

Odysseus as beggar presents ambiguous conduct that he can disown at the slightest sign of aggression or refusal. Equivocating with his positions and postures at the door, around the table, and near the feasters, he signals subordination but improvises challenges by word and gesture. By *their* rules he bluffs, postures, and lies his way into the *megaron* and into more elevated dignity. He playfully *and* seriously feints and moves closer. By submissive

---

49. See Stanford 1965, xxi, "Significant Names," and Russo ad 18.5–7 for more telltale names.

50. G. Rose 1979 discusses dog characters; canine similes and metaphors; Odysseus' hardy, protective, watchdoglike behaviors; and the "barking heart" simile of 20.13–23. The "barking heart" simile "reverses" gender and genus, as Odysseus becomes the protector bitch facing foreign intruders. It is at once perverse and precisely right. Beck 1991 explains the "anticipatory echoes" in this passage. See 17.375–79, 18.357–64, and 21.288–310 for condescending lectures; cf. Adkins 1969. Gillin 1929 briefly surveys attitudes and legislation concerning vagrancy, especially medieval English edicts pursuing able-bodied panhandlers with threats of branding and slavery (427). See Goffman [1955] 1967c for "face-work"; Holoka 1983; Lonsdale 1989.

51. Potter 1962 wittily describes for another, nonheroic society how to be "courteously clever," forestalling objections to specific gambits, while gesture, posture, and words make competitors uncomfortable.

self-assertion, he tricks the suitors into faulty anticipations and insults that rebound to their own dishonor. They mistakenly calculate social stratigraphy and ethical registers. Employing Pierre Bourdieu's concepts, we examine one incident, Eurymakhos' challenge.[52]

"The challenge confers honour."[53] Eurymakhos, to debase the stranger, first mocks his bald pate (κερτομέων . . . γέλω), drawing everyone's attention to a "badge" (uncontrollable physical trait) of advanced age, then offers him hard work on a distant estate to remove him from the premises. He will provide pay, food, and clothing (18.346–64). The condescending offer, like that of Agamemnon to Akhilleus in the *Iliad*, would turn the stigmatized but unbonded stranger into his vassal and client and, moreover, into his bondsman and servant. He practically withdraws the offer by the end of his outburst, when he alleges that the stranger would prefer easy begging. The trapping, quasi-command formula of challenge to work in another's fields (ironic in itself because it emanates from the apparently leisured suitor and is addressed to the legal owner of many more fields) constitutes elaborate insult to the strength and skill of a presumed inferior male, in the macho and status-ridden Mediterranean manner.[54] Odysseus, however, seizes the opportunity to retaliate in kind, turns it around, and challenges Eurymakhos to a one-on-one "working contest" (νῶιν ἔρις ἔργοιο), allowing him to choose his weapon: sickle or plough and oxen. He thereby *wittingly* arrogates equality for himself by means of a status-lowering counterchallenge, an effective retort to his taunter (366–75).

Odysseus then at once revises *his* challenge to shield and spear, thus claiming martial as well as agricultural *arete* and a salient heroic equivalence. He finally accuses Eurymakhos of bullying and cowardice (376–86). He does not thus admit weakness but diminishes his opponent by alienating sympa-

---

52. Odysseus' verbal conflict on effete Skheria with Eu*ry*alos turns on manners suited to athletic challenges (cf. Dickie 1983, 257). Taunt and response provide an "anticipatory doublet" for this contest of words. There, he tries to avoid "head-to-head" comparisons, because he is welcomed *xeinos*. The "home-court" challenger, however, forces him to participate, contrary to the usual xenic protocols. When Ithakan Eu*ry*makhos taunts him with "working-class" physical and spiritual inadequacy, the beggar proposes that they see who can labor better. The work competition, ἔρις ἔργοιο (18.366), has been turned against the taunter. Eurymakhos cannot evade the effective "put down."

53. Bourdieu 1977, 10–14, 22, 192, supplies the quotations in the following paragraphs.

54. No one expects a "Protestant work ethic," of course, but a normal *aristos* has heroic jobs cut out for him: free and bonded workers to supervise in their appointed tasks (cf. 15.321–24), plowing and reaping (to judge from Odysseus' challenge), booty and *kleos* to acquire regularly, and festal obligations to peers to fulfill. Sarpedon voices Homeric ideology: *basileis* earn their magnificent keep (*Il.* 12.310–28). Thus, Telemakhos, Odysseus, and even the energetic dairy-farmer Polyphemos contrast to the lackadaisical suitors and the lax Phaiakians with their partly self-cultivating gardens.

228 *Sardonic Smile*

thy. In response, angry Eurymakhos nonverbally threatens his presumed inferior with formulaic (but no less essential) nonverbal dark looks, affronts him with talk of injury, and alleges inappropriate (or ironically appropriate) and incautious drunkenness. Finally, the big man assaults the vagrant with the lowly footstool (387–98; on drunks, cf. 21.295–304). The threefold, unmodulated overreaction undermines his front of superior dignity. The unprivileged wanderer appears more successful in handling matters of manners than the *aristos*. The dark look does not "work," the threat of violence comes to naught, and the footstool misses. Moreover, a chorus of suitors noisily condemns their fellow's obscene infraction of etiquette. In the paratactic and "repetitious" oral mode of Homeric epic, Telemakhos then boldly returns the insult of drunkenness on the suitors (407) in a way that again drives the suitors to nonverbal lip biting. Their own colleague Amphinomos, the good "bad guy," also censures Eurymakhos' hostile words and attempted violence against the helpless stranger (414–16). The powerless have their own power. In seventy packed lines, Odysseus maneuvers the suitors into ethical faults and social lapses, both by word and act *and* by commission and omission.

Eurymakhos issued a challenge suitable to silence or remove subordinates. Odysseus counterchallenged him, however, as equal. A master's job offer was countered by a peer's call for level competition. Eurymakhos responds not only to insults but to covert claims of equality latent in the challenge. The aristocrat has been verbally boxed in. If he accepts the beggar's presumptuous "offer," he treats him as a worthy peer; if he refuses it, he must appear cowardly. So he tries to avoid the lethal social dilemma with nasty looks, words (ἆ δείλ'), and a humiliating physical assault. By reacting so strongly, he dishonors himself. The attack boomerangs on the attacker. He, not his opponent, loses face because "the disparity between the two antagonists is unequivocal." Odysseus merely crouches in self-defense to avoid the stool. He momentarily returns to acknowledged inferiority, via passivity, to make the suitor look foolish and unbalanced. His humility, "by emphasizing his weakness, highlights the arbitrary and immoderate character of the offence." Eurymakhos has let slip the "contempt gambit" of abstaining from dignifying reply. In any case, disdain here might have been read as "a mask for pusillanimity."[55]

---

55. Pucci 1987 alleges that the *Odyssey* here intertextually "answers" the *Iliad*'s confrontation between contemptible Thersites and elite Odysseus—weak, bad, and ugly heckler versus good and heroic institutional leader. Humiliation at Troy edifies the masses as well as penalizes the immediate culprit. Expedient self-denial in Ithaka trumps vulgar pride based on power. Stillness can speak louder than aggressive abuse from any mouth. The differences may outweigh

Odysseus' task as beggar is to foreground defenselessness, but Athene desires the disguised hero to provoke egregious and reckless offense (18.346–50). Always on guard, he repeatedly catches the suitors off guard. Odysseus quickly grasps sympathetic Eumaios' cues and, like Penelope, locates fissures among the insolent banqueteers. "Every exchange contains a more or less dissimulated challenge." All objects are chess pieces in games of face, shame, and honor. The body, face, and mouth also maintain or damage honor. Odysseus levers limited recognition of a beggar's honor to insinuate himself into *megaron* society. Telemakhos contrasts their own full bellies to his obligation of feeding the beggar (18.408, 20.262–67). With a woman's submissive self-assertion, Penelope manipulates their residual sense of normal spousal duties and "fair play" to secure delay for shroud production and a beggar's (modified) chance at the bow.

More often than not in real life, "moves" are unexplained and unargued. Social practice, a part of the ideology of everyday life, depends on implicit rules. Charity to the weak, handouts to the hungry, and generosity to the guest are axioms that not even the suitors, guests themselves, can *openly* contradict. The concepts wear the cloak of universality. When Aithon stops being humble or when the wielders of power quietly stop feeding him, the crisis requires disattention, repentance, or explicit reconfigurations of ideology.

Zeus Xenios suffuses the narrative's system of rewards, crimes, and punishments. Omnipresently invoked in concatenated scenes of fulfillment or violation (books 9–12), he yet remains notably absent from the suitors' repertoire of social exchange (except at 17.481–87). Disguised Odysseus must mobilize his material and political interests under the guise of divine authority, social institutions, and ethical impeccability. He conceals "real" high status to put himself further in the right by assumed low status. He beats the "kinglets" at their own games (including *megaron* mobility, strength, manners manipulation, and archery), abides by their implicit rules (for the most part), accepts their verbal forms and performs their chores, and even "wins [some of] the group over to his side by ostentatiously honouring the values the group honours." The dominant suitors have the greatest interest in maintaining publicly recognized virtues and marks of honor. The suitors' stage should reflect their front of power and eminence: regulated competition for the bride and spontaneous generosity to those disadvantaged by gender, age, wealth, or other marks of status (Penelope, Telemakhos, Iros, The-

---

the similarities in interchanges, but both "little guys" engage our sympathy and probably the original audiences'; see Thalmann 1988, 25.

oklymenos, and Aithon). Noblesse oblige precludes their showing overt hostility. Their comic shuffling meets with deserved destruction. In both the *Iliad* and the *Odyssey,* Homer questions equations of heroic moral and military excellence with divine or high birth. The suitors expose the deficiencies of the old order determined by birth.[56]

The suitors cannot, finally, control or alter the rules, because the rules are bigger than all of us. They misread omens from *Odyssey* 2 on, they fall for Penelope's ruses, and Telemakhos outwits them in his route and time of return, even before Odysseus does. They abuse the beggar, the vagrant, and the fugitive. Even when dead, sadder but no wiser, Amphimedon grotesquely misinterprets Penelope's proper cleverness (24.167–69); he is still misreading women, children, and beggars. Misdirection is a Laertid and Homeric hallmark technique for foiling peer (and audience) anticipation. The suitors' shoddy perversions of heroic rituals dismantle the *Iliad*'s more heroic paradigm. Traditional concepts of moral nobility through lineage often appear here to be superficial and hollow, shopworn relics of another era, although (or because) Nestor and Helen still swear by them. Personal virtue emerges rather from humble men and women and from the currently lowest not least—Eurykleia, Eumaios, Philoitios, and disguised Odysseus.[57]

"Take and give. I do not begrudge you. In fact, I command [you or it]," says presumptive owner Telemakhos to the presumptuous suitors (17.400).

---

56. I. Morris 1986, 123–27, believes, to my surprise, that the poems glorify *basileis,* "legitimize a desired structure of social dominance," and enshrine the "right" sort of society from an "elite viewpoint." Homer was no Karl Marx, but insecure, backpeddling Agamemnon, remote Akhilleus, and the preposterous suitors provide a poor mirror for nobility; contra, P. Rose 1988; Thalmann 1988, 26–28.

Part of the house itself, servants usually acquiesce silently, a nonverbal sign of accepted submission, as with Phemios, Medon, and even "remarried" Penelope (23.361–65). Their suggestions are routinely rejected, and their fidelity needs testing. Some servants dismiss proper behavior (16.305–20; Olson 1992b, 222). Nevertheless, the humble retainers Argos, Eumaios, Eurykleia, and Philoitios (20.194–96) are better mannered, more noble spirits, and more perceptive players than the wooers. We should only cautiously surmise ideology from (assumed) contemporary audience expectations, since we must confess ignorance about the social stratigraphy of Homer's audiences.

57. The bondsmen Eumaios and Eurykleia are of noble lineage (15.413, 1.429). One can argue two ways from this confusion, as oral tradition conducts a dialogue about social and political issues of nature versus nurture. Either Homer cannot abandon the traditional measure of spiritual worth—heroic temper requires good *aristos* blood—or power and station are ephemeral even for *basileis* and heroes (20.195–96; Herakles at 11.621–22), and moral character therefore depends on upbringing, personal integrity, and the gifts of chance. Both *basileis* and bondsmen can be good or wicked; Philoitios is generous and brave, while bitch Melantho does not reciprocate Penelope's signal kindnesses. Such ambivalence in oral epic parallels theological uncertainty concerning glaring Herakles' nature (heroic or divine?) and his precise whereabouts (11.601–26: god on Olympos or shade in the Otherworld?).

Not mere peevishness and staccato sarcasm (thus Stanford and Russo ad loc.), Telemakhos intentionally goads the suitors to abuse *xenie* once more and in a worse way, before other publics. They will not comply with his orders. Again the Laertids box the suitors in, because as the suitors violate Telemakhos' command, they violate Zeus' expectations. Athene desires their social missteps (e.g., 18.346–48, 20.284–86). Thus, they maltreat the code of behavior that they pretend to uphold. The suitors fail to maintain an "acceptable self," fail to manage "expression games," and fail to repay obligations of indebted *basileis*.

Overt and covert symbolic acts indicate disassociation and injured innocence in this narrative. The suitors, Athene, and, repeatedly, the Laertids bring to public attention their opponents' overstepping of recognized limits. Antinoos and, later, others rehearse Penelope's successful evasions and deceptions of the suitors in the *agore* confrontation to curry public sympathy (2.85–128). Antinoos admits the suitors' humiliation at the hands of a "mere" woman in order to assign to her the first offense. The candid account of her alleged transgression and of the suitors' being duped is meant to "justify" the suitors' unparalleled occupation.

More clearly yet, the beggar's deferential postures, lowered and distant positions (proxemics), and gestures of acknowledged inferiority ("face") in the *megaron* emphasize his weakness, social more than physical. This social admission multiplies the suitors' offenses (Lateiner 1992b, 144–50). The shrewd hero draws moral and social strength from flaunting his socioeconomic weakness. He converts personal need into public disapprobation for suitorial deeds.[58] They push obvious advantages too far. Even some of them realize this and expostulate (17.481–88, 20.322–25). Homer baits the bungling hopefuls into compounding sins, well beyond the parameters of Zeus Xenios or heroic banquet standards (two expressions for the same thing). The generous sprinkling of incidents of ungenerosity doubles the audience's satisfaction in their extirpation. The suitors cannot control the symbolic

---

58. Bourdieu 1977, 11–12, discusses *elbahadla*, "extreme humiliation publicly inflicted," among the North African Berber Kabyles. I thank Gregory Crane for sending me this exposition. Roisman 1990a, 236, marks Odysseus' interest in provoking self-revelatory emotional reactions. See Heubeck ad 24.315–17, on κερτομίοισι; P. Jones 1989, 248, on "heart-cutting" provocations. The epic's social codes for self-lowering and elegantly wounding others must be excavated from the text. Full awareness of the rules governing face-to-face interaction enhances our appreciation. Contemporary anthropological studies of Moroccan and Greek kinship, gender, and African-American status interactions (e.g., East Coast urban cutting contests known as the "dozens") offer assistance. Most 1989a, 124–33, discusses verbal self-defense in ancient Greece, the preservation of *autarkeia* and social elbowroom.

meanings of their words[59] or body movements. Their comedy portrays social ineptitude and a fragile, ad hoc social order.[60]

The suitors' very words backfire, just as their nonverbal behaviors do. Thrown bones and kicks eventually recoil to destroy the pampered perpetrators.[61] Irony is present, repeatedly enhanced by the suitors' misapprehensions of the realities of power. In an out-of-awareness behavior, they bite their lips in exasperation at Telemakhos' increasing boldness. The string of strange nonverbal events in book 20 is ominous in every sense: a crack of thunder; a friendly hand extended to the homeless; a bird omen; and involuntary human acts, such as lip biting, unnatural silence, and crying. The portents climax in the suitors' surreal hysterical fit of loud laughter (20.101, 197, 242, 268, 320, 345–49). Homer favors paralinguistic phenomena to characterize bad manners.

Odysseus chooses the right moment for speech, silence, gesture, and/or action. "Timing" is thematic in the *Odyssey*, an epic about chronemics, the human use of time (see the appendix). Offence and vengeance, threat and execution, prediction and actual upshot, and temptation and fulfillment must await their *hora*, or timeliness. By determined self-abnegation, Odysseus carefully waits for his "own good time." The *Odyssey* esteems endurance and prudent patience, but also, if we observe the same temporal intervals from the opposite end of the looking glass, the poem values deferral, an aggressive sense of careful "timing," knowing *when* "time is on your side," *kairos* in later Greek.[62]

---

59. Unintentionally ominous words, κληδόνες, presage meaning to privileged auditors within or beyond the text. The suitors hope that the beggar gains all that his heart desires (18.110–17). Odysseus rejoices at the superficially jolly words. Hirvonen 1969, 15 examines meaningful, but unintentional, human signs. Stanford 1965, 2: lvii-lviii, considers dramatic irony. See also Russo ad 17.541, 18.117.

60. They are inadequately alert to undertones and overtones of body and word. Although the suitors fail to perceive it, the swineherd, the cowherd, and the lady's maid realize—nearly at once—that this vagrant is no ordinary fellow (14.508–11; 20.194; 19.379–85; cf. Roisman 1990a, 216, on Eumaios' perspicuity.

61. 18.112–13, 353; 21.91, 402–3; cf. 2.33–34, 20.120. Ktesippos, convivial "Son of Overbold" or "Too Much Thersites," who hurled the cow-hoof ξείνιον at the beggar, is struck down by cowherd Philoitios, an example of perfect poetic justice, explicitly noted as such by the bucolic retainer (a counter-ξεινήϊον). The cowboy's phrase originated a proverb according to Eustathius, quoted by Stanford ad 22.290–92.

62. Stanford 1950; Pucci 1987, 47, on τλήμων, πολύτλας, a common formulaic epithet of the hero; Austin 1975, 87–88, on "proper season." The appendix sketches some aspects of time and deferral in the epic.

4. Nonverbal Leakage

Unintended self-disclosure, sometimes ungovernable bodily expression ("leakage"), usefully reports to us others' hidden agendas. We covertly read and check attempts at misleading and self-aggrandizing self-presentation (social "face"). In a warrior's world of braggadocio and macho posturing, the Laertid clan is remarkable for skill in verbal and nonverbal self-control, in hiding true sentiments and emitting false revelations of weakness, as family members engineer others' expectations of their moves. Lip service and "limb service" in deference to societal norms presents a veneer of consensus that allows them to respond in unexpected ways. These disruptive and divisive maneuvers embarrass the pretentious companions' modus vivendi, and they delight the safely separate audience.

One comic element arises from clashes of verbal and nonverbal signals. People usually discern the truth in such conflicts by the nonverbal channel. Iros talks big but shrinks from actual combat; Eumaios talks poor and humble but entertains with lavish, well-nigh princely generosity.[63] Odysseus begs and pleads for bread and gentle reception but never flinches from kicks and blows. The suitors brag about the power and prestige of a *basileus* but then crowd together and cower before few opponents. This nonverbal act subverts the deflatable rhetoric.

Other characters appear less skillful in face-to-face heroic encounters than Odysseus, in part because they leak self-betraying signals unawares, as do the lip-biting suitors, smiling Telemakhos, or insufficiently discrete or crowing Eurykleia (18.410, 16.476–77, 19.476–81, 22.408). "Leakage" surfaces while the chiefs struggle unsuccessfully to deceive, that is, to suppress spontaneous affect displays, such as tears, laughter, verbal frustration, or anger (2.24 and 81, 20.358, 21.248–50, 20.268). Their nonverbal behavior includes psychophysical signals indicating their loss of social control. Situations begin to elude their will. Interlocutors receiving "noncongruent messages" (contradiction among verbal, vocal, and visual channels) depend on nonverbal behavior for more reliable data. Verbal arrogation of status or

---

63. Even if subconsciously he covertly realizes, now or later, that the stranger before him is his former master, as Roisman 1990a, 219–21, well argues, Eumaios repeatedly emphasizes Zeus' laws and expectations; he would provide equivalent entertainment for another vagrant (14.56–61, 388–89, 402–6). Roisman believes, however, that the "best fat hog" of the second meal would be felonious waste for any guest other than the herder's master (229). Odysseus repeatedly hints at his true identity in various encounters, verbally and nonverbally "giving himself away" to those whom he would like to trust.

234 Sardonic Smile

statements of approval, if conflicting with body language, fail to persuade children and even alert adults.[64]

Telemakhos and Odysseus chronically step "out of line" to expose pseudogallantry and the political order constructed by the *basileis*. Odysseus' "faulty interaction" punctures the ideological assumptions that undergird their semipublic proceedings. Instead of renewed submission to authority, one observes passive resistance and strategic transgression of rank. The wooers' words and gestures defend the established order; Laertids deflect weapons of the dominant class and turn them against their mouthpieces. Telemakhos' and Odysseus' challenges remind the suitors of their "dissensus," that they have contrived a false comradely reality. Everyone has coherent patterns of appropriate, unconscious conduct, but the suitors want to be what they are not. The expressive masks of congeniality that they deploy in face-to-face interaction with Telemakhos drop, or "go out of play," when he leaves the (banquet) scene.[65] Homer conveys this disjunction by showing them squabbling with each other over the beggar's table-rights or dividing over how to disestablish Telemakhos.

Odysseus' situational improprieties of word and gesture would be deemed psychotic in an equal, but they appear downright suicidal in an unempowered inferior. His attempt to "hustle" co-participation in the focused "action" of the bow ignores status hierarchy, assigned roles and space, and exclusionary turn taking. The deflating request intentionally uncovers issues of politesse and hierarchy acknowledgment. The bold move doubles the suitors' humiliation (questioning status and skill). Its inappropriate audacity nearly leaks out Odysseus' entire disguise and plan of revenge. Odysseus cuts off his assumed "nose in order to destroy the other's face."[66] His grudging

---

64. Bugental et al. 1970, 652, 654, cited by Holoka 1991.

65. Goffman 1959, 121, discusses social masks. For example, at 4.659–74, when they learn of Telemakhos' unexpected escape, the suitors sit in a huddle, their contests stop, and Antinoos develops blazing eyes and emits grunts at being baulked: ὄσσε δέ οἱ πυρὶ λαμπετόωντι εἴκτην— / "Ὢ πόποι. . . ." A brief doxography of attitudes toward Thersites in *Iliad* 2 illustrates the pitfalls of attributing "univocal intention of the bard" even there; see P. Rose 1988, 6–11. Thersites presents an indictment of Agamemnon "Most Kingly" parallel to Akhilleus' vociferations. He expresses the grudges and discontents inarticulately shared by the soldiers. His explicitly ugly appearance does not undercut his perfectly rational and logical challenge. Homer is aware that appearance and reality do not always jibe as the very theme of the return of the disguised husband proves. Thalmann 1988, esp. 26–28, sketches issues of "heroic ideology" in the *Iliad*, especially the Thersites incident, as he liberates that epic from univocal "aristocratic" ideology. Odysseus of the *Odyssey* achieves precisely what Odysseus of the *Iliad* prevented Thersites from doing. In any case, "class" and status differences are more ubiquitously enunciated and examined in the *Odyssey*. "Intonational quotation marks" (Thalmann 1988, 20, borrowed from Bakhtin) pervade Thersites'and Aithon's parodic use of aristocratic *xenic* propriety.

66. Goffman 1967a, 114, 135, 194, 222 (quote).

acceptance by the companions as privileged local beggar has implicitly pledged him to maintain his (low, distant, subjugated, "knows his place") position in the ceremonial order. His status should have *no* slightable self. He should *desist* from any activity whenever requested to do so, but he, then Penelope and Telemakhos, *resist* and *insist* on some version of privilege. His turn at the divinatory instrument, the bow, would put the established suitorial social selves in jeopardy, as is made explicit, for he is baser (χείρων) and yet *might* turn out to be better (ῥηϊδίως [ἂν] ἐτάνυσσε, 21.325–28). The suitors' illusions of self-determinacy at risk taking are exposed. What seemed an avoidable but chosen and acceptable risk (a game, that is) with high reward becomes dangerous and other-imposed, altered by the ephemeral noble.

Antinoos urgently tries to exclude the vagrant from bow competition among the volatile nobles (21.285–310). Recalling, in a minatory manner, the intruder's originally unearned "gift" of a fair portion of food, his real but limited license to conversation, his exclusive position of welcome beggar at the *megaron*'s table, and the cautionary paradigm of the drunk centaur Eurytion, the chagrined nobleman now threatens Odysseus with negative "gifts," mutilation and bondage. He tells him to sit down, keep apart, and shut up. He wants the vagrant to "keep his place, stay put." Antinoos strenuously tries to ring down the stage manager's (the dominant class') curtain of propriety, but in the bow contest, Odysseus makes the competition happen. He takes crucial possession of the bow only with Telemakhos' support. The wanderer's very composure doubly disgraces them: under pressure in the theater of competitive public performance, they bluster, threaten, pale, huddle, and scatter—that is, they leak fear. As Iros' trembling betrays his fear, so the suitors' labile complexions growing pale, wild glances, and mindless stampeding reveal perturbation. They unheroically "leak"; they express "overflow of affect."[67] Their fear is palpable. The beggar both outpoises and outshoots them.

The suitors at Ithaka besiege the holdings of Odysseus, perhaps an intertextual parody of the Akhaian siege of Troy. They penetrate outer defenses but never the bedroom citadel. They are comic in their repeated gulling by the ruling family and its retainers. They wage ineffectual war to dispose of one woman and her minor son. Their total failure in battle inhibits serious lamentation of their gory deaths. Their indoor epic minibattle inverts both the odds and the antecedent gestures and postures of dominance and submis-

---

67. Lateiner 1989, on 1.381–82; 18.410–11; 20.268; 22.43, 298–300. See also 18.77, 88, 98–100; 21.412; 22.43, 298–300; cf. 11.529 for the paradigmatic and admirable self-control of Neoptolemos.

sion, lord and liege. Odysseus, his slave and peasant crew, and one bird-goddess in the rafters handily rout a much larger, scrambling force of *basileis*. Cowardly nonverbal behavior punctuates the wooers' paltry self-defense (Stewart 1976, 101, 129).

5. Conclusions

The suitors' stratagem intends to convert Odysseus' private estate into public property (δήμιος, 20.264–65). By dining without permission, against the heir's or master's will (1.374–80, 403 [hypocritical]; 2.311; 3.213; ἀέκητι, 16.94), and in their despite (14.164; ἀτιμάζοντας, 18.144), without counter-service or reciprocated meals (1.375–76 = 2.129–40; νήποινον, 1.160, 377 = 2.142; 14.417; 18.280), the suitors intend to impoverish or remove Telemakhos. Telemakhos is wasting away: τὰ δὲ πολλὰ κατάνεται (2.55–67, 17.537, 19.530–34). He becomes victim, not companion, a source of booty and mirth, rather than a granter of big-man largesse. The suitors act without warrant as banquet masters (κοιρανέουσι: 13.377, 20.234; ἀνάγκη), commanding food and epic poems while mishandling sacral libation, sacrifice, and secular *geras* (20.297), one mark of exceptional consideration. Their friendly words and gestures for Telemakhos are decoded by derisive sounds and lethal preparations for his murder.[68]

Telemakhos' original denunciation, a plan to eject them through help of an assembly, had exposed their villainy. Their elaborate show, however, cannot be fully discredited by ordinary male means or womanly tact and guile, but only by superior force or *another* show that manipulates rules that everyone acknowledges. In disguises, Odysseus employs less confrontational stratagems of deferral that succeed by temporarily acknowledging the orthodox codes endorsed by drovers or enforced by the suitors themselves. Although beggars may be disqualified by social status from the noble "game," he and Penelope know that the concept of letting the "best man win" (something) has even wider legitimacy.

At the climax, the suitors have resumed eating Telemakhos' inheritance (as Agelaos notes at 20.336). Homer deploys a strong alimentary metaphor after Theoklymenos' anticipatory vision. He closes the final scene of merriment with the suitors laughing over their sweet, "heart's desire" dinner (δεῖπνον . . . ἡδύ τε καὶ μενοεικές) and grand, numerous sacrifice. Their actual end-of-day supper (δόρπον) was to be the most unpleasant possible—the attack that Odysseus and Athene will "set before" them (20.390–94).

---

68. See 2.301–22, 4.663–73, 16.369–73, and 16.383–92 for various strategies to dispose of Telemakhos.

They will be forced to eat their death. Odysseus, after his prefatory bowshot, resumes the grim metaphor: νῦν δ' ὥρη καὶ δόρπον 'Αχαιοῖσιν τετυκέσθαι / ἐν φάει, 21.428–29, "Now it's time for the Akhaians to order their supper, in daylight." Odysseus repeats only the latter, less feast-like term for a meal. Their life-task becomes a metaphor for their death. Further, Antinoos has raised the wine cup when the arrow hits him fittingly in the gullet. He drops the cup, he upsets bread and meat with a spastic kick, and, in long-delayed recompense, he bleeds measureless quantities like a pipe (22.8–21). Cup, bread, and meat are likewise spilt, spoiled, and scattered by his clone, Eurymakhos (22.83–88). The epic nearly ends where it began: mannerless banqueteers despoiling another man's *megaron*. But Odysseus now cleans out the moral mess.[69]

In book 22, Odysseus has shed mendicant's cover, an assumed identity as victim and "game," for heroic identity and posture as lethal bowman. The suitors' artificial group loyalties are exposed by ludicrous fission and attempts to shift blame to the ringleaders. They try to ransom their lives by golden reparation and to desert longtime comrades (22.48–59). The social and personal identities that they have long since freely chosen cannot, however, now be lightly shrugged off. Their chosen self-images imprison the cowards. Their disclaimers evince a sudden, equitable, cooperative prudence—transparent at once and, as soon as their plea-bargains are rejected, soon belied. When their mask, or front, of superiority has been spoiled, the surviving suitors, bargaining in a pinch, with a dropped "front," try to negotiate as equals. The abortive effort to realign themselves fails because no bonds of obligation survive. They turn to force, but just as princes keep "table dogs"—dogs that have no strength or skill—for show, so the handsome suitors, Penelope's ornamental geese of the dream, muster inadequate fight (17.307–17). Tactical failures mirror social failures and misrecognitions. Their nonverbal behaviors both display and emphasize incompetence in heroic give-and-take. Their freedom of movement is now controlled by the hero's lethal force. They are cattle, then fish caught in a net and stacked in a pile (22.299–300, 383–89), sacrificial victims or less. The showdown not only resolves the plot's crises for son, wife, and master but also reverses again, now right side up, the foregoing, suitor-imposed inversions of face and place.

What causes the suitors' shared problems? In a modern "real-life" clinical analysis, we might diagnose such individuals and the gang as having brain dysfunction, emotional difficulties, criminal tendencies, or lack of proper

---

69. This paragraph is indebted to Simpson 1992, 190–91.

experience for learning appropriate etiquette and nonverbal behavior. Obviously, such an approach does not apply to oral-traditional or literary creations, folkloric villains, and/or creatures of a "tale-type." The suitors exist to practice villainy and to prove the heroes' merit, courage, prudence, and martial skill. Their faux pas highlight the heroic couple's pas de deux. Their brutality serves as a foil to the heroes' punctilious etiquette. They are not biologically dysfunctional or ready for "remediation."[70] Their deficits—social, economic, heroic, and verbal and nonverbal—acts of commission and omission, advance the narrative. They are, in terms of storytelling desiderata, necessary evils, delightfully wicked devils, some with individualized traits, who oscillate between oppressive interference (blocking moves) and ineffective one-upmanship. Their "character" is defined by the semirigid deployment of an epic Gestalt and of folktale motifs that they embody. Their words, acts, and gestures proliferate, as Homer walks us through their objectionable daily routine, by turns villains and clowns. Homer allows the squatters little sympathy.

The suitors demonstrate noteworthy *dyssemia, nonverbal communication deficit*. Such a deficit has two aspects. First, they fail to read correctly the signals that others emit. This *receiving* category includes their obtuse reactions to Telemakhos' growing impatience, Theoklymenos' prophecies, the beggar's foreshadowing fight with Iros and passive aggression toward his "betters," and Penelope's penultimate "flirting and fleeing" maneuvers. They mismanage even verbal quarrels, in which the beggar successfully denigrates his opponents. Second, they fail to emit appropriate and effective signals of their own. This *sending* category for the suitors includes rowdy crowding into the manor house, speaking out of turn and out of place, and social-control maneuvers that misfire and appear as unwarranted bullying (e.g., "ageist" insults and "cracks" about baldness, 2.178, 18.355). Homer ascribes to them nearly everything nasty but halitosis and body odor. They show systemic disrespect for, and disregard of, others' time and territory. They are out-of-bounds "space invaders," short on "excuse me" awareness.[71]

---

70. One of my students correctly notes, with incorrect spelling, that "the suitors seem to have no manors." Allen 1939 believes that the indefensible behavior and legal position of the suitors respond to audience desire for unsympathetic villains and victims of righteousness. Nowicki and Duke 1992, 138, 149, surveys physiologically dysfunctional nonverbal behavior and useful interventionist responses.

71. The beggar's opponents include Melantho/ios, Antinoos, Eurymakhos, and Ktesippos. For explicit "disputatious" νεικ- words, see 17.215, 239, 374; 18.9; 20.267. Martin 1989, 68–75, supplies Iliadic parallels to Teutonic flyting. Lateiner 1987, 108–12, provides a Homeric list of the channels of nonverbal communication. See Nowicki and Duke 1992, 7, 43, 47.

The suitors inhabit a pleasant present, an option that Odysseus rejected in Lotus-land, among Kirke's well-fed pigs, and faced with Kalypso's offer of her eternal youth. They misconstrue social amenities and divine signs. They fail to control Penelope, then Telemakhos, then even the vagabond, and eventually their own actions.

The blundering louts pose no threat, as Athene knows, but Austin is wrong to deny them "any significant part" (20.49–51; Austin 1975, 223). By the bow contest, Penelope invites them to compete with memories of the hero who disappeared twenty years ago. Their failure even to string it proves once again their unworthiness, even in brute strength. They fail many tests in both *metis* and *bie;* this test is but the penultimate. Their inadequacy plays the foil to Odysseus' ambidextrous competence.

The suitors' collective bad faith consistently tries to box in and define Laertid personnel. Melantho/ios is suborned. Laertes and Eumaios are driven far off. Telemakhos is nearly silenced and removed by threats and taunts. And Penelope is severely constrained by gossip and by the automatic gender policing that patrols women's narrow perimeters on Skheria or Ithaka.[72] The princess and the once feckless prince must bluff their gendered ways past jailers. They must control time and tempo, even when they cannot restore altered social rules. Their mobilizing capacity (fighting men) is small, so also their redeemable symbolic capital (favors owed, prestige acquired, and honors due). The suitors' grip on institutions seems effective, until one outlander refuses to remain complicitously silent. The idlers' socially sanctioned usurpation, or "euphemized violence"—Penelope's unpleasant spousal choice, Telemakhos' precarious inheritance, and *one* beggar's right to handouts—shows superficial respect for persons.[73] Nevertheless, their gifts, piety, and social honor barely mask the physical force and verbal violence (browbeating, taunts, and talk of mutilation) lurking in the wings for all "unequals." The suitors will not decamp until Penelope chooses one of their number, they try to kill the legitimate heir, and they assault and batter the Zeus-protected beggar. All household servants and extramural parasites live under perpetual threat. The suitors' latent violence honors the heroic code of conduct mainly "in the breach."

---

72. By the weapons of the seemingly submissive (cf. chap. 11), she has neutralized the suitors, much as Kirke did with her boisterous, incautious male visitors. The foolish beasts idle at a tethered distance, impotent to advance their cause or to leave the enchanting female (2.55, 205–7; 17.534; cf. leaders' jingling names, e.g., Eurylokhos and Eurymakhos at 10.205–20, 238).

73. 2.198–200: μνηστὺς ἀργαλέη, "undesirable courtship," 18.285–89; 20.341–42; 17.446–52. See Bourdieu 1977, 191, for the useful, insightful quoted phrase.

The suitors, although their part is more essential to the story than Thersites' to his, are easy to reduce to bumptious clowns, to caricatures of swains and villains.[74] They are, indeed, multifunctional, serving the folktale's necessity for heroic competitors for the bride's hand, upstart challengers and unjust guests, and indictments of the *basileis* system. The *Odyssey*, like Hesiod's *Works and Days,* criticizes the system endorsed by greedy *basileis*. For instance, King Alkinoos needs reminding about accepting a suppliant, Menelaos' gatekeeping companion Eteoneus forgets his manners, the "upper-class" suitors ignore Athene/Mentes at the door, and Menelaos disregards his own proverbs about excessive hospitality. Penelope's praise of Odysseus clearly implies a less-satisfactory average ruler (4.686–95, cf. 2.230–34). The abuses and gaffes of noblemen and "kings" are opposed to generous receptions provided by the poor and/or (relatively) powerless: Nausikaa, Telemakhos, Philoitios, Penelope, and the swineherd Eumaios—the perfect host who shames supposed superiors and exhibits best the disjunction between imposed status and true civility.[75]

Thus, the suitors' nonverbal behavior belies and overrides their words. This incongruity between external forms of approved behavior and internal sentiment is thematic.[76] In book 1, Telemakhos suppresses Athene's epiphany and misleads his "guests" and his mother while he prepares for departure; Eurykleia is suborned to deceive Telemakhos' mother; Odysseus develops identities and suitable mannerisms for friend and foe; Eumaios entertains the veteran (and perhaps recognized master) lavishly, while apologizing for furnishing meager fare to a stranger; Eurykleia recognizes Odysseus' scar but is forbidden to announce it; Penelope recognizes her husband before her gestures admit it; and Eurykleia is again prohibited from voicing immense joy. Mopping up corpses is disguised as a wedding feast. Body language is designed to deceive. Suitors' smiles hide lethal plans; beggarly

---

74. Comic elements suffuse the *Odyssey,* even when it is read as a romantic adventure tale. We smile at the oafish, slapstick, and black humor of the Kyklops in his cave and the Keystone Cops antics, leaky self-control, and cross-purposes of the suitors, fighting among themselves (18.401–404) and outsmarted by an abandoned woman, a decrepit vagrant, and cannier Telemakhos. The suitors' behavior, peculiar as Penelope details it (18.275–80), finds some justification in Penelope's deceptions and equivocations (2.93–110, 19.139–56, 24.126–48). Neither heroes nor pitiable victims, they elicit (from me, at least) a limited and brief sympathy for understandable frustration and *funny* impotence.

75. Williams 1986 lists six stages of formal reception that are "parodied" in *Od.* 14; Levy 1963, 149–52, describes outstaying your (Homeric) welcome; Roisman 1990a describes Eumaios' insight and politesse.

76. Indeed, an infinite regress of deceptions yawns open already from Akhilleus' duplicity in *Il.* 9.312–13, when he denounces duplicity and significant omission. The following list of fakers could be greatly extended.

humble postures and gestures conceal Aithon's plots to seize control; Telemakhos manipulates a false image of helpless youth; and Penelope's seductive cameo appearance(s) support a stalling strategy, not a sexual surrender.

Expressive behaviors often convey the polar opposite of actual intent or sentiment. The poet's ultimate ironies center on significant, even defining, objects, the bow and the bed. The beggar entreats a try at the bow and muses about strength destroyed (21.281–84). The mistress scorns suitors who fear losing the grand prize (her) by means of the bow to the stranger/guest *of* Odysseus (ὁ ξεῖνος 'Ὀδυσσῆος). Telemakhos claims authority over the bow. Eumaios oscillates in fear while toting the symbolic bow. Finally, while seated, Odysseus examines the string and horn and controls the bow. The text here is verbally so like, while the acts are utterly unlike, Eurymakhos' ineffective fondling and wrestling with the bow.[77]

... ὁ δ' ἤδη τόξον ἐνώμα
πάντῃ ἀναστρωφῶν, πειρώμενος ἔνθα καὶ ἔνθα.

... Odysseus now handled the bow,
Turning it up and down every which way, testing it here and there.

The pattern insists that things cannot be trusted to be what they seem. The obtuse suitors have not learned that basic fact. They only analyze correctly when they sarcastically and insincerely praise the stranger as "connoisseur, bow thief, bow owner, bow maker, expert at villainy" (21.397–400). Odysseus has set up the suitors for a surprise. Homer sets up the blind audience repeatedly for thwarted expectations. Odysseus tests and scrutinizes everyone and everything before revelation. The *Odyssey*'s most ominous nonverbal communication is the twang emitted by the tested bowstring, like a swallow's intelligible speech: χελιδόνι εἰκέλη αὐδήν.[78] Only here and only now do the suitors understand their perilous situation—somewhat prematurely and beyond the facts as Homeric analysts point out—and their responding emotion, "big fear," leaks an involuntary nonverbal behavior, a sudden enjambed pallor: πᾶσι δ' ἄρα χρὼς / ἐτράπετο. Mightily does this display of frightened affect override verbal communication in the ensuing lethal interaction.

---

77. 21.393–95, cf. 245–46; there is also an implied comparison to their respective modes of courting.

78. 21.411. Kalypso is frightful *except* for her *aude, human* voice (10.136, etc.). Cf. Ino at 5.334; 6.125; and Clay 1974. Hanna and Joseph Roisman and Rick Newton improved this chapter.

One's familiar environment is constituted by the unquestioned objects, words, gestures, and taken-for-granted values that structure personal and social experience. This situation also obtained for Homeric audiences. Lived experiences and a hierarchy of "goods" allow certain oral traditional poems to gel. We might call this "Homeric ideology"—flexible enough, like any influential ideology, to allow grumblers to vent (like comic Thersites and tragic Akhilleus) without breaking down, and firm enough to serve and preserve marginal and evanescent spirits like fugitive Phoinix, prophet Theoklymenos, and Aithon the choosy beggar.

Chapter 11
Gendered Weapons: Penelope's Nonverbal Behaviors

1. Gender Asymmetry

Uncertain but resourceful Nausikaa, beleaguered but prudent Penelope, and also Helen, Arete, Klytaimnestre, and Eurykleia employ drastic and devious interactional expedients with men to protect their different interests as women—gendered nonverbal and verbal behaviors and coverbal gestures, whether functional or seemingly redundant. A multidimensional analysis of gender asymmetry, complementary to recent feminist anthropological research and narratalogical criticism of the Homeric poems, may observe their ingenious maneuvering that both preserves their own and their male kin's honor and diminishes public and private antagonism, mockery, and shame.

Women, the young, and the poor can only begin to neutralize the hierarchies that control them. They do this by openly submitting to those hierarchies' demands. Legally and symbolically disadvantaged by the institutionalized instruments for maintenance of the symbolic order, Penelope, Telemakhos, and the beggar (representing the three categories just listed) must respect dominant men of mature age and overwhelming resources, physical and economic. The aspirations of the unempowered—not to hear Trojan death-songs, to be left alone by importunate unpaired males, to sail off from Ithaka or ride away from Sparta, to share meals from a heavily laden table, or to play bow games as an equal—require permission, because they disturb the rulers' self-evident and natural habits. They suspend largely unquestioned rules of legitimacy, the assumed authority of what has always or, here, recently been real and right. The suitors' expectations constitute an order that "goes without saying" for most of the poem's twelve thousand verses.

Like her modern Greek counterpart, Homer's Penelope, as wife and mother protects the house and family, its stores, scion, and honor, by screens of nonverbal evasion, verbal ruses, and unfulfilled promises (ἀπάτη).[1] Penelope weaves Laertes' shroud and unravels it for three years; she extracts ever-more gifts from suitors, who deliver them happily; and she sweetly argues before them that grumbling Telemakhos is too young to pose a threat to them (thus her enforcement of his extended adolescence). Her successes are real.

Penelope tries to bid for authority and control her circumstances, but all the free men thwart her. Telemakhos upbraids her for unwomanly interference and stubbornness, from the poem's beginning to its end (1.346–50, 21.350–53, 23.97–103). When the suitors unmask her deceptions, they righteously demand an end to the charade. Consequently, she prays to Artemis for immediate death—the only available escape from her own unwanted sexual allure and the suitors' unseemly suit. Eventually, as her last card, she chooses to rely on the male stranger's assurances, and after his identity of housemaster has been established, she returns to subordinate female status—back in the bedroom, instructed to keep her kissable mouth shut (23.364–65). Her failures, too, from book 1 to 23, are equally real.[2]

Family goals remain foremost while women steadily promote their legitimate agendas within the constraints of androcentric societies. Penelope has an equal story of endurance through pseudosurrender (see 23.301–5 for the telling). Like her "pre-echo" Arete, Penelope fulfills difficult to reconcile patriarchal duties and self-interest by means of sex-dichotomized nonverbal and verbal behaviors.[3]

---

1. The divine paradigm of female wiles and seductiveness, Hera in *Iliad* 14, offers interesting parallels in verbal misdirection and nonverbal sex-appeal techniques. Arete, in her fact-gathering manners, preechoes Penelope's protective caution, perception, and intuitions about her child's interests and potential suitors.

2. Modern Greek comparative material on gender roles may be found in the classic anthropological studies of Friedl 1962, Campbell 1964, du Boulay 1976, and Peristiany 1965; and, more recently, in the volumes edited by Dubisch (1986) and Loizos and Papataxiarchis (1991). I have derived substantial benefit from modern recorders of Greek gendered habits. Other analysts of antiquity from alien climes might gain similar profit. Professor Nancy Felson-Rubin read and improved an earlier draft of this chapter. I was able to read before publication only one chapter of her book *Regarding Penelope*.

3. Blok 1981; Felson-Rubin 1987; Naerebout 1987, 127–28. Winkler 1990, esp. 134–36, should be qualified by Cohen's 1989 methodological caveats about the difference between sex segregation and isolation. Goffman [1955] 1967c describes various categories of "rituals of accommodation." Nausikaa presents Penelope's young, erratic but promising doublet (cf. Van Nortwick 1979). By "legitimate agendas" I mean means and ends conducive to their self-fulfillment on a hypothesized assumption of gender equality. While this might seem anachronistic, anthropologists who study gender in highly unequal societies (e.g., modern Greece and Arab countries) report various forms of private male acknowledgment of women's power at the same time that public manifestations of it are strictly prohibited. The continuing debate and dispute over Penelope as "character," sign, voice, and impenetrable collection of predicates was con-

Penelope's behavior "has demonstrated the undesirability of the alternatives," the prior presentation of negative models of female sexuality. *Deinai* Kirke and Kalypso, dangerously fecund goddesses in forest retreats and unpatriarchally independent of male control, present unreliable and inhuman helpers. They are female threats to male autarchy, and they represent the potential loss forever of competing for ordinary heroic prizes. Human Nausikaa and Arete speak of active female control in private and public spheres (6.276–89, 303–15; 7.71–74; 11.335–41), however insufficient they prove in dominating their milieux or detaining the attractive sailor. Helen also, like her shadowy, destructive sister, Klytaimnestre, shares male functions as head of household and font of wisdom: offering *xenia*, prophesying, and initiating conversations (15.123–30, 170–72, 4.135–37). Her drug, a synecdoche of sexual power, like Penelope's beauty, unmans men—makes them forget obligations to kith and self (4.22–27, 18.212–13).[4]

Disguise, deception, and misrecognition dominate the 12,110 verses of the *Odyssey*. Athene and Hermes conceal or reveal themselves by sex, complexion, pitch of voice, age, clothes, and so forth. Humans, in every case, stumble when perceiving divinities, divining what they are (cf. the ignorance and complaints of Diomedes and others at *Il.* 5.115–28, 20.131, 21.599–605). Nevertheless, peculiar gait and other strange nonverbal behaviors betray divine deceits.[5] Athene has appeared as mortal man, young woman, adolescent boy, girl-child, and bird in the *Odyssey* (1.105, 2.267–68, 8.194; 6.22; 13.221–22; 7.20; 3.371–72, 23.239). She appears slightly unseemly, at least to twentieth-century audiences, boasting of her third deception at the expense of protégé Odysseus (7.20, 8.194, 13.299–302). Homer's gods, however, have a peculiar sense of humor. Odysseus also, by his inveterate posturing and *metis*, seems unnecessarily and intemperately sadistic in his dedication to, or imprisonment in, deception. For instance, he deceives his son, wife, and father—long after the suitors are entirely disposed of (see chapter 9). Mutual pride in prize-winning concealment and detection of fraud emerges from the heroic boasting competition of goddess and mortal.

---

firmed once again in a panel devoted to her puzzles at the meetings of the American Philological Association in Washington in 1993.

4. Wohl 1993, 19, 24, 28–32, 43, and Katz 1991 point out Penelope-Helen parallels: *Il.* 3.180 and *Od.* 19.315; Penelope cites Helen in her own peculiar *apologia* at 23.218–23.

5. *Il.* 13.61–62; *H. Dem.* 2.111. Vergil also exhibits identification of rare species by mien, breath, gait, odor, and clothing (*Aen.* 1.314–20, 5.647–49). Cf. H.J. Rose 1956, "divine disguisings"; Clay 1972; Stewart 1976; Murnaghan 1986, 1987. Simultaneous seating and "hunkering down" close against the bowl of an olive tree nonverbally seal the *homophrosyne* and mutual acuity of the goddess and the hero (13.372–74, 296–300).

They enjoy fomenting *méconnaissance:* ποικιλομῆτις, κλεπτοσύνη, δόλοι (13.292–93; 19.137, 396 [Autolykos, the father of Odysseus' mother]).

Diligent practice in secrets, indirection, and nonverbal misdirection unifies the *Odyssey*. Whispers at intimate distance or mere nods commence or punctuate important conversations in hostile surroundings. Eumaios sidles up to Telemakhos to avoid suitors' ears (ἄγχι σχὼν κεφαλήν: 17.592 = 1.157 = 4.70, 21.228–29). While an assassination is plotted apart from inconvenient crowds, Medon overhears the suitors' incautious conspiring and at once reports to Penelope (1.132–35, 16.412). The beggar insists that the queen defer her wish for a fireside conversation until a less visible and audible time and place (17.569–73, 580–84). Men and women cautiously keep voices and heads down, together (ἀσσοτέρω: 17.572, 19.506 only), to conceal intentions from the public world. The palace's jolly wedding song and dance after the slaughter ironically disguise the actual bloody mop-up operation and further machinations against vendetta (23.130–52).

Women need to rely at all times on social barriers, impediments to male affront and aggression, nonphysical tactics for self-defense and ego preservation. Strategic planning, especially for women, is perpetually necessary in tightly watched houses and island villages. There, jealous mistrust and ruses (7.307; δόλους τολυπεύω, 19.137), guardedness, and cunning miscues stymie curious neighbors and shrewdly preserve family privacy and social space from male invaders. Nonverbal behavior, differentiated by gender, partly constructs the *Odyssey*'s gender-conscious plot. The beggar Odysseus' covert glances, concealed smiles, and subtle nods also punctuate, contradict, ironize, and dramatize open acts and public words. By dint of the suitors' superior manpower, the hero is forced to employ further subterfuges, other registers of resources with which to negotiate.

Winkler isolated one contrast in nonverbal behavior that violates audience's gender expectations. Eumaios weeps and Philoitios the oxherd wails in public grief when Penelope coolly announces the decisive contest (21.65–83). Soon after, Odysseus nonverbally and verbally reveals himself to the loyal men outside. Tough Greek farmers weep again, now for joy, an action castigated by Odysseus, not for unmanliness, of course, but for fear that some hostile observer might see and report suspicious activities to the insiders (21.82–83, 228–29). The farmers have forfeited male self-reserve in an inappropriate venue—a possibly public scene. These men cry, but the abandoned wife maintains heroic self-control in public—except to gain a specific point by parading a show of female weakness. Penelope, by designed contrast, remains stonily self-contained, unemotional, poised, and suspicious, despite the grand, optimistic (and not unprecedented—see 14.124–

30) salvation that prophet Theoklymenos projects and that the vagrant beggar asseverates will occur in the nick of time. She shows equal aplomb and control before subsequent, more insistent affirmations by her beloved body-attendant Eurykleia, her son Telemakhos, and her admiring husband (17.157; 23.59–64, 97–103, 112–16). The gender games of the second half of the *Odyssey* avoid monotony and provide a principal source of surprise by violating expectations of unsuspecting characters and audiences.

Penelope represents sweet prestige, the main chance for country boys to prove manliness by capturing a female trophy. Male bonding, planning, and competitive equality promote solidarity and promulgate meaning among otherwise repetitive and undistinguished male careers in the *Odyssey* and in general. Public performance in courting rituals provides social recognition on modern Greek islands as well. The man who is successful in his charm and wealth display and can parade the beautiful woman acquires thereby substantially enlarged symbolic capital. Meanwhile, male gender orthodoxy, badinage, and coffeehouse pastimes immobilize putatively heroic and productive energies. "In . . . drinking, gambling, or rhyme contests, just as in animal theft, men demonstrate strong masculine" bonding, observers of modern Greek masculinity and its small pleasures have noted.[6]

Penelope's very inarticulateness defends her against domineering intruders. Like her modern counterpart's strategies, her "normative submissiveness" or lack of performance deforms conventional, male-defined behavior. The suitors' bombastic intimidation of Ithakan and outlander males and their querulous, garrulous ineffectiveness against one lone female satirize their (un)manliness with regard to heroic gender roles. Penelope, Telemakhos, and the vagrant all play the victim and fool and suceed in proving their dupes even greater fools. Homer allows the downtrodden denizens' muted voices to subvert the collective dominant discourse of the self-serving suitors. For example, Penelope stresses her loss of beauty, figure, reputation, and even freedom from remarriage in a sustained anticonjugal discourse, while Odysseus/Aithon stresses his loss of (Cretan) house, health, wealth, and freedom as a consequence of Belly's commands. Telemakhos stresses his loss of household autonomy and his shame, comparative athletic weakness, and social incompetence. Their speeches ostensibly endorse unavoidable submission to the Big Men. Their complementary, pseudocompli-

---

6. Loizos and Papataxiarchis 1991, 17. Zinovieff 1991 describes *kamaki*, modern Greek male "harpooning" of female tourists, the slang name for (bachelor) prestige, semipublic seduction, occasionally leading to marriage. The practice presents humorous modern analogues of unheroic men jostling for (secondary) sexual prizes, unwilling or unable to joust for more traditional sources of male honor, money and political power.

mentary tactics deserve mention. Their true ripostes are bodily declarations, ironic gestures and postures that silently speak resistance and rebellion. Their disguises of weakness artfully control their opponents.

Penelope's weaving and grieving, Telemakhos' leaving and returning, and Aithon's passive aggression in invasive begging all allow an explicit counter-discourse, not of confrontational words, but of superficially irresistable yet infuriating actions. Each of these silent protests and counterthrusts drives the seething suitors to the boiling point. Incorrigible Penelope is to be "forced to choose" (18.288–89, 19.528–29 in their double-speak), obstructive Telemakhos will be murdered, Aithon will be battered, castrated, and further butchered for social temerity. Beset by paradoxes of inverted Laertid family power, the humble of the earth (categorized by gender, age, and status) speak respectfully and wave flags of exaggerated submission. These charades mask strenuous undercutting of courtship and deference codes curtly and discourteously invoked by uninvited guests.[7]

Penelope, the most thoroughly conceived female personality in Homeric poetry, assimilates elements from all preceding females, partly because of oral formulaic pressures (scenes of female entrance, allurement, etc.),[8] partly to demonstrate her many-sidedness (beauty, intelligence, cunning, and gendered social-negotiation skills). "She" (a literary figment) has been produced by oral-formulaic dynamics, but that does not make her any less real. All humans indulge in "generic thinking" on the level of words, situational expectations, and prosaic life experience.

Penelope's coherence, if she has coherence, must be reconstituted from deception—from hoodwinking her suitors, of course—but also from clever management of her "guests," son, maids, and husband, and the audience. Woman as paradigm of negative qualities—deceiver, seducer, adulteress, and femme fatale—is numerically the dominant pattern of the *Odyssey*. Thus, we encounter the ambivalent, but not at all schizophrenic, formula for attitude-versus-behavior dichotomies (2.92, 13.381, 18.283): νόος δέ οἱ ἄλλα μενοινᾷ. We mention Klytaimnestre, Helen, Aphrodite, Kirke, Kalypso, and Melantho. Odysseus expects tricks or traps from Kalypso, Leukothea, Arete, and Athene, even when there is none and they have only treats in mind (5.170–79, 356–57, 13.324–28). He expects, recognizes, and approves Penelope's bamboozling all *other* men (18.281–83, 23.300–305).

---

7. 18.251–70; 17.415–74; 20.311–19; 21.131–35, 370–77. Herzfeld 1991, 80, 82, 92–96, examines modern Greek female subversion of apparent submission, guarded hostility. Women's effect in nontriumphalist, real-life village contexts seems unsurprisingly puny.

8. Nagler 1974, 64–86; Katz 1991, 79, 163–64.

Postmature Penelope, similar to but angrier than premature Nausikaa,[9] repudiates avowed interest in marriage, in her case, remarriage to one selected suitor. Her age for such activities has passed. She subsequently disclaims erotic suitability for the pretender who alleges that he is her wedded conjugate of twenty years plus (6.63–67; 18.251–55, 272–80; 19.136–57; 23.10–17, 63–65, 214–17). We can explain this psychologically—as fixed and frozen emotions—and/or intellectually—as preternatural feminine perceptivity that realizes that, after twenty years, the two partners need to reenact their courtship and wedding and to make a new deal, now with less insistence on macho posturing. Heroic gendered role-modeling needs to be reformulated in recognition of Penelope's heroic and noteworthy achievement.

Penelope's opacity has been interpreted by analysts as a result of different mythic and poetic traditions and by unitarians as a result of the narrator's andrifocal point of view or of Penelope's "femininity" (illogical, emotional,

---

9. Nausikaa may appear the only deception-free female protagonist, but two counterarguments obtrude. First, she schools Odysseus (!) in deception strategies for her townsmen; and second, I believe that by offering *xenia*, gifts, and marriage, she and her family try indirectly to immobilize or capture the handsome stranger. To avoid owing greater debt than that which he cannot avoid, Odysseus refuses elements of Skherian hospitality from every principal (her maids' bath, her mother's questions, her father's marriage offer, her brother Laodamas' athletic invitation, and her suitor(?) Euryalos' challenge). Odysseus also tries to avoid another untitled bride contest with "the many and noble young men" of Phaiakia, among whom these last two are preeminent (8.110, 115–18). He does not want to win the bride inadvertently. Cf. Van Nortwick 1979, 275; Segal 1967, 330–31; Most 1989b, 27 and n. 60. Odysseus' anxiety to ensure that he will be sent home free frames the claustrophobia and impatience of books 9–12, the *apologoi*.

Lest this view seem far-fetched, compare Odysseus' *rejections* of hospitality, an elaborate one-downmanship displayed in his transactions with Kirke (invitation inside, to eat, to stay, etc.), Kalypso, Nausikaa, and even Penelope. He rejects several formulaic aspects of the mistress' ritualized and deeply articulated welcome of strangers. For instance, he refuses a private daytime interview, courteous or importunate questions about identity, a bath from the maids, fleecy bedding, and later, no longer clearly guest or yet husband, the awesome olive-posted bed allegedly to be trundled from the spousal bedroom (17.569–70; 19.105, 166, 317–20, 340–44; 23.183–89). Some refusals to increase debt can be explained otherwise, but the cumulative weight of his "refusal pattern" suggests an awareness of how to evade, nonverbally and verbally, unpayable heroic debts or undeniable obligations to a goddess, princess, or queen. So Donlan 1993 best explains Akhilleus' strategic refusals of Agamemnon's lavish reparations and "gifts." Odysseus positions himself for return to *kyrios* status in Ithaka; cf. Katz 1991, 151. The motif of "hospitality refused" can be followed in Telemakhos' response to Spartan Menelaos' and Helen's hospitality also. Premature princess Nausikaa's culturally imposed embarrassment about hopes and candidates for marriage is explicit (6.66–67, 244–45, 273–89). Nausikaa is policed by the threat of nonverbal teasing and verbal taunts, should she be seen as followed by an eligible man even at a distance (proxemics). Her grown-up personality is still forming; her "stream of conduct" must project a self acceptable to dominant, patriarchal elders and male acquaintanceship.

confused, i.e., the "weeping and sleeping" pathetic beauty). The narratological issue seems to be, What did she know and when did she know it? Katz, who carefully summarizes such positions as the last, essentialistic one of Penelope's pathetic presentation, clarifies the discussion. She suggests that the lady's very "indeterminacy" is rooted in an anomalous social context, one estranged from the usually available Ithakan social safety nets and from the narrator's usual—that is, traditional and inherited—paradigms of womanhood. Her stubborn withholding of acknowledgment from spouse and her devious determination of his identity and intentions match Odysseus' own hard-heartedness. Her ambivalent utterances and acts always preserve deniability, forfend male either-or reductiveness, and conserve survivable outcomes.[10]

Penelope, to maintain privileged status as mistress and emotional equilibrium in singlehood, wants to hear only praise songs of master Odysseus. So, in tears when first we hear her voice,[11] she rejects Phemios' depressing account of Odysseus' bitter homecoming and perhaps death (1.336–44, 354). Such themes are obviously attractive, even exhilarating, to the suitors who consume his house and hope to usurp it. Telemakhos, sparring for *kyrieia* of his ancestral estate, hopes either to preserve or succeed the absent patriarch. So, to assert his own authority, he harshly rejects Penelope's attempts to command events and rudely returns her, with a gendered formula, to women's work and place (1.356–59 = 21.350–53). In this early scene, he ranks his mother as more dangerous, or more defeatable, than the local predatory gentry.

Penelope's "formula," her default-master delaying tactic, withholds and defers decisions—not only with the suitors but with her husband and son. She must betray one or the other of the latter, whether she stays or leaves. Telemakhos is as much exasperated with her seeming disloyalty to (what he sees as) *his* estate as the suitors are with her coy deferrals of marital plans. Sentimental readings (and translations) play down the mother-son conflict, since Penelope's most unambiguous efforts seem to forward her inevitable choice, her son's present bid for all that absent Odysseus had once acquired as booty and patrimony. Telemakhos, however, is now, after his heroic jour-

---

10. Cf. 23.86, 95, 100–103 with 13.333–36. See Katz 1991, 193. Her helpful approach in reviewing previous positions eventually leads her to run dangerously parallel to one essentializing view of women (that she rightly rejects) as labile, fickle, and impressionable creatures. For ambiguities, see also Ardener 1987, 123, 137; Felson-Rubin 1994; Laurel Bowman sent a perceptive public electronic network message on the Classics network, 3 September 1992, available from its file transfer protocol archive.

11. δακρύσασα. Consult Waern 1985 for (male) heroic tears; also Monsacré 1984 and Arnould 1990, 51–68, reviewed by Lateiner in *AJP* 113.3 (1992): 448–52.

ney, already on his own, ready and willing to head the Laertid dynasty and holdings or to die trying. Meanwhile, his mother's interest—both as individual and also as wife and Laertid affine—is to defer any transfer of *kyriotic* power over her body and her son's presumptive house and properties.

Penelope holds the keys to the estate. The house now belongs to her de facto. She inhibits Telemakhos' freedom and delays the returning master's assertion of power. Penelope is *its* bride. She is married to the house, which she terms κουρίδιον, an adjective describing a wife's husband, bed, and/or house (15.22; *Il.* 15.40, 19.580 = 21.78). The house has its keeper (ταμίη: e.g., 2.345–47, 18.169) and servants, but Penelope, from the beginning, controls its deepest spaces, her permanent alibi. Penelope's fugues over impending departure lament in advance the loss of the house, its beauty and wealth (18.579–81). That estate and the position of mistress are the only current καλά in sight, not the husband from twenty years previous who is of dubious present reality.

Telemakhos eventually claims that the house belongs first to Odysseus and then to himself (20.265–66, cf. 20.336, 369). He competes with both his mother and her Ithakan and overseas admirers. In this light, the suitors and Telemakhos both have strong motives for pressuring Penelope, to force her weak (social) hand to a decision that restores male authority in the land. Like Kirke, but more by sexual than by magical means (if the distinction holds a difference), Penelope has frozen all male initiatives. Yet she too entrances the bemused males; *thelxis* applies to her as well as to Kirke and the Sirens. The other "alternative plot," adultery and murder—enacted by Aigisthos and Klytaimnestre in Mykenai—provides no reassurance of his mother's good faith to the young Ithakan Orestes figure.[12]

The suitors of Penelope, however they chose to arrive in Ithaka, have received some real, if misleading, encouragement in their suit (2.91–92; 13.380; 18.160, 212–13). Certain modern critics question Penelope's fidelity. Penelope leads men on but never delivers the gendered goods. Her duplicitous strategy and nonverbal flirtation pattern, advance and retreat, partly provoke invasive insolence. In her weak position of deferring and waiting, she intrigues with feeble allies and, by playing one swain off against the others, turns adversaries into helpers. Although to imagine Penelope as lusting after her goosey suitors seems far-fetched, one may draw attention to her attempt to escape patriarchy's prison. Ambivalence and provocative be-

---

12. Katz 1991, 152, 30, 36–37, 40; Murnaghan 1992, 262. In effect, Penelope has designed and deployed a *kyrios* gridlock to create a realm of female freedom. She has made herself a new Klytaimnestre, "renowned for her wooers." She refuses to remain jailed within a patriarchally allotted sphere.

haviors emerge: secret messages; favored competitors, such as Amphinomos; and even explicit assertion of inclinations to depart with a suitor, however brutal, oily, crude, or glozing he may be (2.91–92, 16.397, 19.524–29). The audience, knowing Odysseus' whereabouts, is reluctant to debit the twenty-year war-wife with sexual disloyalty and emotional frustration. Better, they believe, that she be too good to be true, as in the perennial and relevant fairy tales of the long-lost husband's homecoming. The Homeric truth is muddier. Penelope grieves sincerely for the suitors' death, at least in a dream (the geese in her dream are identified as the suitors), perhaps because they are known quantities; Odysseus no longer has a clear profile.[13]

Penelope's social competence in male-dominated rooms appears when she polices suitors (e.g., 16.409), refurbishes and restores Laertid wealth, and questions visitors, holding the family together as wife, mother, and house protector (23.355). She maintains heroic standards of hospitality. She protects herself and hers, attends to her own needs as woman and beauty queen, and cheerfully accepts the idea that the resident suitors can be extirpated (19.569). Their demise is a separate issue, however—not a guarantee of Odysseus' return.

2. Women's Weapons

Indirect are her woman's glance and investigative tactics, her plot previews in reporting dreams, proposing tests, and interrogating new arrivals. Her elaborate, sneaky testing trick shows she can outwit her husband as well as cheat the suitors in her private space—rooms of her own (2.90; 23.107, 181–82; 19.137–56). She is a brooding Kirke to the suitors, who feed like animals (geese) at her trough (19.535–37, 548–50; 18.275–80). She likes to watch her tethered denizens (19.537—geese = suitors). She outwits fanatically cautious Odysseus, where even goddess Kirke had failed. Penelope is the only human who consciously puts Odysseus to a decisive proof that he "fails."[14]

---

13. 19.536–48. Rankin 1962, 622, represents the unlikely view of a sorely tempted Penelope; cf. Katz' 1991 catalog of opinion (146).

14. 23.177–83; cf. 19.215–21—Penelope was too candid. Odysseus easily parries any preannounced test that she sets, yet he still complains about her hard tasks (19.116, 166, 221 [*argaleon*]). Antianalytical and anti-intuitionist Emlyn-Jones suggests (1984, 8–9) that the "near-recognitions" of book 19 are "spoofs" of recognition scenes from popular tradition or inferior poets. He refers to Penelope's dangerous (probing?) remarks on Aithon's resemblance to Odysseus (sagacity, 350–52, hands and feet, age, 358–59), Eurykleia's similar observations (nonverbal items, such as build, voice, and feet, 380–81), and his nurse's later attempt to draw Penelope's attention to her startling discovery. In this reading (cf., earlier, Kakridis 1971, 157–58), oral poets repeatedly frustrate audiences' vulgar expectations of revelation to increase dramatic pleasure and suspense. Count the legend's many recognitions on Ithaka alone (i.e.,

Tentative communications, not yet deeds, are modulated or modified by face and gestures, withdrawn, or explained away as need be. Penelope makes brash suitors into collective protectors by setting the contemptible deviants against one another. Women's ramified rituals and gestures of accommodation to superior male power, both when feigned and genuine, require endurance and hermetic expertise in piloting through shark-infested waters. In the *Odyssey,* rituals of dining, greeting and parting, and suppliancy are often honored, but, critically for the plot, they are not rarely dishonored by those pretending to uphold tradition. *Xenia,* verbal and nonverbal, is central, a "costly and elaborate gift economy . . . encumbered with personal considerations." Penelope and her hostly congeners share and give. Because they only take, the suitors' "means eat up the end," their tactics undermine their goals of power.[15] Penelope even boasts of success, as men too often do to their cost, but she only does so behind the female veil of reported dream and dreamed, male (husband) dream interpreter. Here, in uniquely total transparency but claiming total ignorance, she presents the suitors as tame, domestic geese subject to their housemistress.[16] Her speech, through veils and darkly, reveals and conceals her thoughts (the geese are loved but killed, the suitors hated but fed, fattened, and baited). Her speech shields her from gender-based opprobrium or suspicion of inadmissable knowledge.[17]

Circumspect (περίφρων) Penelope must remain beware of eavesdropping maids—intramural, gossipy, impulsive, and traitorous women ready to betray their sex and mistress. Besides this, she must fend off the extraneous,

---

leave aside Helen's, Kalypso's, Antikleia's, Polyphemos', etc.): Athene, Eumaios, son, dog, wife, nurse, loyal servants, suitors, maids, and more. I agree with the ascribed performative intent of audience teasing in a teasing tale, but not with the (in any case) unprovable "spoof" hypothesis. Felson-Rubin 1987, 74, analyzes Penelope's effective tactics to enlist the attractive stranger.

15. Bourdieu 1977, 165, 172, 184; Marquardt 1985, 37; Murnaghan 1986; Winkler 1990, 160. Penelope, point by point, matches the extraordinary tenacity and caution of Odysseus (cf. Telemakhos' imperceptive comments at 23.100 and 168). Although she never enjoys the epithets πολύτροπος or πολύμητις, reserved—like many πολυ- compounds for Odysseus alone—she receives the sonically similar πολυμνήστη (4.770, 23.149) and the semantically and thematically similar (but less ambitious) epithets περίφρων and ἐχέφρων (1.329, 4.111, etc.; cf. Stanford 1950, Marquardt 1985).

16. 19.536, 548. The immobilized geese present the obverse of the same book's sexually predatory hound, another Odysseus, grasping the dappled, struggling fawn on the metal clasp, or the relentless young hunter who met and subdued the savage, wild boar.

17. Roisman 1990a develops a good case for Eumaios' justified suspicions about the beggar's identity and covert recognition. The delicate procedures devised by hog-master and spouse (cf. Roisman 1987) to disenvelope the intruder explain many otherwise inexplicable words, deeds, and gestures. Penelope's behavioral agility is self-contradictory on purpose, hard to nail down.

lusty, and greedy adulterers. Nausikaa has stated succinctly to the wanderer the gendered dangers facing even momentarily imprudent maidens.[18]

The young maidservants' failure to groom decrepit Argos and their tittering laughter are in character with their unforgiveable faithlessness to the *oikos* and their sexual promiscuity. Even loyal Eurykleia's brief laughter is silenced or censured.[19] This prudent and admirable old servant had dropped her washbowl (a noisy gesture that would leak stupefaction), nearly shouted when she touched the beggar's scar, and then unthinkingly tried to catch her mistress' eye at a dangerous moment (19.468–77). She thus conforms to emotional, excessively expressive, and incautious female stereotypes beloved by misogynists everywhere. Women are criticized for excessive deviousness, insufficient caution, heated emotionalism, *and* ice-cold reserve.

Gods too play tricks on incautious men and women. They are ready to cuckold other gods or pose as mortal husbands (Ares and Hephaistos in book 8 and 23.63–65; Amphitryon at 11.266–68). Malicious gossipers could and do fault Penelope's hasty(!) courtship and remarriage (13.287–328; 23.63, 148–51). Thus, one appreciates her "guarded negotiations" with her son, the suitors, and the beggar. Also, her bed trick tests and successfully tricks the master trickster, showing us that, for Homer, *metis* is not sex-specific. Despite her self-dramatized despair in sexual limbo, Penelope controls a mind just as mistrustful (ἄπιστος, 23.72), firm, and capable as Odysseus'. Truly they deserve the epithet ὁμοφρονέοντε—like-minded.[20]

Penelope spends considerable time grooming and preening herself (self-adaptors) while denying both the act or justification for it. Her "cultural display rules" as apparently widowed wife argue for little visibility and *minimal* self-presentation, that is, they allow public performances only as grieving matron or widow. Nevertheless, her strategy of deferral and delay, imposed by the suitors' and others' social, prescriptive definitions of her person and available roles, requires maintaining the intrusive men's hopes of resolution. Bourgeois audiences who reprehend "flirting with the boys" as

---

18. 6.273–88. Odysseus later compliments her remarkable poise and careful manners (7.293–94). See Du Boulay 1976; Winkler 1990, 149, 153, 158–60.

19. Goldhill 1988, 15, on 17.318–19; Levine 1987, 24, 27, on 18.320; 20.8; 22.407–12; 23.1, 59. Note the uneuphonious (Stanford's observation ad loc.), gender-biased sounds of κιχλίζω and καγκαλόωσα. Gildersleeve (*AJP* 28 [1907]: 209) notoriously remarked "feminine syntax" in Homer, for example at *Il.* 14.331–36.

20. Odysseus employs this thematic participle with Nausikaa for the partners in a fine marriage, the noun for the resultant marital concord (6.181, 183; cf. 9.456, 15.198, for sheep and male camaraderie). Interpersonal borrowing and entrainment between spouses in matters of vocabulary, nonverbal mannerisms, gesticulation, and intonation is often casually remarked in the sociological literature; cf. Poyatos 1986, 494. So the formulaically induced adjective has sociolinguistic warrant.

disloyal or selfishly materialistic (anticipated by Penelope herself at 19.525–34; cf. Telemakhos at 1.245–51) seem oblivious to her lack of viable alternatives. Her predicament leads her to empathize even with her catastrophic mirror-image peer, Helen, and to "launder" her own accounts of coquetry with the suitors.[21] Her nightly crying jags convey nonverbally her public image and her self-image as lonely, but loyal, wife and mother, a very real victim. Her deeds, words, and teasing nonverbal behavior with the suitors produce successful stalls that retard their haste and replenish Laertid stores. Athene's beauty treatments, "advanced night repair," reverse aging processes only for heroes, but for them both: Odysseus and Penelope (6.229–37, 18.188–96). Heroic courage and actual power over would-be oppressors create a her-story equal to her husband's history of endurance and craft. Her superiority to supposed peers of either sex becomes plain.[22]

Her flirtatious behavior-displays conform to "approach-and-flight" patterns, a nonverbal and conveniently ambivalent set of sexual messages associated with coy sexual acquaintanceship ritual in many societies, especially within the parameters of acceptable "feminine" zigzag roles. Both her conscious and her unconscious behaviors excite males, that is, make her "pretty" and sexually desirable to them. They disarm usual caution and misdirect attention. Consequently, the wooers are distracted from discovering an exit from the wooing impasse. To the extent that Penelope intends to stimulate wooers' lust to produce premarital paraphernalia but no marriage, her nonverbal behavior is deceptive, and her clothing, jewelry, posture, and so forth function as deceptors. "All is fair in *their* love and *her* war."[23] Her bow contest traps them dead.

3. Women's Masks

Nagler explores one significant woman-associated body-adaptor, the mysterious *kredemnon* with its related concepts and expressions. Various mentions of "head ribbons," veils, or whatever this archaic word denotes, all subconsciously or consciously evoke associations with inviolability, chastity, and especially female sexual modesty. Nagler's analysis links Penelope, Nau-

---

21. Felson-Rubin 1987, 66–69, emphasizes, perhaps unduly, the teasing, but not simulated, encouragement of suitors by sexually starved (for twenty years), "increasingly sensuous Penelope." I can easily endorse in imagination the bio-logic of this perceived "horniness," but Penelope remains a literary character.

22. 19.326, 23.301; Levine 1987, 26.

23. Poyatos 1986, 502; Eibl-Eibesfeldt 1972, 302–3; Murnaghan 1986, 109, 113. Rutherford 1992, 32, denies Penelope any plan; Roisman 1990b analyzes the comparable Iliadic vocabulary of *kerdos*, profit and shrewdness.

sikaa,[24] and Ino, but also Thetis, Hera, Andromakhe, and Persephone, on the level of word, motif, and type-scene, but more deeply on the level of gendered cultural "givens." The object, its metonyms and metaphors, externalize internal states. Penelope herself explains her situation; she needs and wants female companions as chaperones *and* her decorous head-covering as a token of protection when she comes downstairs. Otherwise she would be shamed (αἰδέομαι δέ: 18.182–84, 206–11; cf. *Il.*24.90–94).[25] Penelope observes all Homeric nonverbal conventions of woman's relative physical seclusion, including proxemics, veils, and chaperones (the last two are body-adaptors). Her tact, a convenient name for verbal and nonverbal social strategies, could not be improved upon.

The disguised guest Aithon describes, to pass a test, another Penelopean shift, an alter-adaptor with gendered overtones. The indications of power and mortality carry vast symbolic import. When Odysseus sailed off for Troy, Penelope presented him with a parting gift. She gave him an artful (*daidalon*) golden brooch showing a hound seizing and strangling a struggling fawn. The mention here of Penelope's nonverbal expression, token of affection and image of symbolic submission, in preparation for lengthy absence marks their firm bond on three levels: depicted image of quasi-erotic hunt and conquest, valued gift to bind closely one's loyal spouse, and confirming token of claimed identity as *xenos,* as Aithon successfully describes the object. The stunning role of junglelike struggle (*aspair-* stems twice) and animal violence is reaffirmed in even this, the gentlest context of civilized prestation and wifely love. The *ekphrasis* reminds audiences of the thin veneer of social contract and agreement glued onto a substrate of anomic brutality and bestial rapine.[26]

The narrative's implicit negative comparison of Nausikaa's impulsive,

---

24. She removes protective *kredemnon* at the shore; she strips off clothes and bathes; she alone meets Odysseus without attendants or chaperones (6.100, 96, 84 and 139). Van Nortwick 1979, 271–72, compares her to Penelope at 18.184.

25. Nagler 1974, xxiv, 45–47, 64–67, daringly extends analysis of head-coverings to males and even to besieged Troy's physical integrity and violation. Hoekstra ad *Od.* 13.388 discusses the nature of this object. Tuareg male veils with up to forty indigo strips are worn at *all* times and have multivalent meanings (Youssouf et al. 1976, 803, 818–19 nn. 21–23; Hawad-Claudot 1992). These African veils, expensive indicators of status and body adaptors, communicate all manner of affect and intent, including foppery, indifference, fury, and masked focus. Fans held in the hand once served a similar function for preindustrialized Eastern and Western societies. The current North Atlantic equivalent is sunglasses, sold more for sex appeal and privacy than for eye protection; Poyatos 1986, 515. A worthy project might study face-hiding body-adaptors across time and cultures.

26. 19.226–31, 255–57; cf. Felson-Rubin 1987, 70–71, n. 29, who describes the significant object as a combination of erotic and hunting motifs and a binding gift; also Russo ad loc.

winning candor to Penelope's cautious wisdom justifies once again Odysseus' perseverance in pursuing his homeward quest. Nausikaa's ingenuous forwardness at the strand, in contrast to Penelope's equivocations, violates several firm rules of Homeric female modesty. She does so for good cause, the audience may think, but the damage that could have resulted not only to her repute but to her male and female relatives' honor can hardly be calculated. Odysseus helps save her social standing from her human yet immature hankering by what he says and does at both the nearly deserted beach and the busy palace. He responds with care to Arete's justifiably suspicious (and only half-formulaic) questions, after she observes her handiwork and family clothes on the suppliant's back. His catalogs of queens in the Otherworld play up to both women's "natural" interests.[27]

Ikarios' daughter thus presents the mortal woman's positive paradigm: reclusive apartheid with significant exceptions. We encounter the heroine virtuously working home-produced wool to honor and protect her father-in-law's eventual corpse, the remains of her replacement father. She is working with incomprehensible womanly dexterity, until, unfortunately, another clever woman exposes to the men her woven wile. The female, textilic craft demonstrates equal and complementary gendered *metis*—agile, dactylic dexterity combined with sinister motive. She delays besieging suitors and postpones indefinitely unwanted betrayal of her adopted house, an act that will bring her only obloquy or ridicule (see 23.148–51 and Telemakhos' juvenile, unjustified jab at 16.33–35). Fine textiles are status trappings, valuable gendered capital, suitable for *xenia* or ransom, and proof of a virtuous and capable wife's proper pursuits. The textiles nonverbally demonstrate the house's wealth and economic energy. Textiles ubiquitously prove the producer's womanly excellence, personal achievement, and acknowledgment of her socioeconomic niche.[28]

The *Odyssey* shuffles masks and disguises, supplementing costumes and postures with assumed social identities. Odysseus' rags construct a social identity that makes him invisible as a warrior. Penelope too hides behind cloth, material manifestations of matronly excellence. She shelters her marital fidelity behind weaving Laertes' shroud for three years, and she dons a veil when she condescends and descends to the suitors. Her composure here and

---

27. Doherty 1991 examines gendered audiences internal to the *Odyssey*, sexual segregation among the Otherworld's shades, and Odysseus' use of Agamemnon as a "smoke screen" for his own mistrust of Penelope (161). This last point persuades me less than her others, because (a) no hero in Homer needs to hide male suspicion of females and (b) Agamemnon's "other ending" is of great interest and importance to the Homeric cycle for itself and as a foil.

28. Cf. *Od.* 2.89–110; 5.346–50; 8.424–25, 440–41; 24.276–77; *Il.* 16.223–24, 24.228–31; Jenkins 1985, 115, 123.

"leaked" simulated helplessness in flagranti delicto, when her shroud trick has been unveiled, assure suitors that patriarchal social controls are still working. Her bodily silences before their desire and again in the showdown with her self-proclaimed spouse excel and conquer all male self-control.[29] Penelope's indecipherable mien protects her from prying and probing; the veil and her occluded face symbolize hidden resources and ambiguous messages (ἀκριτόμυθοι, like dreams, 19.560). These nonverbal behaviors suggest all her baffling multiplicity and reserved strengths.

Penelope's loom is another significantly gendered object: it serves as a nonportable *kredemnon,* another social line of defense and instrument of opacity. It obtrudes "a permanent available activity," a three-year alibi. It imperiously calls her to another space, a separated universe, an obligation to one set of men that removes and preserves her from another.[30] Male restrictions, then and now, on "woman's place" give rise in Greece to circumventions, self-expression through "creative submission" that allows women to mock male hegemonic discourse. Structural powerlessness develops therapeutic and effective counterstrategies. Penelope "caves in" to suitors' wishes only in circumscribed ways that keep her safe from them and expose their inferior wit. Recall the three-year compromise of Laertes' shroud, the exploitation of standard wooing prestation protocols in a totally anomalous (because fatherless) context (of her devising) that makes Odysseus smile, and the contest of the bow—a rash act to some critics, but the lethal checkmate in the outcome. Women develop submissive self-assertion ploys to escape social effacement. Penelope and Eurykleia literally hold the keys to the kingdom.

In the *Odyssey,* the "normal" paradigm triumphs over the "deviant" in issues of hospitality, marriage, disposition of resources, property, and control of space. Men have the last word. Indeed, the *Odyssey* is no more important as sociological source for Homeric practice than as validating paradigm for patriarchal authority in the classical period. These later customs include androcentric arrangements of separate spheres for men and women, the

---

29. An oft-repeated formula creates and cues audience expectation. Homeric speakers reply 150 times with "winged words," whether that means "wrought up," "swift to escape," "quickly transmitted," "soon evaporating" or "evanescent," (nonverbal behavior) quickly responding in "turn taking," or something else. Combellack 1950/51, 24, selects "transitory, ephemeral," citing Schol. B and T on *Il.* 16.101. Four times in the climactic last third of the *Odyssey,* a woman is so stunned by orders from usually uncommanding Telemakhos (once from lowly Eumaios) that her μῦθος or speech is ἄπτερος, "wingless" (17.57, 19.29, 20.386, 22.398). She is silent, deliver zero-grade verbal response. The audience's narratival and aural expectation is thwarted. Oral epic gains impact from the breach as well as the honoring of formula. A deformation of a ubiquitous speech-formula produces nonspeech, eloquent (nonverbal) silence.

30. See the oral poetics of Nagler 1974, 44–67, and the gender analysis of Bourdieu 1977, 160.

increased seclusion of women, and an ideology that forced Athenian women to pursue most goals by quiet indirection.[31] Penelope is not a blood kin, so her social tie and loyalty to the Ithakan royal house is ever suspect, impermanent, and hypothetically replaceable. Consequently, her testing by the seed of Laertes never stands complete, as both Athene and Odysseus acknowledge (11.177–79, 13.336, 18.257–70). She must run to stay in place.

Penelope must keep the besieging suitors out of her quarters, her bed, and her body.[32] Odysseus' male absence accounts for all her special female problems and privileges. She achieves these difficult goals of exclusion by providing objects and unrefusable offers for the dishonorable suitors to misread. Odysseus must penetrate the palace and regain control of its activities, marital bedroom,[33] and mistress. "Deliberate misdirection," misleading smiles, and reassuring tones contribute to controlled "public personalities." These ploys conceal more than reveal family intentions. From book 17 to 22, the skill of the family in manipulating others through their own apparent weaknesses asserts itself more clearly person by person, scene by scene.

Penelope projects herself frequently as defeated, downtrodden, and essentially resourceless. Nevertheless, her apparent and advertised lack of independence, power, and prestige contrasts starkly with her successful manipulation of her relationships with her family, household, and visitors. This last category currently comprises the irritable, invasive suitors for marriage and the impressive but evasive aristo-vagrant (19.116).

Penelope sees, unlike some recent critics, that Telemakhos' emergence into manhood requires a new, improved family strategy that will empower him among *aristoi*. Her sexually arousing appearance before the suitors implements that switch. She tells Odysseus as much (19.159–61, 530–34). Mean-

---

31. Like Penelope, Athenian women are often described as conducting nonverbal negotiations behind veiled faces, at a distance, and through shared forms of ambiguous discourse. Ceaseless cunning and calculating sangfroid inflects their gendered needs. Isaeus 3.13–14 reports the clichés of gossip. Slander was attached to nonconforming Athenian women; quarrels, parties, and casual sex with all comers were the typical charges. Women did go out to fountains and fields; though separated from *men*, they were not isolated from all social life, enjoying parallel institutional structures and psychological independence (Cohen 1989). Without some hypothesis of limited but real liberties, Aristophanes' three plays centered on gendered amusement become barely comprehensible.

32. Haptics (who touches whom, where, and when) in Greek epic, tragedy, and comedy would provide a suitable topic of a monograph. Kaimio 1988 and Mastronarde 1979 offer first steps. Same- and opposite-sex body contacts strongly exhibit self-disclosure motives, asymmetrical sexual taboos, other gendered behavior (such as economic roles), and societal norms.

33. Proxemic elements of Penelope's marital chastity and gendered no-man's-land distinguish her current upstairs (ὑπερῴιον), single-sex sleeping quarters from the linguistic allomorph, the heterosexual marriage chamber or θάλαμος (16.34–35, 19.600–604, 1.362, 23.295). See Nagler 1974, 72–79; Vidal-Naquet 1986, 35 n. 63, on Penelope's unique situation.

while, she remains apart except for emergencies (1.340–41, 16.411, 19.53–56, 21.63–66) and summons her female retinue to or from the upper, secluded rooms (4.675–715; 16.412–13; 17.505–9, 544, 574–78). The motions of female semiseclusion, veiling, and employing body-attendants underline Mediterranean gender expectations and rules but also allow forms of subversive obedience.[34]

Penelope's notorious laugh, ἀχρεῖον δ' ἐγέλασσεν, emblematizes her gendered mystery. Like Odysseus' analogously unique sardonic smile (18.163, 20.301–2), the verbal hapax also produces a crux. It cannot be read with certainty, at least not now, because the language has no matrix of known meaning. These two facial expressions have no intended internal audience (communication target) and are "devoid of [their] usual meaning," indecipherable, perhaps even to their emitters. They signal deception only to the mind-reading hearer or reader, not to the copresent, internal audience. The laugh is neither inane giddiness nor helpless impulse, but affect leakage that signals another scheme—something up her capacious sleeve.[35]

With rare exceptions, we cannot divine Penelope's thoughts—for example, the thinking behind her public screen of ambivalence (23.85–87; cf. 16.73, 18.164, 19.524). Homer makes all his audiences into pleased yet puzzled Odysseuses, and he surprises them too by her bed trick. Some narratologists, I among them, would credit this Homer with an intentionally occlusive Penelope. Her repeated words and actions are meant to leave internal and external audiences confused—either misled or confident but bamboozled—about both her motives and her intentions, even beyond first hearing. Nearly all her moves preserve "deniability" to *all* audiences.

The "hermeneutics of suspicion" criticizes Penelope for enjoying her gaggle of suitors (19.537, 541). This approach views her death-wish soliloquy addressed to Artemis (20.62–90) as a forlorn prelude to an unavoidable choice of just one husband, an unwanted marriage, and an end to her status as "belle of the ball."[36] It misapprehends with perverse relish her bizarre,

---

34. H. Foley 1978, 9–10; Murnaghan 1987; Felson-Rubin 1987, 77. Katz 1991, 119, will not allow her such autonomy and perspicacity. Her exemplary summary of previous views should be consulted. Hawad-Claudot 1992 describes nonverbal expression in (male) veil manipulation in a contemporary African society.

35. δόλοι at 19.137; cf. 18.283. See Büchner 1940, 143; Levine 1983a, 174. Byre 1988 suggests that the laugh indexes her uncertainty; see also Katz 1991, 82, 89. It may also mask apologetic embarrassment before her silent servant. Gestures, like words, are often elastic and multivalent.

36. Felson-Rubin 1987. Katz 1991, 147–52, rejects the hedonistic woman but accepts one that is resigned to transferring husbands and relinquishing Ithakan residence. Sarah Isles Johnston, reconsidering reference to pathetic Pandarids, has suggested to me that Penelope's recollection of their aborted motherhood reflects a (momentarily) miserable view of her

exaggerated revisionism in which former marital reality (husband Odysseus) seems but a dream, and current dreams seem a "realer" reality (19.579–81 = 21.77–79, 19.541–49). She seems to begin to "leave before she leaves" Ithaka, just as, in tandem, Odysseus returns before he returns (in propria persona). Telemakhos too attempts to clear some space for himself in the four-way jockeying for Ithakan mastery. He paradoxically succeeds best when he knowingly pretends possession to the suitors in the course of his disguised father's reestablishment. Penelope gains ground on his "coattails." Her son's security is her foremost, unswerving goal amid all charades. Warm feelings toward *xeinoi*, Theoklymenos and Aithon, provide the closest homologous positive relations to her absent husband. The noteworthy intimacy of confabulation, the ὁμιλία, suggests long-suppressed willingness to show warmth to a nonsuiting, "platonic" spouse substitute—or secret knowledge.

Penelope stalls men by withholding information. She invents or recalls suddenly the patriarchal significance of Telemakhos' beard. Odysseus' "parting words" and significant gestures emerge when and where they do to extract more bride-price property (18.269). Penelope "reports" that Odysseus, when he left Ithaka, took his wife by the wrist—a ceremonious gesture of mutually acknowledged familial and gendered authority. Her reports to the suitors and her husband convey his patriarchal power and serious behest. He deputized her to care for *everything* at home until Telemakhos grew a beard. Then he authorized Penelope to marry *at that time and not before* whomever she then wished (18.258, 266–70). Suspiciously prescient and generous (but rational) advice for the bride of a soldier sailing off to war, a missing person in the making!

Penelope's report of this "event" may be "fact," merely delayed admission of a genuine valediction. It still enables her to stall the suitors just a bit longer by justifying her choice of a spousal selection mechanism (while she expects the recently prophesied quick return of her husband). Otherwise, and more logically, it may be another Penelopean invention to pry out additional fancy jewelry before the slaughter, because the credible stranger has asserted that the lethal moment of truth has almost arrived. She must believe the stranger, since she *now* (and not before) announces the bow contest. Odysseus finds her performance pleasing—the homophrosynic couple, by (his own) definition, causes grief to enemies (6.180–85). Penelope's own description of the house's economic difficulties (19.530–34) certainly makes her implied social and economic transfer and her prior receipt of bride-gifts and bids into

---

own. See 20.61–78 and cf. Russo ad 19.518–24, for another Pandarid myth with a different plot but the same child-damaging theme.

plausible policy. She must defend herself against public and private reproach with respect to the suitors and the attractive beggar (16.73–77, 19.527). She has developed for this purpose a unique listening post, an aperture (?; κατ' ἄντηστιν, 20.387) expressed by a unique word.

Penelope's new decisiveness has transparent meaning. She is now, at the moment at least, finally ready to do what she says: to leave and remarry. This seductive possibility is defended by Katz for books 18–21, where she recognizes a tergiversating queen who wants to remain Laertid yet recognizes a need to decamp, both to scatter unruly parasitic princelets and to free the scion from would-be assassin squads.[37] This apparent willingness to marry, the apparent collapse of her resistance, cannot be ignored. The issue remains, Why now?[38] Penelope is not capricious, not foolish, and not irrational. She has received oaths and assurances promising Odysseus' immanent arrival (17.155–59, 19.269–72). But she is one suspicious lady, always distrustful of good news. She inclines to believe no one (cf. 14.122–23). Unbelief is her most consistent characteristic, impervious to dangerous hope.[39]

What options are available to the audience? We may regard Penelope as a precipitate fool for not waiting another day, as a quiet genius for penetrating Odysseus' disguise, or as an oppressed, exhausted caretaker who can no longer cope with the fierce pressure. Theorists of the next century, I am sure, clogging the text with interpretive models to make sense of the narrative or to deconstruct any apparent literary unity (one uncertain victory of oral poetics), will devise new approaches that further minimize the reader's desire and need to shape a character. Acknowledging all the unavoidable problems involved with reading a character out of a bunch of black marks on white paper, it still seems most economical to recognize both Penelope's ferocious tenacity in her hard-won, hard-maintained corner of limited freedom and also her inching acceptance of profuse, certified signs of spousal return—cushioned and couched by the wary woman in repeated, formulaic, and psychologically verisimilitudinous denial. The signs include Telemakhos' re-

---

37. Katz 1991, 120–28, 153, argues that Telemakhos and Odysseus "misread" Penelope repeatedly to their own patriarchal satisfaction, but patriarchal texts are not likely to authorize *consistent* ineptitude for patriarchal heroes. The present analysis discovers maximum credit for both the lord and the lady.

38. Combellack 1973, 32–40, addresses this impasse of plot construction, "the great defect."

39. Thornton 1970, 105; Katz 1991, 102–3, 131; but cf. 14.127–28. Perhaps this is another reason why Odysseus wishes to "prod" her, as well as the female servants, into self-revelatory behaviors (16.304–5; δμωὰς καὶ μητέρα σὴν ἐρεθίζω, 19.44–45). Homer's careful reader and scrap collector, the dramatist Aischylos, has his Prometheus describe hope as both a snare and a delusion.

port of Proteus' news that Odysseus lives; Theoklymenos' prophecy of Odysseus' imminent presence in Ithaka and plans to recoup the castle; Telemakhos' sneeze (which she herself optimistically interprets); her persuasive proofs from the grizzled interlocutor about knowing Odysseus; her own dream and its self-contained, dreamed interpreter, eagle-eyed Odysseus; and the beggar's confirmation of her dreamed interpretation (17.142–44, 157–59, 541–50; 19.250 = 23.206 = 24.346; 19.535–58). She elects to disregard them all, or so she says, and so we are led to believe. Book 19 provides male-female double deceptions reminiscent of the double bluff in book 13, where Athene in disguise greets Odysseus in mufti on Ithaka.[40]

Thus, the timing for the drastic contest becomes unenigmatic. Although Penelope suspects the beggar's identity to be Odysseus (and it could also be an avenging god, as she perceptively protests later to Eurykleia at 23.62–68), her resistance is worn down, her son is grown up, and her options are few with thugs all about. Indeed, while the plot requires her to maintain (truthfully) that another marriage would be "hateful" (στυγερὸς γάμος, 18.272; cf. 1.249, 16.126, 24.414), such an outcome seems better than further open-ended abuse of her son, his estate, herself, and their impossible situation. Some form of Harsh's hypothesis of recognition proves less problematic than other evaluations of "all the facts" presented.[41]

Odysseus needs to confirm two personae, to express both alignment and disalignment to suitorial hegemony in Ithaka by small behaviors. He ignores slights, abases himself verbally and physically, and withdraws, in passive if impassive obedience, from tormenters. Thus, he develops a screen by which to hide furious reactions. With Penelope, he expresses diametrically opposed sympathies by both word and proxemic presumptions (chair, propinquity, assertiveness about the future). The suitors face a similar quandary. Plundering behaviors ill fit their expressed sympathies for the plights of Penelope and Telemakhos. Their own jury-rigged and jerry-built social stage verges on

---

40. Russo ad 20.82 claims that Penelope's heartbroken prayer for death proves that "she has no suspicion" that Odysseus is now returned. Odysseus' return, however, as Leokritos pointed out early on (2.246–51), does not in any way guarantee his victory or even his security—or her victory. The estimable and always reasonable Russo resorts to special pleading to explain the cliff-hanging, teasing caesura at 19.358–60: νίψον σοῖο ἄνακτος—ὁμήλικα.

41. I here anxiously align myself against most Homerists and with the "prescient Penelope" school of Harsh (1950), Amory (1963, 103–6), Stewart (1976, 103), and Winkler (1990, 143, 155). These critics certainly disagree about aspects and details, e.g., the moment of recognition and conscious, subconscious, or unconscious (whatever that might mean) identification. Choosing the precise moment and line in the text of Penelope's recognition seems a naive fallacy of literary "realism," unwarranted psychologism, or a pedantic parlor game. But I hope to persuade readers that her recognition in stages long precedes her verbal admission. Winkler reasonably calls the bride contest a calculated gamble.

collapse. They cannot cope with two different audiences, although their leaders play with irony in comforting Telemakhos. The cleavage that results from attacking the vagrant, the quarrels attendant on plans to murder Telemakhos, and Amphinomos' various kind (if vain) gestures as the anomalous "good suitor" all suggest a nearby breaking point. Even their unanimous, unmotivated, derisory and hysterical laughter suggests faulty presentation of self, problems of discipline and disconcerting divinities. Antinoos presents himself as "tactful," someone cognizant of rules of decorum and embarrassment, yet his botched encounters with Aithon thoroughly discredit this self and the suitors' communal self-presentation. Embarrassment spreads in widening circles. In "destroying another's image, he destroys his own" (Goffman 1967a, 102, 106).

The mendicant originally presents a face that the suitors are comfortable with: a new Iros. But his demands assault their lingering attachment to known roles of vagrants. His isolation as an unhoused person leaves him vulnerable. His irregular status in a stigmatized role strips off the usual social insulation: networks, friends, and dependable small talk. He has nowhere to turn, his world is shrunk to whatever ground the suitors will afford him. While they josh Telemakhos, pretending not to mean what they really do, their banter with the beggar is serious prodding on all levels, an attempt to force him to fill the only role that they wish to allow him. Trial by taunt and threat is their chief communication to both the beggar and the prince's son.[42]

Penelope, meanwhile, progressively defines the vaguely eligible stranger, if not as lost husband, then at least as one very much like that very special man. Her confidence grows, not only because of his augural skills and photographic recollection of the gift of a buckle, significant as those talents are, but also because of his body cues. The comparable age, shape, and size of his hands and feet are explicitly remarked by high and low persons among "palace" personnel. His movements and sequences of word and deed repeatedly earn her approbation in books 17–21 (e.g., 17.586, 19.253–54, 350–53, 589–90). Distant and near signals of cooperative activity anticipate the nature of future events. She notes his superior sense and manners, comparing

---

[42]. The bow contest reverses judge and defendants at trial. The unreticent and sexually deprived suitors (1.365–70, 18.212–13) certainly will precipitate change by managing the bow. The resolution will be read either, by the sympathetic, as Penelope's inauthentic "choice," because the existence of her own will has been denied, or, by the unsympathetic, as just a "quick and dirty" solution that will depose and expose her grown son, Telemakhos, after an extended, demeaning wait for a miracle that never came. The time limit for missing persons has expired. But, like impatient Telemakhos, our expectations are frustrated again. Teasing hints and false leads are habitual with Penelope and Odysseus (and Homer), not least in dealing with each other (19.134, 157, 350; 19.235; 23.202).

them most positively to the abusive suitors' (ἀνέρες ὑβρίζοντες ἀτάσθαλα μηχανόωνται, 17.580–88). The very comparison implies that she regards the once-noble beggar as an equal and match for the suitors, if not as the marriage match for her. This man and woman share an affinity, nonverbal wavelengths that augment mutual confidence. They recognize shared fluency and even signals in micromessage encoding and decoding. They are an entrained couple, married or not.

For instance, Odysseus shows good sense in displacing and delaying any hasty heterosexual, private (οἴην), face-to-face conversation—such a conversation would have been a serious violation of Homeric etiquette, had Odysseus acceded, since Penelope intended it to occur in her women's quarters (17.529–30, 569–73). Further, when they do converse, their give-and-take shows quick comprehension of accepted and refused requests and offers of beds and bath (19.104–5, 116, 340–52). The narrator of the *Odyssey* reduces the quantity, as any narrative composer must, of the sensorial nonverbal behavior and verbal data, but readers reamplify and fill in not only words but expressive gestures, a "vocabulary beyond the lexicon," an underworld of communication and meaning.[43]

Odysseus tells Telemakhos there will be no other Odysseus that returns. Aithon alleges that he and Odysseus suffered "one and the same hardship" (ὁμὴν δ᾽ἀναδέγμεθα ὀϊζύν, 17.563). Penelope permits to the familiar stranger greater proxemic liberties than Greek protocol of any era, including the present, endorses (17.505–10, 19.94–101). The stranger is—amazingly and explicitly—physically like Odysseus in build, feet, and voice (δέμας φωνήν τε πόδας τε). Helen already penetrated a similar tattered disguise, perhaps—paradoxically—his "signature" other self (ἀνέγνων τοῖον: 4.250; 19.358–59, 379–91). The stranger has befriended Odysseus; he saw him twenty years ago (19.222), heard of his near approach just days ago, and reports it unmistakably and undeviously: νημερτέως γάρ τοι μυθήσομαι οὐδ᾽ ἐπικεύσω (19.268–69). He is "almost come, very near and not far" (19.300–301). The stranger interprets dreams well and urgently confirms her apparently risky, certainly sudden, and seemingly precipitate contest plans: μηκέτι νῦν ἀνά-βαλλε . . . / πρὶν γάρ τοι ἐλεύσεται . . . / πρίν (19.584–86). Skeptical and poker-faced Penelope may reason (here I speculate): "Be he god [and we

---

43. I owe this phrase and many insights into nonverbal behavior to the pioneer of "literary anthropology," Fernando Poyatos. Fenik, in his 1974 study, which contains much that compels admiration, denies literary and psychological coherence to Penelope and other epic characters (119–20). For his Homer, irony and plot outweigh character and motivation. The purpose of these pages is to show the gain from treating Penelope as a comprehensible literary character. An analyst's shrug of literary abstinence may be logically comfortable, but it robs other readers of demonstrable artistry and pleasures.

know they do come as beggars: 16.178–200, 17.485, 23.63] or man, he's the closest thing I'll ever find to my long-gone husband. I'll fall in with his plan and live [like Madame Martin Guerre] with the consequences. They can't be worse than what I've got." In the words of Odysseus, the world's record-holding doubter (16.202–5):

Τηλέμαχ', οὔ σε ἔοικε φίλον πατέρ' ἔνδον ἐόντα
οὔτε τι θαυμάζειν περιώσιον οὔτ' ἀγάασθαι·
οὐ μὲν γάρ τοι ἔτ' ἄλλος ἐλεύσεται ἐνθάδ' Ὀδυσσεύς,
ἀλλ' ὅδ' ἐγὼ τοιόσδε, παθὼν κακά, πολλὰ δ' ἀληθείς.

Telemakhos, it's not right for you, with your father before you,
Either to wonder too much or gape about.
No other Odysseus will ever come here for you;
I'm it, all there'll be, having gone through hell and wandered back.

Wanderer and sufferer, he is no god or sorcerer-demon. In the end (book 23), we encounter not lucky intuition but a woman in a cul-de-sac and meditations on identity. Imagine your intimate or lover of twenty years ago, the loved one unseen since then, now suddenly back and very bloody.

Penelope, like Kirke, commands and controls her enchanted flock. Both spin fine textiles and tales while they nurture docile herds of sexually enthralled men (θέλγειν: 18.282; 10.213, 291, 318, 326, cf. 329). Homer's formulae construct a womanly, seductive, and magic package or Gestalt. He calls it, at various times, Kalypso, the Sirens, Athene, and Penelope (1.57, 12.40–44, 16.298), although it is not entirely sex-specific, since Odysseus, Hermes, Aigisthos, and bards also know how to entrance with words (14.387, 16.195, 5.47; 3.264, 1.337). Homer repeatedly shows us some men devirilized by hearing what they wish to hear, soothing messages that sing their own sweet superiority.

Already living in the pleasant haze of the spousal past, womanly Penelope early on and only once tries to halt poignant and public male memorializings of her husband's conflicts and even death. Telemakhos and Odysseus encourage, however painful the pleasure, stories of masculine heroism at home and abroad.[44] Newton suggests that the root of Penelope's epithet *polymneste* conjures up another Gestalt of her unyielding memories as well as plentiful wooing. "Very mindful" Penelope, having learned of the murder intrigue,

---

44. 1.340–42, 350, 354–55; 8.489–98, 521–23; cf. Odysseus' pleasure in recalling lost Ithaka, poor and limited in heroic opportunity, but home and therefore right for him (5.219–20, 9.27–36).

prays for death and cries out that Athene should remember (μνῆσαι, 4.765) Odysseus' many offerings and save their son. One suitor (μνηστήρ) comically misinterprets her shriek of pain before ritual blood-spilling (ὀλόλυξε, cf. 3.450) as part of woman's ritualized preparation for marriage, ignorant of death-plots hovering over her son (οὐδέ τι οἶδεν). They can only focus on the disposition of the "much wooed" (πολυμνήστη) lady. They imagine that she forgets her old husband and does not know their plot. The narrator, however, pointedly tells audiences that she has just been informed of the plan, she has mentioned her beloved Odysseus, and the wooers are, in fact, the unknowing ones.[45] The other significant (*kledonic*?) occurrence of the formulaic epithet appears in an equally ignorant, and therefore equally ironic, mouth: that of the passerby at the pseudosuitors' pseudobanquet but very real Laertid dance over the dead suitors (23.149).[46]

Penelope responds to the stranger with a revival of heretofore dormant sexual and social energy. She wants to see him quickly and up close; "almost improper intimacy" characterizes her late-night familiar chatter about her bed "in there" and his bed—the beggar's—"in here." Penelope had hastened imprudent face-to-face encounter; he deferred it at first. She revels in the stranger's reports of Odysseus, his *xeinos* long ago in Crete; and she delights in tears produced by his precise description of the symbolic clasp (τάρφθη πολυδακρύτοιο γόοιο). That news of long ago and the report of her husband's near arrival are "too good to be true." Like his eerily familiar presence, reasonable dream interpretation, and confident prophecy, the signs (announced and leaked) are too overwhelmingly desirable to be accepted as true or rejected out-of-hand as false.[47]

---

45. 4.766–72, the two last lines contrast two parties, repeating the two same verbs, οἶδα and τεύχω, for "know" and "prepare" or "bring about".

46. Newton 1991, 140–41. Eumaios expected Odysseus to grant him a "polymnestic" consort (14.64). The word here suggests not parody, mindless *Märchen* (sic Hoekstra ad loc.), or nodding formula, but one element of the three ordinary "best wishes" of house, land, and mindful (obedient to her vows and sexually loyal?) wife.

47. Russo (Russo et al. 1992, 5–13, esp. 11–12) reviews the difficult, perhaps unresolvable (as Katz 1991 would assert), issue of Penelope's "personality" and recognitions. I support his arguments against the analysts' hypothesis of a "clumsy remnant of another version." His own "'submerged' recognition" hypothesis stumbles not so much in its psychologism (cf. Emlyn-Jones' 1984 eloquent gripe against the "mental" Homer) but in its unfalsifiability and failure to explain Penelope's carefully chosen moment of total, irreversible risk. Russo might regard some of these objections as inadequate to impugn his view, since he (13 n. 13) wants some interpretation that "account[s] for all the phenomena." But no solution is tidy enough to satisfy everyone. Perhaps the idea of *one* solution, or any, for the partial picture of Penelope's mind is to be rejected already in principle, because Penelope, whatever she is, is not a person. At this moment of interpretive *aporia*, let us conserve paper.

The stranger's latent power and proven social survival skills and his uncannily familiar presence and body language all intensely stimulate her. She is acting in a new way (self-display to strangers, more publicly cried tears, and irreversible decision). Her disclaimers, for example, of the obvious dream, are knee-jerk defenses, feminine ramparts of repudiation, deniability gambits that make no sense, except as psychological "buffers" against ubiquitous *nonsooth*sayers (14.124–32, 23.215–17). Most importantly, her nay-saying has *no consequences*. She says, preserving deniability, "No Odysseus, never ever again," but she determines to go ahead with the contest anyway. She takes an ultimate, nonwithdrawable risk *for the first time,* just as the supposedly unknown knockabout urges. She is never anyone's fool—least of all here.

4. Penelope's Sub-mission

What is the plan? Penelope wants to force Aithon, the beggar-friend (from her point of view), now a crypto-wooer (since he is Odysseus), to reveal information about the husband-hero (presumed dead or absent Odysseus, a third-person topic). Her means will be the brainstorm of the bow contest. As she confidently manipulates the suitors for self-interest, so she, suspecting or at least probing the beggar's identity, halts his overcautious maneuverings and penetrates heretofore invulnerable secrecy and otherness. She extracts more information when she elevates him from pitiable beggar to respected friend. The ploy is proxemic—giving him a chair in close proximity (19.253–54; cf. Russo ad loc.) Then a significant object focuses her coherent strategy of discovery. Penelope tells the stranger that the stiff and precious bow will be brought out to decide her lord and its master. He could strenuously object to this apparently foolhardy proposal—but he does not. Why not, and what does she learn by this nonact? First, he says the hero is near; soon after that, he says the hero is very near; and finally, Penelope's constructed situation boxes him in so tightly that he asserts as fact that Odysseus will arrive on the spot before any suitor strings the bow (ἀγχοῦ, ἄγχι μάλ', ἐνθάδ' Ὀδυσσεύς, 271, 301, 585).[48]

Time has run out for dear Odysseus, she says, as she simultaneously has become increasingly intimate in positioning, addressing, and complimenting the stranger.[49] Penelope mentions the hero's bow and her and the beggar's

---

48. This toxic feat will be a nonverbal sign and proof of Odysseus' arrival and identity—probably it was the original folktale proof—just as much as the bed will be. Each object receives its own disgression, because each object is just as important as Odysseus' famous scar in establishing the precious link between past and present.

49. Rutherford 1992, 33: ξεῖνε, ξεῖνε φίλε, and praises (19.309, 350–51, 589–90).

beds together (19.583–99), a meaningful collocation of highly marked, sexualized objects, before retiring alone for the night. She may want to jar the calm assurance of the smug stranger-friend of Odysseus, shock him into some more active mode of helping her, or prepare him (Odysseus?) to give up his sheaf of false personae. She campaigns by feints, swoons, and faints in the conjugal poker game, a war of nerves over identity and self-revelation.

Penelope's insomnia at midnight,[50] weeping, and rapid heart-flutter reveal her heightened emotional tension, caused by a plethora of signs that something untoward is in the air: friendly prophecies, *kledones,* insults, heartening dreams, and a sudden stranger who seems phenomenally familiar. Her behavior is flirtatious toward the unwashed, slovenly Cretan veteran with astonishing recall of Odysseus' outfit twenty years previous. Penelope's command for a *foot*bath at an intensely emotional moment reminds us that often heroes recognize each other by feet as much as face, a phenomenon known from other historical cultures. Indeed, the feet of the vagrant are remarked for similarity to those of the hero by both Penelope and Eurykleia (19.358–59, 381). Another aspect of his body, the thigh's scar—not a look, smile, or smell (heroic pheromones?)—supplies the *coup de grâce* for the penetrable disguise. Penelope and the sanitized, foot-bathed Odysseus later move closer to the fire and each other, a formulaic symbol of trust and companionship, a gendered symmetry, somewhat like, yet even stronger than, the shared dining table or meal (19.55, 506; e.g., for fire: 14.518–19, 16.2).

Penelope tests the stranger ever more rigorously and, as he passes every hurdle, progressively accepts him as a trusted friend of the *oikos*. Their interchanges resemble those of man and wife, although only negative acknowledgment surfaces: Penelope, having complimented his all-night staying power, directs them both to separate beds, an odd topic for unrelated Homeric male and female. Who else but Odysseus, she must wonder, could know so much of her husband's past wardrobe, present whereabouts, and future plans, not least the astonishing information that he is currently nearby and pondering *disguised* return (19.296–99).

Penelope's determined behavior belies her emphatic denials. She insists her quondam husband is dead and wonders whether he ever existed. This formulaic and emotional hyperbole is typical of her gendered rhetoric. But her generous words, gestures, and proxemics bespeak vulnerable trust and rapidly growing affection—however tactemically distanced from the vagrant

---

50. 19.515–17, 600–601; cf. Odysseus' similar complaint and restlessness at 19.340–42, 20.24. Both of them are tranquilized by Athene; how alike can you get? But Odysseus is still baldly lying to his wife about lying (19.269): νημερτέως γάρ τοι μυθήσομαι οὐδ' ἐπικεύσω, "I'll tell you truly and conceal nothing at all."

(e.g., 19.309–11: τάχα γνοίης φιλότητα). Her queries have elicited, after resistance, only a name and "ancient history," but she has conjured up her "dead" husband's double by probes and tests. She sees encouraging identities beneath disguises—just like cousin Helen.

The next day, she proceeds to yet another test of skill, nerves, and disguised traps. The stranger enthusiastically supports it and swears assurance of Odysseus' presence in good time for the contest (19.584–87). The decision to mount the contest, inevitably decisive as it will be, declares confidence in the mantic stranger. After Penelope conceives and devises rules of the game, she herself, astonishingly, intrudes at the crisis and climax of masculine assertions. She weighs in on behalf of the befriended vagrant's turn. Penelope countermands and openly confronts enemies only here, when push comes to shove and no gendered alternative exists.[51] Her endorsement of the hobo's participation nonverbally, by his very turn, discredits all the gentried idlers. Thereby she herself mocks their heroic pretensions. She calms the suitors' fears, or at least verbally boxes them in, with assurances that the tramp's turn "does not count." They lose face long before they die, a double indemnity designed by the wife and her husband (21.148–74, 184–87, 245–60, 285–88, 22.322–29). She leaves, he wins at archery, and the suitors lose all. Penelope is roused from female exclusion to return to where the action is and to consider carefully the vagrant's permanent inclusion as alleged mate. Their own contests of assertion should be over, one might think—but wrongly.

Penelope exercises a limited form of power, while fervently denying, by both words and body language, that such possibility exists.[52] She cannot prevail in violence, but she has cannily forestalled defeat for years. Her social status, defined by gender in the first place and rank in the second, prohibits physical confrontation with male strength. She never questions *expressis*

---

51. Her angry speech to hypocritical Antinoos, who is plotting to assassinate her son—delivered at a distance and from behind her veil—minces no words (16.415–33). But her most notoriously opaque gesture, the private, embarrassed(?) laugh before flirting and arousing the suitors, conceals socially "inappropriate" interests in flirtation from the servant Eurynome (ἀχρεῖον δ' ἐγέλασσεν, 18.163). The paralinguistic act is vaguely apologetic. It also screens the climax of sexual deceptions and assertive family-protection strategies. See Levine 1983a, 172, 174–75; Clay 1984; Felson-Rubin 1987, 70.

52. Murnaghan 1986, 110–12, calls Penelope powerless and victimized, but this view overlooks the motif of *homophrosyne*, here, gendered, symmetrical employment of stigmatized victim-roles. Penelope just plays it better and plays it even with her heroic husband. We are rarely allowed to peek into her mental closets. In the *Odyssey*, women's weapons are deception and treachery, whether they be good or evil, for instance, Klytaimnestre, Aphrodite, Helen, and Nausikaa. Cf. du Boulay 1986 for women's establishment of respect in a modern Euboean village; du Boulay 1976 analyzes the social dynamic of lies and mockery in the same village.

verbis the essential gender premises of patriarchal Homeric society, in our hearing, but she never relaxes her continual care, nor does she surrender legal, emotional, and physical control of the dicey situation—until she believes that the lord of the manor is returned. At that point, she declares the contest. After that, she needs to make him understand her heroism; thus, she pulls the bed trick. Only then does she restore authority to the right male. She is not placed under male authority; rather, she controls herself, and, paradoxically, she puts herself in her "natural" position of social inferiority.

Odysseus had rejected a restorative bath, clothes, and a bed as a guest or *xeinos* in book 19. It would compromise him in more ways than one. After the suitors' slaughter, he provides himself (as returned and uncontested master) with a bath and clothes—thus, he becomes his own guest and no one else's (23.153–55). He protects his claims. Telemakhos, the servants, and the nursemaid have accepted him, but his bedmate Penelope has not, so he orders another bedstead from Eurykleia (23.171). The *xeinodokos* role itself is not easily expropriated from Penelope, though. She regains initiative once more, by specifying which bed, the best and with the best covers, to provoke self-revelation, the unwitting self-betrayal of the one remaining, sole-surviving suitor.[53]

"We all act better than we know how" (Goffman 1959, 74). Others' punctilious dedication to self-presentation(s) makes one, especially battered Penelope, wary of being taken in—again (cf. 14.126–29). The once noble stranger has flirted with her and wooed her—better than any other, she implies (19.509, 589–99). Now he claims her, body and soul, but Penelope rejects both masks, beggar and prince, and even the less fungible scar that so fully satisfies all others' suspicions. She wants to perceive the "backstage" Odysseus, wants to offend him to have him reveal a regressive, socially disapproved, but more candid, self. She wants to discern a "sloppy," off-guard, emotional posture, not his successful controlling ruses. The Homeric metaphors of spreading out, relaxed or impulse-driven, versus tightness, alert or self-possessed, are found in the suitors' πετάσειε θύμον and Odysseus' ἀγχίνοος.[54] Penelope knows her man, his discretion and behavioral *polytropy*. She wants to evoke his asocial, sullen irritability, his relatively unmediated self, not a persona who segregates audiences and suitable characters for performance. In the *megaron,* Penelope expresses indecision verbally and nonverbally (with her distance, silence, and a glance: 23.85, 89, 93, 91). She "gives off" confusion and rejection. However ingenuous her

---
53. Katz 1991, 177–78. Goffman 1959, 74, 128, 137, 141–43, provides the theory for the next two paragraphs.
54. 18.160, 13.332. Katz 1991, 82, follows Thornton 1970, 97.

behavior seems as she sits down, Homer expressly credits her with disingenuous testing of her spouse at her time and on her terms (114; 116; 168–69; 181, cf. 114). The successful trick requires an unscheduled, unrehearsed response at a moment when the stage lights are turned off. Odysseus thinks that the examination period has apparently recessed.

We attend a comedy of secrets. Secrets presume an "us" against a "them." The following "teams" in social intercourse vary their membership from conflict to conflict. First, "inside" secrets belong to every "team." They comprise shared, "in-the-know" information that builds solidarity among a united group. The spousal "team" of Penelope and Odysseus share uncommon knowledge of Odysseus' scar (23.72–76, 107–14). Odysseus tells Telemakhos that he expects Penelope will want several of these team-exclusive indicators. Second, "strategic" secrets hide one team's intentions and capacities from another as limited information is released. Here we distinguish female team Penelope's vital awareness that the marriage bed has not been moved, about which she purposely misinforms male team Odysseus to lead him to betray himself. Third, the "entrusted" secret of masqueraded Odysseus' return belongs to the "Home Team" including Eurykleia, Philoitios, and Eumaios—but apparently not to the non-"hometown" player, Penelope. Fourth, "dark" secrets may never be revealed by one team to another. Their very existence cannot be admitted—sometimes even to oneself. The depth of Odysseus' vanity in "mind games" and pleasure in manipulating others may be one of these, although Penelope penetrates his still and cryptic mysteries. Odysseus' greed may be another, misrepresented by him as aristocratic punctuality about prestation in his self-serving travel accounts to the Skherians and his own son (16.230–32). Penelope's unarguable and invincible distrust, disclaimed only when no alternative at all remains, provides another "dark" secret. Who is *this* man, and why, anyway, did he encourage her to convene the contest and "go for broke," if not to cash in all the chips for himself?[55]

Odysseus has intended, at least from Athene's early admonition, to test *her*, his wife. Agamemnon thought that you cannot be too careful. Her cool and reserved nonverbal presentation in book 23 is justified psychologically by a distrustful, deceiving husband, who further insults her proven integrity, trustworthiness, and pride. Her chagrin at being informed that everyone but

---

55. Issues of personal identity are raised most trenchantly and variously by Ovid in his *Metamorphoses*. Among modern treatments of spousal awareness, we note Janet Lewis' novel *The Wife of Martin Guerre* (San Francisco, 1941) and N.Z. Davis' study of the same sixteenth-century historical event, *The Return of Martin Guerre* (Cambridge, Mass., 1983).

she had long since learned or been entrusted with the bum's identity can easily be imagined (23.29, 75, 113–15, 168–70).[56]

Her grief for her son's situation and husband's absence has been intolerably prolonged. Furthermore, the testing never ends. Does she know the catastrophic denouement of Kephalos and Prokris' folktale of spousal mistrust (11.321)? Penelope's measured and cautious response to good news delays apocalyptic Odysseus' resumption of mastery and compels him to taste his own bitter medicine—sentiments deformed and disguised for profit and humiliating spousal deception, first in public, but also alone together in book 19. Her self-contradictory messages in this final contest of champion status manipulators (proximity but separation, gentle tone but firm disbelief) brilliantly protect and promote her own fragile interests. Her movements and moves should be read as wiliness, not confusion—if not consciously strategized, then still learned and gendered social survival skills. These nonverbal, hard-to-detect, harder-to-expose tactics keep the disclosed master from erasing or ignoring the past twenty years and especially the last two days.[57]

Mobility and imprisonment have been the axes of Odysseus' experience. Escape from dangerous enemies—described earlier in Odysseus' reports of arrival, reception, and deception in the faerylands—represents the negative virtue of male mobility, its minimal benefit of survival. The positive side of male mobility is access to inner and restricted areas, such as sanctuary, asylum, or privileged, private space—for example, visitation privileges to Penelope's personal chamber. Odysseus' next move is motionlessness. The aggressive force and rhetoric that penetrated the suitors' perimeter and then demoralized and disposed of them[58] is now reversed for a nonverbal impassivity that is able to await the final goal of Penelope's assent to, and acceptance of, the idea of this alluring, if violent, vagrant as her lawful, wedded husband.

To the distress of the bystanders Eurykleia and Telemakhos, Penelope does not accept bald statements about the "facts" of the situation. Her silence meets his silence. In their ultimate pre-remarital interview, Odysseus

---

56. This sentence does not concede that she did not *know* who the bum was, only that she had not been trusted by her mate, despite good evidence of her trustworthinesss.

57. Those who deny Penelope's prior awareness of Odysseus' identity still must allow her now to recollect in book 23 the hero's recent fainéant history while on Ithaka. Roisman 1987, and Murnaghan 1992, 261–63, perceive Penelope's indignation.

58. At 22.1, Odysseus, like an athlete dressed in a new body, literally strips for battle, revealing his true (physical) identity; but at 22.487–89, Eurykleia politely objects to his still wearing ragged clothes. Either he has resumed them or his earlier ecdysis was incomplete.

274   *Sardonic Smile*

stops talking, freezes his body in a lowered position,[59] and averts his gaze downward. His lips are sealed. When they speak, it is not to each other but to, and therefore through, Telemakhos. Odysseus awaits, in his still ragged and blood-spattered outfit, her informed consent to his latest assumed identity (23.90–95). But it is too soon or too uncertain. She wants other signs, so the hero smiles and goes off for an attended bath. On his return, however, nothing seems to have changed. She still holds her ground. She accepts her friend's invitation to assume openly the active role in determining results (ἦ τοι μητέρ᾽ . . . / πειράζειν ἐμέθεν, 23.113–14). Penelope invisibly orders the proxemics, chronemics, and turn taking, and she engineers both his decisive bluff ("get me another bed") and her trumping counterbluff (*the* bed).

In this colloquy, man and wife both first address each other as δαιμονίε, "weird, dear creature"—he in true postbloody bewilderment at her implacable reserve, she in deft "entrainment," verbal and nonverbal tailgating mimicry, ironic *homophrosyne*.[60] The world's two most preternaturally cautious heroes realize their complementarity, as they emerge through dyadic marital therapy from prolonged, benumbed isolation. Odysseus identifies spiritual and emotional harmony between spouses as life's *summum bonum* (6.181–85, widely athetized; cf. 15.198). His expectation of sharing it with Penelope on Ithaka motivates rejections of (at least) three paradises that land in his lap: Aiaia, Ogygia, and Skheria. The synchronized and sympathetic couple suggests an ideal far removed from the subtle, but real, fracas simmering between Menelaos and Helen or even from the calm but repeatedly awkward and backfiring management of affairs (misunderstood by Nausikaa) visible in the marriage of perspicacious Arete and hesitant Alkinoos. The latter ruler shows consistent slowness in picking up signals, the opposite of hasty "tailgating."

Homophrosyne can exist in nonspousal relations. Telemakhos and Pisistratos reach a special peer accord. Odysseus' sympathetic days and evenings with Eumaios bespeak more than careful pretence and Zeus-commanded charity. His relations with Telemakhos and, briefly, with Laertes suggest easy alignment and shared wavelengths, chronemic and proxemic. Penelope's withdrawal from house management is partly remedied—without negotiation—by Eurykleia's automatic advance to fill the breach, to guard the stores. Eurykleia, echoing mistress Penelope, remarks the beggar's un-

---

59. Cf. Odysseus' knowledgeable nonverbal response to Eumaios' fierce guard dogs: he lowers himself, drops his staff, and waits for the master to call them off (14.30–35).
60. 23.166, 174. The formulaic footwork never disproves apt application. The name-calling retribution is true-to-life entrainment, to judge from my experience. He repeats the verbal sign of incomprehension, a pet name (?), at 23.264.

canny physical and paralinguistic, not to mention prudential, similarity to the lost nursling and master (17.580–86, 19.350–53; Austin 1975, 200–238, esp. 231–32, 276 nn. 16–21). Like-mindedness in the *Odyssey* expands to more and more arcane matters in books 17–23. The vagrant's generous reception is fostered by Theoklymenos' mantic promise of Odysseus' local preparations and by Telemakhos' *kledonic* sneeze at the mention of Odysseus' name (17.155–61, 541–47). Penelope laughs and seizes on the spousal omen. She summons the guest into her presence, but why? She herself happily interprets the sneeze as foretelling death for the idlers, but why? Her smiles have not come easily or often. Her laugh here changes the book's musical key. When their deferred tête-à-tête takes place later that night, almost a prelude to pillow talk, she praises her absent husband's commanding skills and semantic subtlety, her own supreme female mental strategy and *metis*, and the present stranger's nicely chosen words and prudence (σημάντορες, νόον καὶ ἐπίφρονα μῆτιν, μάλ' εὐφραδέως πεπνυμένα πάντ' ἀγορεύεις, 19.314 and 326, 352; cf. Austin 1975, 216–19). Are they "three" of a kind? The explicit first identification of the long-lost *basileus* is Eurykleia's, but Penelope's extensive and active probes from books 17 to 23 should be seen as more than refreshments and story hour.

Perhaps to some minimalists it smacks of documentary fallacy, even psychologism, to assert that the intelligent and intuitive heroine Penelope could hardly be so stupid as *not* to pick up the energized vibrations emitted by Odysseus, informed Telemakhos, and old nurse Eurykleia, all "in the know" by book 19. Nevertheless, that book's late-night physical and psychic proximity and its hair-trigger heightened sensibilities, Penelope's tears and coquettish charms, and her shift from *noblesse oblige* generosity for a starving vagabond to conspiratorial request for his valued advice (guidance from a never before and very sudden "dear friend", 19.350) demand that either she suspect the tramp's identity or—I mean this seriously—that she be more obtuse than Polyphemos and more promiscuous than Helen. I prefer the former hypothesis.

In the final quiet showdown with her alleged husband, Penelope equals Odysseus in heroic self-restraint. Her marked failure to show socialized, sociable surrender—indeed anticipatory, official submission with body contact to "the man of the house"—elicits the noncomprehending chorus' disapproval. She maintains her caution in every test. The earlier and the next generation, the aged serving-lady Eurykleia and her son Telemakhos (23.5–79, 96–110), voice traditional expectations of gendered behavior. Unappreciative Eurykleia and indignant Telemakhos browbeat Penelope for impenetrable female caution but do not criticize Odysseus for his still-strange behavior. "Mother, no Mother," Telemakhos says. Women in the toils of Homeric social reproductive systems are not supposed to know how to suppress impulse, calculate against men, and be distrustful. Does Odysseus agree with their objections (23.97, 166–72)? He seems to withold judgment.[61]

Penelope instructs the internal audience, who are expecting thoughtless emotion, that gods are involved one way or another. She is correct. She needs a special sign. By this she turns out to mean an unintentional giveaway, a kind of *kledon* on the human level—in this case, verbal and nonverbal unintentional semiosis, a "leak" from Mr. Cool. Odysseus smiles a knowing and yet unknowing smile. She is beyond his grasp. Odysseus sits in expectant comprehension, ready, at the verbal cue, to deliver histories on his infamous, rites-de-passage scar, to play "Twenty Questions," or to supply an answer to whatever enigma she poses. The problem, however, is that Penelope wants only something he is not prepared to give her. Testing him, as Homer explicitly says, the female trickster gets what she wants—an unintentional rise.

Odysseus explicitly accepts Penelope's demand for further negotiation. Meanwhile, denied his wife's affection and conjugal pleasures, he realizes the desirability of a "false" wedding, another stratagem conceived to throw the town off the track (23.113–52). The conscious ruse to disinform snooping publics by nonverbal ritual serves to provide, however, a real (if unconscious) basis of renewal for the couple's marriage. Penelope's silence also replicates procedures of conventional marriages (23.93; cf. the ending of Euripides' *Alkestis*). The sign of the bed, a symbol of original spousal sexual union, recalls Odysseus' own youthful exertion in making it and reasserts the sturdy, immovable olive tree as synecdoche for that union, the emblematic instrument of conjugal and personal satisfactions. The recreation of the bed also re-creates and realizes his original marriage-making. The woman's bed trick finally strips off Odysseus' mask of controlled heroic reserve and self-assumed signorial mastery.[62]

Penelope drives her stressed husband to thoughtless male rage, just the fault that has led so many of his companions, enemies, and competitors to destruction, long ago and earlier this day. Thus, having proved full equality

---

61. Telemakhos' criticisms of his mother deserve cataloging. They include inter alia, his own uncertain paternity, her excessive weeping and interference, her poor aesthetic judgment, her imposition of her female self in men's affairs, his potentially threatening maternal grandfather, her inadequate cleanliness for sacrificial vow (17.48–51), her absence from the productive loom, her anticonjugal reserve, and, finally, her stony, therefore unfeminine, stubbornness.

62. Katz 1991, 168, 179, neatly compares the hero's epic history of the bed (*lechogony*) to his catalog or litany of Laertes' patrimony of trees. The latter re-creates sonhood as the former re-creates husbandhood. Both reconstitute true, irreplaceable personhood and legitimacy in ways that mere savage scars cannot.

or complementarity to blustering Odysseus, and only then, on her own terms (in a patriarchal text, nevertheless), she runs across the room to kiss him, a complex gesture and proxemic act of gendered, hierarchical deference. Touching taboos (haptics) exhibit societal rules at their strongest. Now, by this touching act, her quotidian and long-expected womanish tears save *his* "face." She reverts to gendered script.

A demonstration of *polytropic* cunning,[63] Penelope's ploy has forced an overconfident Odysseus, his front damaged by her successful trick, to lose his temper and reveal himself in a unique, embarrassing way. She finally forces Odysseus' hand and mouth; his precise knowledge of the bedpost and his blustery manner equally expose the truth. This exposure forces Odysseus to be, of all possible people, Odysseus. As she wheedled, fooled, and defeated unwelcome suitors, so she deceives and defeats her welcome suitor, Odysseus. His defeat alone permits his peculiar, neoheroic victory: a *Wieder-zu-sich-selber-Kommens* return to himself as grounded man, husband, father, and prince.[64]

Body language, here a leak of anger that for once benefits this (for once) unwary communicator, leads to carnal knowledge. Penelope the shrewd (κεδνὰ ἰδυῖαν, 23.182), in the service of the supreme female virtue (in male eyes) of sexual fidelity, has outwitted the wittiest man about bedroom furniture arrangements. The bed is immovable, ἔμπεδα; he is not. Her bloodless heroism rates its own climax free and clear of Odysseus' slaughter of the suitors.[65]

---

63. The vexed issue of precisely when Penelope intuits, senses, guesses, or knows the hobo's "real" identity (a literary and philosophical problem of its own) is unresolvable precisely because the male bards and male audiences rarely, if ever, view the *Odyssey*'s action from her estranged point of view. For good discussions of the *anagnorismos* question, curious readers may consult—before Russo's recent (Russo et al. 1992) "Introduction"—Marquardt 1985; Murnaghan 1986; Winkler 1990, 150–58; and Katz 1991, 97–99, 164–66, 175–76.

64. Stewart 1976, 121, 143 n. 12, 145 n. 14; Schadewaldt 1959, 24. Only at Odysseus' unintended self-revelation (23.181–82) is he stripped of every epithet, a hero deprived of guise, disguise, and attribute. (The ancient scholiasts note deficiencies of epithet at moments of high emotion.) Only here does he speak in anger (ὀχθήσας). Homer rarely penetrates Penelope's intention, and importantly he does so here; she is πόσιος πειρωμένη, "testing her husband," as he has tested her repeatedly (13.336; 19 passim). She too enjoys inflicting sorrow on others (23.306–8). Which narratological commentator points out that gods would as easily know bedroom details as any other detail of puny mortal physical reality? It is the hero's disconcerted reaction, however, not his inside information, that proves him both human and her husband.

65. Emlyn-Jones 1984, 11, 14, remarks that Penelope is just doing her queenly job in the circumstances by arousing but denying the suitors. She is protecting Odysseus' estate, following alleged orders (18.257–70), and relieving the pressure on the heir apparent, Telemakhos, as well as she can. Her report of Odysseus' departing wishes should not be assumed veracious; Stanford ad loc. argues against her now inventing it. Rutherford 1992, 36, describes her role in the bow contest as unwitting.

"By dispossess[ing him] of what determines his identity," his own bed, Penelope forces him to reconstitute, not merely resume or reclaim, intimacy. Penelope alone reveals Odysseus to Odysseus. The bed incorporates the earth-rooted tree; the bedchamber encloses the bed; the farmhouse encloses the bedchamber. The bed has roots into earth, into nature. Like marriage, it combines elements of nature and culture, biology and man-made significances.⁶⁶ Union in the bed, with the bed, and about the bed reactivates a marriage with a twenty-year hole in it.

5. Conclusions

The prudent wife, then, nonverbally reassumes her subordinate position in the traditional power structure of the heroic family. She falls slack, openly weeps tears, and, breaking the salutation gridlock, runs over to embrace her husband and kiss his head, one clear Homeric nonverbal token of male and female submission and "greeting up" (23.205–14; cf. the act of servants at 21.223–25). Words confirm and explain her earlier, courteous but otherwise inappropriately cool, first nonverbal "greeting": οὕνεκά σ' οὐ τὸ πρῶτον ... ὧδ' ἀγάπησα (23.214).

This woman's coy perspicacity and nonverbal ruses redeem the general absence of heroic prestige allocated to women in Homer. Without much intellectual esteem, political power, and open control of bodies and lives (as we recall from the object-status of Khryseis and Briseis; cf. Iphigeneia, Andromakhe, and Helen), Homeric women chart necessarily idiosyncratic paths to self-fulfillment and limited autonomy. Penelope is consistent and comprehensible as a disadvantaged competitor in male status competitions and the ultimate trickster.⁶⁷

---

66. Pucci 1987, 93; Katz 1991, 177, 181.

67. du Boulay 1986 describes women and their roles in modern rural Greece. On Homeric etiquette and courtesy, especially gender-based manners, H. Foley 1978, 8–10, describes Penelope's inversion of gender roles; Hohendahl-Zoetelief's 1980 monograph does not do justice to this extensive topic. Sealey 1990, 110–50, argues for Penelope's "right" to choose a new husband and to arrange the contest, but he sees Homeric women as markedly passive, except for goddesses on Olympos, a locus of female initiative and recalcitrance (122–23, 147). We could equally well say that divine femininity "reflects" some perception of real and known mortal women. Felson-Rubin 1987 has presented the strongest case for an empowered Penelope; Emlyn-Jones 1984, Murnaghan 1986, and Rutherford 1992, 27–38, offer the most lucid denials of insightful, strategic Penelope. If Penelope is but a pathetic pawn, or the sum of social limitations on Homeric women, the poem becomes less interesting. Furthermore, such an unperceptive woman poorly motivates Odysseus' dogged determination to return home and the suitors' goofy infatuation. Such feebleness assigned to the heroine also fails to explain the suitors' repeated failure over several long years (2.89–90) to get the wedding march played for one of their band.

Homer's version, I speculate, gave Penelope her deserved renown that reaches over earth and up to heaven. In this version, she alone puts Odysseus in his place. We end where Homer began (with Odysseus and Telemakhos: ἀοιδὴ νεωτάτη, 12.452–53, 1.351–52), reminding peasant listeners and even academic readers steeped in traditional elements that heroic audiences, like all others, reject artless repetitions of well-told tales and welcome performance novelty. Penelope's perceptions and ploys may be our Homer's greatest novelty in the traditional folktale of the "returned husband."[68]

---

68. See Kakridis 1971 for later Greek ballads and other folksongs on this theme; Hansen 1990, for another Odyssean folktale motif's transmogrifications, here "the unrecognized implement." The *Odyssey*'s version of this idea is arguably the oddest.

Conclusion: "More Than Words Can Say..."

Body-talk enables us to understand each other. We use the body as a tool of expression in every encounter, to persuade and to deceive. This separate channel of communication affects interpersonal power and public status as much today as it did three millennia ago. In daily life, every act, tone, and word counts *all* the time. Although we still lack a universal, standardized taxonomy of communicative acts for explicit analysis, we cannot, as social units, dispense with any available channel. As Edward Sapir said in 1927, body language is "an elaborate and secret code that is written nowhere, known by none, and understood by all." Homer cannot include every body movement, snicker, or sneeze. Therefore, he narrows the channels in oral or written delivery. But everything he chooses to mention means something—or else why did he mention it?

So I was disturbed when a philologist bluntly asked, "So what? How does this material change my understanding of Homer in Greek or help me teach epic in translation?" The subject illuminates both reciprocal and nonreciprocated interchanges in daily life, he admitted, but his classical handbooks offered it scant space.[1] At first blush, it seemed to him a nonstarter, a nonsubject. Perhaps skeptical readers who have persevered this far have been convinced that attention to nonverbal behavior offers valuable insights into literary texts, especially into oral epic (which must have been "acted out" to some degree that is impossible to reconstruct confidently).

Nonverbal messages override verbal messages in importance; out-of-awareness corporeal manner overrides formulaic or nonformulaic addresses and even consciously deceptive acts. Odysseus' "pushy" crowding (proxemics) outweighs abased verbal requests as a homeless beggar. The formal genuflection and supplication by Trojan warriors defeated on the battlefield (Adrestos, Dolon, and Lykaon, e.g.) and the parallel gestures and postures of

---

1. One may peruse articles by H.J. Rose, *OCD*, 2nd ed., (1970) 465–66; B. Kötting, *RAC* 78 (1978): 895–902; W.H. Gross, *Der Kleine Pauly* (1979), 2:707–8; and Lateiner, *OCD*, 3d ed., forthcoming 1995.

submission of Ithakan servants groveling for clemency on the *megaron* floor (Leodes, Phemios, and Medon) echo the driving thought—rather, the words echo and clarify the more urgent and expressive gesture. Greek visual *and* verbal art excel in evoking ceremony and transitory moods by means of posture and gesture. Gaze, facial expression, and bodily bearing express the soul, as Xenophon's Sokrates noted (*Mem.* 3.10.3–5).

Different groups within a society enjoy different nonverbal repertoires: Homeric noblewomen have a veil, old men get turn-taking speech priority, and authority figures nod with curt head-talk at sailor crews, servants, and sons. Clearly, the suitors' prolonged malaise and social disorientation as well as their external assaults against Telemakhos, Penelope, Laertes, and beggar Aithon make us question the stability of their corporate self-estimation and even the coherent "front" of these stymied squatters. Different situations summon different gestures. Effective public speakers emphasize their arguments by gesturing with the herald's staff (cf. 3.218–20; Kirk 1985, ad 2.109: Homeric scepters). Power, age, and gender, we have seen, both limit and contribute to the individual's gestural spectrum. The majesty (γέρας, γεραρός: 3.170, 211) of a god or *basileus* imposes respect, whether he sits or stands, but this majesty is largely his bearing and relative location, body-talk that transmits dignity.[2] The adept emitter of nonverbal behavior in a group will be labeled "cool," refined and articulate, for using all available channels and for using them appropriately.

A study of the small change of human interaction cannot and need not describe in full detail perceptible and complex Homeric ideologies. Yet both my own conceptions of Iliadic and Odyssean society and the accumulated incidents of challenge and response, social expectation and violation, and power confronting established authority encourage, if they do not require, generalizations about Homeric social assumptions and conventions. While the chapters of this book presume some static or momentarily stable—that is, predictable—set of social conventions and rules for encounters, a common canon of courtesy and exchange, Peter Rose (1992, 58) seems right to declare that, in implicit ideology, the Homeric poems exhibit at every level a "tension between traditionalism and radical negation." Behavior *according* to the usual rules, for these plots, proves to be exceptional. The rules prove to be an illusion—qua unbreakable constraints. Agamemnon kills his own child. He rejects, despite choral mumbling from his own troops, the alien

---

2. In ancient fictions, reported nonverbal behavior is usually socially determined, often ceremonial (e.g., feasting and prayer), but a group's emotional attitude is *embodied* in an expressive individual. Lateiner 1992a compares Roman to Greek, secondary to primary, epics' expressions of silence and stillness—nonverbal behaviors communicating paralysis.

priest's rich and appropriate ransom of his daughter Khryseis. The possession of property is said to depend on martial prowess and automatic, patrilineal inheritance—but high and low persons, Agamemnon, the suitors, and their henchman Melanthios decisively dismember behavioral and ethical norms by daughter killing; aggression against all Trojans, including the innocent; outrageously unfair intra-Akhaian distribution (and fumbling antiheroic reappropriation, *dasmos,* at Troy); insulting the beggar; and plain theft of the Ithakan *basileus'* resources. Supplication is repeatedly denied and compensatory payments refused.

The cynic or historian might note that rules are usually observed only so long as they benefit the rulers. Agamemnon is a fiction that exists to collect obloquy. He rarely does anything right; he just "doesn't get it." The violations highlighted by the two plots intensify "the inherent insecurity of political power" and demonstrate "the constant necessity to prove oneself" in any unstable or mobile society. Merit, proven and proven again by the indispensable superwarrior, yet does not gain Akhilleus his just desserts. The dominant institutions neither provide Akhilleus with a court of appeal nor guarantee exposed Telemakhos his privacy at home or an exercisable option to boot out the interlopers. Agamemnon's "gratuitous brutality" matches his clumsy negotiations, strategic incompetence, and battlefield cowardice. His authoritative communiqués come a cropper or fall hilariously flat (e.g., *Iliad* 2).[3]

In fact, one can intertextually read Iliadic Agamemnon as the Odyssean protosuitor. He consumes other men's fair shares and abuses them for it all the while. Men and gods (Zeus and Dream) encourage him to make a fool of himself, just as Athene does to the suitors. The ruling-class ideology of warrior merit rewarded could hardly look emptier than when greedy Agamemnon mouths it in *Iliad* 1 and 9, when the army does not prevent his violent deviations from the heroic code, and when Akhilleus suffers for and from its iniquities. He repeatedly rejects the heroic system in *Iliad* 1, 9, 18, and 19. His incurious ultimate acceptance of Agamemnon's material requital and Priam's costly ransom of Hektor is emotionally indifferent, courteous yet ultimately apathetic. Like skulking Bellerophon before and Odysseus after, he seems himself a "dishonored displaced person."[4] This image of an

---

3. P. Rose 1992, 58, 62–63, citing the instability of old king Neleus' realm, *Il.* 11.688–760; 70–72, citing 9.37–39, 14.83–94, 13.105–14. Chap. 6 and Clay forthcoming discuss Agamemnon's unintelligent manners and/or intentional insults—"dissing" in current African-American slang—even when apologizing to Akhilleus.

4. P. Rose 1992, 88; ἀτίμητος μετανάστης, 9.648; cf. 6.202, 9.447, 16.59, 23.85–88, 24.531–33; cf. *Od.* 23.28.

unanchored, stigmatized wight offers a Homeric theme worth pursuing. Few audiences, I wager, have found blustery Agamemnon more persuasive than his young opponent who indicts wholesale the kingliest *basileus,* his silent-majority supporters, and his meretricious system. Few Hellenic or modern readers misread the Phthian's return to battle as a return to Akhaian politics and rewards as usual. As always, Akhilleus conforms to some convenient forms, bending them to his advantage whenever possible. It is a delicious, Odyssean irony when Agamemnon the bully and Amphimedon the suitor— quondam *xeinoi* in Ithaka—meeting on the gangways of the Dead, review the errors of their respective ways as would-be, but murdered, sexual consorts (24.102–16). Agamemnon here relishes the role of establishment chastiser of marital disloyalty and adultery, but we well remember his offensive, public devaluation of Klytaimnestre as wife, wit, weaver, and sex partner in *Iliad* 1.113–15. The "double standard" of heroic sexual infidelity is not double enough to exculpate him.

Therefore, Rose appears oddly self-contradictory and doubly wrong in positing that the *Iliad* takes place in "the transition from a meritocracy to a plutocracy," neither of which ever was. It dumbfounded this reader of his Marxian chapter 1 to read in chapter 2 that the *Iliad* represents a world where "political power and status truly correspond to demonstrable excellence." Homer—like bitter Hesiod (of the *ainos,* gift-gobbling kings, and judicial legerdemain), Arkhilokhos, and Hippias of Erythrai, all of whom Rose invokes—describes his modest Ithakan community as an urban aggregate (i.e., less than a polis, more than a village) where power has been usurped by ferocious oligarchs. Hippias' self-selected and exclusive group of Erythraian *basileis* or *tyrannoi* confiscate King Knopos' privilege and position. They dress elegantly (wearing diadems and fancy footwear), banquet frequently (partaking of conspicuous consumption, perhaps potlatch), and with uncensored sadism, humiliate disempowered fellow "citizens" at their feasts. With whips and blows, they force fellow townsmen to serve as public "street-sweepers." The *basileis* abuse the demos and their wives, daughters, and children. The weirdly Odyssean echoes culminate in the East Aegean king's and demos' savage revenge on the pillaging oligarchs and their women. The *Odyssey* does not, in my view, support, stridently or otherwise, a "ruling-class outlook." Odysseus, the good king of twenty years ago, like the lonesome hobo of the present, is a convenient stick with which to beat self-aggrandizing, contemporary oligarchs. The Odysseus of the future *may* restore the social fabric, but he has not yet done so in our poem. Here, the beggar quietly, if comically, bellyaches against nature (γαστήρ: 15.344, 17.286, 473–74), the hustler fights over food, and the defender of *dike* and the heavenly host slaughters the stale and arrogant upper-crust banquet-consumers—almost staging a Bakhtinian pie-fight. It is a pretty ugly picture of a dysfunctional society, reminiscent of the *Iliad*'s paralyzed demos and righteously outraged Phthian hero.[5]

Body-boundary anxiety, the fear of violation, invasion, or deformation of the flesh—alive or dead—provides a term for rational and irrational concerns of the individual about rape, mutilation, incorporation, disintegration, and transformation. The *Odyssey* sets before us human bodies sucked into oblivion or, more frequently, eaten—by such instruments as Kharybdis the black hole, Zeus-forswearing Kyklops, the Laistrygones, and barking Skylla. We hear of bodies transformed into animals (Kirke's pets before Odysseus arrives, then his crew, and also Athene); corpses unburied or rotting and shriveled up (Elpenor and the Sirens' victims); men drowned and lost (Odysseus' crew after the Thrinakia layover and Odysseus almost so in the Skherian breakers); folk tortured, castrated, and hanged (the suitors' threats to the disguised vagrant and Iros and the Laertid treatment of miscreant Melanthios and the sluttish maids). These intense, nightmarish physical sufferings and violations remind the secure listener of the fragile, permeable, and vulnerable human somatic state.

The spirit has its own envelope, an ego territory, or self-hood, with boundaries that are equally or more brittle, frail, and frangible than the body's. Already in the *Iliad,* we encounter Thersites beaten, if not entirely stilled, and Briseis' role as trafficked merchandise in flesh but also as Akhilleus' lover and Patroklos' sincere (if notedly self-reflecting: *Il.* 19.302) mourner. Human personality damage and repair permeates the *Odyssey.* Eumaios grows grander as the noble *basileis* shrink. He lords his domain as host, protector, and dispenser of hospitality more effectively than they do theirs. Nonverbal behavior in literature can only reflect ego violation that has a sensible, visible or audible, component, but of these there is no shortage. Secular and sacred ceremonies provide a transterritorial claim, and desecrators of hallowed custom forfeit sympathy.

Students of ancient literatures may learn from students of contemporary alien cultures. Anthropologists and sociologists can enrich classicists' awareness of underrated factors in both the literature and reality of antiquity. We

---

5. P. Rose 1992, 94–102, 119 (for quotation). Karl Marx did not see the Akhaian freebooters in the Trojan mudfields as his Utopia. On 112 n. 37, Rose notes Penelope's significant and unflattering criticism of partial and unjust *basileis* at 4.686–95. They seem more the rule than the exception. Hippias of Erythrai (F. Jacoby, *FGrHist* IIIB 421 = Athen. 258f-59f), perhaps Hellenistic in date, offers a most suggestive portrait of archaic Ionian *hybris,* perhaps itself modeled on this Ithakan epic.

can become literary anthropologists and study ceremonial and everyday acts and behaviors of ancient men and women in texts as well as in art and archaeology. Characters, genres, and authors and their individual works offer clues into social structures and personal conflicts to literary critics alert to nonverbal behavior. Petronius' Trimalchio, bumblers and confidence men in Apuleius' *Metamorphoses,* and the ancient novel as a whole collect Roman imperial nonverbal behavior data in different strata, provinces, and epochs.[6]

We have not, to be sure, discovered a subject untouched by philologists. Commentators, especially W.B. Stanford, are at times alert to body language in ancient literature, in passages remarked for a negative nod, a sardonic smile, or a trembling body. But the topic is rarely explored except ad loc.[7] To my knowledge, no one, since meticulous Sittl, has explored the range even of hand gestures alone in ancient literature or presented categories serviceable to students of other ancient texts. Neither the importance of proxemics and chronemics (see chapter 7 and the appendix) nor the terms themselves had surfaced in 1890. The study of nonverbal behavior does not supply a golden key to the secret of great literature. It cannot reveal when the Hellenic epics were first composed in their present form, when they were written down, or whether Homer was not Homer but another person—perhaps female—of the same name, or not a person at all, but a multigenerational guild of bards served well, we might presume, by a final redactor, given the *Odyssey*'s dense cross-references.

Some students, still imprisoned in the maze of unitarian, analytic, and neo-unitarian views, tabulate feast formulae, devote years to one choice word or theme, struggle to unravel Homeric vocabulary of the mind and divine motivation, or compare Homer's poems to living oral epic and Caribbean "rap." To the traditional and innovative projects thus enumerated, nonverbal behavior can be added, to provide the Homeric consumer with the third central channel of (underappreciated) meaning. Students can find explicit Homeric data on individual and group behavior and the sociology of

---

6. Martin 1989 makes good use of Herzfeld 1985; I hope to collect, analyze, and publish some of the material from the ancient novels.

7. Merely as illustration, an entry for "gestures," the comparatively well-appreciated aspect of nonverbal behaviors, appears in only one of the six indexes to G. Kirk et al. 1985–93, which runs to 2,342 pages; Richard Janko's volume 4 has eight references. The authors comment throughout on obviously expressive acts—e.g., Kirk illuminates scepters' various symbolic utilities at 2.109—but the absence exemplifies the truth that philologists, by definition as well as inclination, are less concerned with, and aware of, nonverbal communication. David Bevington, *Action is Eloquence: Shakespeare's Language of Gesture* (Cambridge, Mass., 1984), offers a welcome exception, but theater is a visual art to begin with.

some coherent society, even if it were only an imaginary one. I believe that reported nonverbal behavior reflects actual communicative practice in the epoch of the existing redaction.[8] First of all, oral tradition tends to delete words, things, or behaviors that audiences fail to understand.[9] Moreover, universal gestures and postures change slowly, if at all, and even ethnogests require unreflecting comprehension from interactants and also from audiences.[10]

Interwoven in the complex plot and subplots are clues and misclues, suggested denouements and deferrals, keys and traps. Virtually every Odyssean character poses sometimes or always as someone he or she is not. Fear of exposure informs every individual's self-presentation and interaction. Every self on view is discredited or discreditable or both. No one wants to show his cards.[11] The reader or listener to the text finds both psychological and social subtleties of characterization without psychologizing. One deduces from peripheral, but not parenthetical, hints the carefully observed social interplay of public etiquette and ritual, on the one hand, and personal predilection and emotion, on the other.

The study of nonverbal behavior in past societies, through imaginative literature as well as through images and material artifacts, is yet young, if not infantile. The Greek body in art, literature, and daily life reveals personality and sentiment within and advertises, to its various publics, status and social expectations. Performative gestures of stylized ceremony (such as scepter handling and beverage toasts) and peripheral gestures of daily informal

---

8. Rhapsodic performers (as distinguished from theatrical actors) certainly incorporated limited dramatic movements, such as pointing, whispering, and drawing themselves up majestically. Plato's Ion offers some helpful hints on this topic. Bérard 1918, following a hint of Croiset, considers the Homeric poems as performance literature expecting gesticulation by bards or rhapsodes; cf. Boegehold 1986, Stanford's 1965 commentary, e.g., 1:xxiv-xxv, ad 1.159, 3.321, 4.776, 11.134, 17.447; J. Foley 1990, 1992. Performers' style and audiences' demeanor modulate *every* face-to-face interaction, informal and formal. A *bard's* or *speaker's* postures, gestures, facial expression, clothes, and intonation and an *audience's* response and attentiveness (head-cock, taut posture or tired shoulder slump, eyelid movement, or great yawns) all affect every minidrama, visual performance and overheard dialogue.

9. Especially egregious anachronisms and archaizings, such as the notorious boar's-tooth helmet, may survive just for exotic, distancing qualities; cf. I. Morris 1986, 89.

10. For instance, African laughter indicates discomfort or wonder more often than amusement, while Japanese hissing and Masai spitting are gestures of respect. Posture and gesture possess semantic content in both formal and informal social intercourse. See La Barre 1947, 49, 51, 56; Eibl-Eibesfeldt 1972, 305–6, 311; Youssouf et al. 1976; Poyatos 1986, 471–72, 506; Holoka 1991. Poyatos posits nineteen categories of nonverbal behavior, which subdivide Ekman and Friesen's six major varieties: emblems, illustrators, externalizers, adaptors, emotional displays, and regulators.

11. Holoka 1992, 241, makes these points about Petronius' novel, another social satire. See also Newbold 1992.

discourse (such as smiles, head-tilts, and beetled brows) are indispensable features of social interaction and literary expressiveness. Bodily comportment encourages trust and lubricates sociability. Equally important are inverse processes that allow control of the body and voice to discriminate oneself, to convey and emphasize social differentiation, including age, gender, and social rank.

Posture—the static body—and gesture—the dynamic body—underlie and underline language. They amplify nonrational motives, belie intentions, and "leak" true sentiments of the communicator—willy-nilly. Gestural and postural communities vary for class, time, and place, as European hand and finger gestures quickly reveal to the unwary. Body language shapes, directs, and binds groups; it communicates power and social identity. Body language also reveals invisible character by physical person, as ancient students of drama, forensics, and philosophy assert. An individual's symbolic actions have as much efficacy and as many consequences as instrumental deeds for interactants within texts and for "live" audiences.

We have examined examples from the Homeric repertory of "natural" fretting and strutting and common rituals, ceremonies, and stately assembly procedures—the complex choreography of social equality and inequality. Behaviors suggestive of the animal kingdom's cockfights, canine coital dances, pecking orders, and feral sulking suggest an inventory opening unique windows on ancient Mediterranean behavior and the mimetic skills of Homer. Let us look in, in tragedy, comedy, oratory, and history, as well as in epic.

Strutting one's stuff, *Imponierverhaltung,* permeates Greek life and literature. From blustering Agamemnon of Mykenai and the Ithakan suitors demonstrating their "authority" to the stately pomp and pomposity of late antique Byzantine courts and the modern Greek customshouse officer, Hellenes throw themselves "body and soul" into persuasion and enforcement. "Quiet gestures," however, also evoke Hellenic approval: for example, Eumaios' gracious cottage-*xenia* and Odysseus' gestic self-restraint, celebrated long after, from Plato's ostentatiously modest Sokrates to Longos' orderly and model Lesbian gentleman of the Roman imperial era. Nonverbal behavior provides another script for the drama of human experience.[12]

Literary art, especially the result of a lengthy oral poetic tradition, distills essential body-knowledge, a quintessence of gesture and posture. The *Odyssey*'s descriptions of the suitors' aggressive threat-displays and Odysseus'

---

12. See D. Morris et al. 1979 for contemporary European gesture; Bremmer and Roodenburg 1991, 7 (Thomas); 19 (Bremmer), on walking, standing, and sitting; Newbold 1981, 1988.

stigmatized abasement provide a credible shorthand for Hellenic macho assertion and insistent possessiveness, on the one hand, and another, equally significant repertory of Hellenic self-effacement and enforced public consent to social grades and creative degradation, on the other. The suitors jockey for dominance through position and gesture as well as speech, and they show solidarity and aggregation by sitting at the table, forming the pugilistic circle, and, at the showdown, huddling together defensively. These expressive acts transmit a parallel text, not a mere echo of spoken words, but a separate orchestration or ballet of human responses. Penelope's withdrawals, elevational collapses, and exhibitionist body movements, for instance, nourish the senses in the audience's imagination, as her exhausted words nourish the spirit. Similarly, the suitors' "ritualized competitive interaction," their attempts to create and maintain power differentials, while drinking, gaming, and wrestling the bow, encapsulate their desire, ultimately frustrated, to embody and communicate marriageable manliness.[13]

The poet plays with audience expectations, hinting by nonverbal behavior at truths only later, if ever, verbally proclaimed by a character or the narrator. Body language, expressions of (dis)respect, age-based hesitation, and gendered proxemics both present enlivening detail and concretely express emotion. Acts echo metaphors, as the hero's uncomfortable writhing on the floor the "night before" echoes his thematically canine "barking heart." Homeric formulae and objects gain resonance from repetition; so do gestures. Cedric Whitman once said that Homer's repeated phrases grow like snowballs in meaning when they reappear, regardless of co-occuring mechanical phenomena of oral-formulaic theory. The same is true of body language, widely defined. Nonverbal behavior in Homer constitutes a significant facet of the poems, mimetic and expressive elements nuanced by engaging issues, such as age, gender, and social status.

---

13. See Driessen, in Bremmer and Roodenburg 1991, 238, 242–43, on contemporary Spanish male barroom behaviors, including hoisting of the crotch of the pants and attendant testicles on crossing the public threshold. I note that I have never encountered more self-effacing and modest people than certain quiet male and female Greeks of the Aegean Islands.

Appendix: Chronemics

Chronemics studies time as cultural artifact, an organizing and communicative system that varies across cultures. Along with place and proxemics, chronemics—the peculiarly human awareness of existence as a changing process—is the chief mode of human self-situating. Persons perceive time both as implacable advance and in "warps": speeding up, slowing down, and even stopping. They can distinguish clock time, "profane" time, sacred time, life-stage (biological) time, and circadian time, keeping one's internal clock in phase with the external environment—for example, when combating "jet lag" problems. Humans believe they share peculiar "time frequencies," synchronizations that allow easy communication with lovers, game-partners at cards, or close relatives.

Rhythm denotes regularized timing, or pacing of activity, by the body (by biorhythms), by the sun, or by family, colleagues, or superiors and inferiors. Some rhythms, perhaps most, engage us subconsciously, as when we synchronize dialogue turn taking. We employ different response patterns for our child and for a powerful magistrate. The adjustment of pace and tone, sometimes called "entrainment," the process of one or both parties fitting behaviors to the other, continues until a mutually satisfactory rhythm establishes itself. We take social synchronization for granted—until we sense its violation: a foreigner's ignorance of American tacit talk-interruption permissions; a teenager's misguided haste or hebetude in answering the telephone; or an employee's resentful, slow pace on the job, apparently not "up to speed" for the boss on purpose.[1] Humans also provide each other with temporal "cues" or "adumbrative moves" that foreshadow one's next action in an "action chain," a shared sequence—like the act and reaction that extends one right forearm and expects another's reciprocity in Euro-American handshake greeting procedures.

Chronemics names the regulation of ancient and modern social intercourse as well as studies humanity's sense and manipulation of time. Austin

---

1. Hall 1984 identifies nine varieties of time in chap. 1 and discusses *entrainment* in chap. 10. His promise of examining "what literature can teach us" (134–35) remains unfulfilled.

(1975, 88, 266 n. 7) observes that the *Odyssey* is grounded in ὥρα—judicious timing: "*Hora* is the motivating impulse of the poem." This wise observation can be extended from critical developments in the plot to a microchronology of strategic interactions.

Homer multiplies incident and withholds climax. The first half of the *Odyssey* propels us rapidly through a hall of mirrors with simulated courtship, brides, and simulated weddings—real and sham feasts. The second half of the *Odyssey* repeatedly blocks resolution between Odysseus' arrival on Ithaka and his reunion with Penelope. Time is their enemy; they have less of it as age advances. Its pressure moves them toward inexorable decay and death. They clearly enunciate these inevitable changes. Non-, semi-, and pseudorecognitions show us how far Greeks enjoy deception, teasing, and conversational as well as sexual foreplay. Suspense—a pleasure unknown to gods and dogs—is prolonged for mortal characters and listeners. Kyklops' soliloquy and thoughts expressed out loud to his favorite ram (to which poor Odysseus precariously clings) heighten tension and retard the plot just as artfully as digressions on the scar and the bow or mythological hortatory, cautionary, or consolatory tales (cf. Austin 1966, 1991; Willcock 1964, 142).

Time is a human construct of constant motion (it "marches on," as we say), but it is a variable of literary narrative. Authors may speed up or slow down the stream of time, drive it forward or backward, make it skip or repeat, and juxtapose different parties'—genders' or cultures' or individuals'—experience of time. The suitors seem frozen in time; Odysseus expands it, as it throbs and beats against him. Time can heal or exacerbate wounds, depending on the culture. Deep structural differences separate, for instance, Hopi Indian, Homeric Greek, and Euro-American experiences of time (Hall 1984, chapter 2 and p. 104). Tempo in social experience varies for solitary walking, for reacting to a rival's threat, slight, or gift—from Akhilleus' lightning-fast, hair-trigger "verbal tailgating" of Agamemnon in *Iliad* 1 to Aias' silent snub of Odysseus in the Otherworld, or Orestes' paternal revenge plotted and executed only many years later. In such bloodmatters as this last, even generations may pass; the passage of time does not matter, only the right opportunity for a social person trapped in a long-past moment with consequent obligations. The suitors of Penelope shoot from the hip and "forget the clock." Meanwhile, the denizens of the Laertid establishment stall for time, bide *their* time, and finally choose their time and force a decision.

Repetitions of words, events, and even gestures—whether individual, familial, or communal—are not popular in our "trendy" and novelty-craving society. Intervals are rarely repeated; rarely are identical events enjoyed. The modern era rejects rhythms—repeating sequences—in ideology and entertainment, hence the primacy of superficially distinct television sitcom episodes and "*nov*els." The modern individual is so hostile to repetition, except for a few political and religious events, that one can hardly appreciate its value in traditional societies—in their work, their play, and their poetry.[2]

Heroic time, if we may here so nominate the passage of days in the *Odyssey*, includes the narrator's forward pace of the story, accelerated and decelerated incidents, parallel and recurring scenes, manipulations and "distortions" of flashes back and forward, the characters' similar manipulations in internally recounting events that occurred elsewhere and necessarily prior, their augury or prediction of future events, and their psychic perceptions of time passing quickly or slowly. Emphatic *incongruence* between "real-time" action and description—for instance, slowing down the pace to emphasize the appropriate *moment,* καιρός—characterizes Homeric epic (Austin 1975, 87–89). The description of the scar or bow and the slow-motion narrative of Odysseus twanging it mark seconds to savor, saturation in fulfillment.

Homer's poetic economy describes persons, actions, and objects by their effects—human reactions—rather than by detailed psychological analysis, narrators' licensed intrusions. Human reactions are often nonverbal, and chronemics can be a salient aspect of a gesture or conversational interaction. Pause or absence of pause in interchange often conveys a clearer message than words. Physical hesitation or paralysis, by inserting a stillness into interaction, sends a clear message to an interactant (e.g., Dolios' Sicilian woman and his children before Odysseus: 24.391–92) or to an audience. At the Skherian palace, as later at the Ithakan manse, Odysseus stops still in his tracks to admire the imposing structure (7.81–83, 133–34; 17.260–71). The prefatorial nonverbal immobility of the hero, bracketing and extending beyond the stopped-time *ekphrasis,* emphasizes the magical beauty, the timeless, paradisiacal qualities of the faerylike place, decorated and defended by precious metals and talismanic dogs. Extended description of Kirke's palace or Kalypso's cave not only paints a pretty picture and fantasy but retards the character's and the audience's progress in the story. Homer's *Odyssey* moves crabwise, perversely scuttling aslant expected paths. Every frustrated anticipation of the reader may betray the master performer's master performance. Similarly, the *ekphraseis* of the bow, the scar, and the shield of Akhilleus, and the many extended similes as well, emphasize by literary pace a critical

---

2. Teenagers' commercial music and obsessive dance furnish an interesting exception here, but as Hall 1984, 214, 178, says, these two highly specialized activities "release" rhythms that are already present in our psychophysical being. F.G. Naerebout is preparing a study of the social functions of dance in ancient Greece.

moment (Austin 1966). Chronologically, the plot is stalled, while the audience's anticipation (based on chronemic experience) accelerates. In all these cases, forward movement of the main character is arrested—if only in narrative time. Retardation of the narrative rhythm slows down both characters in question and synesthetically slows down the impatient audience. Critics need to examine the retarded chronemics of persons in the plot, of the author who paces the plot, and of the reader/listener who experiences the tale (*Rezeptionstheorie*).[3]

Time drags in the *Odyssey* when the body clocks of its characters expect more or different (preferable) circumstances. The twelve, drawn-out Ithakan books narratologically present fifty ways to invert the peaceable kingdom, while Telemakhos and others await a momentous impetus. The pace reflects the hero's stubborn difficulties, his tactical need to delay while he tests, and his lack of allies. Telemakhos—nearly alone in Ithaka, Pylos, and Sparta—suggests the slower, indeed sometimes interminable, pace of time experienced by the young, whether undirected or not yet empowered.[4] When crying by the seashore on Aiaia, Odysseus seems to experience seven years of endless ennui after one year of ecstatic sex. On Kirke's island, the men, if not the hero, impatiently note the passage of the year, seasons, months, and "long days" (all are synesthetically mentioned: 5.151–58, 7.259–61, 10.467–72). The Laertids' psychic time quickens after Odysseus reveals himself to his son at the pigsty.

Time usually "flies" in the *Odyssey*, but it does so spasmodically, when danger mounts to a life-threatening degree. Time compression ("my whole life flashed before me") is a widely acknowledged experience of the concentrated mind (in the presence of, e.g., danger, a job deadline, or a series of track hurdles) as well as a cliché of melodrama. Athene apparently has the power to retard or advance astronomical time (23.344–48).

Re-creation of a rhythm, or a return to cosmic and human synchronic phase for master and slave, father and son, and husband and wife, re-inverts the Ithakan world of disturbed classes and inappropriate proprietors. Of the suitors, bold Antinoos alone accuses Telemakhos of overbold speaking: Τηλέμαχ' ὑψαγόρη' (2.85 = 303, 17.406; cf. 1.385). Part of the chief wooer's

---

[3]. In the contrary, comically accelerated Kyklopian scene, after the giant Polyphemos enters his cave, the fear-crazed humans, startled, hurry back into the dark corners (9.236). Other compressions one might cite include the catalog of women in book 11; the sojourn on Kalypso's island, off the beaten track of even Hermes; and the reciprocal summaries of 23.300–41.

[4]. At the meetings of the American Philological Association in New Orleans in 1992, S.D. Olson argued against Delebecque 1958 and resynchronized Telemakhos' chronology with Odysseus'. Modern theory of the novel is much interested in different treatments of time; for a helpful start, see A.A. Mendelow, *Time and the Novel* (London, 1952).

own characterization in a poem "sensitive to rank and occasion," the epithet ironically suits the speaker better than the addressee. Bold speaking concerns content, of course, but also pace, tone, and rapidity of turn taking, verbal "tailgating." Telemakhos develops from potential to active hero, a nonverbal miniversion of Odysseus' feet, hands, hair, and physique (as Helen and Menelaos note). He even has his father's gaze. The stranger is characterized by his scaled-down Odyssean manner, gestures (4.113–16, 16.213–24), and speech, which is πεπνύμενος.[5]

Hosts speak first to guests, as does Telemakhos to Mentes, Nestor's son and Menelaos to Telemakhos, Eumaios to disguised Odysseus, and Penelope to the wayfarer (1.122–24, 3.43, 4.60, 14.37, 19.103; cf. 19.415). Giving priority is a universal chronemic recognition of social inferiority. Indeed, inexperienced Telemakhos breaches speech-initiating and turn-taking decorum by speaking before his Spartan host when at the table, even though in whispers, a meaningful paralinguistic incourtesy (4.71–75). Menelaos graciously picks up the conversational ball. Thus, the narrator silently characterizes both men by chronemic manners as well as by words.

Characters observe and violate time-taking permits. Thus, they ratify or disturb imputed or assumed social roles. As a suppliant on Skheria, Odysseus follows the pattern and "passes" for what he presents himself as: a suppliant. But when he disguises himself as a beggar and suppliant on Ithaka, congruence disintegrates: pig-drover Eumaios senses something special and uncanny about his superficially modest visitor, suitors become ill at ease and angry with the alms-taker, and Penelope becomes suspicious or, at the least, unusually trustful of an upstart vagrant's promises. Feedback is incongruent, expected "action chains"[6] break down, resentment builds up, and ordinary timing and ceremonious procedures are interrupted and unsettled. Meanwhile, jarring challenges and responses substitute for daily patterns as suitors try to shape and cue the "misfit" and agitatedly recall him to his permitted social role. The beggar misses cues and "makes waves," and the wave patterns themselves interfere with each other. Telemakhos asserts that the hungry beggar is insufficiently aggressive; Antinoos asserts that he is too much so in his spacing and timing. One major dimension of aggression is the frequency and speed at which one interacts with others—chronemics.

---

5. 1.361, 4.141–50, 21.355: an epithet of heralds and unseasonably mature talk from young males, (therefore) inferiors. See Austin 1975, 64, 79, 263 n. 52. No suitor is ever πεπνύμενος—except when cannily diplomatic Telemakhos calls them so at 18.65, in a warning.

6. We refer here to sequence expectations, interactional patterns of biological and social behavior, such as eating protocols, bullying hierarchies, gendered courtship routines, toasting patterns, and alms begging. Visser 1991 places Homeric banqueting in a larger historical and cross-cultural context.

Rhythm sharing, chronemic phasing whether by luck, chance, or long practice, in fact, all "in-sync" behaviors characterize practiced athletes and dancers, "copasetic" family members, and so-called alter egos. This sort of synchrony emerges in the *Odyssey* between guest and hostess (She: "When should I do it?"; He: "Do it now!" in book 19), son and father, and compatible spouses.

Hidden moral and social energies are released by the tense moment before Odysseus draws the bowstring taut. His hands caress and test his long-lost possession, the backbent bow, in the interstices of time. Then he strainlessly strings it and tests the very bowstring. A further test of the bow and string's compatibility also serves as a gesture of notification in the pause, a twang in the stillness, "dead time." The suitors respond with an affect display: color drains from their faces. The vibrant moment demonstrates not mere virtuoso narrative technique but the hero's inner enjoyment of long-deferred καιρός, the perfection of excellence all in its good time.[7] Not only strength but deep tuning appears to embrace the archer, bow, arrow, string, and targets at a moment of the gods' choosing.

Later, husband and wife tap the chronemic wellsprings of romantic, connubial synchronization and stop-time. Their transtemporal recognitions, the Laertid clan's celebratory dancing, and the couple's long-deferred lovemaking (while Athene uniquely holds back the dawn: 23.344–48) show a final sensitivity to the primacy of timing and chronemic awareness. The topic of time offers many opportunities for further research, if only one has time.

---

7. Odysseus can draw the mighty bow even in a sitting position. Posture here signals superior rank as well as strength, to judge by humorous Olympian jumping-up protocols when Zeus the boss arrives in *Il.* 1. Hall 1984, 97, discusses archery's rhythms, referring to Eugen Herrigel, *Zen in the Art of Archery* (1971). William Faulkner once said of chronemic awareness, "There is no such thing really as was, because the past is."

Bibliography

Adkins, A.W. 1969. "Threatening, Abusing, and Feeling Angry in the Homeric Poems." *JHS* 89:7–21.
Alexiou, Margaret. 1974. *The Ritual Lament in Greek Tradition*. Cambridge, Mass.
Allen, W. 1939. "The Theme of the Suitors in the *Odyssey*." *TAPA* 70:104–24.
Amory, Anne. 1963. "The Reunion of Odysseus and Penelope." In Taylor 1963, 100–121.
Apthorp, M.J. 1980. "The Obstacles to Telemachus' Return." *CQ* 30:1–22.
Ardener, S. 1987. "A Note on Gender Iconography: The Vagina." In *The Cultural Construction of Sexuality*, ed. P. Caplan, 113–42. London.
Arend, W. 1933. *Die typische Scenen bei Homer*. Berlin.
Arieti, J.A. 1986. "Achilles' Alienation in *Iliad* 9." *CJ* 82.1:1–27.
Arnould, Dominique. 1990. *Le rire et les larmes dans la littérature grecque d'Homère à Platon*. Paris.
Auerbach, Erich. 1953. *Mimesis: The Representation of Reality in Western Literature*. English trans. W. Trask. Princeton
Austin, Norman. 1966. "The Function of Digressions in the *Iliad*." *GRBS* 7:295–312. Reprinted in *Essays on the Iliad*, ed. J. Wright, 70–84. Bloomington, 1978.
———. 1969. "Telemachos *polymechanos*." *CSCA* 2:45–63.
———. 1975. *Archery at the Dark of the Moon*. Berkeley.
———. 1983. "Odysseus and the Cyclops: Who Is Who." In *Approaches to Homer*, ed. C. Rubino and C. Shelmerdine, 3–37. Austin.
———. 1991. "The Wedding Text in Homer's *Odyssey*." *Arion* 3: 227–43.
Bates, J.A. 1975. "The Communicative Hand." In Benthall and Polhemus 1975, 175–94.
Beck, William. 1955–. "Δόμος, δῶμα, μέγαρον." In *Lexicon des frühgriechischen Epos,* ed. B. Snell and H. Erbse. Göttingen.
———. 1991. "Dogs, Dwellings, and Masters: Ensemble and Symbol in the *Odyssey*." *Hermes* 119:158–67.
Belmont, D.E. 1967. "Telemachus and Nausicaa: A Study of Youth." *CJ* 63.1:1–9.
Benardete, S. 1963. "Achilles and the *Iliad*." *Hermes* 91:1–16.
Benson, R.G. 1980. *Medieval Body-Language: A Study in . . . Chaucer*. Copenhagen. *Anglistica* 21, monograph.
Benthall, J., and T. Polhemus. 1975. *The Body as a Medium of Expression*. New York.
Bérard, V. 1918. "La geste de l'aède et le texte homérique." *REG* 31:1–38.
Bergren, A. 1981. "Helen's 'Good Drug': *Ody.* 4.1–305." In *Contemporary Literary Hermeneutics and the Interpretation of Literary Texts,* ed. S. Kresic, 201–14. Ottawa.

Birdwhistell, R. 1970. *Kinesics and Context. Essays on Body Motion Communication*. Philadelphia.

Bloch, M. 1974. "Symbols, Song, Dance and Features of Articulation: Is Religion an Extreme Form of Traditional Authority?" *Archives Européennes de Sociologie* 15:55–81.

Block, E. 1985. "Clothing Makes the Man: A Pattern in the *Odyssey*." *TAPA* 115:1–11

Blok, A. 1981. "Rams and Billy-goats: A Key to the Mediterranean Code of Honor." *Man* 16:427–40.

Boegehold, A.L. 1986. "Gestures and the Interpretation of Greek Literature." *AJA* 90.2:181.

Bogucka, Maria. 1991. "Gesture, Ritual, and Social Order in Sixteenth- to Eighteenth-Century Poland." In Bremmer and Roodenburg 1991, 190–209.

Bourdieu, P. 1977. *Outline of a Theory of Practice*. Trans. R. Nice. Cambridge.

Braswell, B.K. 1982. "The Song of Ares and Aphrodite: Theme and Relevance to *Odyssey* 8." *Hermes* 110:129–37.

Bremmer, Jan. 1983. "Scapegoat Rituals in Ancient Greece." *HSCPh* 87:299–320.

Bremmer, Jan, and H. Roodenburg, eds. 1991. *A Cultural History of Gesture*. Ithaca, N.Y.

Brewer, W.D. 1951. "Patterns of Gesture Among the Levantine Arabs." *AA* 53:232–37.

Brown, C.S. 1966. "Odysseus and Polyphemus: The Name and the Curse," *Comp. Lit.* 18:193–202.

Büchner, W. 1940. "Die Penelopeszenen in der Odysee." *Hermes* 75:129–67.

Buck, R. 1984. "The Development of Emotion and Emotion Communication." In *The Communication of Emotion*, 121–68. London.

Bugental, D.E., et al. 1970. "Perception of Contradictory Meanings Conveyed by Verbal and Nonverbal Channels. *Journal of Personal and Social Psychology* 16:647–55.

Burgoon, J., and Th. Saine. 1978. *The Unspoken Dialogue: An Introduction to Nonverbal Communication*. Boston.

Burns, Tom. 1992. *Erving Goffman*. London.

Byre, Calvin. 1988. "Penelope and the Suitors before Odysseus: *Odyssey* 18.158–303." *AJP* 109:159–73.

Calbris, G. 1990. *The Semiotics of French Gesture*. Trans. O. Doyle. Bloomington.

Calhoun, G.M. 1934. "Classes and Masses in Homer." *CP* 29:192–208, 301–16.

Campbell, J.K. 1964. *Honour, Family, and Patronage*. Oxford.

Clarke, H.W. 1963. "Telemachos and the Telemacheia." *AJP* 84:138–45.

Clay, Jenny S. 1972. "The *Planktai* and *Moly*: Divine Naming and Knowing in Homer." *Hermes* 100:127–31.

———. 1974. "*Demas* and *Aude*: The Nature of Divine Transformation in Homer." *Hermes* 102:129–36.

———. 1983. *The Wrath of Athena*. Princeton.

———. 1984. "Homeric ἀχρεῖον." *AJP* 105:73–76.

———. 1995. "Agamemnon's Stance (*Iliad* 19.51–77)." *Philologus* 139:72–75.

Cohen, D. 1989. "Seclusion, Separation, and the Status of Women in Classical Athens." *G&R* 36.1:3–15.

Colakis, Marianthe. 1986. "The Laughter of the Suitors in *Odyssey* 20." *CW* 79:137–41.
Combellack, Frederic. 1946/47. "New Light on Homer's Profession." *CJ* 42:210.
———. 1948. "Speakers and Scepters in Homer." *CJ* 43:209–17.
———. 1950/51. "Words That Die." *CJ* 46:21–26.
———. 1965. "Some Formulary Illogicalities in Homer." *TAPA* 96:41–56.
———. 1973. "Three Odyssean Problems." *CSCPh* 6:17–46.
———. 1981. "The Wish Without Desire." *AJP* 102:115–19.
Cowan, Jane. 1991. "Going Out for Coffee? Contesting . . . Pleasures in Everyday Sociability." In Loizos and Papataxiarchis 1991, 180–202.
Cramer, Owen. 1976. "Speech and Silence in the *Iliad*." *CJ* 71:300–304.
Crane, Gregory. 1992. "Power, Prestige, and the Corcyrean Affair in Thucydides 1." *CA* 11:1–27.
Crystal, D. 1975. "Paralinguistics." In Benthall and Polhemus 1975, 162–74.
Culler, J. 1981. *The Pursuit of Signs*. Ithaca, N.Y.
Danforth, L.M. 1982. *The Death Rituals of Rural Greece*. Princeton.
Delebecque, Ed. 1958. *Télémaque et la structure de l'Odyssée*. Aix.
———. 1980. *Construction de l'Odyssée*. Paris.
Denniston, J.D. 1966. *The Greek Particles*. 2d ed. Oxford.
Denny, F.M. 1987. "Postures and Gestures." In *Encyclopedia of Religion*, ed. M. Eliade, vol. 11, 461–64. New York and London.
Dickie, M. 1983. "Phaeacian Athletes." *PLLS* 4:237–76.
Dimock, George E., Jr. 1956. "The Name of Odysseus." *Hudson Review* 9:52–70. Reprinted in Taylor 1963, 54–72.
———. 1989. *The Unity of the Odyssey*. Amherst, Mass.
Doherty, Lillian. 1991. "The Internal and Implied Audiences of *Odyssey* 11." *Arethusa* 24.2:145–76.
Donlan, Walter. 1971. "Homer's Agamemnon." *CW* 65:109–15.
———. 1982a. "The Politics of Generosity in Homer." *Helios* 9.2:1–15.
———. 1982b. "Reciprocities in Homer." *CW* 75:137–75.
———. 1989. "The Unequal Exchange Between Glaucus and Diomedes in Light of the Homeric Gift-Economy." *Phoenix* 43:1–15.
———. 1993. "Duelling with Gifts in the *Iliad*: As the Audience Saw It." *Colby Quarterly* 29:155–72.
Douglas, Mary. 1970. "The Two Bodies." In *Natural Symbols*, 65–81. London.
———. [1971] 1975. "Do Dogs Laugh? A Cross-Cultural Approach to Body Symbolism." *Journal of Psycho-Somatic Research* 15:387–90. Reprinted in *Implicit Meanings*, 83–89. London.
Drerup, H. "Griechische Baukunst in geometrische Zeit." In *Archaeologia Homerica*, ed. F. Matz and H.G. Buchholz, Göttingen.
Dubisch, Jill, ed. 1986. *Gender and Power in Rural Greece*. Princeton.
du Boulay, Juliet. 1976. "Lies, Mockery, and Family Integrity." In Peristiany 1976, 389–406.
———. 1986. "Women: Images of Their Nature and Destiny in Rural Greece." In Dubisch 1986, 139–68.
Ebeling, H. 1880. *Lexicon Homericum*. Leipzig.
Eckert, C. 1964. "Initiatory Motifs in the Story of Telemachus." *CJ* 59:49–57.

Edwards, Anthony T. 1993. "Homer's Ethical Geography: Country and City in the *Odyssey.*" *TAPA* 123:27–78.
Edwards, Mark W. 1975. "Type-Scenes and Homeric Hospitality," *TAPA* 105:51–72.
———. 1987. *Homer: Poet of the Iliad.* Baltimore.
———. 1991. *The Iliad: A Commentary.* Vol. 5. Cambridge.
———. 1992. "Homer and Oral Tradition: The Type-Scene." *Oral Tradition* 7.2:284–330.
Edwards, Viv, and T.J. Sienkewicz. 1990. *Oral Cultures Past and Present: Rappin' and Homer.* Oxford.
Eibl-Eibesfeldt, I. 1972. "Similarities and Differences between Cultures in Expressive Movements." In *Nonverbal Communication,* ed. R. Hinde, 297–311. Cambridge.
Ekman, P. 1981. "Mistakes When Deceiving." *Annals of the New York Academy of Science* 364:269–78.
———. 1992. *Telling Lies: Clues to Deceit in the Marketplace, Politics, and Marriage.* Rev. ed. New York.
Ekman, Paul, and W. Friesen. 1969a. "Nonverbal Leakage and Clues to Deception." *Psychiatry* 32.1:88–105.
———. 1969b. "The Repertoire of Nonverbal Behavior: Categories, Origins, Usage, and Coding." *Semiotica* 1.1:49–98.
———. 1972. "Hand Movements." *Journal of Communication* 22:353–74.
Emlyn-Jones, C. 1984. "The Reunion of Penelope and Odysseus." *G&R* 31:1–18.
Evans, E.C. 1930. "*Quo modo corpora voltusque hominum auctores Latini descripserint.*" Ph. D. diss., Harvard University. *Non vidi.* Summary published in *HSCP* 41 (1930): 192–95.
———. 1969. *Physiognomics in the Ancient World.* TAPhS 59. Philadelphia.
Falkner, Thomas. 1989. "ἐπὶ γήραος οὐδῷ: Homeric Heroism, Old Age, and the End of the *Odyssey.*" In *Old Age in Greek and Latin Literature,* ed. T. Falkner and J. de Luce, 21–67. Albany.
Faraone, Chris. 1992. *Talismans and Trojan Horses.* Oxford.
Felson-Rubin, Nancy. 1987. "Penelope's Perspective: Character from Plot." In *Homer: Beyond Oral Poetry,* ed. I.F. De Jong et al., 61–83. Amsterdam.
———. 1994. *Regarding Penelope: From Character to Poetics.* Princeton.
Fenik, B. 1974. *Studies in the Odyssey.* Hermes Einzelschrift 30. Wiesbaden.
Fingerle, Adolf. 1939. *Typik der homerischen Reden.* Ph. D. diss., Munich.
Finley, Moses. 1978. *The World of Odysseus.* 2d ed. New York. First edition published in 1954.
Firth, R. 1969. "Postures and Gestures of Respect." In *Exchange and Communication: Mélanges Lévi-Strauss,* ed. P. Miranda and J. Pouillon, 188–209. The Hague.
———. 1972. "Verbal and Bodily Rituals of Greeting and Parting." In *The Interpretation of Ritual: Essays A.I. Richards,* ed. J.S. La Fontaine, 1–38. London.
———. 1973. "Bodily Symbols of Greeting and Parting." In *Symbols: Public and Private,* 299–327. Ithaca, N.Y.
Fisher, N.R.E. 1992. *Hybris: A Study in the Values of Honour and Shame in Ancient Greece.* Warminster.
Foley, Helene. 1978. "'Reverse Similes' and Sex Roles in the *Odyssey.*" *Arethusa* 11:7–26.

Foley, John M. 1990. *Traditional Oral Epic: The Odyssey, Beowulf, and the Serbo-Croatian Return Song*. Berkeley and Los Angeles.
———. 1992. "Word-Power, Performance, and Tradition." *JAF* 105:275–301.
Fränkel, H. [1962] 1975. *Early Greek Poetry and Philosophy*. Trans. M. Hadas and J. Willis. Oxford. Original published in New York, 1951.
Friedl, E. 1962. *Vasilika: A Village in Modern Greece*. New York.
Friedrich, Rainer. 1987a. "Heroic Man and Polymetis: Odysseus in the *Cyclopeia*." *GRBS* 28:121–33.
———. 1987b. "Thrinakia and Zeus' Ways to Men in the *Odyssey*." *GRBS* 28:375–400.
———. 1991. "The Hybris of Odysseus." *JHS* 111:16–28.
Geddes, A.G. 1984. "Who's Who in Homeric Society." *CQ* 34:17–36.
Gillin, J.L. 1929. "Vagrancy and Begging." *AJSoc.* 35:424–32.
Goffman, E. 1959. *The Presentation of Self in Everyday Life*. Garden City, N.Y.
———. 1963. *Stigma: Notes on the Management of Spoiled Identity*. Englewood Cliffs, N.J.
———. 1966. "Engagements Among the Unacquainted." In *Behavior in Public Places*, 124–48. New York.
———. 1967a. *Interaction Ritual*. Garden City, N.Y.
———. [1956] 1967b. "The Nature of Deference and Demeanor." In *Interaction Ritual*, 47–95. Garden City, NY.
———. [1955] 1967c. "On Face-Work: An Analysis of Ritual Elements in Social Interaction." in *Interaction Ritual*, 5–45. Garden City, N.Y.
———. 1969. *Strategic Interaction*. Philadelphia.
———. 1971. "Supportive Interchanges." In *Relations in Public*, 62–94. New York.
———. 1976. *Gender Advertisements*. New York.
Goldhill, Simon. 1988. "Reading Differences: The *Odyssey* and Juxtaposition." *Ramus* 17.1:1–31.
Gombrich, E.H. 1966. "Ritualized Gesture and Expression in Art." *Phil. Trans. of the Royal Soc.*, ser. B, vol. 251:393–401. Reprinted in *The Image and the Eye*, 63–77. Oxford, 1982.
———. 1972. "Action and Expression in Western Art." In *Non-verbal Communication*, ed. R.D. Hinde, 373–92. Cambridge.
Goody, E. 1972. "'Greeting,' 'Begging,' and the Presentation of Respect." In *The Interpretation of Ritual: Essays A.I. Richards*, ed. J.S. La Fontaine, 39–71. London.
Gould, John. 1973. "'IKETEIA." *JHS* 93:74–103.
———. 1991. "Give and Take in Herodotus." Fifteenth J.L. Myres Memorial Lecture. Oxford.
Grajew, F. 1934. *Untersuchungen über die Bedeutung der Gebärden in der griechischen Epik*. Ph. D. diss., Albert-Ludwigs-Universität. Freiburg.
Griffin, Jasper. 1977. "The Epic Cycle and the Uniqueness of Homer." *JHS* 97:39–53.
———. 1980. *Homer on Life and Death*. Oxford.
Gruber, M.I. 1980. *Aspects of Nonverbal Communication in the Ancient Near East*. 2 vols. Rome.
Gutglueck, J. 1988. "A Detestable Encounter in *Odyssey* VI." *CJ* 83:97–102.
Hall, Edward T. 1959. *The Silent Language*. Garden City, N.Y.

———. 1966. *The Hidden Dimension*. Garden City, N.Y.
———. 1984. *The Dance of Life: The Other Dimension of Time*. Garden City, N.Y.
Hallpike, C.R. 1969. "Social Hair." *Man. Journal of the Royal Anthropological Institute* 4.2:256–64.
Halverson, John. 1985. "Social Order in the *Odyssey*." *Hermes* 113:129–45.
Hansen, W.F. 1990. "Odysseus and the Oar." In *Approaches to Greek Myth,* ed. L. Edmunds, 241–72. Baltimore.
Harsh, Philip W. 1950. "Penelope and Odysseus in *Odyssey* xix." *AJP* 71:1–21.
Hawad-Claudot, H. 1992. "The Veiled Face and Expressiveness among the Tuaregs." In Poyatos 1992a, 197–211.
Hellwig, Br. 1964. *Raum und Zeit im homerischen Epos. Spudasmata* 2. Hildesheim.
Henley, Nancy. [1977] 1986. *Body Politics*. New York.
Henley, Nancy, M. Hamilton, and B. Thorne. 1985. "Womanspeak and Manspeak: Sex Differences and Sexism in Communication: Verbal and Nonverbal." In *Beyond Sex Roles,* ed. A.G. Sargent, 168–85. St. Paul, Minn.
Herman, G. 1987. *Ritualised Friendship and the Greek City*. Cambridge.
Herzfeld, Michael. 1985. *The Poetics of Manhood*. Princeton.
———. 1991. "Silence, Submission and Subversion: Towards a Poetics of Womanhood." In Loizos and Papataxiarchis 1991, 79–97.
Heubeck, A., S. West, et al. 1988–92. *A Commentary on Homer's Odyssey*. 3 vols. Oxford.
Hewes, G. 1957. "The Anthropology of Posture." *Scientific American* 196:123–32.
Hirvonen, K. 1969. "Cledonomancy and the Grinding Slave: *Od.* 20.91–121." *Arctos* 6:5–21.
Hoekstra, A., and A. Heubeck. 1989. *A Commentary on Homer's Odyssey*. Vol. 2. Oxford.
Hohendahl-Zoetelief, I.M. 1980. *Manners in the Homeric Epic*. Leiden.
Holoka, James. 1983. "Looking Darkly: Reflections on Status and Decorum in Homer." *TAPA* 113:1–16.
———. 1991. "Homer, Oral Poetry Theory, and Comparative Literature: Major Trends and Controversies in Twentieth-Century Criticism." *Colloquium Rauricum* 2:456–81.
———. 1992. "Nonverbal Communication in the Classics: Research Opportunities." In Poyatos 1992A, 237–54.
Hölscher, U. 1960. "Das Schweigen der Arete." *Hermes* 88:257–65.
Horowitz, M.J. 1964. "The Body-Buffer Zone: An Exploration of Personal Space." *Archives of General Psychiatry* 11:651–56.
Houston, G.W. 1975. "*Thronos, Diphros,* and Odysseus' Change from Beggar to Avenger." *CP* 70:212–14.
Irvine, J. 1974. "Strategies of Manipulation in the Wolof Greeting." In *Explorations in the Ethnography of Speaking,* ed. R. Bauman and J. Sherzer, 167–91. Cambridge.
Jenkins, I.D. 1985. "The Ambiguity of Greek Textiles." *Arethusa* 18:109–32.
Jones, Chr. P. 1987. "*Stigma*: Tatooing and Branding in Graeco-Roman Antiquity." *JRS* 77:139–55.
Jones, Peter V. 1988a. *Homer's Odyssey: A Companion*. Carbondale and Edwardsville, Illinois.

---. 1988b. "The *Kleos* of Telemachus: *Odyssey* 1.95." *AJP* 109:496–506.
---. 1989. "*Iliad* 24.649: Another Solution." *CQ* 39:247–50.
Jourard, S., and J.E. Rubin. 1968. "Self-Disclosure and Touching: A Study of Two Modes of Interpersonal Encounter and Their Interrelation." *Journal of Humanistic Psychology* 8:39–48.
Kaimio, Maarit. 1988. *Physical Contact in Greek Tragedy*. Ann. Ac. Sci. Fen. 244. Helsinki.
Kakridis, J. 1949. *Homeric Researches*. Lund.
---. 1971. "The Recognition of Odysseus." In *Homer Revisited*, 151–63. Lund. Originally published in Greek in 1957.
Kapsalis, Peter T. 1946. *Gestures in Greek Art and Literature*. Ph.D. diss. Johns Hopkins University, Baltimore.
Katz, Marylin. 1991. *Penelope's Renown: Meaning and Indeterminacy in the Odyssey*. Princeton.
Kendon, Adam. 1973. "A Description of Some Human Greetings." In *Comparative Ecology and Behaviour of Primates,* ed. R.P. Michael and J.H. Crook, 591–668. London and New York.
---. 1982. "The Study of Gesture: Some Observations on Its History." *Recherches Sémiotiques/Semiotic Inquiry* 2:45–62.
Kennedy, G. 1972. *The Art of Rhetoric in the Roman World*. Princeton.
Kirk, G., B. Hainsworth, R. Janko, M. Edwards, and N. Richardson. 1985–93. *The Iliad: A Commentary*. 6 vols. Cambridge.
Knox, M.O. 1970. "'House' and 'Palace' in Homer." *JHS* 90:117–20.
Kullmann, W. 1984. "Oral Poetry Theory and Neoanalysis in Homeric Research." *GRBS* 25:307–23.
Kurz, G. 1966. *Darstellungsformen menschlicher Bewegung in der Ilias*. Heidelberg.
La Barre, W. 1947. "The Cultural Basis of Emotions and Gestures." *Journal of Personality* 16:49–68.
Lateiner, Donald. 1987. "Nonverbal communication in the *Histories* of Herodotus." *Arethusa* 20:83–119.
---. 1988. Review of *Literature's Silent Language: Nonverbal Communication,* by Stephen Portch. *Style* 22.4:664–70.
---. 1989. "Teeth in Homer." *LCM* 14:18–23.
---. 1992a. "Affect Displays in the Epic Poetry of Homer, Vergil, and Ovid." In Poyatos 1992a, 255–69.
---. 1992b. "Heroic Proxemics: Social Space and Distance in the *Odyssey*." *TAPA* 122:133–63.
---. 1993. "The Suitors' Take." *Colby Quarterly* 29.3:173–96.
Lattimore, Richmond. 1951. *The Iliad of Homer*. Chicago.
---. 1967. *The Odyssey of Homer*. New York.
Levine, Daniel. 1982a. "Homeric Laughter and the Unsmiling Suitors." *CJ* 78:97–104.
---. 1982b. "*Odyssey* 18: Iros as Paradigm for the Suitors." *CJ* 77:200–204.
---. 1983a. "Penelope's Laugh: *Odyssey* 18.163." *AJP* 104:172–78.
---. 1983b. "Theoklymenos and the Apocalypse." *CJ* 79:1–7.
---. 1984. "Odysseus' Smiles: *Odyssey* 20.301, 22.371, 23.111." *TAPA* 114:1–9.

———. 1987. "*Flens matrona et meretrices gaudentes:* Penelope and Her Maids." *CW* 81:23-27.
Levy, H.L. 1963. "The Odyssean Suitors and the Host-Guest Relationship." *TAPA* 94:143-53.
Lloyd-Jones, H. 1992. "Becoming Homer." *New York Review of Books* 39.5:52-57.
Lohmann, D. 1970. *Die Komposition der Reden in der Ilias*. Berlin.
Loizos, Peter, and E. Papataxiarchis, eds. 1991. *Contested Identities: Gender and Kinship in Modern Greece*. Princeton.
Lonsdale, S.H. 1989. "If Looks Could Kill: Παπταίνω and the Interpretation of Imagery and Narrative in Homer." *CJ* 84:325-33.
Lorimer, H.L. 1950. "The Homeric House." In *Homer and the Monuments*, 406-33. London.
Louden, Bruce. 1992. "Homeric Puns: An Attempt at Classification." Paper presented at the annual meeting of the American Philological Association, New Orleans.
Lowenstam, Steven. 1981. *The Death of Patroclus*. Koenigstein.
———. 1992. "The Uses of Vase Depictions in Homeric Studies." *TAPA* 122:165-98.
Lyne, R.O. 1983. "Lavinia's Blush: Vergil *Aeneid* 12.64-70." *G&R* 30:55-64.
Mackie, G.M. 1899. "Gestures." in *Hastings Dictionary of the Bible*, vol. 2, cols. 162b-163b. New York.
Macleod, Colin W. 1982. *Homer: Iliad XXIV*. Cambridge.
Marquardt, P.A. 1985. "Penelope *Polytropos*." *AJP* 106:32-48.
Martin, Richard P. 1989. *The Language of Heroes*. Ithaca.
———. 1993. "Telemachus and the Last Hero Song." *Colby Quarterly* 29.3:222-40.
Mastronarde, D.J. 1979. *Contact and Discontinuity: Some Conventions of Speech and Action on the Greek Tragic Stage*. Berkeley.
Mauss, Marcel. 1935. "Les techniques du corps." *Journal de la psychologie* 32: 271-93. English translation published in *Economies and Sociétés* 2.1 (1973): 70-88.
———. 1967. *The Gift*. Trans. I. Cunnison. New York. Originally published as *Essai sur le don*. Paris, 1925.
Meister, K. 1921. *Die homerische Kunstsprache*. Leipzig.
Millar, C., and J. Carmichael. 1954. "The Growth of Telemachus." *G&R* 1:58-64.
Miner, H. 1956. "Body Ritual Among the Nacirema." *American Anthropologist* 58:503-7.
Mondi, R. 1983. "The Homeric Cyclopes: Folktale, Tradition, and Theme." *TAPA* 113:17-38.
———. 1990. "Greek Mythic Thought in the Light of the Near East." In *Approaches to Greek Myth*, ed. L. Edmunds, 142-98. Baltimore.
Monsacré, H. 1984. "Weeping Heroes in the *Iliad*." *Gestures: History and Anthropology* 1:57-75.
Morris, Desmond, et al. 1979. *Gestures*. New York.
Morris, Ian. 1986. "The Use and Abuse of Homer." *CA* 5:81-138.
Most, Glenn W. 1989a. "The Stranger's Stratagem: Self-Disclosure and Self-Sufficiency in Greek Culture." *JHS* 109:114-33.

---. 1989b. "The Structure and Functions of Odysseus' *Apologoi.*" *TAPA* 119:15-30.
Motto, A.L., and J. Clark. 1969. "Isê dais: The Honor of Achilles." *Arethusa* 2:109-25.
Murnaghan, Sheila. 1986. "Penelope's *Agnoia:* Knowledge, Power, and Gender in the *Odyssey.*" *Helios* 13.2:103-15.
---. 1987. *Disguise and Recognition in the Odyssey.* Princeton.
---. 1992. "Maternity and Mortality in Homeric Poetry." *CA* 11.2:242-64.
Myres, J.L. 1932. "The Last Book of the *Iliad.*" *JHS* 52:264-96.
Naerebout, F.G. 1987. "Male-Female Relationships in the Homeric Epics." In *Sexual Asymmetry,* ed. J. Blok and P. Mason, 109-46. Amsterdam.
Nagler, M.N. 1974. *Spontaneity and Tradition.* Berkeley and Los Angeles.
Nagy, Gregory. 1979. *The Best of the Achaeans.* Baltimore.
---. 1992. "Homeric Questions." *TAPA* 122:17-60.
Neumann, G. 1965. *Gesten und Gebärden in der griechischen Kunst.* Berlin.
Newbold, Ronald. 1981. "Space and Scenery in Quintus of Smyrna, Claudian, and Nonnus." *Ramus* 10.1:53-68.
---. 1988. "Polysemy and Authority in the Late Roman Empire." *Semiotica* 71:227-42.
---. 1992. "Nonverbal Communication in the *Satyricon* and in Apuleius' *Metamorphoses.*" *QUCC* 41:127-36.
Newton, Rick. 1983. "Poor Polyphemus: Emotional Ambivalence in *Odyssey* 9 and 17." *CW* 76:137-42.
---. 1987. "Odysseus and Hephaestus in the *Odyssey.*" *CJ* 83:12-20.
---. 1991. "Michael Herzfeld, Cretan Dishonesty, and Homer's *Odyssey.*" Unpublished CAMWS abstract.
Nimis, Steve. 1986. "The Language of Akhilleus." *CJ* 79:217-25.
Nöth, Winfried. [1985] 1990. *Handbook of Semiotics.* Bloomington.
Nowicki, Stephen, and Marshall Duke. 1992. *Helping the Child Who Doesn't Fit In.* Atlanta.
O'Hanlon, M. 1983. "Handsome Is as Handsome Does: Display and Betrayal in the Wahgi." *Oceania* 53:317-33.
Olson, S. Douglas. 1990. "The Stories of Agamemnon in Homer's *Odyssey.*" *TAPA* 20:57-71.
---. 1992a. "Ancient Disjunctions and Modern Mechanisms: the Problem of Time in Homer's *Odyssey.*" Paper presented orally at American Philological Association, annual meeting.
---. 1992b. "Servants' Suggestions in Homer's *Odyssey.*" *CJ* 87:219-27.
---. 1994. "Telemachos' Laugh (*Od.* 21.101-105)." *CJ* 89.4:369-72.
Page, Denys. 1955. *The Homeric Odyssey.* Oxford.
Parry, Adam. 1956. "The Language of Achilles." *TAPA* 87:1-7.
Parry, Milman. 1971. *The Making of Homeric Verse.* Ed. A. Parry. Oxford.
Pedrick, Victoria. 1982. "Supplication in the *Iliad* and the *Odyssey.*" *TAPA* 112:125-40.
---. 1988. "The Hospitality of Noble Women in the *Odyssey.*" *Helios* 15:85-101.
Peppmüller, R. 1876. *Commentar zu Ilias Ω.* Berlin.

Peristiany, J.G. 1965. "Honour and Shame in a Cypriot Highland Village." In *Honour and Shame: The Values of Mediterranean Society,* ed. J.G. Peristiany, 173–90. Chicago 1974. Originally published in London 1965.
———, ed. 1976. *Mediterranean Family Structures.* Cambridge.
Perysinakis, I.N. 1991. "Penelope's EEΔNA Again." *CQ* 41:297–302.
Pitt-Rivers, Julian. 1977. "The Law of Hospitality." In *The Fate of Shechem, or the Politics of Sex,* 94–112. Cambridge. Originally published in *Les Temps Modernes* 253 (1967):2153–78.
Podlecki, A.J. 1967. "Omens in the *Odyssey.*" *G&R* 14:12–23.
———. 1969. "Guest Gifts and Nobodies in *Odyssey* 9." *Phoenix* 15:25–33.
Portch, Stephen. 1985. *Literature's Silent Language.* New York.
Potter, Stephen. 1962. *One-Upmanship . . .* New York.
Poulsen, F. 1945. "Talking, Weeping, and Bleeding Sculptures." *Acta Arch.* 16:178–95.
Poyatos, Fernando. 1981. "Silence and Stillness: Toward a New Status of Non-Activity." *Kodikas/code* 3:3–26.
———. 1983. "Literary Anthropology . . ." In *New Perspectives in Nonverbal Communication.* Oxford.
———. 1985. "The Deeper Levels of Face-to-Face Interaction." *Language and Communication* 5.2:111–31.
———. 1986. "Nonverbal Categories as Personal and Sociocultural Identifiers: A Model for Social Interaction Research." In *Iconicity: Essays on the Nature of Culture for Thomas Sebeok,* ed. P. Bouissac, R. Posner, and M. Herzfeld, 469–525. Tübingen.
———, ed. 1992a. *Advances in Nonverbal Communication: Sociocultural, Clinical, Esthetic, and Literary Perspectives.* Amsterdam and Philadelphia.
———. 1992b. "Aspects of Nonverbal Communication in Literature." In *Traducere Navem: Festschrift K. Reiss,* ed. J. Holz-Mänttäri and Chr. Nord, 137–51. Tampere, Finland.
Pucci, P. 1987. *Odysseus Polytropos: Intertextual Readings in the Odyssey and the Iliad.* Ithaca, N.Y.
Qviller, B. 1981. "The Dynamics of Homeric Society." *SO* 56:109–55.
Rankin, A.V. 1962. "Penelope's Dreams in Books XIX and XX of the *Odyssey.*" *Helikon* 2:617–24.
Redfield, James. [1967] 1973. "The Making of the *Odyssey.*" In *Parnassus Revisited,* ed. A.C. Yu, 141–54. Chicago.
———. 1975. *Nature and Culture in the Iliad.* Chicago.
Roisman, Hanna. 1987. "Penelope's Indignation." *TAPA* 117:59–68.
———. 1990a. "Eumaios and Odysseus: Covert Recognition and Self-Revelation." *ICS* 15:215–38.
———. 1990b. "*Kerdion* in the *Iliad*: Profit and Trickiness." *TAPA* 120:23–35.
Rose, Gilbert. 1967. "The Quest of Telemachus." *TAPA* 98:391–98.
———. 1969. "The Unfriendly Phaeacians." *TAPA* 100:387–406.
———. 1971. "*Odyssey* 15.143–82: A Narrative Inconsistency?" *TAPA* 102:509–14.
———. 1979. "Odysseus' Barking Heart." *TAPA* 109:215–30.

———. 1980. "The Swineherd and the Beggar." *Phoenix* 34:285–97.
Rose, H.J. 1956. "Divine Disguisings." *HThR* 49:63–72.
Rose, Peter. 1988. "Thersites and the Plural Voices of Homer." *Arethusa* 21:5–25.
———. 1992. *Sons of the Gods, Children of the Earth: Ideology and Literary Form in Ancient Greece*. Ithaca, N.Y.
Roth, H. Ling. 1889. "On Salutations." *JRAI* 19:164–81.
Russo, Joseph. 1983. "Interview and Aftermath: Dream, Fantasy, and Intuition in *Ody*. 19 and 20." *AJP* 103:4–18.
———. 1987. "Oral Style as Performance Style in Homer's *Odyssey*." In *Comparative Studies in Oral Traditions*, ed. J.M. Foley, 549–65. Columbus, Ohio.
Russo, Joseph, M. Fernandez-Galiano, and A. Heubeck. 1992. *A Commentary on Homer's Odyssey*. Vol. 3, Books 17–24. Oxford.
Rutherford, R.B. 1992. *Odyssey: Books XIX and XX*. Cambridge.
Saïd, S. 1979. "Les crimes des prétendants, la maison d'Ulysse, et les festins de l'*Odyssée*." *Etudes de Littérature Ancienne*, 9–49.
Schadewaldt, W. 1959. "Kleiderdinge: Zur Analyse der Odyssee." *Hermes* 87:13–26.
Scheflen, Albert E. 1964. "The Significance of Posture in Communication Systems." *Psychiatry* 27:316–31.
———. 1972. *Body Language and Social Order*. Englewood Cliffs, N.J.
Schein, S. 1970. "Odysseus and Polyphemus in the *Odyssey*." *GRBS* 11:73–83.
Schiffrin, Deborah. 1977. "Opening Encounters." *ASR* 42.5:679–91.
Schmiel, R. 1972. "Telemachus in Sparta." *TAPA* 103:463–72.
Schwartz, G.S. 1975. "The *Kopros* Motif: Variations of a Theme in the *Odyssey*." *RSC* 23.2:177–95.
Scott, John A. 1917/18. "The Journey Made by Telemachus and Its Influence on the Action of the *Odyssey*." *CJ* 13:420–28.
———. 1921. *The Unity of Homer*. Berkeley.
Sealey, R. 1990. *Women and Law in Classical Greece*. Chapel Hill.
Seelinger, R.A. 1986. "Spatial Control . . . Lucius' Progress." *TAPA* 116:361–67.
Segal, Charles. 1967. "Transition and Ritual in Odysseus' Return." *PdP* 22:321–42.
———. 1971. *The Theme of the Mutilation of the Corpse in the Iliad*. Leiden.
Shelmerdine, Cynthia. 1969. "The Pattern of Guest Welcome in the *Odyssey*." *CJ* 65:124.
Shewan, A. 1926/27. "Telemachus at Sparta." *CJ* 22:31–37.
Shive, David. 1987. *Naming Achilles*. Oxford.
Simpson, Michael. 1992. "Manners and Morals: Hospitality in the *Odyssey*." In *The Odyssey and Ancient Art*, ed. D. Buitron and B. Cohen, 186–92. Annandale-on-Hudson, N.Y.
Sittl, C. 1890. *Die Gebärden der Griechen und Römer*. Leipzig.
Spain, Daphne. 1992. *Gendered Spaces*. Chapel Hill.
Spitzbarth, Anna. 1946. *Untersuchungen zur Spieltechnik der griechischen Tragödie*. Zurich.
Stanford, W.B. 1950. "Homer's Use of Πολυ- Compounds." *CP* 45:108–10.
———. 1963. *The Ulysses Theme*. 2d ed. Oxford.
———. 1965. *The Odyssey of Homer*. 2d ed. 2 vols. New York.
Stewart, Douglas. 1976. *The Disguised Guest*. Cranbury, N.J.

Sulzberger, M. 1926. "*Onoma eponumon*: Les noms propres chez Homère et dans la mythologie grecque." *REG* 39:381–477.
Taylor, Charles, ed. 1963. *Essays on the Odyssey*. Bloomington.
Thalmann, W.G. 1988. "Thersites: Comedy, Scapegoats, and Heroic Ideology in the *Iliad*." *TAPA* 118:1–28.
Thornton, A. 1970. *People and Themes in Homer's Odyssey*. London.
———. 1984. *Homer's Iliad: Its Composition and the Motif of Supplication*. Göttingen.
Trager, G. L. 1958. "Paralanguage: A First Approach." *Studies in Linguistics* 13:1–12.
Trahman, C.T. 1952. "Odysseus' Lies (*Odyssey* Books 13–19)." *Phoenix* 6:31–43.
van Gennep, Arnold. [1908] 1960. *The Rites of Passage*. Trans. M.B. Vizedom and G. Caffee. Chicago.
Van Nortwick, T. 1979. "Penelope and Nausicaa." *TAPA* 109:269–76.
Van Wees, Hans. 1986. "Leaders of Men? Military Organization in the *Iliad*." *CQ* 36:285–303.
———. 1988. "Kings in Combat: Battles and Heroes in the *Iliad*." *CQ* 38:1–24.
———. 1992. *Status Warriors: War, Violence and Society in Homer and History*. Amsterdam.
Vidal-Naquet, P. 1986. "Land and Sacrifice in the *Odyssey*: A Study of Religious and Mythical Meanings." In *The Black Hunter*, trans. A. Szegedy-Maszak, 15–38. Baltimore, Originally published in *Annales, E.S.C.* 25 (1970): 1278–97.
Visser, Margaret. 1991. *The Rituals of Dinner*. New York.
Volkmann, R. 1885. *Die Rhetorik der Griechen und Römer*. 2d ed. Leipzig.
Wace, A.J.B. 1962. "The Homeric House." In *A Companion to Homer*, ed. A.J.B. Wace and F. Stubbings, 489–97. London.
Waern, Ingrid. 1985. "Der weinende Held." *Eranos* 83:223–29.
Walcot, P. 1977. "Odysseus and the Art of Lying." *Ancient Society* 8:1–19.
Webber, A. 1989. "The Hero Tells His Name: Formula and Variation in the Phaeacian Episode of the *Odyssey*." *TAPA* 119:1–13.
Wender, D. 1977. "Homer, Avdo Mededovic, and the Elephant's Child." *AJP* 98:327–47.
Wescott, Roger W. 1966. "Introducing Coenetics." *American Scholar* 35:342–56.
West, Stephanie. 1993. "Homeric Hospitality." *Omnibus* 25:11–14.
Whitman, C. [1958] 1965. *Homer and the Heroic Tradition*. Cambridge. Reprint, New York.
Wilamowitz-Moellendorf, Ulrich von. 1927. *Die Heimkehr des Odysseus*. Berlin.
Wildeblood, J. 1965. *The Polite World*. Oxford.
Willcock, M.M. 1964. "Mythological Paradeigma in the *Iliad*." *CQ* 14:141–54.
Williams, F. 1986. "Odysseus' Homecoming as a Parody of Homeric Formal Welcomes." *CW* 79.6:395–97.
Windeatt, B. 1979. "Gesture in Chaucer." *Medievalia et Humanistica* 9:143–61.
Winkler, John J. 1990. "Penelope's Cunning and Homer's." In *The Constraints of Desire*, 129–61. New York and London.
Wohl, Victoria. 1993. "Standing by the *Stathmos*: The Creation of Sexual Ideology in the *Odyssey*." *Arethusa* 26:19–50.

Woodhouse, W.J. 1930. *The Composition of Homer's Odyssey.* Oxford.
Youssouf, Ibr., A. Grimshaw, and C. Bird. 1976. "Greetings in the Desert." *Am. Ethnologist* 3.4:797–824.
Zinovieff, Sofka. 1991. "Hunters and Hunted: *Kamaki* and the Ambiguities of Sexual Predation in a Greek Town." In Loizos and Papataxiarchis 1991, 203–20.

Index of Passages Cited

Most passages cited as supporting evidence are not included. Pages referenced include passages in footnotes.

Arist.
  Poet. 1460a18–19: 163, 175
  Rhet. 1380b22–25: 174
    1403b20: 6
Athen.
  Deipn. 258f–59f: 285

Cic.
  Or. 17.55: 40
  de Off. 1.37: 72
  de Orat. 2.189: 155
    3.221: 57
    3.213–21: 6

Dem.
  Or. 54.9: 185
Dion.
  Dem. 53: 7

Eustath.
  Comm. ad Od. 6.363: 6

Gilgamesh Epic, 6: 82

H. *Aphr.* 171–83: 84
  180–84: 153
H. *Dem.* 101–2 and 275–76: 180
  111: 245
  268–80: 84
Hdt.
  Hist. 1.45: 47
    7.225: 47
Hes.
  Erg: 240
  Erg. 128–39: 127

Hippias
  FGrHist IIIB 421: 285
Homer
  Iliad
    1: 32, 35, 115, 296
    1.26–31: 52
    1.104: 43
    1.105: 43
    1.113–15: 284
    1.148: 43
    1.165–68: 217
    1.185: 54
    1.199: 45
    1.225: 43
    1.245: 46
    1.299: 76
    1.366–80: 53
    1.490: 40
    2: 28, 217, 234
    2.144–53: 44
    2.212–46: 41
    2.625–37: 218
    3.2–9: 13
    3.221: 91
    3.418–20: 13
    6.51–53: 36
    6.224–25: 207
    6.224–33: 72
    6.253: 32; 57
    6.343–49: 150
    6.466–70: 58
    9: 35, 54, 115
    9.30–56: 218
    9.39–43: 217

Iliad (continued)
9.160: 98
9.160–61: 54
9.179–81: 57
9.192–94: 66
9.312–13: 29, 240
9.318–20: 191
9.378–92: 12
9.400–9: 47
9.443: 40
9.648: 283
10.523: 13
11.382–83: 44
11.623: 24
11.631–36: 13
11.645–46: 74
11.765–79: 38
11.775–80: 66
12.310–21: 216
12.310–28: 227
13.61–62: 245
13.71–72: 84
13.278–86: 43
14: 42, 182
14.159–353: 182
15.84–89: 35
16.46–47: 52
16.225–30: 13
17.694–700: 13
18.22–34: 13
18.111–15: 55
18.423: 57
19.7: 57
19.51: 54
19.54–276: 97
19.76–77: 54
19.77: 97
19.137–50: 55
19.194–98: 217
19.302: 285
19.580: 251
21: 175
21.64: 45
21.489–92: 57
22: 35
22.9–10: 84
22.491–99: 58

22.492–97: 120
23.101: 46
23.207–8: 58
23.587–90: 139
24: 31–32, 35, 60
24.9–13: 43
24.15–17: 33
24.32: 51
24.51–52: 33
24.101–2: 13
24.127: 56
24.160–65: 34
24.200: 56
24.233–37: 13
24.247–52: 51
24.260–62: 196
24.305–21: 48
24.328: 33
24.352: 51
24.360–61: 51
24.416–21: 33
24.417–18: 57
24.472: 39
24.473: 51
24.477–78: 41
24.482–84: 37, 46
24.483: 45
24.483–85: 41
24.486: 37
24.505–6: 41
24.507–22: 38
24.508: 51
24.509–10: 44
24.510: 41
24.559–60: 12
24.568–71: 12
24.581–82: 34
24.591: 56
24.629–32: 44, 57
24.633–35: 41
24.635–40: 47
24.671–72: 57
24.673–75: 52
24.707–20: 55
24.710–12: 34
24.719–24: 34
24.743: 58

24.746: 56
24.747: 34
24.760: 56
24.761: 34
24.775: 44
24.802: 55
Homer
  Odyssey
    passim: 202
    1–2: 144, 155
    1.1–10: 9
    1.3: 100
    1.89: 156
    1.104: 122
    1.113–20: 66, 74
    1.118–20: 96
    1.121: 66
    1.136–40: 32
    1.166: 208
    1.189–90: 109
    1.208–19: 142
    1.225–29: 165
    1.234: 146
    1.243–44: 146
    1.250: 217
    1.274–75: 145
    1.274–97: 147, 225
    1.277–78: 216
    1.308: 146
    1.336–44: 250
    1.351–52: 279
    1.356–59: 250
    1.386–404: 208
    1.414–16: 214
    2–3: 158
    2.12: 155
    2.26–28: 212
    2.26–32: 215
    2.26–34: 208
    2.36–37: 96
    2.50–55: 216
    2.55–67: 236
    2.58–60: 145
    2.76–79: 148
    2.80–81: 74
    2.85: 294
    2.85–128: 231

    2.89–110: 88
    2.89–90: 278
    2.90–92: 252
    2.92: 88, 248
    2.94–110: 14, 126
    2.129–40: 236
    2.132–33: 212
    2.178: 238
    2.178–93: 219
    2.203: 211
    2.203–5: 215
    2.246–51: 211, 263
    2.255–56: 116
    2.301–36: 144
    2.323–26: 116
    2.332–36: 160
    2.371–72: 80
    2.400–404: 196
    3–4: 149
    3.12–74: 206
    3.14–24: 74
    3.22–24: 114
    3.30: 74
    3.32–35: 96
    3.35: 69
    3.58–59: 211
    3.122–25: 148
    3.207: 118
    3.218–19: 149
    3.313–16: 214
    3.346–55: 80
    3.371–73: 84
    3.406–9: 93
    4 and 15: 151
    4–16: 142
    4.1–75: 206
    4.22–27: 245
    4.30–31: 117
    4.48–50: 66
    4.71–77: 106
    4.72–75: 132
    4.113–17: 150, 295
    4.113–46: 149
    4.136: 98
    4.148–50: 148
    4.149–54: 150
    4.156–57: 149

Odyssey (continued)
 4.161–67: 151
 4.221–28: 150
 4.246–51: 182
 4.561–70: 168
 4.587–99: 161
 4.590: 80
 4.612–19: 80
 4.625–27 = 17.167–69: 220
 4.659–74: 126
 4.667–68: 156
 4.675–715: 260
 4.686–95: 240, 285
 4.716–20: 88
 4.766–72: 267
 4.767–71: 178
 4.768–75: 211
 5.11: 154
 5.55–148: 208
 5.151–58: 294
 5.170–79: 248
 5.219–220: 266
 5.222: 154
 5.346: 14
 5.346–50: 14
 5.356–64: 14
 6.56: 108
 6.121 = 9.176 = 13.202: 219
 6.129: 181
 6.141–47: 110
 6.143–47: 133
 6.145–47: 69
 6.149–57: 71
 6.180–85: 261
 6.181: 254
 6.229–37: 255
 6.230–301: 48
 6.240–43: 169
 6.273–99: 205
 6.300–301: 140
 6.300–302: 130
 7.81–83: 293
 7.91–94: 130
 7.135–54: 94
 7.139–54: 206
 7.155–68: 96
 7.159–66: 78

 7.162: 93
 7.162–65: 204
 7.169–71: 74
 7.170–71: 94
 7.199–210: 179
 7.216–21: 189
 7.233–38: 80
 7.294: 139
 8.80: 59
 8.83–93: 89
 8.110: 249
 8.115–18: 249
 8.158–64: 9, 78
 8.400–15: 77
 8.449–56: 66
 8.457–62: 80
 8.457–68: 80
 8.469: 93
 8.505–6: 59
 8.523–31: 170
 8.546–47: 209
 9–12: 73, 210, 229
 9.27–36: 266
 9.214–19: 72
 9.224–29: 196
 9.228: 172
 9.229: 78
 9.231–32: 173
 9.266–71: 78, 99
 9.269–71: 204
 9.270–71: 72
 9.273–78: 85
 9.275–77: 221
 9.312–13: 83
 9.315: 91, 172
 9.374: 91
 9.395: 91
 9.413–14: 171
 9.468: 78
 9.504: 174
 9.506: 91
 9.513–15: 169
 9.515: 162
 9.552–55: 173, 175
 10.31–48: 217
 10.310: 122
 10.410–15: 45

Index of Passages Cited   315

10.428–42: 217
10.467–72: 294
10.496–99: 43
11.177–79: 259
11.184–87: 211
11.185: 223
11.203: 167
11.205–11: 72
11.233: 113
11.321: 273
11.326–27: 167
11.356–61: 81
11.359–60: 195
11.363–69: 179
11.392–94: 72
11.409–15: 191
11.488–91: 191
11.494–503: 208
11.501–3: 211
11.539: 80
11.563: 80
11.563–65: 134
11.621–22: 230
12.358: 221
12.452–53: 279
13: 263
13–24: 294
13.10–15: 196
13.19–90: 67
13.24–28: 82
13.28–41: 82
13.29–30: 49
13.56: 97
13.81: 88
13.135–216: 82
13.141–45: 173
13.142: 216
13.163–64: 48
13.197–200: 87
13.287–301: 9
13.287–88: 83
13.288–90: 84
13.291–99: 82
13.292–93: 246
13.299–302: 245
13.306–10: 170
13.307–10: 188

13.324–28: 248
13.398–402: 143
13.399: 48
13.434–38: 188
14: 240
14.30–31: 95
14.45–48: 70
14.45–52: 66
14.56–58: 204
14.62–67: 79
14.93–95: 215
14.96–108: 213
14.109–20: 10
14.122–23: 262
14.122–31: 9
14.124–30: 246
14.126–29: 271
14.165–70: 9
14.230–34: 76
14.259–70: 217
14.318–20: 176
14.363–66: 9
14.372: 109
14.387–92: 9
14.459–512: 167
14.508–10: 9
15.19–20: 118
15.19–23: 88
15.22: 251
15.44–47: 117
15.64–66: 116–17
15.68–79: 210
15.88: 117
15.113–17: 80
15.114: 157
15.126–27: 119
15.198: 254
15.321–24: 227
15.344–45: 189
16.14–16: 68
16.33–35: 257
16.35 = 8.280: 195
16.41–45: 96
16.41–48: 152
16.42–53: 207
16.69–89: 224
16.71: 155

Odyssey (continued)
16.105–11: 121, 153
16.160–62: 153
16.173–76: 143
16.178–200: 266
16.178–79: 169
16.179–85: 153
16.192–200: 169
16.202–5: 168, 266
16.204: 153
16.207–12: 153
16.213–16: 108
16.213–24: 295
16.214–15: 93
16.273: 180
16.274–80: 200
16.303–4: 118
16.310: 74
16.342–408: 126
16.361–62: 15
16.375–82: 225
16.383–86: 130
16.400–402: 225
16.415–33: 270
16.424–30: 209
16.424–33: 217
16.430–33: 79
16.435–39: 196
16.641: 113
17–19: 129
17–21: 120, 264
17–22: 152, 259
17–23: 275
17.26–30: 15
17.45–51: 74
17.46–51: 57, 161
17.48–51: 276
17.63: 155
17.65: 112
17.65–66: 101
17.75–83: 79
17.83: 216
17.85–97: 66
17.101–6: 161
17.107–49: 160–61
17.155–61: 275
17.170–77: 15

17.215: 238
17.234–35: 42
17.238–46: 91
17.239: 89
17.260–71: 293
17.286–89 and 470–74: 189
17.291: 72
17.297–99: 132, 209
17.334 and 339: 98
17.339: 95
17.339–22.120: 121
17.339–67: 226
17.340–41: 197
17.342–45: 158
17.365–67: 95, 120, 176
17.375–79: 101
17.393–408: 99
17.397–400: 79
17.397–402: 217
17.397–404: 163–64
17.400: 230
17.400–404: 220
17.406: 294
17.406–8: 101
17.413–62: 134
17.415–17: 71
17.415–23: 217
17.419–23: 189
17.419–24: 192
17.446–47: 121, 123
17.446–49: 9
17.446–62: 200
17.453–64: 134
17.460–88: 159
17.462–91: 194
17.463–64: 22
17.465: 90, 159
17.473–74: 284
17.478–80: 221
17.481–87: 136, 229
17.483–87: 99, 192, 213
17.491: 90, 159
17.541–47: 275
17.563: 265
17.569–73: 246, 265
17.580–88: 265
18–21: 262

Index of Passages Cited

18.8 and 17: 171
18.10: 110
18.41: 112
18.48–49: 226
18.55–59: 86
18.61–65: 158
18.76–89: 134
18.100 and 102–3 and 111: 111
18.101–7: 134
18.110–17: 125, 232
18.111–23: 219
18.153–55: 224
18.153–57: 127
18.163: 195, 260
18.182–84: 256
18.188–96: 255
18.206–11: 256
18.212: 216
18.215–25: 216
18.216–20: 155
18.227–32: 160
18.235–39: 114
18.245–49: 99
18.251–55: 249
18.257–70: 259, 277
18.258: 261
18.266–70: 261
18.272: 263
18.274–83: 88
18.275–80: 79, 212, 240
18.280: 236
18.283: 88
18.285–89: 239
18.288–89: 248
18.320–36: 216
18.346–48: 231
18.346–50: 229
18.346–64: 227
18.355: 48
18.357–64: 192
18.360–64: 224
18.365–75: 209
18.366–75: 227
18.376–86: 227
18.384–86: 122
18.387–98: 228
18.394–404: 194

18.394–96: 95
18.395: 124
18.395–96: 184
18.403–4: 136
18.404: 90
18.414–16: 228
19: 24, 175
19.22–23: 196
19.27–28: 213
19.44–45: 262
19.104–5: 265
19.107–22: 10
19.116: 259
19.124–25: 150
19.137: 246
19.137–59: 212
19.159–61: 259
19.167–68: 86
19.183–98: 10
19.194–98: 76
19.203: 176
19.209: 135
19.209–12: 85–86, 185
19.213 = 19.251 = 21.57: 69
19.226: 207
19.226–31: 256
19.239–43: 76
19.253–54: 157, 268
19.268–69: 265
19.271: 268
19.296–99: 269
19.300–301: 265
19.300–307: 196
19.301: 124, 268
19.309: 102, 268
19.309–11: 270
19.309–16: 9
19.317–20: 66
19.325–28: 102
19.340–42: 269
19.340–52: 265
19.350–52: 147
19.358–60: 263
19.396: 246
19.401: 124
19.468–77: 131, 254
19.476–77: 89

Odyssey (continued)
19.476–81: 233
19.482–83: 124
19.509: 271
19.515–17: 269
19.525–34: 255
19.530–34: 261
19.535–37: 252
19.535–58: 263
19.560: 258
19.579–81: 261
19.583–99: 269
19.584–86: 265
19.584–87: 270
19.585: 268
19.589: 102
19.589–90: 268
19.589–99: 271
19.600–601: 269
20: 232
20.14–15: 226
20.24: 87, 269
20.49–51: 239
20.62–90: 260
20.150: 132
20.184: 90, 159
20.194–96: 230
20.262–67: 155, 229
20.264–65: 118, 236
20.267: 238
20.279–83: 223
20.284–86: 231
20.284–320: 158
20.293–400: 99
20.295: 220
20.295–300: 222
20.297: 236
20.299–302: 193
20.301–2: 12, 260
20.304–8: 200
20.322–25: 231
20.345–47: 161
20.345–49: 232
20.346: 201
20.346–49: 223
20.348–57: 222
20.358–83: 193

20.364–72: 127
20.367–70: 194
20.373–84: 75
20.376: 213
20.384: 164
20.387: 262
20.390–94: 236
21.8–9: 131
21.11–41: 76
21.24–30: 191
21.26–30: 210
21.48–49: 131
21.55–57: 198
21.68–77: 128
21.77–79: 261
21.82–83: 246
21.101–5: 115
21.102–5: 141, 160
21.106–10: 152
21.125–35: 161
21.129: 78
21.131–2: 141
21.131–33: 162
21.141: 113
21.228–29: 246
21.281–84: 241
21.285 = 17.481: 198
21.285–310: 235
21.285–87: 197
21.288–310: 226
21.295–301: 191, 210
21.295–304: 211
21.305–29: 197
21.311–42: 128
21.325–28: 235
21.330–33: 99
21.331: 215
21.331–35: 102
21.344–53 and 369–75: 158
21.348–49: 218
21.350–53: 250
21.393–400: 198
21.397–400: 241
21.404–22.68: 200
21.410–13: 90
21.411: 91, 241
21.412–13: 71

21.420: 24, 96
21.424–25: 159
21.428–29: 224, 237
22.1: 193
22.1–2: 95
22.2: 103
22.8: 197
22.8–21: 237
22.27–30: 159
22.34–38: 199
22.48–59: 237
22.83–88: 237
22.200–201: 128
22.239–40: 84
22.281–84: 87
22.290–92: 232
22.299–300: 237
22.308: 91
22.383–89: 237
22.408: 233
22.480–94: 15
22.488: 193
23.5–79: 275
23.62–68: 263
23.72–76: 272
23.90–95: 274
23.93: 276
23.96–110: 275
23.97–103: 161
23.100: 253
23.107–14: 272
23.113–14: 274
23.113–52: 276
23.141–52: 165
23.144–51: 178
23.146: 125
23.148–51: 257
23.153–55: 271
23.155–63: 201
23.166: 174, 274
23.177–83: 252
23.182: 277

23.207–8: 129
23.214: 278
23.295–96: 108
23.296: 202
23.300–341: 294
23.306–8: 277
23.344–48: 294, 296
23.364–65: 202, 244
24.106–16: 284
24.129–45: 208
24.150–56: 177
24.167–69: 230
24.226–31: 183
24.242–55: 99
24.387–411: 140
24.391–411: 69
24.391–92: 293
24.480–86: 213

Isaios *Or.* 3.13–14: 259

"Longinus" *de subl.* 9.2: 22
Longos *Daphnis and Khloe*: 288

Ohio Revised Code: 219

Plato *Ion* 535b–c: 6
    Ion: 287

Quint. *Inst.* 1.11.17: 6
    11.3.2: 40
    11.3.65: 40
    11.3.65–184: 6
    11.3.66: 32
    11.65–184: 40

Thuk. *Hist.* 7.86: 47

Verg. *Aen.* 1.314–20: 84, 245
    5.647–49: 84, 245

Xen. *Mem.* 3.10.3–5: 282

Index of Important Subjects and Persons

Abasement, 96, 289
Absence, 36
Abuse, macho, 219
Acceptance, phantom, 191
Access, 67, 79, 96, 182, 191
Accostability, 191
"Action chains," 295
Acts: instrumental, 3, 16, 199, 288; intended, 3; lack of, 195, 268; symbolic, 16, 141, 199, 231, 288
Adaptors, 180
Adolescents, x, 74, 114, 117, 128, 143, 148, 213, 244; disguises, 156; ineptitude, 160; resources, 156; transitions of, 164
Adornment, 180, 182n.25
Adult, 8, 142
Adultery, 248
Adventurer, 173
Aeikelios (ἀεικελίως), 143
Affect displays, 5, 12, 21, 83, 185, 233
Affect, viii; overflow, 235; overrides speech, 241
Affection, 86
Affiliation, 127
Affinity, spousal, 265
Agamemnon, 8, 17n.21, 29, 36, 40, 42, 52, 54, 76, 93, 97–98, 168, 218, 282–84
Aganophrosyne (ἀγανοφροσύνη), 167
Age, 39, 80, 152, 180
Agendas, 244n.3
Aggression, 295; heroic, 145; passive, 248
Agora, 132, 144, 231
Aias, 80

Aideomai (αἰδέομαι), 256
Aidos (αἰδώς), 114, 116
Aigisthos, 191
Aiolos, 80
Airs, of superiority, 196
Aithon, 86, 101, 176, 229, 256; forced to fish or cut bait, 268; manners, 264; undevious!, 265
Akhilleus, 8, 36, 40, 46, 53–54, 76, 80, 97, 142, 175, 184, 240n.76, 249n.9, 283, 284
Akhreion (ἀχρεῖον), 260
Akikus (ἄκικυς), 161
Aklees (ἀκλεής), 147
Akritomythos (ἀκριτόμυθος), 258
Aliens, 225
Alignment, 204, 263
Alkinoos, 35, 81, 173n.11, 274
Allegiance, groups, 211
Alter-adaptors, 41, 86, 94
Alternants, 91, 112
Amphimedon, 230, 284
Amphinomos, 124, 205, 224, 228
Analysis: psychological, ix, 6, 8, 53, 98, 108, 136, 157n.23, 263n.41, 267n.47, 275, 287, 293
Analysts, 25
Anamorphosis, 143, 179
Andalusia, 100
Andromakhe, 191, 217n.25, 220n.30
Anger, leaked by Odysseus, 277
Angkhi (ἄγχι), 108n.9, 124, 268
Angkhinoos (ἀγχίνοος), 271
Animals, 72, 256
Anthropology, x; literary, xiii, 105, 265n.43, 286
Anticipation, 197n.42

321

Anticipatory doublets, 202n.49, 204n.3, 211, 226n.50, 227n.52
Antiheroic, 28, 171
Antikleia, 211n.16
Antilokhos, 42, 89
Antinoos, 75, 79, 86n.4, 90, 121, 123, 134, 147n.9, 159, 176, 190, 205, 217, 220–21, 223–25, 231; bold accusations, 294; strategies, 235; toasts, 237
Anxiety, 87; body-boundary, 285
Apate (ἀπάτη), 244
Aphonia, 124, 134n.50
Aphrades (ἀφραδής), 219
Aphron (ἄφρων), 160
Aplomb, 129
Apologies, 54–55, 97, 139, 144, 161
Apologoi, 210n.14, 249n.9
Aporia, 267n.47
Appearance, 40, 49
Approach, 67, 109, 114
Apteros (ἄπτερος), 257n.29
Arbitrariness, 106n.4
Arete, 42, 244
Argos, 87n.5, 125n.37, 131, 185
Arguments, cumulative, ix
Arignotos (ἀρίγνωτος), 84, 140
Aristos (ἄριστος), 148, 173n.11, 176, 207, 209n.12, 227n.54, 228, 259
Arrivals, 67–72
Art, visual, 29n.12
Artemis, 42, 57
Assassination, subplot, 151
Assemblies, 40, 97n.8, 212, 214, 221n.35, 236
Assertiveness, 121; macho, 289; proxemic, 136
Asylum, 151, 165
Atasthal- (ἀτασθαλ-), 118, 173n.9, 265
Athene, 35, 54, 84, 146, 149, 153, 163–64, 169, 179–80, 182, 245; epiphanies, 240; tranquilizes favorites, 269n.50
Atim- (ἀτιμ-), 216, 283n.4
Attack, physical, 185
Aude (αὐδή), 84, 90–91
Audiences, viii n.2, 26–27, 29, 87–88, 92, 102, 123, 135–36, 141, 168, 171–72, 177, 179, 183–84, 200–201, 205, 233, 252, 288; Homer informs, 267; blind, 241; comprehension of character, 287; comprehension of gestures, 287; confused, 260; expectations, 230n.56, 246, 270, 289; frustrated, 252n.14; gendered, 257n.27, 277n.63; impatient, 294; inclinations, 284; internal, 176, 260, 276; judgment of Penelope, 257; options as plot unfolds, 262; original, 229n.55; reactions to flirting, 254; take values for granted, 242; teased, 253n.14
Augury, 48
Authority, 13, 124, 146, 147n.9, 192, 213, 234
Awareness, 3, 56, 71, 88–89, 108, 110–11, 126, 181, 207, 232
Away, 126, 128
Axis, central, 94

Badges, 48n.38, 153, 155, 180, 227
Badinage, 158, 219, 247
Baldness, 84, 169, 238
Banquet, 14, 173, 231, 284
Bargaining, 192
Barking, lack of, 153
Basileis (βασιλῆες), 114, 118, 123, 126, 157, 162, 164, 173n.11, 178n.19, 196, 205, 207–25, 213n.20, 227n.54, 230n.56, 236, 240, 284, 285
Baths, 143, 150n.14, 181, 206, 249n.9, 271
Battlefield, 39, 89, 208
Beard, 169, 261
Bed trick, 88, 201, 215n.22, 254, 271; audience surprised, 260; strips off reserve, 276
Bed, 128–29, 157, 195n.41, 198, 202, 249n.9, 267, 269; immovable, 277–78; its history, 276n.62; marriage, 272; *sema* (σῆμα), 276; widow's, 207
Beggar, 23, 86, 95, 99–100, 103, 119–20, 123–25, 134, 169, 171, 177, 180, 182, 187, 189, 205, 207, 225,

229, 295; routines, 188n.35, 190, 198–99
Behaviors: age-based, 58; congruent, 186; control, 111; gendered, 275; giveaway, 276; unintended, 128
Belches, 172
Bellerophon, 283
Bellow, 131
Belly, 193, 247, 284
Betrayal, 85
Big man, 142, 212n.17, 247
Big talk, 142
Bildungsroman, 156n.22
Biography, implied, 199
Birth, 148
Blanch, 71, 85, 181, 201, 235, 241
Blanket, help with, 185
Blemishes, 192
Blink, 85
Bluffs, 140, 149, 158, 165, 186, 193, 239, 274; double, 263
Blurting, 200
Blush, 181
Bluster, 233, 288
Boar, 253n.16
Boasts, 245, 253
Bodies, 95; Odysseus', 168; penned in, 113; piled, 113; women's controlled, 278
Body: Penelope's, 259; badges, 84; boundary anxiety, 162n.28; buffer-zone, 107; contacts, 66, 259n.32; control, 88; display, 180; envelope, 37, 49, 108, 121, 136; instrument, 88; liminal, 188; orientation, 51; placement, 155n.21; static and dynamic, 288; talk, 281; tonus, 108, 124n.36; tool of expression, 281
Body-adaptors, 180–82, 188, 199
Bonding, 139; male, 247
Bonds, obligations, 237
Booty, 209, 215, 217, 236
Boundaries, 107
Bourdieu, Pierre, 227
Bow, 75, 90–91, 157–58, 161, 197–98, 200–201, 235, 239, 241, 264n.42, 289, 296

Breast baring, 107
Bride, 57n.48, 72, 199, 240
Briseis, 54, 76, 162n.28, 278, 285
Brooch, 14, 267; token of affection, 256
Browbeating, 156, 184; Penelope, 275
Brows, 38, 77; beetled, 288
Build, 84, 148, 252n.14, 265
Bullies, 111, 162, 187–88, 195n.41, 204, 224, 227, 238
Burial, 55
Business, ordinary, x
Bustle, 178
Butt, of insults, 192

Caesura, teasing, 263n.40
Cant: beggar's, 188, 192n.38
Capital, 217; Laertid, 210; gendered, 257; symbolic, 247
Caress, 296
Cash flow, 212n.17
Castration, 211, 248, 285
Catalog, 17
Ceremonies, 13, 53–54, 141, 207, 208; idioms of, 99n.13; rotten, 226; sacred and secular, 285
Chairs, 47, 94
Challenges, 75, 93, 96, 122, 158, 226–27, 229, 295
Channels, 105; communicative, 19; nonverbal, vii; verbal, 90
Chaperones, 126
Character, x, 9, 19–29, 92, 195, 262; development, 156n.22
Characterization, ix, 75n.16, 136, 154, 165, 295
Charades, 156, 201, 261
Charity, 101
Chastity, 126, 255
Chaucer, 43n.28
"Chicken out," 145
Chiefs, 216, 218
Children, 77, 115, 140, 216n.23
Chin, 161
Chronemics, 14, 37, 41, 106n.5, 121, 190, 200, 201, 291–96; Odysseus', 232; deference, 134; phasing, 296
Civil inattention, 189n.36

Index of Important Subjects and Persons

Claustrophobia, 81, 120, 122, 171, 174, 249n.9, 251n.12
Clinging, 57
Close, 133
Closure, 60, 93
Cloth, 70, 181
Clothes, 14, 46, 157, 176, 180, 185, 197, 202, 271
Clown, 111, 160, 171, 190, 198
Clues, 12, 92, 136; to deception, 149
Cockiness, 201
Code: heroic, 54–55, 173, 283
Coercion, 220
Cohesion, social, 158
Coitus, 125n.38
Collapse, 96n.6
Comedy, 41–42, 75, 79–80, 139, 143, 152–53, 168n.3, 199, 204, 208, 215n.22, 217, 224, 233, 240n.74; Homeric techniques, 219n.29; of manners, x, 70; of secrets, 272
Comfort, too close for, 124
Communication: face-to-face, 206; intended, 15; nonverbal, 107n.6; overrides, 111; symbolic, 7; tentative, 253; unintended, 15, 83
Communities, gestural, 6
Compassion, 53
Competence, social, 239
Competition, 100, 208
Complexion, 202, 235
Complicity, 194
Comportment, 42, 85, 109n.11
Concealment, 184–85
Condescension, 112
Conduct, 99; disowning, 226; stream of, 205
Confidence men, 286
Congruence: emotional, 153; gestural, 295
Constraints, social, 165
Consumption, 216
Contact, 95; rejected, 178
Contest, 102, 160, 198–99, 227, 246, 261, 268, 270; a gamble, 263n.41; bow, 263; declared, 271; plans for, 265

Contiguity, 124
Contradiction, 26, 135
Control, 57; lack of, 22, 94
Conversation, 13, 117n.23, 125, 149n.13, 200n.45, 265
"Cool out," 157n.24
Corpse, 34, 37, 43, 46
Counterchallenge, 227
Counterplot, suitors', 225n.47
Couple, entrained, 265
Courtesy, 93, 147, 282
Courtship, 217n.25, 239n.73, 295n.6
"Cover," 185
Cowards, 237, 283
Cower, 182, 233
Cretan, warrior, 177
Cringe, 94n.3
Crouch, 95, 184, 190
Crowding, 92, 185n.31
Crowds, 34, 36, 44, 112, 125
Crowing, 233
Cues, 92, 94, 105, 148, 206, 229, 295; body, 264; false, 264n.42; temporal, 291
Cunning, 154, 202
Cup, 196, 223–24, 237

Daily life, 140, 206n.6
Daimonie (δαιμόνιε), 274
Dais (δαίς), 222n.38, 223
Dance, 196, 220n.31, 293n.2
Dangers, gendered, 254
Dasmos (δασμός), 283
Daydreaming, 222
De (δέ), 194
Dead, 113, 284
Death, 32n.3, 198
Debts, 212n.18, 217
Decency, 163
Deception, 8, 83n.1, 85–86, 92, 136, 163, 165, 171, 240, 270n.51; detecting, 149; double, 177n.18, 263; intent, 160; spousal, 88, 273
Decoding, 182
Decorum, 99, 199, 224
Defects, imputed, 198
Deference, 37, 55, 86, 98–103, 145,

Index of Important Subjects and Persons   325

152, 159, 191, 199, 204n.3, 205; asymmetrical, 99; codes, 248; coercion of, 147; negative, 99n.14; Thersites', 162n.28
Deferral, 86, 125, 157, 170, 186, 200, 232, 236, 251, 296
Definition: prescriptive, 254; progressive, 168, 264
Degradation, 142, 189n.36, 289
Deikanaomai (δεικανάομαι), 140
Delivery, 40
Demas (δέμας), 84
Demeanor, 42, 55n.44
Demodokos, 59
Demos, 148, 160, 163, 178, 209, 214n.21, 216–17, 219, 284
Deniability, 135, 168, 176, 195, 250, 260
Departure, 73n.12, 79–82
Deportment: gendered, 181–82
Detection, 253n.17
Detention, 80–82, 116
Dignity, 88
Digressions, 292
Dike (δίκη), 225
Din, 125, 211, 222
Diomedes, 44
Dirge, 34
Disassociation, 127n.41, 231
Disattention, 80, 190, 229
Disclosure, guarded, 188
Discomposure, 143
Disconnectedness, 140n.1
Discourse: dominant, 247; male hegemonic, 258
Discretion, female, 103
Disempowered, 37, 96, 123, 136, 176, 178, 180, 183, 186, 188, 193, 198, 228, 243, 247
Disesteem, 196–97
Disguises, 10, 84, 109, 150, 154; divine, 179; penetrable, 177, 269; penetrated, 265; weakness, 248
Dishonor, ix, 83, 102, 134, 199, 215, 227–28
Disidentifiers, 185
Disinformation, 84

Disorientation, 165
Disparity, of challenger, 228
Displacement, 94–96, 98n.10
Displays: dominance, 196; emotional, 21; maleness, 133; negative, 182; reassurance, 65; submission, 129; threat, 288; trophy, 57
Disposition, 108
Disrespect, 99, 191
Dissensus, 234
Dissertation topic, 96n.7
Dissimulator, 142
"Dissing," 99, 142, 283n.3. *See also* Disrespect
Dissonance, communicative, 22
Distance, 187; categories, 108; intimate, 108, 128; maintenance of, 103; personal, 108, 134; public, 108; social, 108
Distribution, of surplus, 208
Distrust, 148, 186
Dogs, 87, 95, 152–53, 199, 226, 237, 253n.16, 292–93
Dolios, 140
Dolos (δόλος), 85, 88, 126, 246, 260n.35
Dominance, 86, 127, 158, 207, 209, 235
Domos (δόμος), 130, 131n.45
Doors, 123, 131
Dora (δῶρα), 47, 212, 212n.17
Double-takes, 199
Doubleness, 194
Down, 128
Dowry, nonexistent, 212n.17
"Dozens," 231n.58
Drawing back, 184
Dreams, 252, 268, 269; Penelope's, 263
Dress, 69
Drug, 245
Drunkenness, 228
Duplicity, 85, 181
Dyssemia, 60, 85, 110, 204, 206, 238

Eating, 222
Echoes, verse, 134
Ego: building, 144n.5; displays, 175; territory, 285; violation, 162

Eidos (εἶδος), 84
Ekphrasis, 14, 207n.10, 256, 293
Elbahadla, 231n.58
Elbowroom, 231n.58
Elevation, 8, 37–38, 54, 94–98, 103, 152, 170, 187, 199, 226, 241, 296n.7; lowered, 88, 120, 274; relative, 96; transition, 96
Embarrassment, 70n.8, 114, 204, 205, 249n.9, 264
Emblems, 41, 94, 180
Embrace, 58, 69, 153
Emotions, 60; betrayal of, 134; communicated by nonverbal behaviors, 187; frozen, 249; suppressed, 92
Encounters: deferred, 267; face-to-face, 267
Endurance, 172, 174
Enjambment, 241
Ennui, 294
Entrainment, 153, 254n.20, 274, 291
Entrance, 93, 117
Envelope: empty, 186; spatial, 50; spirit's, 285
Epic: homeostatic tendencies, 132n.46; oral, 86n.4, 132n.46, 203n.1; paratactic mode, 228
Epiphanies, 84, 160, 179
Epithets, 295n.5; antiheroic, 224n.44; stripped away, 277n.64
Equality, 86, 93, 100, 113, 227, 228, 276
Equity, 223n.40
Erethizo (ἐρεθίζω), 262n.39
Escape, 175
Esteem, 209
Eteoneos, 117
Ethnogests, 21, 29, 78, 92, 106, 135, 287
Ethnopoetics, 165
Ethology, 107, 288
Etiquette, 6, 65–66, 77, 98, 123, 172, 189, 238; gendered Homeric, 265; manipulation, 150; of meetings, 208; public, 287
Eumaios, 35, 74, 152, 162, 177, 233n.63, 240

Euryalos, 77, 100, 170
Eurykleia, 124, 274
Eurylokhos, 95
Eurymakhos, 110, 151, 227, 228; censured, 228
Eurytion, 235
Evasiveness, 160n.26, 186, 194; gendered, 128; screens, 243
Excellence, of humble, 230
Exchange, 35, 76, 197, 229, 282; asymmetrical, 207
Exclusion, 122, 127, 194
Excreta, 172
Excuses, 144; youth's, 146
Exemplars, negative, 210
Exhibitionism, 289
Exorcism, 122n.33
Expectations, 23, 211n.16
Expressions: facial, 106, 205; formal and informal, 96
Expressivity, 22
Eyes, 43, 89, 149, 234n.65

Facade, smarmy, 174
Face value, 83
Face, 5–6, 39, 54, 77, 85, 88–90, 92, 125, 143, 163, 198, 215, 228; destroyed, 234; expressions, 184n.30; hiding, 256n.25; occluded, 258; saved, 277
Face-to-face, vii, 52, 54, 203, 231n.58, 287n.8
Facework, 51, 86, 88–89, 95, 193, 226
Failures, 146
Fair play, 229
"Fake-out skills," 163
Family, 243, 278
Far, 124, 133
Fasting, 34, 152n.18
Father, 194, 196, 215, 217
Faux pas, 238
Favor, 221
Fear, 139, 241
Feasts, 116, 130, 146, 157, 208, 210, 211, 292
Feedback, 85, 295; proprioceptive, 164
Feet, 148, 252n.14, 269

Feints, 86, 155
Femininity, Penelope's, 249
Fidelity: Penelope's, 251, 277
Fidgeting, 120n.28, 190
Filled pause, 195
Fire, focus of proxemics, 269
Flab, 84
Flattery, 175
Flinch, 185, 233
Flirting, 254–55, 269, 270n.51, 271
Fluency, message decoding, 265
Fluster, 144, 164, 176, 204
Folktale: Homer's novelties in, 279; proof, 268n.48
Fondling, 177
Food, 11, 190, 236
Footing, 65, 67
Foreshadowing, 195n.41
Forms, social, 53
Formula, 24, 69n.7, 88n.7, 134, 142, 144, 156, 180, 187n.33, 193, 195, 195n.41, 197, 201n.47, 210, 222n.38, 228, 249n.9, 254n.20, 262, 267, 267n.46, 286; cues audiences, 258n.29; denial, 269; dynamics, 248; entrainment, 274n.60; gendered, 250; of nonverbal behaviors, 4n.2
Framing, of story, 165
Fraud, 146, 245
Friend, 129, 275
Front region, 208
Front, 87, 142, 144, 188, 192, 214n.21, 218, 219n.28, 226, 237
Frowns, 226
Funeral, 33–34, 55

Gabel, E. Marianne, 219n.28
Gaffes, 139, 149n.13
Gait, 180, 206, 245
Gambits, 165; contempt, 228; of courtesy, 226n.51; denial, 268
Games, 85, 155, 188; board, 222; expression, 9, 149, 231; gender, 247; heroic, 174; mind, 272; no-win, 146; parlor, 263n.41; risks of, 235; spousal, 215n.22, 269; suitors', 236; victims', 237; zero-sum, 148

Gameworthiness, 162, 214
Gaster (γαστήρ), 284
Gatekeepers, 109, 117n.24, 120, 122, 125, 130
Gaucherie, 117, 144, 206
Gaze, 41, 43, 56, 77, 82n.24, 89, 148, 295
Geese, 237, 252–53
Gender, 69, 70n.8, 72, 80, 89, 119, 124n.36, 126, 205; Mediterranean expectations, 8, 260; dimorphism, 128, 243–52
Generations, 73
Generosity, 217n.26
Geras (γέρας), 44n.30, 172, 174, 195, 221, 236, 282
Gestalt, trickster, 183
Gestures, 3, 17, 288; authority, 261; coverbal, 67, 243; echoed by speech, 282; expressive, 265; fitting, 175; hand, 286; ingratiating, 86; insincere, 135; ironic, 248; kinetic, 88; loud, 85; negative, 161, 270; neutral, 108; opaque, 270n.51; performative, 287; prevalance of, 135; quiet, 155, 288; resonant, 289; retreat behind cloak, 150; self-surveying, 186; universal, 21, 29, 106
Gift exchange, 93, 203, 222
Gifts, 39, 66, 72–73, 75–77, 80, 82, 128, 157–58, 171, 175, 195–96, 209–10, 212, 216, 217n.25, 235, 239, 272; binding force, 256n.26; bride, 127; brooch, 264; competition, 150; dueling with, 142; guests', 14, 215, 224; negative, 77; traffic, 196; way of possessing, 216
Giggles, 161
Give-and-take, 100, 203, 237
Glances, 12
Glares, 77, 91, 230n.57
Goading, 147n.9
Goddesses, 245, 278n.67
Gods, viii, 35n.11, 84–85, 91, 97, 99, 201, 220n.32, 245, 254, 263, 292; knowledge of, 277n.64; sense of humor, 245; sharing with, 221

Index of Important Subjects and Persons

Goffman, Erving, 7, 156
Gossip, 239, 253-54, 259n.31
Gratitude, 101
Greed, 192
Greeks, contemporary, 128, 244n.2
Greeting up, 67, 72, 86, 208-9, 278
Greetings, 65n.1, 67
Grief, 43, 171
Grins, 89; shit-eating, 172
Groans, 91, 172n.8
Grooming, 48n.38, 254
Ground, 94
Groups: affiliation, 207; behaviors, 286; loyalties, 237; self-defined, 225; solidarity, 272
Grovel, 95
Grumblers, accommodated by flexible ideologies, 242
Grunts, 234n.65
Guest-friendship, 210. See also *Xenia*
Guests, 39, 66, 69-70, 99-102, 115-16, 155, 181, 206
Guises, 22, 152; adopting, 177

Hair, 44, 48n.38; social, 169; tearing, 34n.9
Hall, Edward, 7
Halt, 96
Handicap, exploitable, 215
Hands, 5, 57n.48, 71, 220, 252n.14; grasping, 38; kissing, 38; of marriage, 210; open, 120, 190; shaking, 69, 291; stretched forth, 223; washing, 32n.5
Haptics, 34, 38-39, 41, 49, 53, 259n.32
Harmony, spousal, 274
Harsh, Phillip, 263
Hazing, 144n.6
Head, 69; cocking, 287n.8; ducking, 177; holding, 34n.9; kissed, 278; nod, 89; shaking, 89-90, 159, 183
Healing, 54, 60
Hebe (ἥβη), 156
Hedna (ἔδνα), 85, 146n.8, 212, 216n.24, 225
Heir, 212n.17, 239

Hektor, 34, 48, 58, 283
Helen, 7n.5, 44, 116, 150, 245, 255, 265
Helplessness, 86, 95n.5
Hephaistos, 42, 195n.41
Hepsiaasthai (ἐψιάασθαι), 224n.45
Hera, 35, 42, 182n.25, 244n.1
Herakles, 76, 210, 230n.57
Heredity, 213n.19
Hermes, 35
Hero, 66, 96, 112, 120, 141, 153, 159, 182-83, 193, 213; cautious, 274
Heroic: custom, 75; debt, 120n.29; manhood, 163; outlets, 165
Heroism, 28, 125, 174; less forthright, 186; masculine, 266; feminine, 277
Hesiod, 284
Hetairoi (ἑταῖροι), 215
Heterophany, 179
Hidden agendas, 233
Hierarchy, 8, 51, 67, 77-78, 80, 93, 97, 135, 178, 207, 218, 243
High, 178
Hiketeia (ἱκετεία), 55
Hilarity, 158
Hippias, 284, 285n.5
History, reflected in poems, 203n.1
Hitting back, lack of, 184
Homadeo (ὁμαδέω), 95n.4
Home, 129
Homer, viii, 15, 81, 284; allowance of sympathy, 238; on appearance and reality, 234n.65; attention of, 169; characterization of suitors, 238; explicit credit to Penelope, 272; externalized manner, 108; helpful, 183; highlights, 163; identity, 286; languages of, 141; objective style, 47; reading into, 195; reminders to audiences, 279; representation of space, 130; sensitive to rank, 295; spoofs recognitions?, 252n.14; suggestions, 191; uncertainty of, 146n.8
Homophrosyne (ὁμοφροσύνη), 45n.31, 127, 189, 201, 215n.22, 245n.5, 254, 261, 270n.52, 274

Honor, ix, 54, 99, 101–2, 123, 132n.47, 147, 152, 173, 188, 210, 212, 221, 223; male, 243, 247; paradigms of, 115; relatives, 257
Hoodwinking, 248
Horniness, 255n.21
Horripilation, 53, 199
Hospitality, 72–79, 73n.12, 151, 162, 164, 171n.7, 210, 221, 258; bed and baths, 265; Homeric, 204n.4; management, 144; menu of, 177; negative, 211; rejected by Odysseus, 249n.9
Hostility, 165
Hosts, 70, 73, 80, 86, 96, 99–102, 144, 155, 173, 181, 210, 216, 295
House, 79, 88, 118, 125, 129–33, 197, 199–200, 212n.17, 243; claims to, 158; control, 144–45; economic difficulties, 261; honor of, 132; Telemakhos', 251; wealth, 257
Housemaster, 115, 125, 157, 244, 275
Housemistress, 157, 253, 259
Huddling, 44, 112
Humiliation, 46, 54, 97, 118, 145, 156n.22, 172, 175, 189, 191, 194, 220, 234, 284
Humility, 37, 95, 142, 228
Hunkering down, 245n.5
Husband, 277; long-lost, 252; returned, 279; who?, 273
Hustling, 234
Hybris, 109, 127n.41, 152, 189, 200, 213, 219, 221n.34, 265, 285n.5
Hyperbole, 99
Hyperoion (ὑπερῶϊον), 126, 259n.33
Hyperphialos (ὑπερφίαλος), 120n.27, 171, 224n.44
Hyperthymos (ὑπέρθυμος), 177
Hyphistemi (ὑφίστημι), 98
Hypodra (ὑπόδρα), 77
Hypokrisis (ὑπόκρισις), 40, 187

Identity, 84, 128, 152, 202; assumed, 274; claims, 145, 174; Cretan, 178; determined by Penelope, 278; heroic, 185, 237; imputed, 86, 178; nonverbal, 174; perceived, 270; revelation, 201; social, 145, 147; spoiled, 190; stranger's, 177, 273, 275; verbal and nonverbal, 153
Ideologies, Homeric, 282
Ideology, 28, 229, 230n.56, 293; Akhilleus', 191; assumptions, 234; elite, 225; of elite, 203; gendered, 259; heroic, 172, 224; merit, 283; ruling-class, 284; of suitors, 220
Idiogest, 43n.28, 49n.40, 59
Idomeneus, 43
Ikarios, 212n.17
Iliad, 83, 221, 285
Iliad 1, 32, 35, 296n.7
Iliad 9, 35
Iliad 24, viii, 31–61
Illustrators, 41, 133
"Image, spitting," 148
Importuning, 190
Imputed defects, 120
In, 122–23, 126, 129–30
Indecision, nonverbal, 271
Inferiority, 93, 231
Infidelity, heroic, 284
Inhospitality, 78
Initiation, 124
Insomnia: Odysseus', 269n.50; Penelope's, 269
Institutions, 203n.1, 217, 243
Insults, 68, 77, 139, 169, 173, 190–91, 193, 199, 203, 227–28, 269
Integrity, 132, 135
Intentionality, 15
Interaction; asymmetrical, 281; faulty, 93, 234; social, 28
Interiorizing, 160
Interruptions, 291
Intimidation, 164
Invective, 54
Inversion, 102, 120, 125, 152, 173, 181–82, 184, 189, 196, 202, 210, 215, 288; battlefield, 235; face, 237; gender roles, 278n.67; place, 237
Invitation, 115
Iphitos, 75, 198
Iris, 35

Irony, 22, 26, 92, 105n.3, 124, 135, 141, 162–63, 174, 179, 183–84, 232, 241, 295
Iros, 41, 95, 110, 125, 183, 188, 190
Isolation, 122, 128n.42, 164, 170, 235, 244n.3
Ithaka, 109, 162, 165, 176, 209, 215, 266n.44, 284
Ithyne (ἴθυνε), 197n.42

Jeers, 158, 174
Jewelry, 181
Jokes, 146, 215
Joshing, 151, 211
Journeys, 119, 150, 168, 202, 214
Jousting, verbal, 103

Kairos, 160, 232, 270, 293, 296
Kakoxeinia, 204
Kamaki, 247n.6
Karpos (καρπός), 57
Kathizo (καθίζω), 98
Keimelion (κειμήλιον), 117
Kephalos and Prokris, 273
Kerd- (κερδ-), 109, 172, 174, 255n.23
Kertomi- (κερτομι-), 90, 231n.58
Keying, 85
Khalifron (χαλίφρων), 74
Khryseis, 278
Khryses, 36, 52
Kicks, 81, 111, 184, 191
Kin, 213
Kinesics, 43
Kinesthetic, 80
Kisses, 68–69, 97, 140; deferential, 277
Kledon (κληηδών), 111, 232n.59, 269, 276
Kleos (κλέος), 145, 147, 176, 197, 213, 215, 225, 227n.54
Klytaimnestre, 118, 214
Knee, 94
Knopos, 284
Kouridion (κουρίδιον), 251
Kradie (κραδίη), 87
Kredemnon (κρήδεμνον), 255, 256n.24, 258
Ktesippos, 75, 194, 222

Kyklops, 35, 73, 75, 78, 85, 167, 171–75, 172n.8, 189, 206
Kyrieia, 158, 250

Lackeys, 181
Laertes, 99, 108, 127, 152n.18, 183, 187n.33
Laertids, 99, 102, 112, 133, 180, 189, 200, 203, 215; attempt to box in, 239; celebrations, 267, 296; dynasty, 251; homestead, 225; loyalists, 180, 216; manipulative, 259; masks, 234; misdirection, 230; power inverted, 248; Penelope's desire to remain one, 262; psychic time, 294; respect for, 157; skepticism, 154n.19, 169; strategies, 231, 292; treatment of servants, 285; wealth, 252
Lateiner, Ulysses, 166
Laughter, 28, 44, 45n.31, 74, 91, 111, 134, 159, 220, 223, 227, 232, 236, 254, 264, 287n.10
Leakage, 13, 43, 83–86, 88, 111, 159, 164, 177, 184, 194n.40, 206, 206n.7, 219, 233–36, 241, 276, 288; affect, 260; discrepant, 86n.4
Leering, 124n.36
Legitimacy, 212n.17, 243; gaining, 236
Libation, 75, 82, 221, 224, 236
License, limited, 189, 235
Lies, 9, 167, 176–79, 187, 226; adult, 160; Cretan, 175; spousal, 269n.50
Life, daily, 106
Limbo, 147; sexual, 254
Limbs, 5, 39, 136
Line-initial phrase, 193
Lip biting, 220, 232
Literature; oral, 19–20; written, 19
Loiter, 211, 217
"Longinus," x
Looks, 115, 193, 228; nasty, 44, 228
Loom, gendered object, 258
Loop: emotional feedback, 155; nonverbal feedback, 153; sensory feedback, 183

Index of Important Subjects and Persons   331

Loot, honorable, 172
Love, spousal, 256
Low, 178, 206
Loyalty, 212

Männerbund, 144n.6
Magic, 175, 266
Maidservants, 254, 285
Males, 12, 133; adolescent, 166; adult, 119; bonding, 144n.6; initiatives frozen, 251; insecure, 144; prerogatives, 157; provocations, 186; rage, 276
Management: impression, 149, 193; information, 163
Manhood, 289; emerging, 214; meaning of, 196
Manipulation: pleasure of, 272; status, 165, 273
Manners, 9, 191, 204; chronemic, 295; gendered, 278n.67; lack of, 221n.34; suitors', 232; table, 222
Manure, 132
Mapsidios (μαψιδίως), 220
Marginality, 119, 122–23, 178, 242
Marriage, 57–58, 146, 211n.17, 255, 258, 260–61, 263
Mascot, 198, 226
Masks, 153, 228
Maturation, 154, 214
Meal, 70, 237
Megaron, 114, 119, 121, 130, 132, 208, 237, 271, 282; "queen's," 126
Melanthios/Melantho, 45n.31, 77, 124, 191, 216
Meleagros, 36
Memory, 202
Menace, 156
Menelaos, 35–36, 66, 75, 80, 116–17, 132, 149–50, 168n.3, 210
Mentes, 101, 144
Mermerizein (μερμερίζειν), 81
Messages: noncongruent, 233; secret, 252
Metacommunication: nonverbal, 218; verbal, 66, 89, 146
Metadeception, 269n.50

Metamorphosis, 84
Metaphors, 289; spreading out, 271
Metis (μῆτις), 87, 172, 174, 245, 254; women's, 257, 275
Micromotions, 22
"Mine is the power," 144, 164n.32
Miracles, do not come, 264n.42
Miscues, 246
Misdirection, 129; habitual for Penelope, Odysseus, and Homer, 264n.42
Misinformation, 84
Misrecognition, 245
Mnema (μνῆμα), 197
Moans, 153
Mobility, 56, 273
Mockery, 9, 99n.14, 144, 227; women's, 270n.52
Modesty, 124
Monuments, 34, 146
Morals, 204
Mother, 214, 276
Motifs: absence of, 206; folktale's "unrecognized implement," 279n.68
Motion, lack of, 111
Motives, amplified by nonverbal behaviors, 288
Mourning, 33, 44n.30, 55
Movements; copied, 160; lack of, 96, 134
Muslims, 170
Mutilation, 33, 57, 150, 191, 210–11, 235, 285

Nakedness, 70n.8, 181, 193n.39
Names, 174–75, 187n.34, 222n.38, 226, 239n.72; magic, 210n.14; revelation of, 173n.9
Narrative, 4, 9, 60, 165; advanced by nonverbal behaviors, 238; analysis eschewed, 171; climax, 292; comparisons, 256; indirection, 210n.14; manipulative, 168; pace, 27, 293; parallels, 195n.41; poetry within, 220n.32; quantity of nonverbal behaviors, 265; semiotics, 201; suspense, 292; technique, 5

Index of Important Subjects and Persons

Narratives, 106, 116; false, 178; of suspense, 177n.18
Narrator, 154, 168, 179; hints, 289; superior knowledge, 179n.21
Nausikaa, 80, 86, 110, 166, 181, 205, 249n.9, 256
Near, 115, 124, 265
Negotiations, 94
Neik– (νεικ-), 238n.71
Nepios (νήπιος), 117, 140–42, 146–47, 161, 199
Nepoinon (νήποινον), 109, 236
Nervous system, autonomic, 95
Nestor, 35, 75, 80
Niobe, 33
Nobles, 141
Nobody, 147, 171–72, 174, 177, 192
Nods, 77, 144, 159, 246
Non-events, 183
Nonbeing, 143
Nonverbal behaviors, 5, 15, 206; absence of, 159; age-based, 166; categories, 10, 16; ceremonial, 282n.2; co-occurrent, x; deceptive, 281; faulty receiving, 238; faulty sending, 238; functions, 26–27, 31, 60; gendered, 166, 243; intended, 183; lack of, 36; literature, 286n.7; manipulation of, 105; parental, 83; past societies', 287; patterns, 203; quiet and noisy, 140n.2; significant facet of epic, 289; standards, 23; variety, 6, 223
Nonverbal channel, preferred, 233
Noos (νόος), 88n.7, 248
Norms; manipulation of, 141; of suitorhood, 209; violated, 283; women's, 247
Nudge, 81, 123

Oaths, 262
Obedience, subversive women's, 260
Object; bow, 268; significant, 96; throwing, 121
Object-adaptors, 48, 84
Objects, 46, 195–98; gendered, 256; italicize speech, 282; not wasted, 195; significant, 3, 13, 197

Objectual correlate, 198
Obligations, 102, 109, 212, 292
Odor, 107, 221
Odysseus, 65, 74–75, 79–81, 84–86, 90, 94, 97, 103, 119, 153, 167–202, 211, 228, 239, 245; agendas, 167; badges, 169; caution, 253n.15; comical, 169; crowding behaviors, 281; cruelty, 187n.33; defeats, 252, 277; doubleness, 194; eerily familiar presence, 267; embarrassing self-betrayal, 277; esteem, 187; feet, 265; flaunting weakness, 231; games, 187n.33; godlike, 169; greed, 272; hair, 181; hands and feet, 264; hints of identity, 233n.63; his crew, 174–75, 221; human reaction, 277n.64; improprieties, 234; lack of nonverbal leakage, 183; mistakes, 179n.21; no god, 266; personae, 263; proxemics, 119–25; prize doubter, 266; real-time, 169; scar, 271; skin, 181; stages of progress, 197; stupid, 173n.9; tact, 175; tests, 272; to be shocked, 269; tools, 198; tricks, 187
Odyssey, ix; dense cross-references, 286; disguise motifs, 257; gender-conscious plot, 246; rituals in, 253; source of patriarchal authority, 258
Odyssey 13–24, 294
Odyssey 17–22, 259
Odyssey 17–23, 275
Odyssey 18–21, 262
Offers, 228; condescending, 227
Ogre, 171, 175
Oikos (οἶκος), 131n.45, 132–33, 208, 250, 269
Olive tree, 276
Omens, 151, 230; thunder, 232
Omission, tactful, 167
Oneupmanship, 142, 174, 238
Onomatopoesis, 182n.27
Oppression, 19
Oralists, 23
Orator, 97
Order: "goes without saying," 243; ceremonial, 235; serial, 127; symbolic, 243

Orientation, 80, 108, 133n.48, 170, 199
Orifices, 172
Orymagdos (ὀρυμαγδός), 222
Oudos (οὐδός), 96, 122
Out, 122–23, 126, 128–30
Outbursts, 153
Outrage, 194
Overreaction, 228
Overtones, nonverbal, 232n.60

Pace: acceleration and deceleration, 293; literary, 293. *See also* Narrative
Pais (παῖς), 117
Pandarids, 260n.36
Panhandling, 184
Parade, 82
Paradigms, 191; perverted, 66
Paralinguistics, 7, 16, 41, 56, 90–92, 191, 205, 232, 252n.14
Paralysis, 293
Parasites, 191
Parent, 144
Pariah, 128n.42
Paris, 42, 117n.24, 142
Parody, 11, 73, 80
Passivity, 90, 186, 188
Pathos (πάθος), 44, 47, 58, 60
Patriarchy, 251
Patrimony, 119
Patroklos, 36, 42, 52
Patronize, 145
Patterns, 195; *Odyssey's*, 241; flirtation, 251; refusal, 249n.9; revenge, 151; structural, 73; voyage, 151
Pause, 94, 106, 201, 293
Peers, 144n.6, 223
Penelope, 42, 45n.31, 48n.38, 88, 97, 103, 115n.20, 118, 126–27, 183, 188n.35, 189, 198, 201–2, 208, 211, 216, 219, 244; allurement, 248; ambivalence, 260; analogue, 197; body, 251, 271; chagrin, 272; "choice," 264n.42; criticized, 276n.61; cues, 271; death wish, 260; deceptions, 240n.74, 255; deferrals, 87, 250; denial, 262; dormant energy, 267; endurance, 244; failures, 244, 266; feints, 269; fugues, 251; heroism, 249, 271; Homer rarely penetrates her thought, 277n.64; hospitality, 252; hyperbole, 269; impervious to hope, 262; insulted by Odysseus, 272; manipulates system, 259; mistrust of, 167, 262; notorious laugh, 260; opacity, 249, 260; pattern of behavior, 250; personality, 267n.47; poise, 246, 265; prayer, 263n.40; prescient, 263n.41; prodded by Odysseus, 262n.39; proxemics, 126–29; prudence, 257; pseudosurrender, 244; quarters, 265; recognition in stages, 263n.41; renown, 279; revisionism, 261; risk-taker, 267n.47; self-control, 271; self-disclaimers, 268; self-display, 268; sexually arousing, 259; shrewd, 277, 277n.65; shriek, 267; silence, 276; social standing, 257; strategic skills, 261, 278n.67; stubborn, 276n.61; stupid?, 275; submissive behaviors, 239n.72; survival skills, 268; tears of, 278; tenacity, 262; tricks, 252, 278
Penetration, 182n.28, 188, 198
Pepnumenos (πεπνύμενος), 295
Performance, 9, 218, 247; male, 4n.1; oral, 19; respect, 66
Performative force, 192
Performative utterances, 158, 178
Perimeters, 121, 130
Peripeteia, 200
Periphron (περίφρων), 103, 253
Permission, 243
Person: eaten, 285; emotions, 287; missing, 219n.28, 261, 264n.42; social, 174n.14; unprepossessing, 143
Persona, 14; Cretan, 175; backstage, 271; false, 269; nondecodable, 153
Personality, damage, 285
Pervert, 79
Pestering, 191
Phaiakians, 133, 167, 206, 227n.54, 249n.9
Phasing, 296. *See also* Chronemics

Philos (φίλος), 204
Philotimia (φιλοτιμία), 172, 174
Philoxeinos (φιλόξεινος), 219n.29
Phoinix, 36, 38
Phonation, 90, 103. *See also* Paralinguistics
Phthinytho (φθινύθω), 217
Pisistratos, 74, 81, 145, 149
Pitch, 56
Placation, 190
Place, 187; high, 157; order, 158; yielding, 157
Plot: alternative, 251; assassination, 225n.48; clues and traps, 287; previewed by Penelope, 252; retardation, 292
Ploys, 148; adolescents' flawed, 163; proxemic, 268
Poetics, x, xiv, 179, 232n.61
Poise, 235, 254n.18
Poland, 115
Police, 77, 120, 205, 207, 211, 239, 249n.9, 252
Polis, 109
Pollution, 125
Polymneste (πολυμνήστη), 253n.15
Polyphemos, 171; *See also* Kyklops
Polytropicity, 119, 154, 170, 187, 253n.15, 271, 277
Postures, 58, 93–95, 180, 205, 288; assertive, 165; deference, 231; equivocating, 226; ironic, 248; of submission, 282; sitting, 296n.7; sprawl, 85, 113
Posturing, 226; macho, 196, 233, 249
Potlatch, 216n.24, 284
Poverty, 205
Power, 19, 142, 194, 204, 218n.26; differentials, 289; extortions of, 203; gendered, 57; Penelope's limited, 270
Powerlessness, 144, 171, 220n.30
Poyatos, Fernando, 265n.43
Pragmatics, xiv, 89
Praxis, 7
Prayer, 82, 97
Pre-echoes, 168, 194n.40, 244n.1
Precedence, 108, 113, 136

Preconscious, 124
Prehero, 147
Presence, 84, 163
Prestation, 76, 85, 196, 203n.1. *See also* Gifts
Prestige, 75, 203, 239, 247
Priam, 32n.2, 34–35, 40, 46–47, 51, 55
Pride, 175
Priority-granting, 295
Prisoner, 128n.42
Privilege, 127, 136, 155; arrogation of, 100; marginal, 191
Prize, 128, 130, 197–98
Profit, 88n.7, 109
Projectiles, 46n.34
Prophecy, Theoklymenos, 263
Propriety, 234n.65
Protocols, 114, 141; elevation, 98n.10; jumping up, 296n.7; kinesic, 37; of feast, 220; of visitors, 74; prestation, 258; sexual, 140n.2; suppliancy, 151
Proxemics, 4, 14, 37, 40, 49, 67, 105–13, 105n.2, 187, 190, 249n.9, 264, 269; degree zero, 201; indicate dignity, 282; intended, 111; liberties, 265; loud shift, 199; structure, 111; unintended, 111
Proxy, 54; narrative, 167
Prudence, 180
Pseudo- , 153, 234, 244, 292
Psychology: Homeric, 26; characters', 204; person subordinate to group, 22
Ptokhos (πτωχός), 134, 182
Public address, 40
Punch, 184
Puns, 169n.5, 222n.38
Put-downs, 158
Pylos, 131n.45

"Queens," 257, 262; catalog, 257
Queue, 113

Rags, 14, 180–81, 193n.39, 257, 273n.58
Raise, 95

Rank, 66, 71, 106, 136, 152, 159, 192, 218; social, 23; transgression, 234
Ransom, 46, 257
Rape, 211, 285
Reaction, lack of, 86n.4
Reading, sociocultural, viii n.2
Real life, 202
Reappearance, 151
Reception, 98, 206, 240n.75
Recess, 128
Reciprocity, 35, 65, 68, 86, 93, 109, 191, 203, 211, 216–18, 220, 223n.41, 291; asymmetrical, 217n.26; meals, 236; negative, 68, 79, 212, 215, 221
Recognitions, 292; modes of, 196; moments of, 177n.18; near, 252n.14
Redistribution, 213, 215; of food and booty, 223n.42
Redundancy, 15, 58, 133–34, 194
Regulators, speech, 107n.7
Reinitiation, 129
Remediation, 76–77
Reparations, 200
Repetition, 20, 292–93
Reproach, public, 262
Reputation, 145, 170
Resemblance, thematic, 148
Resistance, siding with, 161
Respect, 83, 85, 98, 108, 217; feigned, 158
Responses, frozen, 187n.34
Restitution, 54, 55n.44
Retaliation, 194n.40
Return, disguised, 269
Revenge, 173, 211, 214, 292
Rhetoric, gendered, 269
Rhythms, 291; psychophysical signs, 293n.2
Riches, 212
Ridicule, of weak, 193
Rile up, 156
Rise, 96–97
Risk taking, 235
Rite of passage, 122, 147–48
Rituals, 5, 11, 31, 60, 80, 209; encounter, 65; food, 33, 253; form of power,
192n.38; friendship, 73; interaction, 218; marriage, 267; mourning, 96n.6; parting, 65; perverted, 230, 253; ratifying, 65; religious, 33; sexual, 255; status, 99; wedding, 276
Roles: discrepant, 188; imputed, 220; strained, 200
Rolling, 43–44, 107
Rooms, women's secluded, 260
Roots, 186
Routines, 218; courtship, 295n.6
Rudeness, 208
Rulers, 225n.48, 240
Rules: bigger than all of us, 230; breakable, 282; implicit, 229
Rupture, 54

Sacredness, 192
Sacrifice, 221, 236
Sadism, 245, 284
Salutation, 35. *See also* Reception
Sapir, Edward, 58
Sarcasm, 163, 217, 231
Sardonic, 194n.40
Satire, 81–82, 247
Scar, 124, 178, 268n.48; Odysseus', 269, 272
Scatter, 112
Scepter, 46, 181, 220
Schlaraffenland, 171n.7
Scream, 91
Screens for behavior, 204, 263
Seat: not taken, 184; of honor, 74, 170, 173n.11, 214, 223; yielding, 152
Seating, 38, 55n.44, 112
Secrets, 149, 194; dark, 272; entrusted, 272; inside, 272; strategic, 272
Segregation, 244n.3
Self: acceptable, 231, 249n.9; discreditable, 287; slightable, 235; sloppy, 271; sustainable, 165
Self-abasement, 172
Self-abnegation, 185, 232
Self-adaptors, 180, 254
Self-aggrandizement, 233
Self-assertiveness, 145, 172, 196, 227; submissive, 229, 258

Self-betrayal, 22, 276
Self-confidence, 145, 164, 194
Self-consciousness, 58
Self-control, 22, 85, 94, 125, 172n.8, 185, 224, 233, 246, 288
Self-criticism, 160
Self-defense, 194, 231n.58
Self-defilement, 34
Self-definition, 143
Self-degradation, 36
Self-denigration, 173n.9
Self-determination, 235
Self-disclosure, 163, 259n.32
Self-displacement, 54, 55n.44
Self-disturbance, 66
Self-effacement, 172, 289
Self-enhancement, 153
Self-esteem, 224
Self-evaluation, 95
Self-exculpation, 156
Self-fouling, 44
Self-image, 67; undignified, 161
Self-lowering, 93, 184n.30, 207
Self-occlusion, 183
Self-possession, 105n.3
Self-presentation, 54, 136, 205, 233, 264, 271
Self-preservation, 173
Self-priming, 110
Self-regulation, 130
Self-respect, 147
Self-restraint, 275, 288
Self-revelation, 85, 87, 146, 194n.40, 269, 271; Odysseus', 277n.64; Penelope, 262n.39
Self-subversion, 22
Self-sufficiency, 58
Sema (σῆμα), 128
Servants, 72, 123, 155n.21, 188n.35, 199, 230n.56, 282
Settings, bounded, 189
Sexuality, female, 216n.23
Shame culture, 145
Shame, 164, 215, 229; women's, 243
Shape-shifting, 179
Share, 52
Shifty lad cycle, 183n.28

Shroud: Laertes', 128, 258
Shudder, 44, 111
Signs, 149, 175, 198, 201; divine, 239; leaked, 267; multiplicity at crisis, 269; nonverbal, 268n.48; psychophysical, 12, 111, 233; slowness in receiving, 274; special, 276; spousal, 262, 274
Silence, 13, 115, 134, 152, 170, 194–95, 201–2, 258n.29, 273; Penelope's, 258; complicitous, 239
Similes, 171, 226n.50, 293
Simulation, 142, 156, 233
Sit, 96–98
Sitting, 296n.7
Skin, wrinkled, 180
Skommata (σκώμματα), 219
Skulk, 207
Slack, 94
Slander, 259n.31
Slaughter, 178
Sleep, 47; heroic, 82
Slight, 292
Smell, 84n.2, 107
Smile: sardonic, 184, 193–95
Smiles, 12, 42, 186; knowing, 276; misleading, 259
Sneers, 203
Sneeze, 160; Telemakhos', 263
Snubs, 199, 292
Social: ascent, 186; context anomalous, 250; controls, 258; death, 220; definition, 185; deviance, 198; differentiation, 288; eccentricity, 198; equality, 288; handicaps, 198; identity, 192, 199, 202, 215, 257; inferiority, 186; niches, 154; order, 191; persona, 181, 206; roles, 202, 220; stigma, 189; synchronization, 291; values, 165
Sokrates, 288
Solidarity, 289; groups, 224; tribal, 212
Soliloquy, nonverbal, 87n.6
Son, 194, 196
Space, 130; establishment, 107; gendered, 126; interior, 93; personal, 106; perversion of social, 107; segre-

Index of Important Subjects and Persons   337

gated, 126; social, 106; transgressions, 107. *See also* Proxemics
Speech, viii, 3, 19, 24, 29, 45, 50, 58, 74, 83–84, 91, 94, 106, 134, 201, 206; a mask, 253; double, 248; formalized, 191; heroic, 175; initiating, 295; otiose, 73
Spit, 182n.27; Masai, 287n.10
Split-screen, 194
Spouses, 202, 205
Spraints, 127
Stability, 58, 179
Staff, 46–47
Stalls, 142
Stampede, 235
Status quo, 126, 192, 224
Status, x, 8, 19, 68, 98–99, 108, 110, 142, 198, 206, 209n.12, 225; acknowledgment, 121n.29; age, 155; anarchy of, 117; *aristos,* 230n.57; arrogation, 95, 141; caste, 125; changes in, 122, 177; characters', 61; competitions of male realm, 278; deceptions, 180; differences, 126, 234n.65, 239; elevated, 118; establishment, 93; of extremes, 178; gendered, 270; as host, 159; impasse, 147n.9; imposed, 240; inferior, 57; instability, 170; *kyrieia,* 249n.9; low, 100, 102, 133, 180, 229; management, ix, 76; manipulation, 215; markers, 185; nonverbal rhetoric of, 136; personal, 213; public, 119; renegotiation, 111; symbols, 185; warriors, 9, 114, 214
Steadiness, 92
Stigma, 24, 121, 169, 182–83, 185–93, 198–99
Stillness, 13, 44–45, 170, 178, 183–86, 200–201, 228n.55, 273, 282n.2
Stinginess, 79
Strangers, 99–101, 116, 267, 268; stratagems, 163; tested, 269
Strategies: Odysseus', 236; deferral, 241; guest's, 210n.14; of interaction, 292
Stratification, social, 143

Strepistics, 15, 90n.10
Stress, 112
Stroking, 117
Strut, 288
Stupefaction, 13n.16, 45, 161
Stupidity, 174
Stupor, drunken, 172n.8
Submission, 86, 184; creative female, 258
Suck, 124
Suitors, 28, 42, 73, 79, 95, 101, 116, 120–21, 127, 134, 162, 164, 173, 178, 190, 198, 203–41, 250, 267; affect displays, 201; as cattle, 237; character, 238; class, 240; comic, 230, 232, 235, 238, 240; deficits, 238; efforts to appease Odysseus, 199; encouraged, 251; exclusions, 220; face lost, 270; as fish, 237; front, 229; goaded, 231; hegemony, 263; high birth, 230; Homer questions, 230; huddling, 289; humiliated, 231; idleness, 188; inclusion, 223; intimidating, 247; lack of control, 231; misinterpretations, 199; mocked by Penelope, 270; non-, 226; nonverbal behaviors, 240; obtuse, 182, 241; outmaneuvered, 228; perimeter, 273; piety, 221; pollution, 222n.37; respect for person, 239; shamed, 197; stage, 229, 263; suspicious, 181; table, 223; villainy, 236; words, 232
Superiors, 217
Suppliancy, 11, 35–36, 52, 72, 102, 173n.11, 176, 281, 283; heroic, 155; honoring, 191; sacred, 221
Surplus, 213, 215
Survival skills, 186; gendered, 273
Suspicion, hermeneutics of, 260
Suspiciousness, 87n.6
Swagger, 141
Sweat, 181
Symbolism: of brooch, 267; proxemic, 128; system, 102
Symmetry, gendered, 269

Synchrony 296; in, 296; out of, 204, 218
System: distribution, 283; exchange, 212

Table, 112, 115; companions, 190; head-of, 93; manners, 106n.5, 134n.50, 295; shared, 269
Taboos: sexual, 259n.32; touching, 277
Tact, 100, 175
Tailgating, 15, 150, 274, 292
"Take," 140
Tales: cautionary, 195n.41, 292; Cretan, 192n.38; tall, 202; types, 238
Talisman, 76
Talk: grooming, 65; small, 218, 264
Tamie (ταμίη), 251
Taste, 107
Taunts, 75, 119, 142, 156, 170, 174, 191, 205, 211, 214, 249n.9, 264
Teams, 219, 272
Tears, 12, 43–44, 69, 141, 144, 153, 246, 250, 255; delightful, 267; Odysseus' lack of, 184, 186; Penelope's, 186; Telemakhos', 187n.33
Teasing, Penelope, 255
Teeth, 43
Telemakhos, 35, 42, 54, 67, 74, 80–81, 101, 114–19, 128, 142, 164, 179, 200, 211, 213, 215, 217–18, 234, 244, 249n.9, 250, 274–75, 294; criticisms of mother, 276n.61; guests of, 222
Terms to eschew: kings, 209n.12; revolution, 209
Territoriality, 15, 53, 99, 107, 122, 126, 130, 135, 186, 207
Territory, 212n.17; portable, 210
Tests, 28n.8, 157, 186, 188, 198, 239, 256, 275, 296; Odysseus, 241; Penelope put to, 259; Penelope's, 270; of Odysseus, 276; of Penelope, 273; spousal, 272
Textiles, 14, 257, 266
Texts: speech-laden, 166; verbal, 21; written, 106

Thalamos (θάλαμος), 126, 130, 259n.33
Thambos (θάμβος), 37, 45, 45n.32
Theft, 54
Thelgein (θέλγειν), 177, 251, 266
Themes: appearance versus reality, 240; children-damage, 261n.36; disguised husband, 199; likemindedness, 254n.20; wedding, 80
Theoklymenos, 127n.41, 151, 193, 222n.37
Thersites, 28–29, 41n.25, 42, 234n.65
Thesmos (θεσμός), 125n.38
Thetis, 35, 51
Thieving, 196
Thigh, slapping, 87n.6
Threats, 101, 139, 145–46, 148, 199, 239
Threshold, 95, 122, 123n.35, 125, 188, 197
Thronos (θρόνος), 24, 39n.18
Thymos (θυμός), 84, 87, 174, 194n.40
Time, 291; accelerated, 294; biological, 291; circadian, 291; clock, 200, 291; compressed, 294n.3; dead, 296; narrative, 200; nick of, 161; profane, 291; sacred, 291; stopped, 293, 296; taking, 121, 295
Time-out, 210
Time (τιμή), 200
Timing, 263, 292
Tisis (τίσις), 211
Tlemon (τλήμων), 142, 154, 174, 232n.62
Toast, 97n.9, 140, 219, 223, 287
Tone, 88, 90, 92, 106, 205, 223
Torture, 164
Touch, 56, 83, 107, 124n.36, 135
Transgression, 165
Trees, rooted, 278
Trembling, 84
Trespass, 107, 135
Triage, 172
Trick, 85; shroud, 258; successful, 272
Triplicity, 121n.30, 194–95, 200, 202
Trophies, 197; Penelope, 247
Troy, 113, 170; parody of siege, 235

Index of Important Subjects and Persons   339

Truth, 140, 176–77
Tuning, 296. *See also* Entrainment
Turf, 49, 56, 68, 120
Turn taking, 40–41, 66, 94, 106, 149, 176, 201, 210, 258n.29; errors, 238; exclusionary, 234; vagrant's, 270
Tutor, 145
Twang, 199, 201, 241, 293
Twitching, 220n.30
Type-scenes, 11, 59, 68, 98, 121n.30, 211n.15, 222; entrance, 248; hospitality, 206n.9, 223n.41; women, 256

Unequal intercourse, 199n.43
Unheroic, 75n.16, 95, 145, 171–72
"Unitarians," 25
Untouchables, 133
Up, 126, 128
Uppityness, 103
Utterance, blocked, 84

Vacillation, 88
Vagabond, 153, 189, 259, 264, 266
Vagina dentata, 167n.2, 202
Vaunts, 55, 174–75, 208
Veils, 182n.26, 197; Penelope's, 257; male, 256n.25
Vengeance, 174
Vergil, 84n.2, 112n.15, 245n.5
Versions, alternate, 176n.17
Victim, 78, 89n.9, 132, 173, 236; blame the, 147n.9; playing the, 247
Victory, neoheroic, 277
Violations, 23
Violence: euphemized, 239; symbolic, 87
Vocalics, nonverbal, 3, 19. *See also* Paralinguistics
"Voices," 131
Volume, 56
Vomit, 85, 139, 172
Vulnerability, 162n.28, 171, 180, 193, 215n.22, 219

Wailing, 34
Wand, 153
Warmth, 68

Wash, 69
Weaklings, 162
Weakness, 190
Wealth, 212
Weaponry, 181
Wedding, 240, 249, 276
Welcome, 23
Wheedling, 184
Whispers, 56, 246, 295
Whistles, 91
Wife, 199–200, 254, 267n.46; bidding for, 216n.24; dangerously beautiful, 195n.41; widow, 254
Wiliness, 273
Wine, 171, 173, 175, 196
Withdrawal, 151
Women, 12, 70, 75, 167, 202, 214; baths, 256n.24; capable of suppressing emotion, 276; captive, 171; chaperones for, 256; control, 127, 143, 245; criticized, 254; deception, 215n.22, 255–68; deniability, 150n.15; dexterity, 257; distrust of, 118, 248n.7; freedom, 251n.12; gestures of accomodation, 253; ministrations of, 181; motifs of sexuality, 255; paradigms, 248, 250; reputation, 170, 270n.52; ridicule, 257; rituals, 253; seclusion, 259; submissive?, 247, 268–78; undependable, 161; vertical axis of, 128; victims, 270n.52; weakness, 246; weapons, 252–55, 270n.52
Wonder, 132
Wooing, 210n.13, 225
Words: "mere," 141, 155, 159; sharp, 161; winged, 258n.29
Worm, licensed, 190
Wounds, licking, 146
Wrinkles, 84
Wrist, 57, 72; grasp of, 261; kisses, 140n.2
Writhing, 85
Wrong, 173

Xeinion (ξεινήϊον), 232n.61
Xeinodokos (ξεινοδόκος), 155, 271

Xeinos (ξεῖνος), 65, 102, 159, 198, 227n.52, 256, 267, 268n.49, 271; Odysseus, 241; Telemakhos', 220

Xenia (ξενίη), 39, 41, 72–73, 75, 81, 84, 99–100, 117, 127, 144, 155, 158, 173, 190n.37, 191, 204, 211–13, 222, 231, 245, 249n.9, 253, 257, 288

Yawns, 287n.8
Youth, 8, 74, 139–66, 215, 294

Zeus, 35, 42, 73, 173, 183, 192, 204, 213, 283, 296n.7; *Dikaios,* 204; disregard of, 221; *Hiketesios,* 204; *Xenios,* 189, 229, 231